THE MAUDSLEY
Maudsley Monographs

MAUDSLEY MONOGRAPHS

HENRY MAUDSLEY, from whom the series of monographs takes its name, was the founder of The Maudsley Hospital and the most prominent English psychiatrist of his generation. The Maudsley Hospital was united with the Bethlem Royal Hospital in 1948, and its medical school renamed the Institute of Psychiatry at the same time. It is now a school of King's College, London, and entrusted with the duty of advancing psychiatry by teaching and research. The South London & Maudsley NHS Trust, together with the Institute of Psychiatry, are jointly known as The Maudsley.

The monograph series reports high quality empirical work on a single topic of relevance to mental health, carried out at The Maudsley. This can be by single or multiple authors. Some of the monographs are directly concerned with clinical problems; others, are in scientific fields of direct or indirect relevance to mental health and are cultivated for the furtherance of psychiatry.

Editor
Professor A. S. David MPhil MSc FRCP MRCPsych MD

Assistant Editor
Professor T. Wykes BSc PhD MPhil

Previous Editors

1955–1962	Professor Sir Aubrey Lewis LLD DSc MD FRCP and Professor G. W. Harris MA MD DSc FRS
1962–1966	Professor Sir Aubrey Lewis LLD DSc MD FRCP
1966–1970	Professor Sir Denis Hill MB FRCP FRCPsych DPM and Professor J. T. Eayrs PhD DSc
1970–1979	Professor Sir Denis Hill MB FRCP FRCPsych DPM and Professor G. S. Brindley
1979–1981	Professor G. S. Brindley MD FRCP FRS and Professor G. F. M. Russell MD FRCP FRC(ED) FRCPsych
1981–1983	Professor G. F. M. Russell MD FRCP FRCP(ED) FRCPsych
1983–1989	Professor G. F. M. Russell MD FRCP FRCP(ED) FRCPsych and Professor E. Marley MA MD DSc FRCP FRCPsych DPM
1989–1993	Professor G. F. M. Russell MD FRCP FRCP(ED) FRCPsych and Professor B. H. Anderton BSc PhD
1993–1999	Professor Sir David Goldberg MA DM MSc FRCP FRCPsych DPM

Maudsley Monographs number forty-nine

Hands-on Help
Computer-aided Psychotherapy

Isaac M. Marks, Kate Cavanagh and Lina Gega

LONDON AND NEW YORK

First published 2007 by Psychology Press

Published 2016 by Routledge
2 Park Square, Milton Park, Abingdon, Oxfordshire OX14 4RN
711 Third Avenue, New York, NY 10017

First issued in paperback 2016

Routledge is an imprint of the Taylor and Francis Group, an informa business

© 2007 Taylor & Francis

Typeset in Times by Garfield Morgan, Swansea, West Glamorgan
Cover design by Lisa Dynan

All rights reserved. No part of this book may be reprinted or
reproduced or utilised in any form or by any electronic,
mechanical, or other means, now known or hereafter
invented, including photocopying and recording, or in any
information storage or retrieval system, without permission
in writing from the publishers.

Notice: Product or corporate names may be trademarks or
registered trademarks, and are used only for identification
and explanation without intent to infringe.

British Library Cataloguing in Publication Data
A catalogue record for this book is available from the British Library

Library of Congress Cataloging in Publication Data
Marks, Isaac Meyer.
    Hands-on help : computer-aided psychotherapy / Isaac M. Marks,
Kate Cavanagh and Lina Gega.
        p. ; cm. – (Maudsley monographs, ISSN 0076-5465 ; no. 49)
    Includes bibliographical references and index.
    ISBN-13: 978-1-84169-679-9 (hardback)
    ISBN-10: 1-84169-679-X (hardback)
1. Computer-assisted psychotherapy. I. Cavanagh, Kate, 1975–
II. Gega, Lina. III. Title. IV. Series.
    [DNLM: 1. Psychotherapy–methods. 2. Mental Disorders–
therapy. 3. Self Care–methods. 4. Therapy, Computer-Assisted.
W1 MA997 no. 49 2007 / WM 420 M346h 2007]
    RC489.D35M37 2007
    616.89'140078567–dc22

                                                            2006033285

ISSN: 0076-5465
ISBN 13: 978-1-138-87199-1 (pbk)
ISBN 13: 978-1-84169-679-9 (hbk)

When the ingenious Sumerian who invented writing first carved those cuneiform symbols in stone along the Tigris River some 6000 years ago, a skeptic standing nearby predicted with concerned countenance that people would soon stop talking to each other.

(Slack, 2000)

Contents

List of tables	xi
Foreword by Sir David Goldberg	xiii
Preface	xv
List of abbreviations	xvii
CP systems	xvii
Other abbreviations	xviii

1. Introduction — 1
- Reasons for and scope of the monograph — 2
- Why have computer-aided psychotherapy (CP)? — 8
- Modes of access to CP — 16
- Functions of CP — 20

2. CP for phobic/panic disorder — 23
- Chapter summary — 23
- Desktop and PC systems — 24
- Net systems — 29
- Handheld-device systems — 43
- Display exposure systems — 48
- Direct non-immersive display systems — 53
- Immersive Virtual Reality (VR) systems for anxiety disorders — 60

3. CP for obsessive-compulsive disorder and post-traumatic stress disorder — 61
- Chapter summary — 61
- CP for OCD — 62
- CP for PTSD — 69

viii   CONTENTS

4. CP for general anxiety and emotional problems — 73
Chapter summary — 73
Nonclinical studies — 77
Desktop and PC systems — 79
Net systems — 83
USA: Palmtop system — 84

5. CP for depression — 85
Chapter summary — 85
Standalone computers — 89
Internet — 98
Phone-Interactive Voice Response (IVR) — 106

6. CP for eating problems — 109
Chapter summary — 109
Desktop and PC — 113
Handheld computers — 115
CD-ROM systems (Table 6.2) — 120
Internet — 127

7. CP for substance misuse — 137
Chapter summary — 137
Smoking reduction — 143
Alcohol problems — 150
Drug misuse — 161

8. CP for miscellaneous adult problems: pain, tinnitus distress, insomnia, sexual problems, schizophrenia — 169
Chapter summary — 169
Pain: headache in adults — 172
Pain: chronic back pain — 175
Pain during burn wound dressings — 175
Tinnitus distress — 176
Insomnia — 177
Jetlag — 178
Sexual problems — 179
Schizophrenia — 183

9. CP for problems in children and teenagers — 187
Chapter summary — 187
Phobias and anxiety — 188
Depression — 192
Headache — 193
Brain injury — 194
Autism spectrum disorder — 196
Encopresis — 197
Childhood asthma — 198

10. Synthesis — 207

Scope of CP studies — 207
Mental health problems CP has helped — 209
Virtual clinics? — 210
Screening suitability for CP — 210
What is CP? — 212
Human support of CP users — 212
Time users spend on CP — 214
Education and age of users — 215
Live therapist vs CP — 215
Constraints and patients' preferences — 216
CP effect on symptoms and functioning — 216
CP uptake, completion and attrition rates — 217
Cost, cost effectiveness, and CP's place in healthcare provision — 218

11. Conclusion — 221

Appendix I: search method — 225
Appendix II: availability of and contacts for CP systems reviewed — 229
Appendix III: CP references by clinical problem — 235
References — 239
Author index — 257
Subject index — 267

List of tables

1.1 Some functions allowed by various ways of guiding psychotherapy — 21

2.1 CP for **phobia/panic disorder** – London desktop system and UK *FearFighter* (*FF*) system — 25–26

2.2 CP for **phobia/panic** via internet – Swedish, Australian and Canadian systems — 32–33

2.3 CP for **phobia/panic**: handheld devices aiding homework between ftf sessions — 44–45

2.4 CP for **phobias** – vicarious display system: *Computer-Aided Vicarious Exposure* (*CAVE*) — 49–50

2.5 CP for **phobia/panic disorder** – direct display systems — 54–55

3.1 CP for **obsessive-compulsive disorder (OCD)** and **post-traumatic stress disorder (PTSD)** — 62–63

4.1 CP for **general anxiety** and **emotional problems** — 74–76

5.1 CP for **depression** — 86–88

5.2 CP for **depression** *Beating the Blues* (*BTB*) — 92–93

6.1 CP for **eating problems** on desktop, PC, handheld computers and other devices — 110–112

6.2 CP for **eating problems** on CD-ROM and internet — 121–125

7.1 CP to reduce **smoking** — 139–142

7.2 CP for **alcohol** misuse — 151–153

7.3 CP for **drug** misuse — 162–163

8.1 CP for **pain, tinnitus distress, insomnia, jetlag** — 170–171

8.2 CP for **sexual dysfunction** — 180–181

8.3 CP for **schizophrenia** — 184

xii   LIST OF TABLES

9.1 Problems in **children** and **teenagers – phobias, anxiety, headache, brain injury, autism, encopresis**   189–191
9.2 Problems in **children** and **teenagers – asthma**   199–200
10.1 Number of CP systems by clinical problem, system type, country of origin/testing, type of study   208–209

Foreword

The first Maudsley Monograph that Isaac Marks wrote used what I had always thought an unpromising instrument – Osgood's semantic differential – to amazingly good effect. It illuminated important points about both obsessional illness and psychopathic personality. I read it during my training, during which time he worked closely with Michael Gelder developing behaviour therapy and familiarizing psychiatrists with its use.

Although he is not an epidemiologist, Isaac has always appreciated the enormous gulf between the disorders seen in the clinic and those occurring in the community, and has grappled with the problem of how treatment can possibly be made available on a wide enough scale.

His first major departure was to enable nurses to carry out behavioural treatments, rather than having them confined to the inadequate numbers of psychologists and psychiatrists available in the UK's NHS. This venture was highly successful, but still failed to provide the large numbers of therapists that will be needed to deal with the scale of the problem.

He was one of the pioneers to recognize the potential that computers offered to psychiatry, and at first interested himself in using them to help measure treatment outcome and its cost. He soon moved on to develop treatments based on computers, and from the first experimented with a range of computer technologies in collaboration with UK and US colleagues. Their well-known programs for phobias, depression and obsessional states used a variety of different technologies, and he characteristically

xiii

xiv FOREWORD

carried out controlled studies to compare the results obtained by the computer-aided treatments with those produced by live therapists.

In the past 15 years a wide range of computer-aided therapies has been developed, and it is now timely to review the field and discuss their advantages and limitations. The first chapter of the present monograph does this in a comprehensive way, explaining the possible advantages and describing a wide range of problems. There are now almost 100 different treatment packages available. This monograph reviews about 175 different studies evaluating these packages, giving about 300 references. It is indeed a veritable milestone, and even though it is certain that new technologies and refinements of existing packages will continue to become available, it is extremely valuable to have the present state of knowledge described.

As the authors themselves acknowledge, it is no more sensible to ask whether computer-aided therapies are effective than to ask whether drugs are effective – one has to ask which package, for which kind of patient, with which type of support. It emerges that some of these packages are of only marginal benefit to patients, while others are highly effective, and certainly comparable with results obtained by face-to-face therapists. But just as there are patients who do not get on with their live therapist, there are those who cannot work creatively with a computer.

Before I retired, I had the good fortune to work with Isaac and others in assisting Judy Proudfoot to produce *Beating the Blues*, a computer-aided package for depression. One of the things that interested us as we carried out the evaluations of the package was the part played by the nurse who familiarized the patient with the computer, and subsequently greeted the patient when he or she came for a further session with it. These were general nurses working in the practice and had no experience of the treatments that the computer was guiding. Nonetheless they appeared to play an important role, so that the combination of the live nurse expressing interest and concern for the patient, combined with the systematic self-help guided by the machine may well have accounted for the results we obtained.

Isaac has been greatly assisted by his co-authors Kate Cavanagh and Lina Gega, and together they have produced a thorough account of present knowledge. As computers develop, it is likely that the treatments which are developed will cease to be mere copies of those available in clinical settings, but exploit the versatility of the machines as more refinements become available, and clinicians develop new strategies. Meanwhile, the careful description of the present state of knowledge will be appreciated by those interested in the field including developers of the next generation of computer-guided treatments.

Sir David Goldberg
Institute of Psychiatry

Preface

The authors of this review are from the disciplines of psychiatry (IMM), psychology (KC) and nursing (LG). Reviewing the English-language literature on computer-aided psychotherapy (CP) has been a humbling experience. Between us we have spent decades developing and testing eight computer-aided psychotherapy (CP) systems and have published our results in dozens of papers, while a recent NICE review covered four of those systems plus another two. When we looked around carefully at what else has been happening in the world it was astonishing to find 97 CP systems tested in 175 studies of which 103 were randomized controlled trials, and we're still counting. Quite a few of the studies were excellent. We'll see that this fertile ferment has already helped thousands of people who had mental health problems or were at risk of developing them. CP in diverse forms seems likely to play important parts on the psychotherapy and perhaps prevention stages. Only time will tell what those roles will be within different countries' healthcare organizations. CP may also enhance teaching and research in psychotherapy.

ACKNOWLEDGEMENTS

We thank the many authors of studies reviewed in this monograph who patiently answered our questions, often over repeated email exchanges, to clarify aspects of their work. Any errors remaining are our responsibility, and we would welcome corrections to those for future updates of our review. Dr David Mataix-Cols gave much help in the early stages of the Monograph and valuable comments on it. We are also grateful to Professors Lee Baer, Pim Cuijpers, John Greist and Dave Peck for sapient suggestions about the manuscript.

The senior author (IMM) shares intellectual property rights in the *FearFighter*, *BTSteps* and *Cope* systems.

Abbreviations

Reports of computer-aided psychotherapy (CP) adopt many abbreviations to shorten cumbersome text. This review adopts many and adds a few more and some symbols, especially in the tables. They are listed below for ready reference. *The abbreviated and full names of CP systems are usually in italics.*

CP SYSTEMS

AA = Air Academy: The Quest for Airtopia
AC = Asthma Command
Acont = Asthma Control
AF = Asthma Files
BRAVE = Body signs, Relax, Activate helpful thoughts, Victory over fear, Enjoy yourself
BSCPWIN = Behavioural Self-Control Program for Windows
BTB = Beating the Blues
BTS = BT (behaviour therapy) Steps
BTWL = Behavior Therapy for Weight Loss
CADET = Computer-Assisted Diet and Exercise Training
CAE = computer-aided exposure

CARL = computer-assisted relaxation learning
CAVE = Computer-Aided Vicarious Exposure
CLCS = Captain's Log Cognitive System
CQ =Committed Quitters™ Stop-smoking Plan
DAVP = Drug Abuse and Violence Prevention
DCS = PLATO Dilemma Counselling System
DCU = Drinker's Check-Up
DL = Drinking Less
ESPWC = Empowerment Solution for Permanent Weight Control CD
FF = FearFighter
FPS = Family Problem Solving

xvii

ABBREVIATIONS

GDA = Good Days Ahead
GSI = Girls' Stress Intervention
IMPACT = Interactive Multimedia Program for Asthma Control and Tracking
IRCAE = internet relaxation computer-aided exposure
ITEMs = automated individually-timed educational messages
MA = Managing Anxiety
MAP = Mastery of Your Anxiety and Panic
MES = Motivational Enhancement System
NAPFD = Net assessment and personalised feedback for problem drinking
OB = Overcoming Bulimia
Panic Online (PO)
OD1 = Overcoming Depression by Bowers
OD2 = Overcoming Depression by Calipso
ODIN = Overcoming Depression on the Internet
Q = QuitNet
QSN = QuitSmokingNetwork
SB = Student Bodies
SBI = Screening and Brief Intervention
SHTC = Self-Help Traumatic Consequences
SODAS = Stop, Options, Decide, Act, Self-praise to think, not drink
SS = StopSmoking
ST = Stop Tabac
TC = Totally Cool
TLC-Eat = Telephone-Linked Communications-Eat
TLP = Therapeutic Learning Program
UCPT = U-Can-Poop-Too
WDTA = Watch, Discover, Think and Act

OTHER ABBREVIATIONS

AUDIT = Alcohol-Use Disorders Identification Test
BAC = Blood Alcohol Concentration
BDI/BAI = Beck Depression/Anxiety Inventory
BED = binge-eating disorder
beh = behaviour
BES = Binge-Eating Scale
BMI = body mass index
BSQ = Body Shape Questionnaire
CBT = cognitive behaviour therapy
CD-ROM = compact-disk read-only-memory
CESD = Centre for Epidemiological Studies Depression Scale
CIDI = Computer-aided Diagnostic Interview
CIS-R = Clinical Interview Schedule–Revised
CORE-OM = Clinical Outcomes in Routine Evaluation – Outcome Measure
CP = computer-aided psychotherapy
disc/discu = discussion
DO = dropout
DSM = Diagnostic and Statistical Manual
DVD = digital-videodisk
EDI = Eating Disorders Inventory
ERP = exposure and ritual prevention
ES = effect size
FQ = Fear Questionnaire
ftf = face-to-face
fu = follow-up
h/hr = hour/s
GAD = generalised anxiety disorder
GHQ = General Health Questionnaire
gp/s = group/s
GP = general practitioner
h = hours
HamD = Hamilton Rating Scale for Depression
HMQ = Health Maintenance Questionnaire

ICD = International Classification of Diseases
ID = identification
*imp = improved/improvement
inc/incl/inclu = including
info = information
instru = instruction
IOSR = immediate on-site recording
IRC = Internet Resources Comparison
IT = information technology
ITT = intention to treat analysis
IVR = interactive voice response
KCM = Keep a Clear Mind
m = month/s
MADRS = Montgomery-Asberg Depression Rating Scale
min/s or ' = minute/s
n = number of subjects
net = internet
NET = Neurocognitive enhancement therapy
NHS = National Health Service
NICE = National Institute for Clinical Excellence of England and Wales
ns = not significant
OCD = obsessive-compulsive disorder
odf = online discussion forum
PC = personal computer
pts = patients

PGI = Patient Global Impression of Improvement
PTSD = post-traumatic stress disorder
RCT = randomised controlled trial
RDC = Research Diagnostic Criteria
SCID = Structured Clinical Interview for DSM
sess = session/s
sig = significant/ly
SMS = short message service
SUDS = Subjective Units of Discomfort Scale
TAU = treatment as usual
v/vs = versus
VA = Veterans' Administration
VR = virtual reality
w/wk = week
WL = waiting list
WSA = work and social adjustment scale
y/yr = year/s
' = minute/s
↑ / ↓ = increased/decreased
≥ = more than or equal to
≤ = up to or equal to
→ = followed by
> / < = improved significantly more or better than / less or worse than
YBOCS = Yale Brown Obsessive-Compulsive Scale

Note

* To avoid repetition in the text and tables, 'imp', 'improved' and 'improvement was greater/more' mean 'statistically significantly' unless otherwise specified.

CHAPTER ONE

Introduction

Early in a new development it is hard to see the big picture, the wood for the trees. Does the advent of computer-aided psychotherapy (CP) herald a revolution in psychological treatment, or is its rosy promise a glistening bubble about to burst? Early enthusiasm for videophones decades ago gradually gave way to the sober realization that when answering their phone few people want to be seen in pyjamas or hair curlers or with an illicit partner. Videophone sales did not boom, though video screens are now on many mobile (cell) phones.

Computer-aided psychotherapy shows signs of being no bubble. It seems to be evolving into a further avenue of help for mental health problems. After a halting start over decades new CP systems and research are mushrooming across the world in the way fax, computers, printers and email spread in the late twentieth century – now it is hard to remember how we ever managed without them. Some journals devote significant space to studies of computer uses for mental health care,[1] though one recently ceased publication.[2] More journals, including some high-impact ones, put CP into the mainstream of research and practice by publishing CP articles.[3]

---

1 For example, *Computers in Human Behavior, Computers in Human Services, Cyberpsychology and Behavior, Journal of Telemedicine and Telecare, Journal of Medical Internet Research.*
2 *MD Computing.*
3 For example, *American Journal of Psychiatry, Archives of General Psychiatry, Behaviour Research & Therapy, Behavioural & Cognitive Psychotherapy, Behavior Therapy, British*

2 HANDS-ON HELP: COMPUTER-AIDED PSYCHOTHERAPY

There are caveats. Current costs and some snags of CP resemble those of computers, printers and international phone calls decades ago, but technology costs tend to fall and efficiency rises as a field matures, infrastructure grows, and people learn to use it. Government and private health funders are naturally wary of having to pay for new forms of healthcare, yet they slowly began to fund new medications, devices, renal dialysis, scans and the like as benefits became obvious. What used to be innovations became a routine part of healthcare. The National Institute for Health and Clinical Excellence (NICE) for England and Wales in its (2002) appraisal of CP did not recommend any CP for routine care. NICE's (2006) reappraisal, however, recommends for the National Health Service two CP systems – *Beating the Blues* for mild and moderate depression and *FearFighter* for phobia/panic. This might be the first recommendation of CP by a government regulatory body anywhere.

Following NICE's (2006) recommendation, some English health authorities have started to fund CP as a routine care option. Implementing NICE's recommendation, however, is harder than implementing a recommendation for a new drug. Health authorities and the NHS Purchasing and Supply Agency can follow well-trodden paths to fund prescriptions of recently approved medications, and post-marketing surveillance has long tracked their spread and monitored adverse events. In contrast, CP is a new beast. Organizations have little experience in funding, implementing and auditing CP and tread understandably warily.

REASONS FOR AND SCOPE OF THE MONOGRAPH

Why survey CP yet again given the plethora of reviews over the last ten years[4] and given that quite a few of these are detailed and valuable? This monograph is broader in scope. It tries to cover the world literature on all types of CP for mental health problems that have appeared in English.

Journal of Clinical Psychology, British Journal of Psychiatry, Canadian Journal of Psychiatry, Cognitive & Behavior Therapy, Comprehensive Psychiatry, Journal of Behavior Therapy & Experimental Psychiatry, Journal of Clinical Psychiatry, Journal of Clinical Psychology, Journal of Consulting & Clinical Psychology, Neuroscience & Biobehavioural Reviews, Psychological Medicine, Psychotherapy & Psychosomatics, Psychiatric Services.

4 For example, Cavanagh and Shapiro (2004); Cavanagh, Zack, Shapiro, and Wright (2003); Copeland and Martin (2004); Finfgeld (1999); Kaltenthaler, Shackley, Beverley, Parry, and Chilcott (2002); Kirkby and Lambert (1996); Marks (1999); Marks, Shaw, and Parkin (1998b); Maheu, Pulier, Wilhelm, McMenamin, and Brown-Connolly (2004); Murray et al. (2005); Newman (2004); Newman, Consoli, and Taylor (1997a); NICE (2002, 2006); Oakley-Browne and Toole (1994); Proudfoot (2004); Przeworski and Newman (2006); Tate and Zabinski (2004); Wooton, Yellowlees, and McLaren (2003); Wright and Katz (2004).

1. INTRODUCTION 3

Translation costs regrettably bar a review of CP papers in other languages. We review CP for phobia/panic, general anxiety, depression, obsessive-compulsive disorder, post-traumatic stress, eating disorders and obesity, smoking and alcohol and drug misuse, headache, pain, tinnitus distress, insomnia, jetlag, sex dysfunction, schizophrenia, and diverse problems in children such as anxiety, headache, brain injury, autism, encopresis and asthma.

The present book deals qualitatively with 175 published and unpublished randomized controlled trials (RCTs), case reports, and small pilot and larger open studies of 97 CP systems. It discusses the screening of would-be users, effectiveness and efficacy, cost-effectiveness, socio-political barriers to the dissemination of CP within health services and ways in which these might be overcome, and scenarios for organizing CP in health services, including human support for CP users, who might give that support and how, and the way supporters might be trained. It surveys CP's current place in mental health care.

Issues about RCTs and systematic reviews

RCTs are often regarded as a 'gold standard' of trials to evaluate treatment and an impressive methodology has developed to grade and compare RCTs in meta-analyses. Cochrane's 'systematic' reviews (e.g. Murray, Burns, See Tai, Lai, & Nazareth, 2005) and NICE health technology appraisals (e.g. Kaltenthaler et al., 2002, 2005) use such methods to decide the efficacy and cost-effectiveness of treatments for mental health problems. In RCTs of psychotherapies some desirable features are hard to design: e.g. blinding both patients and therapists to treatment group (www.phru.nhs.uk/casp/casp_rct_tool.pdf), though research staff can be successfully blinded. Moreover, though efficacy and cost-effectiveness are clearly crucial, they may not tell us which ingredients of psychotherapy packages yielded a given result. Improvement might merely reflect supposedly adjuvant aspects of therapy rather than the treatment itself – e.g. classic placebo or Hawthorne effects if the controls are on an unsupported waitlist expecting not to improve until they have treatment later and who are not attending a clinic for scheduled sessions. Careful exclusion of known therapeutic aspects of control group packages can give such clues. Systematic testing of each aspect over a series of RCTs in diverse conditions builds up a picture of what affects outcome.

Unlike Cochrane or NICE reviews, the present monograph does not confine itself to RCTs with comparisons of relative risks, standard mean differences, confidence intervals, effect sizes and other statistics, concealment of randomization, dropouts at each stage, and testing of rater blindness etc. which growingly sophisticated meta-analyses rightly require.

4   HANDS-ON HELP: COMPUTER-AIDED PSYCHOTHERAPY

Efficacy is obviously critical, especially if a regulatory body like NICE is to recommend the widespread use of particular CP systems. Much else is relevant too, however. Examples include:

1 The types of clients/patients/volunteers treated.
2 Where they were recruited and referred from.
3 Where and how they were screened.
4 Where and how they did CP.
5 The CP components tested.
6 The type of contrast groups if any.
7 The duration of human support given during CP.
8 Who gave that support, where and how.
9 Whether that support was scheduled or on demand.
10 Other staff contact during CP.
11 The measures used.
12 How often patients were asked to return measures.
13 Whether patients returned to a clinic to do ratings.
14 How important confidentiality was.
15 Funding issues.

A common belief is that RCTs can have an ideal control group. In fact any control group chosen advances knowledge only to the extent that it can answer the particular question/s posed in the RCT. It is vital to scrutinize the potentially therapeutic ingredients in each group compared. As an example, many RCTs compared CP plus human support with a waitlist (delayed treatment) or treatment as usual (TAU) group; commonly CP turned out to be superior in such studies. That superiority might reflect the greater activity, attention-placebo and/or expectancy accompanying CP rather than the CP per se. Such confounds cannot be compensated by the big sample sizes, masked randomization, blind ratings, low dropout rates, and rigorous statistics that get good grades in systematic reviews.

A second example: in an RCT comparing CP with face-to-face (ftf) therapy for depression (Bowers, Stuart, & McFarlane, 1993) the CP omitted the behavioural activation and individualized homework ingredients included in the ftf therapy, so CP's inferiority in the RCT might have reflected that omission rather than the use of CP per se. In a third illustration, when interactive CP for depression turned out to be no better than a less interactive information program covering similar ground, each with similar human phone support (Christensen, Griffiths, & Jorm, 2004a), that questioned the role of interactive CP in improving depression. The design of RCTs for CP springs especially many traps because we know so little as yet about the essential ingredients of effective psychological treatments (Marks, 2002; Zeiss, Lewinsohn, & Munoz, 1979).

1. INTRODUCTION   5

This monograph is a narrative review complementing 'systematic' reviews, not substituting for them. Systematic reviews, like RCTs, are commonly held to be a 'gold standard' for reviews, but may attend too little to crucial qualitative issues beyond efficacy. We explore qualitatively lessons to be learned not only from vital RCTs and cost-effectiveness analyses, but also from naturalistic trials and even single-case reports and observations on how to implement CP in practice. An unduly restrictive review can overlook critical nuances in the young technology of CP, which when used on the internet might eventually transform self-help for populations in whole regions and countries. We deliberately desist from giving each study a Procustean 'good' or 'poor' rating except to highlight work which seems especially promising in particular ways. One inspiring anecdote might open up vistas missed by conventionally 'excellent' RCTs. Our narrative review can also serve as a springboard for systematic reviews that require updating or have yet to be done.

Our search method is detailed in Appendix I and includes methods used by systematic reviews to find 'grey' literature. The field is growing so rapidly that any search, however thorough, is bound to miss some studies, even excellent ones. Years can elapse between their completion, analysis, write-up, acceptance and publication in print or electronically. To be as comprehensive as possible, we cover as yet unpublished studies whose authors permit citation of available results.

Independent testing of CP?

Very few studies of CP systems were independent of their creators. This source of bias is inevitable in a new field. Fresh approaches are naturally tested first by their originators with a vested interest in success, be it personal, ideological, professional or financial. Regulatory approval is not withheld from a new drug just because its RCT was sponsored by the manufacturer, though potential prejudice in such an RCT should be scrutinized especially closely. There is, of course, no substitute for independent testing, but that usually comes later. A new treatment's full potential and drawbacks can only emerge once it has spread widely, but its chances of spreading widely are small until it is approved by a regulatory body. Some CP is entering that phase. CP is a long way from an even later phase when treatments have become so sanctioned by hallowed usage that negative results are met with disbelief.

Self-help books vs CP

Self-help can be as effective when guided by a book as by CP (e.g. Ghosh, Marks, & Carr, 1988). Why bother with CP? Looking at this closely, in Ghosh et al. (1988), self-help with the book *Living With Fear* improved phobias as much as not only CP but also ftf CBT. We would not therefore argue for abolishing ftf care, only for offering bibliotherapy too as an option in care. Bibliotherapy is more than the reading of a self-help book. The Ghosh et al. RCT asked every patient to attend a clinic repeatedly for ratings, so testing the value not just of reading a self-help book per se, but of a therapist firmly asking the patient to read it and come back to the clinic at intervals. This is more than merely buying a book in a shop. Some patients of Ghosh et al. had bought *Living With Fear* in a shop but failed to read it until they joined the RCT, were randomized to bibliotherapy, and had the therapist ask them to carefully follow the book's instructions.

Compared to a book with the same content, CP can confer at least four important advantages. These include greater interactivity and individual tailoring to users' needs. Two further benefits flow from CP on the net or phone interactive voice response (IVR) compared to bibliotherapy. CP speeds updates of self-help guidance, saving the expense of withdrawing outdated books, replacing them with updated ones, and distributing of the new books. CP can also expedite anonymized auditing of the progress of thousands of users throughout a region or country. There is an obvious caveat. Giving the wrong guidance misleads whether given by CP, book, or face to face.

Books are often said to be cheaper than CP. Yes and no. Actual books cost more than free CP on the net but less than CP systems requiring a licence. Somebody somewhere is paying to produce, publish and update both books and 'free' CP. The question is relative cost-effectiveness of each book and CP system for each disorder taking into account issues of user support, production, dissemination, updating and audit population-wide. Such information involves complex economic analyses not easy to do with clinical RCTs. As we saw earlier, RCTs resolve certain issues and leave others wide open.

Meaning of computer-aided psychotherapy (CP)

In this monograph CP refers to any computing system that aids talking treatments by using patient input to make at least some computations and treatment decisions (Marks et al., 1998b). This definition excludes video-conferencing and ordinary phone and most email consultations, chat rooms and support groups. Those expedite communication and overcome the tyranny of distance, but hand over no treatment tasks to a computer or other electronic device. It excludes too electronic delivery of educational materials and electronic recording of clinical state or behaviour where those allow no more interaction than do paper leaflets and workbooks. We do include studies where patients' entries into either devices (e.g. *Mandometer* for eating disorders; Bergh, Brodin, Lindberg, & Södersten, 2002, Table 6.1) or computer questionnaires (e.g. *NAPFD* for problem drinking; Cunningham, Humphreys, Koski-James, & Cordingley, 2005, Table 7.1) led to simple computed feedback designed to help treatment. Also included are CP systems resembling workbooks with a little interaction added which have been called netbibliotherapy (Carlbring et al., 2006b). Today's virtual reality (VR) systems are largely employed to enhance exposure treatments and few take over therapists' tasks, so we omit almost all of them except for brief mention of VR which might ease pain from burns in a unique way (Hoffman, 2004).

CP covers diverse systems, just as drugs, medication and pharmacotherapy cover a vast range of compounds and ways of getting them on to or into the body. Just as drugs might be delivered as an ointment, powder, drops on the skin, eyes or ears, inhaled as a spray, put under the tongue, swallowed as a tablet, capsule, powder or wafer, injected subcutaneously, intramuscularly or intravenously, or inserted as an anal or vaginal pessary, so CP systems might be delivered on a range of computing devices such as standalone or internet-linked computers, PCs, palmtops, phone-interactive-voice-response, CD-ROMS, DVDs, cell phones and VR devices. The title, abstract and even main text of some CP reports leave unclear exactly what the CP consisted of.

Why say computer-aided rather than computerized psychotherapy? Because unlike withdrawers of cash from an automatic teller machine, to do which they need no human help at all, users of most CP systems still have at least brief contact at some time with a human who is usually a clinician. CP systems vary greatly in how much they take over the screening and therapeutic role of the clinician. Some are basic aids to just one aspect of treatment, dealing with perhaps 5% of the tasks and time required of a clinician, while others cut these by 30–70%, and a few execute 80–95% of the treatment tasks required with only minimal time needed from a clinician. Reports of CP systems often lack information to allow judgement of how much screening and subsequent support time those systems require of a clinician or other person. Often too, information is skimpy about how many therapist hours are required without CP in real-time, face-to-face, phone or email therapy where a human makes all the decisions. Deciding how much therapist time CP systems save is also hard because some try to enhance current therapies rather than save time, so they replace nothing, though, for example, delegating education and other basic therapy tasks to CP frees clinicians to offer a fuller therapy plan over the same number and length of ftf sessions.

We know fairly little about how much completely computerized psychotherapy helps users who have no human screening or support or requirement to send progress ratings, without which benefit is hard to judge. Open studies and RCTs try to raise compliance in participants, so their results may not reflect those usually found with routine care or website access.

8   HANDS-ON HELP: COMPUTER-AIDED PSYCHOTHERAPY

Huge attrition (dropout) is seen in casual visitors to unmoderated CP websites which give no human support at all (Christensen, Griffiths, Korten, Brittliffe, & Groves, 2004b; Eysenbach, 2005; Farvolden, Denissof, Selby, Bagby, & Rudy, 2005). In studies doing screening, and these are the great majority, most of the attrition is at the pre-entry stage of winnowing out 'unsuitable' subjects who don't meet trial criteria.

Why say computer-aided psychotherapy (CP) rather than computer-aided cognitive behaviour therapy (CCBT)? Because a few CP systems deliver nonCBT psychotherapy and their number may grow and be sub-sumed under CP. Most current CP systems guide CBT as it seems to be so specifiable. CBT itself is a package with many components that are present in differing proportions across different CP systems. Component variations may affect outcomes and need factoring into the interpretation of results.

Once research shows conclusively which psychotherapy ingredients are essential to improve particular problems, then developers can try to build those into future CP systems. Those ingredients cannot be taken for granted. Though it has long been held that building a trusted therapy relationship and analysing the transference is vital for psychotherapy, CP has actually been effective without those ingredients. Certain non-exposure and non-cognitive approaches have improved some anxiety disorders. What works for whom under what conditions will take generations of research to sort out in reliable detail. CP can play a major role in this endeavour by speeding the process and reducing the cost of giving psychotherapies with and without particular ingredients and by easing the collection of outcome data.

Psychotherapy or psychological treatment are not unambiguous terms in defining the scope of this monograph. Various types of relaxation and biofeedback, for example, are hardly 'talking treatments' yet are often described under a psychotherapy rubric and form part of certain CP systems. The same applies to meditational methods, some of which may become computer-aided in time. Our definition covers any system designed to help users overcome mental health problems.

Snares also await us in defining 'mental health' problems for this review. Asthma, headache, tinnitus distress and jetlag are seldom regarded as mental health issues but worsen with 'stress' for which CP stress-management systems have been tried to change relevant behaviour and feelings. Drawing the line of exclusion is inevitably arbitrary.

WHY HAVE COMPUTER-AIDED PSYCHOTHERAPY (CP)?

Advantages of CP

Climbers may scale mountains just because they are there, but better reasons than the mere advent of computers drive the development and use of CP. Not all patients need the same type and intensity of help (Haaga, 2000). Some benefit from reading a self-help book, watching an instructional video, or doing CP, others by joining a brief educational group run by a paraprofessional, and still others by long-term individual therapy from a highly trained professional therapist with specialized expertise. Patients should get all the time, expertise and individual attention they need, but not more. CP is a new self-help arrow in our quiver of care options. Some functions facilitated by various ways of delivering psychotherapy including CP are compared in Table 1.1 on page 21.

Access to help widened

CP widens sufferers' access to help by taking over routine aspects of care, so freeing therapists to help many more patients than before and to focus on issues which a computer cannot handle. In most countries the demand for psychotherapy exceeds the supply of trained therapists. One- to two-year waiting lists for CBT are common in the UK and elsewhere. During that time the burden grows on sufferers, their families and communities and the problem gets more entrenched and harder to help.

Different CP systems vary in how much they deliver different aspects of care and hence how much time they free for the therapist. The treatment tasks that CP might take over can include education about the patient's problem and what its treatment involves, screening (assessment) for therapy, helping patients to describe their personalized problems with individually tailored homework tasks to overcome those problems, diaries of tasks done, troubleshooting, monitoring of progress through therapy, and rating (evaluation) and display of clinical status and outcome. Some CP systems consist largely of screen pages like a book with little interaction, while others store entered data and give appropriate feedback. The more that a CP system is interactive and individually tailored, the more the therapist can delegate tasks to that CP system.

Home access

Access is further widened by the convenience of home use of certain CP systems via the internet (net, web) or phone-interactive-voice-response (IVR, see below). Home access to CP systems:

1 Empowers sufferers who prefer it to work at self-help at their own pace in their own time without having to spend hours in the company of a therapist. Some clients prefer dealing with problems by CP rather than personal interaction. When users want a rest or time to think they can leave the computer or phone-IVR link without the embarrassment of

10 HANDS-ON HELP: COMPUTER-AIDED PSYCHOTHERAPY

prematurely exiting the consulting room or putting down the phone during a live phone interview or moving out of camera range during a video interview. Home access by net or phone-IVR is available daily round the clock and the most common time of user access is outside usual office hours.

2 Abolishes the need to schedule appointments with a therapist: though brief phone helpline or email support may be scheduled during office hours until support becomes economically feasible at other times too.

3 Stops the bother and expense (and panic with agoraphobics) of having to travel to a therapist which is especially hard for those in rural areas, in unusual settings such as oil rigs, or with impaired mobility.

4 Lessens the risk of stigma involved in visibly visiting a therapist which is widely felt by many people, including people engaged in healthcare, the police, fire service, politics, media etc., and by people who are sensitive to having obvious disfigurements or to talking about secret sexual or other problems.

5 Eases help for the hard of hearing as CP works more with visual than auditory information.

The benefits of no travel and less stigma also apply, of course, to ordinary telephone, videophone or email consultation from home, but those save no therapist time and an appointment time must usually still be scheduled for telephone, videophone, or online email consultations. CP can cut stigma further by being seen not as psychotherapy but as a computer lesson similar to an evening class, a means of self-improvement rather than a sign of deficit or dysfunction. When applying for a job, sufferers can truthfully write and say they've not seen a therapist, as they merely used a machine.

Confidentiality

Linked to the lessening of stigma is the greater confidentiality of secure CP than human therapy. Users commonly confide sensitive information more to a computer than they do to a human interviewer, e.g. about sex, illicit drugs or excess alcohol, or suicidal plans (cited in Marks et al., 1998b). Confidentiality is not a straightforward issue. When a patient used a system in a primary care centre a nurse asked her permission to watch the computer screen while standing behind her. On seeing information appearing on the screen the nurse exclaimed, 'But you didn't tell me that!' to which the patient replied, 'Of course not. This computer's confidential' and went on happily entering further information knowing the nurse was continuing to watch. Confidential can mean 'I can't tell it face to face' rather than 'I don't want my clinician to know'.

CP reduces inhibition

CP overcomes inhibition from therapist cues in direct contact – gaze, voice and gesture when face to face or on a videophone, voice when on the telephone, writing when contact is by letter or email. Such inhibition is why psychoanalysts sit out of view of their patient and Catholic priests taking confession sit hidden from view. Computers have no eyebrows. Patients have found it easier to tell computers about sensitive issues such as high alcohol consumption, impotence, a past criminal record, being fired from a job, and attempted suicide (reviewed by Slack, Porter, Balkin, Kowaloff, & Slack, 1990). CP systems can be carefully devised to avoid any hint of disapproval and to encourage disclosure without worry about the tone of the therapist's voice and other contextual cues. The complexity of the cues which affect self-disclosure is vividly attested by how some people may conceal intimate personal problems in a face-to-face interview yet broadcast them widely on radio and television shows or tell them to a newly met passenger on an airplane whom they are unlikely to see again and who has no acquaintances in common.

Earlier access to care

Widening and easing access to care also allows earlier access to care, thus reducing the disability from, and chronicity and intractability of, mental health problems and reducing their cost to sufferers and health services. Patient samples in many treatment trials for anxiety disorders tend to have had their problem for a mean of about nine years, testifying to the barriers facing sufferers seeking help. If access is delayed by making prior screening by a health professional mandatory, such delay might be cut by also allowing self-referrals who email or post completed screening question-naires which staff can assess within a couple of minutes.

Therapist expertise

CP can unfailingly convey inbuilt therapists' expertise and ask all the right questions at the right moment without forgetting because they are bored, tired, hungry, or distracted after a row with someone shortly before. 'No doctor has ever been as thorough with me as your machine' a woman said about a self-help program concerning urinary infections (Slack, 2000). CP can be programmed to have endless patience without ever delivering confidence-damaging scorn or reproach, and to give completely consistent responses without excessive expectations or undue investment in the patient's progress or inappropriate reward for not doing vital homework tasks. And computers can't be unduly attracted to or have sex with the patient (www.kspope.com/sexiss/index.php).

Patient motivation

CP may be programmed to enhance patients' motivation by presenting a wide range of attractive audiovisual information with voices giving instructions in whichever gender, age, accent, language and perhaps game format the client prefers. Little is known of exactly which presentational features of CP best inspire patients to complete self-help and improve, apart from the therapeutic appropriateness of the instructions (e.g. to do exposure rather than just relaxation or self-assessment for anxiety disorders). In a rare RCT on this issue postpartum women in an obstetric hospital increased their desire to reduce drug misuse after using a CP *Motivational Enhancement System* (Ondersma, Chase, Svikis, & Schuster, 2005). CP probably has much to learn from the advertising industry on how to spur sufferers to do effective self-help.

Patient progress

Certain CP systems can quickly and automatically report patient progress and self-ratings to (a) users who can print out their progress charts; and (b) a central computer displaying to a manager reports, without personal identifiers, of the progress of a user or group of users. Such rapid and large-scale audit is impracticably expensive without computers.

Research

Research into aspects of psychotherapy process and outcome is advanced by CP systems which record users' every keystroke for subsequent analysis. Compared to human therapy, CP gives better control of which therapy components it can insert or delete to speed dismantling studies that can test which ingredients are effective and which redundant (e.g. Osgood-Hynes et al., 1998; Richards, Klein, & Austin, 2006; Schneider, Schwartz, & Fast, 1995a).

Education of practitioners

CP can facilitate the education of psychotherapists and other healthcare staff if they go through CP systems as pretend patients (Gega, Norman, & Marks, 2006; McDonough & Marks, 2002).

Therapy content

Therapy content can be updated far more quickly with CP (especially net- or IVR-based CP) by modifying a central server than it is by retraining therapists and rewriting manuals.

Disadvantages of CP

It goes without saying that there are also downsides to CP:

1 *Technophobia by the user*: this can be reduced by making CP systems easy to use and offering brief live advice (by phone or email if the user is at home) in the event of problems. Even elderly sufferers commonly improve markedly with user-friendly CP, and most people of all ages are comfortable with the most widely disseminated computer terminal, the telephone. Recent systems for children are in friendly game formats (Table 9.1, pp. 189–191), and *FearFighter*, *BTSteps* and *Cope* assume a reading age of 11 years. In contrast, certain Australian and Swedish CP systems use a workbook format resembling college texts that assume more education.

2 CP *cannot answer all possible questions users may ask*, though replies to a growing proportion can be built in as experience is gained. Therapists may be able to give an accurate answer to a higher proportion of questions asked by patients.

3 CP *can't detect subtle nonverbal/verbal clues to clients' misunderstandings or other difficulties and try to correct them immediately*. Having a supporter phone or email at intervals can help but this is usually after a delay, while users rarely seek such support the moment it is needed, even when encouraged to do so.

4 The *consistency of CP applications can become a weakness* when the more flexible approach is called for that clinicians intuitively use with undefined or unknown processes.

5 Clients may *cherry-pick* from a range of homework options presented in CP, *avoid indefinitely the hardest yet crucial tasks*, and work solely on simpler side issues.

6 *Not all clients find CP acceptable* even though others love it; just as one person may find that a given drug relieves distress with few side effects while another finds the same medication unhelpful with unbearable side effects. Finding out who does best with various CP systems rather than ftf care, and the reverse, is in its infancy. How much partially sighted people can use CP with the help of screen readers remains to be seen.

7 *Inability to detect and deal with complications that were not or cannot be programmed for*: for example, clients' responses may suggest serious suicide risk and prompt a message 'Please see your doctor immediately'. If clients don't act on that and the computer system is truly confidential, it cannot ensure that help is summoned. Is the CP system's owner then legally liable if users kill themselves without having consulted a practitioner? If a CP system on detecting serious suicidal risk automatically sends an alarm summoning human help, is the owner

14 HANDS-ON HELP: COMPUTER-AIDED PSYCHOTHERAPY

illegally breaking confidentiality? Courts have yet to test such issues even with non-computerized advice that has long been offered in books, newspaper columns and media chat shows.

8 CP systems tend to be *tailored to just one type of problem/s* (e.g. phobia, depression, or alcohol dependence). Unlike live therapists, CP can't switch to guide self-help for fresh problems which might appear during use. However, users can then opt for a second CP system to guide help for a fresh problem. We have little experience of patients using more than one CP system beyond a few PTSD sufferers who successfully used *FearFighter* for phobia/panic plus *Cope* for depression, which two types of symptoms cover most features of PTSD (Marks, Mataix-Cols, Kenwright, Cameron, Hirsch, & Gega, 2003).

9 CP systems have *not yet been designed for salient problems* like the reduction of aggression and don't try to detect and manage the risk of harming others, e.g. if the input is 'I'll kill him'.

10 *Vital yet unknown therapeutic ingredients may be absent* from a CP system despite clinicians employing them as unwittingly as they breathe. This deficiency should show up as a lack of efficacy.

11 Some phobics may fear *stigma* or unwelcome attention if they carry around and visibly use CP devices such as palmtops, and may forget to carry them when going out. When the palmtop bleeps as a reminder to do a therapeutic task, users may tell others nearby that it is a reminder to do other things, and alarm times need tailoring to be opportune for each user's needs.

12 An opposite problem is that portable CP devices may come to function as *safety signals* just like tablets in one's pocket, in which case they may diminish the value of self-exposure homework. A handful of OCD users of *BTSteps* began to use it repetitively as a ritual and had to be asked to desist from making IVR calls too often.

13 CP is *inaccessible to clients who can't read or see or hear well or can't speak the language* of the CP system they need (English, Swedish, etc.). Technological advance may widen access by magnifying screens for the visually impaired and translating CP systems, though funding scarcity dictates a long wait for them to be translated into the same plethora of tongues as that for Microsoft Word.

14 *Security failure of a central CP database* could allow hackers to see more people's confidential records than thieves could with a paper record system. This is avoided by never storing personal identifiers on CP systems, merely impersonal IDs and passwords that only link elsewhere to personal identifiers.

15 *CP is currently hard to get because health authorities are reluctant to fund CP.* They are understandably slow to approve recurring revenue expenditure for any new technology in its early phase before its benefits

1. INTRODUCTION 15

have become widely recognized (Whitfield & Williams, 2004) and before funding mechanisms have been established in the way they have been, say, for medication, prostheses or renal dialysis. A computer-aided self-help clinic in west London (Marks et al., 2003) closed when seed research funds ran out and ongoing revenue was not approved.

16 Some fear that if CP becomes readily available, *practitioner numbers could shrink* as happened to bank tellers after the spread of automatic teller machines. This seems unlikely: 'The idea is not to replace the doctor; the idea is to fill a void' (Slack, 2000). There is a vast unmet demand for early care of mental health problems and better communication with sufferers, and in any case many patients want some human contact even when most of the therapy process is computer-aided self-help. As CP takes over repetitive aspects of therapy this is less likely to throw therapists out of work than to free them to deal with the many clinical problems that CP cannot manage, so enhancing job satisfaction and perhaps reducing therapist burnout. Moreover, a new group of practitioners might arise dedicated to brief support of CP users in the way that UK nurses manage NHS Direct calls. These points won't assuage all therapists. Machiavelli observed: 'The innovator makes enemies of all those who prospered under the old order' (cited by Slack, 2000), and George Bernard Shaw noted that 'every profession is a conspiracy against the laity'.

17 *Huge effort* is required *to create*, debug, clinically test and disseminate effective CP systems and get them recognized by regulatory bodies, though this process costs but a tiny fraction of the expense involved in bringing new drugs to market. CP regulation brings some consumer protection at the cost of increasing the expense of getting new CP programs into daily use.

18 *Universities give staff and students little academic credit for creating a CP system* which does not count as a publication. More academic kudos is earned for the later step of publishing clinical trials of that system.

19 *Low uptake and high dropout rates*: we will see later that some studies had high rates of refusal to start CP and of dropout after starting CP. This is especially true for CP with no human contact at all either by preliminary screening or brief subsequent support face to face or by phone, email, or online discussion group. Refusal and dropout rates tend to be lower in research trials than in everyday care. Whether refusal and dropout rates were worse with CP as a whole than more usual ways of delivering treatment outside research studies is hard to tell. It is common to see estimates of 50% refusal and dropout rates for routine drug or psychological treatments.

20 Other disadvantages of CP will emerge in time. Few foresaw a serious adverse effect of the uncontrolled use of computers but not of CP – the

16   HANDS-ON HELP: COMPUTER-AIDED PSYCHOTHERAPY

promotion of suicide. Numerous websites and occasional participants in internet chat rooms, bulletin boards and the like actually encourage people to kill themselves and advise them how to do this. Fortunately, CP systems are produced by professionals trying to help rather than harm sufferers.

MODES OF ACCESS TO CP

Peripheral vs central access

Peripheral CP systems are those not linked to a central computer. Peripheral here does not denote the site of access. Peripheral CP systems are accessed on standalone PCs perhaps via CD-ROMs and DVDs, or on handheld devices, VR displays or biofeedback devices. CD-ROMs and DVDs allow access in clinics, at home, or elsewhere with suitable computers. Problems with peripheral devices include the trouble of installing and maintaining CP on widely distributed standalone computers or other devices, the burden of tracking users' progress by collecting data from their peripheral devices and sending that data to a central computer for analysis, and the hassle of periodic updating of all separate disseminated copies of the program.

Central CP systems refer to those linked to a central computer via the internet (net) or by phone-IVR. Central does not refer here to a particular site of access. NetCP systems allow access anywhere with a net link which may even be by wireless. Access may be at home, in a clinic or public library (UK GP surgeries and libraries have net access), internet cafés, or hotels, airports, stations etc. with wifi or other net links. Central systems allow CP users to get self-help guidance from anywhere with a net link or phone and to get brief support by phone (if in a private space) and/or email. Central systems facilitate self-help at home. They obviate any need to travel to a clinic or other site unless users need a net link unobtainable easily elsewhere or specifically want to get self-help guidance away from home, say in a quiet corner of a library or clinic. Occasionally the referring GP or therapist may have the client access a central CP system mainly in the clinic where ftf monitoring of attendance, progress or risk, or giving adjunctive care may be appropriate. NetCP greatly eases access to CP, its large-scale dissemination and updating, and tracking of users' progress. The number of central CP systems is growing rapidly, especially on the net. Among central systems net access is more convenient than phone-IVR access as: (a) it is quicker to scan information and answer questions on a screen than to go through IVR menus in real time; (b) it removes any need to distribute IVR paper manuals for use during phone-IVR calls. People who can't read or don't speak the language of a CP system can be helped by others who do read and speak the language, just as patients having ftf therapy in a foreign language may need to work through an interpreter. Future netCP systems might reach even more people by greater use of easily understood pictures and logos.

Devices giving access

PCs, workstations, laptops

Personal computers (PCs), workstations or laptops operated by a keyboard and mouse or by a touchscreen are present in most western homes and almost all UK GP clinics, libraries and internet cafés and at other sites. Most have a PC linked to the net, increasingly so by broadband, giving access to those CP systems which are available on the net. Such systems may be password protected. On standalone PCs with no net link, and for CP systems which are unavailable on the net, users can load into the PC those CP systems which are obtainable on:

- a CD-ROM (compact-disk, read-only-memory) e.g. anxiety management program (White, Jones, & McGarry, 2000), *Balance* for anxiety/depression (Yates, 1996b),
- a DVD (digital-videodisk), e.g. *Good Days Ahead* for depression (Wright & Katz, 2004).

PCs store scripts, videos, pictures and voice files on a hard disk, CD-ROM and DVD (floppy disks have too small a capacity to store most CP systems and are going out of use). By operating the PC's keyboard and mouse (or touching its screen for those with touch-sensitive screens and compatible PC systems) users see CP material appear on the screen, sometimes with sound, and on request can input information: e.g. to specify or rate their problem and get customized feedback, as in *FearFighter* (*FF*) for phobia/panic (Kenwright, Gega, Mataix-Cols, & Marks, 2004; Marks, Kenwright, McDonough, Whittaker, & Mataix-Cols, 2004), education for schizophrenia (Jones et al., 2001), *Stresspac* for general anxiety (Jones et al., 2006), *Beating the Blues* (*BTB*) for depression (Proudfoot et al., 2003a).

Some CP gives two-dimensional interactive simulations on a PC screen, directed by the user via a mouse, joystick or screen touch. *CAVE* (*computer-aided vicarious exposure*) is a therapeutic PC game to teach users exposure therapy as they direct a supposedly phobic screen figure to approach and remain in the avoided feared situations shown on the screen until that figure's fear score drops. That supposedly phobic figure's fear-thermometer score on the screen rises with each approach and falls as the figure remains in or avoids the situation. The game gives and displays to users points for moving the figure towards exposure scenes e.g. *CAVE* for spider or lift

18   HANDS-ON HELP: COMPUTER-AIDED PSYCHOTHERAPY

phobia (Fraser, Kirkby, Daniels, Gilroy, & Montgomery, 2001; Gilroy, Kirkby, Daniels, Menzies, & Montgomery, 2000, 2003; Heading, Kirkby, Martin, Daniels, & Gilroy, 2001) and for OCD (Clark, Kirkby, Daniels, & Marks, 1998; Kirkby, Berrios, Daniels, Menzies, Clark, & Romano, 2000).

PCs, workstations and laptops linked to internet

PCs or workstations or laptops which are linked to the net (internet, web) allow interaction with a computer (the internet server) at a distance and can be accessed from anywhere connected to the net. The net link allows patients:

- access at home or elsewhere to those CP self-help systems which are on the net: e.g. *netFF*, *Panic Program*, *Panic Online*, or other systems for phobia/panic (Carlbring et al., 2005; Farvolden et al., 2005; Kenwright et al., 2004; Klein & Richards, 2001; Schneider et al., 2005), *MoodGYM* for depression (Christensen et al., 2004a, 2004b), CP for headache (Ström, Pettersson, & Andersson, 2000), tinnitus distress (Andersson, Stromgren, Ström, & Lyttkens, 2002), and insomnia (Ström, Pettersson, & Andersson, 2004),
- written communication with a therapist by email (e-therapy, online therapy) in real time: e.g. *Interapy* for trauma and grief (Lange et al., 2000a), or by voicemail. E-therapy only qualifies as CP if the system itself rather than the therapist makes some therapy decisions based on the patient's input.

Handheld computers

Handheld computers include small portable palmtops with a keyboard and touch-sensitive screen. They deliver information and process and store inputted material and give customized feedback: e.g. palmtop systems to aid homework between face-to-face sessions for generalized anxiety disorder (Newman, 2000), panic disorder with or without agoraphobia (Kenardy, Dow, Johnston, Newman, Thompson, & Taylor, 2003a), and OCD (Baer, Minichiello, & Jenike, 1987; Baer, Minichiello, Jenike, & Holland, 1988). As further handheld devices apart from palmtops and small capnometers come into use they too can be expected to be harnessed soon for CP: e.g. handheld wireless computers such as Blackberry.

Phone interactive voice response (IVR)

Phone interactive voice response (IVR) systems, unlike live phone consultations or voicemail needing usual therapist time, deliver computer voice files accessed by phone from anywhere (these are clearest on landline phones, which are present in 98% of western homes). Users select pre-recorded voice files by keypresses on their telephone keypad or speaking into the phone, and also input information: e.g. problem ratings, rehearsal of answers, which the IVR system processes to give customized feedback. Users look at a manual while making their calls. Examples are *BTSteps* for OCD (Bachofen et al., 1999; Greist et al., 2002; Nakagawa et al., 2000) and *Cope* for depression (Osgood-Hynes et al., 1998). Both *BTSteps* and *Cope* will soon have PC accessibility on the net, which may replace IVR-phone access to complex CP systems and remove the need to send a manual to accompany IVR calls.

Display systems

Along with therapy guidance, some CP systems give non-immersive displays of static or moving pictures, often with sounds, of phobia-relevant or other situations along a hierarchy to promote exposure therapy. Non-immersive displays might be controlled by the patient or automatically go up a hierarchy as anxiety ratings fall (Bornas, Fullana, Tortella-Feliu, Llabrés, & de la Banda, 2001a; Bornas, Tortella-Feliu, Llabrés, & Fullana, 2001b; Bornas, Tortella-Feliu, Llabrés, Mühlberger, Pauli, & Barcelo, 2002; Bornas, Tortella-Feliu, & Llabrés, 2006). Display systems which are not especially immersive include those for agoraphobia (Chandler, Burck, Sampson, & Wray, 1988), flying phobia (Bornas et al., 2001a, 2001b, 2002, 2006) and spiders (Hassan, 1992; Whitby & Allcock, 1994). One (see *CAVE* above) promotes vicarious exposure by asking the patient to move a supposedly phobic or obsessive-compulsive figure on the screen into frightening situations shown on the screen.

The most common display systems now are *immersive virtual reality* (*VR*) systems giving three-dimensional interactive displays of objects and situations that a user can see, hear and/or feel via sensory input devices such as a head-mounted helmet with visual screens, a body-positioning tracking machine, and stereo earphones. VR systems are available in some clinics but currently cost too much for most homes. Examples are VR systems to simulate exposure environments such as helicopter flying and jungle clearing in Vietnam (Rothbaum et al., 1999a; Rothbaum, Hodges, Ready, Graap, & Alarcon, 2001), World Trade Centre attack (Difede & Hoffman, 2002), spider (Hoffman, 2004), flying (Rothbaum, Hodges, Smith, & Lee, 2000; Rothbaum, Hodges, Anderson, & Price, 2002), and agoraphobic situations (Choi, 2005).

Biofeedback devices

Biofeedback devices record physiological changes and display the result to the patient on a monitor: e.g. computer respiratory biofeedback to aid breathing control in panic disorder (Meuret, Wilhelm, & Roth, 2001).

FUNCTIONS OF CP

Some potential functions allowed by various ways of accessing psychotherapy including CP are summarized in Table 1.1.

1   *Interaction with patient*: this occurs in most kinds of face-to-face (ftf) psychotherapy where the therapist is not usually silent, is present in live phone therapy, is present with delays if therapy is guided by letter, voicemail and some email and SMS exchanges. Some CP systems involve a great deal of therapeutic interaction with the user whereas workbook (netbiblio) CP systems involve only slightly more interaction than that in reading a book.

2   *Link to a central computer*: this only occurs with voicemail, email, SMS and CP on the internet or by IVR. Central data analysis with ensuing automatic-therapy decisions only occur with some netCP or IVR-CP systems.

3   *Elimination of travel to have therapy* occurs with all distance (non-ftf) methods of accessing psychotherapy except where peripheral CP systems have to be used away from home.

4   *Enhanced confidentiality* is especially possible with most distance methods of access, particularly so with central CP systems that are accessed by an anonymous password known only to the patient and an administrator who never sees the patient and has no access to the central computer.

5   *Stigma can be reduced* with all ways of accessing psychotherapy at a distance if arranged so that the patient cannot be seen entering a clinic and administrators know little about the patient–therapist contact. Protection against disclosure is especially secure with central CP where the administrator cannot link the computer's anonymized data to the patient.

6   *Screening of suitability for therapy* varies widely regardless of how psychotherapy is accessed, even with live contact whether ftf, by phone, letter, voicemail or email. Various forms of nonCP psychotherapy screen out or accept widely differing proportions of help seekers. Where CP does screen this may be electronic, by live or IVR phone, or ftf, or a mixture of these.

7–9   Also differing hugely irrespective of how the psychotherapy is accessed are *education* about the nature of the problem and how to deal with it, *setting of problems and goals to do so*, and repeated *rating of progress*. Most CP *educates* patients and supporters about the problem and the treatment rationale, and/or gives brief advice which is customized to varying degrees. This educational aspect saves the clinician time in explaining and can enhance compliance (adherence). Educational leaflets

TABLE 1.1
Some functions enabled by various ways of guiding psychotherapy

Function	1	2	3	4	5	6	7–11	12	13
Mode of guiding psychotherapy	Interaction	Central link	↓ Patient travel	↓ Scheduled appts	↑ Privacy	↓ Stigma	See legend	On-site homework prompts	↓ Therapist time
Face to face	+ or −	−	−	−	−	−	+ or −	−	0%
Live telephone	+	−	+	−	+ or −	+ or −	+ or −	+ or −	0%
Letter mail (post)	delay	−	+	+	+ or −	+ or −	+ or −	−	0%
Voicemail or email	+ or −	+	+	+	+ or −	+ or −	+ or −	+ or −	0%
Peripheral CP	+ or −	−	+ or −	−	+ or −	+ or −	+ or −	+ or −	0–85%
Central CP via net	+ or −	+	+	+	+	+	+ or −	+ or −	0–85%
Central CP via IVR	+ or −	+	+	+	+	+	+ or −	+ or −	0–85%

Notes: + = yes; − = no; + or − = depends on therapist or CP system.
Columns 7–11 are collapsed for the functions '↑ *confidentiality*', '*screening for suitability*', '*therapy education*', '*problems and goal setting*', and '*rating of clinical state*', because every row for those columns shows '+ or −'.

and books may do the same. Where *problems and goals are set* and *progress is monitored* and such tasks are the norm for a given type of psychotherapy, then those CP systems which perform those tasks save much therapist time.

10 *On-site prompting of ratings and homework tasks* has been done by scheduled live phone calls to cellphones and by other pre-set handheld devices. It could in theory be done more by netCP systems (but is still exceptional) and by post-hypnotic suggestions.

11 *Guide self-help* steps which patients work through with only brief support from a clinician. In this regard CP simulates the clinical process most clearly, being designed to empower clients to carry out reliable psychotherapy methods to overcome their difficulties. Many CP systems process information entered by the patient and give interactive feedback, functions which are not possible with self-help by manuals or non-interactive multimedia (video- or audiotape, non-interactive CD-ROM, etc.). Guided self-help can save a lot or a little clinician time depending on the CP system, and saves the patient travel time if the CP system is accessed on the net or by phone-IVR.

The next eight chapters will review CP systems for particular clinical problems, covering only those systems for which there are data for outcome and/or acceptability. Many more systems not reviewed are currently under development and testing, results for which should eventually emerge.

Before reviewing CP for each clinical problem and system, an obvious caveat is essential in considering CP's place in healthcare. One size does not fit all. No drug or other treatment is a panacea. It is unrealistic to expect one or more CP systems to alleviate every problem. Unscreened populations of referrals may include a wide range of difficulties, some of which are thought to respond best to a CP system designed for phobia/panic, others to CP intended for depression, yet others to CP for one of the eating disorders, and further problems which no CP system can help as yet. When a population of referrals contains a wide range of problems, more can be helped by a clinic or website which gives access to a broad range of CP systems each of which aids different clinical problems within that population. CP may also need to be used in tandem with nonCP approaches. Such issues are discussed in Chapter 10. There we will integrate lessons learned from our synoptic summary, a snapshot of a field forging ahead.

CHAPTER TWO

CP for phobic/panic disorder

CHAPTER SUMMARY

More CP systems have appeared for phobic and panic disorder than for any other mental health problems. Since 1979 at least 18 CP systems for phobia/panic disorders were developed in Australia (4), Canada (1), Spain (1), Sweden (2), UK (4) and USA (6), quite apart from immersive virtual reality (VR) displays which are not reviewed as they promote exposure therapy like photos, films, videos, etc. but do not yet make CP decisions or save therapist time, though this may change soon. The CP systems were evaluated in at least 12 open studies and 26 RCTs, mostly for panic with agoraphobia and some for social, flying, spider, dental-injection, examination or mixed phobias. CP systems for phobia/panic vary hugely in mode and site of access, assumed educational level of users, therapy tasks taken on, and amount of therapist time saved. They were studied in single or larger case series, group comparisons and RCTs of varying sophistication. The CP was accessed on desktop or PC systems, CD-ROMs, DVDs, handheld devices to aid homework between ftf sessions, vicarious or direct display systems, and increasingly in recent years, the internet (net).

The UK system *FearFighter* (*FF*) is recommended by NICE, the English regulatory body like the USA's FDA, for managing phobia and panic, and is in commercially licensed use on the internet around the UK. In naturalistic studies and RCTs, *FF* improved phobia, panic, anxiety, disability and comorbid depression when present, in 274 patients in all, while in two RCTs *FF*'s educational version helped medical and nursing students learn about exposure therapy to help *FF* users. Swedish net biblioCBT systems for panic/agoraphobia and for social phobia were also studied extensively in open studies and RCTs. Panic/agoraphobic and social-phobic users of the Swedish workbook-type systems improved more than if they were on a waiting list (e.g. on cognitions, avoidance, anxiety, depression, quality of life), and especially if they also had an online discussion group plus email and sometimes phone support with therapist input to a total of around three hours which is less than is usual in ftf CBT. It is unclear how much users would improve with even briefer support and how well less-educated subjects would improve with the netbiblio systems which demand regular exam-type answers as in a college course. The RCTs using waitlist comparisons did not exclude potential placebo effects. When an Australian *Panic Online* (*PO*) net biblioCBT system was given with substantial support, this helped panic sufferers more than being on a waitlist, leaving open possible placebo effects; adding stress-management modules did not enduringly enhance efficacy. In an open study of the unmonitored Canadian *Panic Program* on a website, massive attrition occurred after session one though the 13% who used the system for ≥ 3 sessions improved. Time spent in ftf CBT for phobia/panic was cut without impairing outcome when sufferers also used CP on handheld devices to facilitate homework or on a handheld capnometer plus an audiotape to promote breathing retraining. Australian *CAVE* vicarious exposure displays on a PC in different RCTs improved adult but not young spider phobics to varying extents and in an open study improved agoraphobics slightly with irrelevant exposure, while a Spanish display system improved flying phobics but saved no therapist time.

DESKTOP AND PC SYSTEMS

London: *Desktop system*

This text-based interactive system to guide self-exposure was used at a desktop terminal in a UK outpatient clinic. Various facets of outcome of an RCT were reported in four papers (Table 2.1; preliminary, Ghosh, Marks, & Carr, 1984; final, Carr, Ghosh, & Marks, 1988; Ghosh et al., 1988; agoraphobic subsample, Ghosh & Marks, 1987). Patients in the RCT had eight sessions over ten weeks in patients who had phobia/panic disorder

TABLE 2.1
CP for **phobia/panic disorder** – London desktop system and UK *FearFighter* (FF) system

Study	Phobia/panic system	Design	Patients	Outcome
Ghosh et al. (1984, early results; 1988, final results); Ghosh & Marks (1987, agoraphobic subsample of above); Carr et al. (1988, subsample of above)	Desktop exposure guidance system at a terminal in psychiatric outpatient clinic.	RCT for 10w: (1) CP (n=28 incl 15 agor) vs (2) ftf-guided (n=19 incl. 12 agor) vs (3) book-guided (n=24 incl. 13 agor). 20 CP cases (of above 28) vs 20 matched historical ftf controls.	London: 71 ICD-9 chronic phobic patients completed treatment. 35 refused entry, 13 dropped out. 20 of 28 CP pts vs 20 pts who had ftf-guided exposure previous year.	All 3 gps improved sig and equally at wk 10 and at 1, 3 and 6m fu. Same result for agoraphobic subsample. Both grs imp sig and equally pre-post and pre-fu.
Shaw et al. (1999)	*standaloneFearFighter* (*FF*) = exposure self-help via PC, keyboard and mouse + brief support ftf.	Open pilots: (1) 10w at IoP, London support by psychiatrist psychol or admin; (2) 7–11 sess at GP surgery, support by admin.	London/Wales: ICD10 agora/claustrophobia: (1) 17 pts in London; (2) 6 pts in Wales.	(1) London: 15/17 completers; imp – 2 marked, 4 moderate, 3 slight, 6 none. (2) Wales: 4/6 completers imp 100% to 13%. No fu.
Kenwright et al. (2001)	*standaloneFF* on PC in outpatient clinic + brief ftf therapist support.	Open pilot over 10 weeks compared: (1) *FF* (n=54) vs (2) historical controls ftf-guided self-exposure (n=31).	54 London pts with phobia/panic disorder.	*FF* patients = historical controls but took 85% less clinician time. No fu.
Marks et al. (2004); McCrone et al. (2007)	*standaloneFF* as in Kenwright et al. (2001) above.	RCT in 2:2:1 ratio to 6 1h sess over 10w of (1) *FF* n=37 vs (2) ftf exposure n=39 vs (3) CP-relaxation n=17. *FF* and relax had brief ftf support. 1m fu.	93 London outpatients with DSM-IV phobia/panic disorder DOs *FF* 16 (*43%*), ftf 10 (*24%*), relax 1 (*6%*) 65 completers post 60 reached 1m fu.	*FF* and ftf exposure imp clinic and stat. sig and = and > relax at w10 and 1m fu. At 1m fu: ES on primary measures 3.7 *FF*, 3.5 ftf, 0.5 relax.

continues overleaf

TABLE 2.1 Continued

Study	Phobia/panic system	Design	Patients	Outcome
Kenwright et al. (2004); Marks et al. (2003)	*netFF* at home + brief support from therapist on phone helpline.	Open pilot compared: (1) *netFF* (n=10) vs (2) historic controls had *standaloneFF* (n=17).	UK: 27 ICD10 phobia/ panic disorder patients Refused/DO: *netFF* 1/0 *standalneFF* 12/16.	*netFF* improved sig, similarly to historic controls. ES 1.8 to 0.4 across measures. No fu.
Schneider et al. (2005)	(1) *netFF* as in Kenwright et al. (2004); (2) *netMA* – managing anxiety at home on net + brief therapist support on phone.	RCT in 2:1 ratio over 10 weeks: (1) *netFF* n=45 vs (2) *netMA* n=23 1m fu. Blindness checked. Self vs blind rater agreement.	UK: 68 ICD10 phobia/ panic disorder. Dropouts: *netFF* 12 (27%), *netMA* 8 (35%).	*netFF* ES 3.4 to 0.4 across measures and self/clinician-ratings. Wk10: *netFF* and *netMA* each imp sig and = 1 mfu: *netFF* > *netMA* on some measures.
Hayward et al. (2007)	net*FF*.	Open.	Scottish Highlands; mixed phobias/panic	imp. in phobias, depression, disability.
McDonough & Marks (2002)	*edFF* – shortened CD-ROM educational version of *FF* using its HTML screens only.	RCT: (1) 90-min teaching session: (1) *FF* HTML screens worked solo (n=19). (2) Face-to-face small-group tutorial (n=18).	London: 27 medical students. All completed pre-post. No fu.	Knowledge ↑ sig. pre-post (by 26% *edFF* – < 34% ftf tutorials). Gp tutorial took 5× > teacher time but > enjoyed than solo *edFF*.
Gega et al. (2005)	*edFF*: improved on the CD-ROM version used by McDonough & Marks (2002).	RCT: 1h of: (1) *edFF* worked solo, or of (2) ftf medium-gp tutorial; then 1h vice-versa.	London: 92 pre-registration nurses. 85 completed pre-post. No fu.	Similar satisfaction, ↑ in knowledge and skills for *edFF* and ftf gp tutorial. *edFF* more efficient for teacher.

2. CP FOR PHOBIC/PANIC DISORDER 27

(ICD-9). It asked them to list their main phobic avoidances, explained the rationale for exposure, suggested appropriate exposure tasks, and asked for ratings of tasks completed and of anxiety.

After a 35-minute screening interview 119 patients were offered randomization (method unspecified) in the RCT, and 35 refused. The 84 consenters continued with a two-hour assessment including one-hour self-rating at the computer. Of the 84, 13 dropped out prematurely, 71 completed it and 70 had six-month follow-up. The 71 had been randomized to carry out one of three forms of self-exposure therapy over ten weeks guided by the computer (n=28) or a psychiatrist (n=19) or the book *Living With Fear* (Marks, 1978) (n=24). All three groups improved significantly at post-treatment and at one, three and six months follow-up with no significant differences between them. The same result was found in the subsample of 46/71 patients who met DSM-III criteria for agoraphobia. In 20 of the CP completers outcome resembled that in 20 matched historic controls who had face-to-face guided exposure in the same clinic the previous year (Carr et al., 1988).

UK: *PC and internet FearFighter (FF)* system

FearFighter (FF) is a CP self-help system for phobia/panic disorder which guides patients through nine self-exposure steps (Hayward, MacGregor, Peck, & Wilkes, 2007; Kenwright, Liness, & Marks, 2001; Kenwright, Gega, Mataix-Cols, & Marks, 2004; Marks et al., 2004; Schneider, Mataix-Cols, Marks, & Bachofen, 2005; Shaw, Marks, & Toole, 1999). It explains the exposure therapy rationale with case examples and helps patients to identify their problems and goals in a step-by-step personalized exposure program, with homework diaries, feedback on progress and troubleshooting advice. *FF* was studied when used on a standalone PC in a clinic or GP surgery (*standaloneFF* – two open trials and a RCT) or used on the internet (*netFF*) mostly at home (two open trials and a RCT). *FearFighter* has been sold to and is in use by many healthcare trusts around the UK.

UK: *PC standaloneFearFighter*

Open trial 1

This *standaloneFF* study (Shaw et al., 1999) was in agora/claustrophobia patients – 17 in a tertiary clinic in London with face-to-face (ftf) support from a psychiatrist, psychologist or administrator, and six in a GP surgery in Wales with ftf brief support from an administrator. The London clinic had 15/17 completers of whom 2 improved markedly, 4 moderately, 3 slightly, and 6 were unchanged. The Wales practice had 4/6 completers who improved from 100% to 13%.

Open trial 2

The outcome of *standaloneFF* (n=54) in a psychiatric outpatient clinic in south London was compared to that of patients in the same clinic the previous year who had face-to-face (ftf) therapist-guided self-exposure (n=31) (Kenwright et al., 2001). The *standaloneFF* patients improved significantly from pre- to post-treatment, as much as had their respective historical ftf controls.

RCT

Concealed randomization was made of 93 London outpatients with panic disorder/agoraphobia, social or specific phobia to one of three conditions in a 2:2:1 ratio: (a) *standaloneFF* + brief ftf therapist support; (b) ftf therapist-guided self-exposure; (c) computer-guided non-exposure self-relaxation with brief ftf therapist support (Marks et al., 2004). Analysis was of 90 patients. The two exposure conditions combined had significantly more dropouts than relaxation (*FF* 43%; ftf 24%; relaxation 6%). In completer and intent-to-treat (ITT) analyses, the *standaloneFF* and ftf-guided self-exposure groups improved significantly and similarly to each other, with comparable satisfaction. Mean effect sizes on primary measures at one-month follow-up were *FF* 3.7, ftf 3.5, relaxation 0.5. Relaxation patients improved significantly but much less than the other two groups. The use of *FF* cut clinician time by 73% without impairing outcome. Patient satisfaction was greater with relaxation than with self-exposure guided by *standaloneFF* or ftf, reflecting relaxation's higher completion rate but not treatment outcome. Assessor blindness was maintained for *standaloneFF* vs ftf-led self-exposure but not for those two self-exposure conditions combined vs self-relaxation. Ratings were reliable (r of self vs assessor ratings medium to large). Relaxation without exposure is one form of treatment as usual, so gains with *FF* were better than with treatment as usual and similar to that of ftf-guided self-exposure. In a cost-effectiveness analysis (McCrone, Marks, Kenwright, McDonough, Whittaker, & Mataix-Cols, 2006) the per-patient cost of *FF*, clinician-led therapy, and relaxation was respectively £331, £453 and £122. Computer-aided therapy was more cost-effective not only than the relaxation placebo, but even than clinician-led therapy if a unit improvement in problems is valued at less than £180.

UK: Educational FF

FearFighter is also available in a short educational version (*edFF*). It is reviewed here because it guides healthcare professionals and students as a pretend patient interactively through individually tailored self-exposure therapy for phobia/panic and can help them to briefly support *FF* users.

RCT 1

One RCT of *edFF* randomized 37 London medical students to learn about phobias and self-exposure therapy for 90 minutes either by going alone through *edFF* or by having a group face-to-face tutorial (McDonough & Marks, 2002). On pre- and post-teaching answers to multiple choice questions, the students' gain in knowledge from a solo single *edFF* session resembled that from the group face-to-face tutorial but required far less teacher time, though the group face-to-face tutorial students enjoyed their session more.

RCT 2

In a second RCT in London (Gega et al., 2007), *edFF* was tested with six modifications from the first RCT: it used a more comprehensive and updated version of *edFF*; it tested 92 pre-registration nursing, not medical, students; its control group was a medium-size group lecture-discussion (*L*) as opposed to a small-group tutorial; it revised the outcome measures to fit the revised content of *edFF* and of *L*; its instruction was for 60, not 90, minutes. The students, after completing an hour of one teaching method (*edFF* or *L*), completed a second hour of instruction by the other teaching method (*L* or *edFF*); 85 gave pre-post measures. Each teaching method led to similar improvements in knowledge and skills, and to similar satisfaction, when used on its own or in tandem with the other method. *edFF* was more efficient than *L* as it saved teacher preparation and delivery time and needed no specialist tutor.

NET SYSTEMS

UK: *NetFearFighter*

FF transferred to the internet is called *netFF*.

Open trial 1

The patients were referrals to a west London stress self-help clinic who had various phobias/panic disorder. The open trial tested the outcome of *netFF* used mostly at home with brief therapist phone support (n=10 after 1 refused, 0 dropped out) with that of users of *standaloneFF* in a clinic with brief therapist ftf support (n=17 after 12 refused, 16 dropped out) (Kenwright et al., 2004; Marks et al., 2003). The two groups improved markedly and similarly, with effect sizes ranging from 1.8 to 0.4 across different measures. *NetFF* patients used it over a mean of 66 days and had slightly longer support (113' by phone vs 99' ftf), having been the first to ever use *netFF*.

30 HANDS-ON HELP: COMPUTER-AIDED PSYCHOTHERAPY

Open trial 2

In a second open trial done independently of *FF*'s developers (Hayward et al., 2007), 32 patients in the rural Scottish Highlands used *netFF* and improved in phobias, anxiety, comorbid depression, and disability with effect sizes ranging from 1.5 to 0.7 across various measures. Depression comorbid with phobia/panic had also improved with *netFF* in the study of Kenwright et al. (2004).

RCT

Concealed randomization was made in a 2:1 ratio to: (a) *netFF* self-exposure (n=45); or (b) net-self-help to manage anxiety with CBT excluding exposure (*netMA*, n=23). Each was used mostly at home with brief therapist phone support (Schneider et al., 2005). *NetMA* comprised anxiety and mood ratings, mood and activity homework diaries, education about anxiety, panic and their management (relaxation, diaphragmatic breathing, coping responses) and omitted exposure instructions. Dropouts were 12 from *netFF* and 8 from *netMA*. Both groups improved significantly and similarly at week 10 post-treatment, but *netFF* including exposure was superior to *netMA* without exposure on some self- and assessor ratings at 14 weeks (one month follow-up). Effect sizes of *netFF* ranged from 3.4 to 0.4 across different measures. The two therapists had comparable outcomes. At week 10 the assessor was truly blind though at week 14 guesses about treatment condition were better than by chance. The study noted self and clinician blind ratings on valid and reliable outcome measures, power calculations, entry criteria, and screening and monitoring procedures. It controlled for time and support-helpline sessions with a clinician, time and sessions interacting with a computer and doing homework, net access, and phobia type. It made only a completer, not an intent-to-treat analysis.

NetFF's effect size was lower than with *standaloneFF* in some earlier studies. This might have reflected home vs clinic access, delayed vs immediate technician and therapist support to resolve problems, and/or small differences in ease of use of net vs standalone *FF*. Because the effect size of *netMA*'s non-exposure was greater than with standalone non-exposure relaxation in the first RCT, *netMA* could not be considered a placebo. It is unclear how much of *netMA*'s greater effect was due to CBT ingredients absent from the standalone relaxation of Marks et al. (2004), e.g. problem solving, time management, cognitive restructuring and pleasant activities.

In brief, the standalone and net *FearFighter* versions for phobia/panic were effective in naturalistic studies and efficacious in RCTs in a total of 274 patients. Its educational version helped medical and nursing students learn about exposure therapy to help *FF* users. *NetFF* is being sold to and in use by UK healthcare authorities and is recommended by both NICE, the English regulatory body, and the Scottish Chief Scientist's Office, for managing panic and phobia.

Sweden: *Net bibliosystem guiding CBT for panic disorder*

This system (Table 2.2: Carlbring, Westling, Ljungstrand, Ekselius, & Andersson, 2001; Carlbring, Ekselius, & Andersson, 2003; Carlbring et al., 2005) resembles a modular workbook of up to 250 pages in its expanded year 2005 version. It originally had about 10% interactivity and has more now. Users are required to give email answers at the end of each module and a therapist gives email support and in one RCT also gave phone support. In three studies the users were asked to contribute to an online discussion group. Four RCTs of this Swedish system were in panic disorder, mostly with agoraphobia. Subjects were self-recruited via a computerized screening interview and had above average education. They used the system mostly at home.

RCT 1: netCBT vs yoked waitlist (Carlbring et al., 2001)

Five hundred responders to advertisements completed an internet-based interview for screening and baseline self-ratings over two weeks. From the completers of baseline ratings, 41 DSM-IV panic-disorder subjects without severe depression were selected. These were randomized pairwise to: (a) a yoked control waiting list (n=20); or (b) net-CBT-self-help (n=21) over six modules – education, breathing retraining, cognitive restructuring, interoceptive exposure, live exposure, relapse prevention. Net users had 14 days to complete each module and had to answer questions at the end of each module before getting the password to the next module. When a net self-help patient was ready to do post-treatment ratings his or her yoked control was asked to self-rate too. A therapist emailed an enquiry about progress between days 10 and 14 and at the start of each new week, spending, over 7 to 12 weeks, a mean total email per patient time of 90 minutes over a mean total of 7.5 email contacts per patient. Of subjects 88% completed net-self-help. At post-treatment, compared to waitlist patients the net-self-help patients improved clinically significantly more on most measures including panic, avoidance and depression. No follow-up was reported. NetCBT

TABLE 2.2
CP for **phobia/panic** via internet – Swedish, Australian and Canadian systems

Study	Phobia/panic system	Design	Participants	Outcome
Kenwright et al. (2004); Schneider et al. (2005)	*netFearFighter*: see Table 2.1.	Open study and RCT: see Table 2.1.	UK phobia/panic pts: see Table 2.1.	See Table 2.1.
Carlbring et al. (2001)	Swedish netCBT for panic in 6 modules + scheduled brief email support – mean 90mins.	RCT over 7–12w: (1) netCBT n=21; (2) yoked WL n=20.	Sweden: 41 pts with DSM-IV **panic disorder**. Dropouts 4/21, netCBT, 1/20 WL.	NetCBT self-help ES 0.9, sig imp >WL on most measures. No fu.
Carlbring et al. (2003)	As in Carlbring et al. (2001) + scheduled brief email support – mean 30mins. No deadline to complete modules.	RCT pre-post 7m: (1) net-CBT-self-help; (2) net-*applied*- relaxation + CD (incl exposure).	Sweden: 22 WL pts with DSM-IV **panic disorder** n=11 per gp. DOs 3/11 CBT, 2/11 *applied*-relaxation.	NetCBT self-help ES 0.4 with trend < net-*applied* relaxation ES 0.7. No fu.
Carlbring et al. (2005)	As in Carlbring et al. (2001) but 10 modules, + online group discuss + scheduled email support 150mins in all.	RCT over 10w: (1) netCBT; (2) ftf CBT, 10 1-hr sess weekly. Fu at 1m and 1y.	Sweden: 49 pts with DSM-IV **panic disorder** on WL for netCBT. n=25 netCBT, n=24 ftfCBT. 3 DOs per gp.	NetCBT = ftfCBT at week 10 and at 1m fu. Respective ESs: wk 10 – 0.8 and 1.0; 12m fu – 0.8 and 0.9.
Carlbring et al. (2007a)	As in Carlbring et al. (2005) + 10 scheduled wkly 10-min phone calls = total 220mins email + phone support.	RCT over 10w: (1) netCBT n=30; (2) WL n=30.	Sweden: 60 DSM-IV **panic disorder** patients 2 DOs.	NetCBT similar imp. and > completers than in 2005 RCT; 80% no longer met PD criteria at wk 14; ES=1.1 at wk 10 and 1.0 at 9m fu.
Andersson et al. (2006)	As in Carlbring et al. (2005) but for **social phobia** + email support + online discuss gp + 2 live gp-exposure sess.	RCT1 for 9w: (1) netCBT n=32 + email support 2h each + 2 live gp-exposure sess 2h each; (2) WL n=32.	Sweden: 64 DSM-IV **social phobics** via national/ regional ads. ??DOs.	NetCBT + live gp expos imp soc anx, dep, gen anx, satisf; ES pre-post 0.9 within-gp, 0.7 between-gps.

Study	Intervention	Design	Sample	Results
Carlbring et al. (2007b) *Panic Online* (*PO*) precursor: RCT 1	As in Andersson et al. + email support + phone support.	RCT 2 for 9w: (1) netCBT n=30 *v*; (2) WL n=30.	Sweden: 60 DSM-IV **social phobics** via newspaper and net ads. DOs 3netCBT, 2WL.	44% attrition from computer- to phone-screen interview. NetCBT > WL, 93% compliance. Imp at 1y.
Carlbring et al. (2006b)	As in Andersson et al. (2006) + email support + online discussion gp. no live exposure gp.	PostRCT WL crossover to netCBT. Open study 9w.	Sweden: 26 DSM-IV **social phobics** after 9w on WL for netCBT in Andersson et al. (2006).	NetCBT imp ES 0.9 at post-treatment and 1.3 at 6m fu.
Klein & Richards (2001) *Panic Online* (*PO*) precursor: RCT 1	Net self-help + brief therapist support ftf and by phone: 2 modules.	RCT 1 over 3w: (1) Net self-help n=11; (2) Self-monitoring=12.	Australia: 23 patients with DSM-IV **panic disorder**.	Self-help ES 0.2–0.5; self-help sig > self-monitoring. No fu.
Richards & Alverenga (2002)	*PO* precursor on net: ↑ Klein & Richards (2001) from 2 to 5 modules.	Open trial: 5-module system over 5–8w. Post-test 3m post-entry.	Australia: 14 patients DSM-IV **panic disorder**.	*Panic Online* ES 0.3; imp at 3m post-entry.
Klein et al. (2006) *Panic Online*: RCT 2	Net*Panic Online* (*PO*).	RCT2: 6w: (1) *PO* + email help. n=19; (2) *MAP* manual CBT + phone help, n=18; (3) net-info WL + phone checks, n=18.	Australia: 55 DSM-IV **panic disorder** clients, 80% with **agoraphobia**. DOs n=1, 3, 5.	Net*PO* and *MAP* imp = to 3m fu, and > net panic-information WL at post-test.
Richards et al. (2006) *Panic Online*: RCT 3	Net*PO* as in Richards & Alverenga (2002) and net*PSO* (*PO*) + stress management.	RCT 3, 8w: (1) Net*PO* n=12; (2) Net*PSO* n=11 (each + email support): (3) net-info WL n=9 + email checks.	Australia: 32 DSM-IV **panic disorder** clients, 78% with **agoraphobia**.	Net*PO* <net*PSO* at w8 but = net*PSO* at 3m fu at 20w post-entry. Net*PO* and net*PSO* > WL at 8w.
Farvolden et al. (2005)	*Panic Program* workbook on *Panic Center* website + bulletin-board support group.	12w open trial of free visitors.	Canada: of 1161 registrants over 18m with an **anxiety or mood disorder**, only 12 reached session 12.	Attrition++: 13%→1% did sess 3→12. Users imp, liked support group, printed *Panic Program's* pdf file.

34 HANDS-ON HELP: COMPUTER-AIDED PSYCHOTHERAPY

users said the system without eye contact eased their confiding of sensitive information such as fear of loss of control.

RCT 2: netCBT vs net-applied relaxation + CD + cellphone text reminders to relax (Carlbring et al., 2003)

This concerned DSM-IV panic-disorder subjects who had spent a mean of 15 months on the 2001 study waitlist. The RCT randomized 22 subjects to either (1) netCBT self-help as in 2001 [but with (a) email therapist support for only 30, not 90, mins given via 25 standardized emailed answers to emailed questions and (b) no time limit to complete each module]; or (2) net-*applied* relaxation (*A*R) including exposure instructions and a CD and cellphone text reminders to relax.

NetCBT users had to email satisfactory answers to questions at the end of each module before getting a password to the next module, and if they did not were emailed what to do to progress. Net-CBT-self-help had six and net-*A*R nine modules, implying fewer emails from the therapist to CBT vs *A*R subjects. Three months post-entry, all subjects were sent an email asking about progress. There were 11 completers per condition. Each group improved significantly, with netCBT being slightly inferior to net*A*R (effect sizes 0.4 vs 0.7). NetCBT's 0.4 effect size was less than half the 0.9 effect size with users in the 2001 study, with subjects completing less of the material than in the 2001 study, perhaps due to subject differences, having been on a waitlist, less therapist support time, fewer and standardized therapist emails, and/or no time limit to complete each module. Subjects wanted prompts and deadlines to reduce procrastination. Though intended as a placebo, *applied* relaxation includes exposure instructions of known efficacy and so was not a neutral placebo. No follow-up was reported.

RCT 3: expanded netCBT vs face-to-face (ftf) CBT (Carlbring et al., 2005)

Forty-nine DSM-IV panic-disorder subjects who had been a mean of seven months on a waitlist for netCBT passed screening interviews by computer and then face to face. They were randomized to: (a) use a more interactive ten-module version of Carlbring et al.'s (2001) six-module system (n=25); or (b) have face-to-face (ftf) CBT (n=24) from a therapist using those modules in manualized form in ten one-hour sessions a week, and after ftf sessions to listen to an audiotape of that session. The year-2001 modules were increased from six to ten in number totalling about 250 pages including socialization material, a hyperventilation test, and assertiveness training, and the pace across different modules was made more even. NetCBT subjects were asked to email answers to each module's questions and within 36 hours were either

2. CP FOR PHOBIC/PANIC DISORDER   35

emailed positive feedback plus the password to the next module or were told how to qualify to go there. In each module subjects had to post at least one message in an online discussion group about a given topic which fellow participants could read and comment on and a warm supportive atmosphere developed. The therapists were not very experienced with panic disorder. Each condition had three dropouts. The two groups improved significantly with no marked differences between them. Effect sizes were respectively for netCBT and ftfCBT: at post-treatment 0.8 and 1.0, and at one-year follow-up 0.8 and 0.9. Mean total therapist time per patient over the ten treatment weeks was 2.5 hours by email for netCBT and 10 hours for ftfCBT. The authors thought netCBT users might do even better with phone support though weekly phone calls had not enhanced headache relief in users of netCBT (Andersson, Lundstrom, & Ström, 2003).

RCT 4: netCBT vs waitlist (Carlbring et al., 2006a)

Sixty DSM-IV panic disorder subjects passed screening interviews by computer and then by phone. They were randomized to ten weeks of either: (a) being on a waiting list (n=30); or (b) using netCBT as in the 2005 study (n=30) including an online discussion group with a warm supportive atmosphere. NetCBT had email support for a per-patient mean of 12 minutes weekly to a total of 120 minutes over 10 weeks (as in the 2005 study), plus an added ten scheduled weekly 10-minute phone calls to a total of 100 minutes in all. Per-patient therapist time over 10 weeks thus totalled 220 minutes (120+100).

NetCBT subjects in the 2006 RCT improved with more completers than in the 2005 RCT (80% vs 28%, and vs 88% for ftf CBT in 2005). From pre- to post-test, netCBT improved more than the waiting list on bodily interpretations, maladaptive cognitions, avoidance, general anxiety, depression, and quality of life. NetCBT subjects finished more modules in the 2006b than 2005 study. At week 14, on blind-assessor ratings 77% of netCBT but 0% of waiting-list subjects no longer had panic disorder. Overall between-group effect size was 1.1 at week 10 and 1.0 at 9-month follow-up. NetCBT's within-group effect size (1.1) more resembled that of 2005 ftfCBT (1.0) than of 2005 netCBT (0.8). On that basis, but not on ceasing to have panic disorder, gains with netCBT were boosted by adding 100 minutes of live phone support to the 120 minutes of email support. Most subjects were satisfied with their treatment.

Sweden: *Net bibliosystem guiding CBT for social phobia*

This netCBT system for social phobia (Andersson et al., 2006; Carlbring et al., 2006a) resembles the Swedish system for panic disorder. It is a self-help

36   HANDS-ON HELP: COMPUTER-AIDED PSYCHOTHERAPY

manual adapted for use on the web, and consists of a workbook of 186 pages in nine modules. Among others it describes social phobia and CBT with cognitive restructuring and behavioural experiments, goal setting, exposure, social skills training and relapse prevention. To progress from one module to the next subjects must answer and pass between three and eight essay questions and also multiple-choice quizzes monitored by online therapists and must post at least one message in an online discussion forum.

RCT 1

Sixty-four DSM-IV social phobics were recruited in Sweden (Andersson et al., 2006) via ads after screening by first a computer interview and then a live SCID interview at the psychology department. They were assigned by a random-number service to nine weeks of either: (a) netCBT by a self-help manual on the web paced to complete one module a week (n=32) plus email therapist support for a mean of 180 mins per patient plus two live two-hour group exposure sessions with six other subjects at the psychology department; or (b) a waitlist whose treatment was delayed to the end of week nine. Dropouts at nine weeks were 3 netCBT, 0 WL. Subjects' mean age was 37 and problem duration 23 years; 62% had been to university (almost twice the national average) and only 8% were unemployed or on a disability pension. Total per-patient therapist time for netCBT was six hours. NetCBT patients improved on social and general anxiety, depression and quality of life, with between-group effect size of 0.7.

In brief, after face-to-face screening, netCBT plus an online discussion forum plus email therapist support plus live therapist-led group exposure in a psychology department, social phobics improved more than those on a waitlist. The design cannot tell how much the superiority of netCBT was due to netCBT, to its mean per-patient therapist contact by email for two hours and face to face in a group for four hours, and to the waitlist having none of those and not expecting to improve.

RCT 2

Adult DSM-IV social phobics without depression were recruited in Sweden (Andersson et al., 2006) via newspaper ads and a web page linked to the home page of the Swedish National Anxiety Association. Of 243 applicants, trial criteria were met by 127 in a computer-screen interview. Of those 127, fully 65 could not then be reached for a phone-screen interview of

2. CP FOR PHOBIC/PANIC DISORDER   37

unspecified duration, but 60 were phoned and met criteria in that interview. The 60 had concealed randomization to nine weeks of either: (1) netCBT; or (2) being on a waitlist. Subjects never met staff in person. NetCBT subjects participated in an online discussion group and had support from student psychologists for an unspecified duration in nine weekly emails on a free encrypted service plus weekly phone calls, each lasting about 11 mins, totalling 95 mins per patient. At week nine, 28 netCBT and 28 waitlist subjects gave data (7% dropout rate). NetCBT improved more than the waitlist with a mean between-group effect size of 1.0 across all measures. At one-year follow-up improvement continued after netCBT (n=28), within-group effect size being 1.0; by then waitlist subjects had been treated. Trial subjects had more post-secondary education than the general population (60% vs 33%).

In brief, in the second RCT, social phobics who had netCBT plus an online discussion group plus weekly email and phone support to a total of 120 minutes improved more over nine weeks than a waitlist and stayed improved a year later. The waitlist design could not tell how much netCBT's apparent superiority reflected an attention placebo effect and the various extra supports given with netCBT, nor whether such netCBT would help less educated subjects. It is also unclear why attrition from computer to phone screening was fully 47%.

Open study (crossover from waitlist of RCT 2 above)

After completing screening interviews by computer and by phone and nine weeks on the waitlist of Carlbring, Gunnarsdóttir, Hedensjö, Andersson, Ekselius, and Furmark (2007b), 26 of the 32 social phobic controls had netCBT for nine weeks plus email contact as in the RCT and were asked to contribute to an online discussion group (Carlbring, Furmark, Steczkó, Ekselius, & Andersson, 2006b). Unlike the RCT's netCBT group, this crossover netCBT group had no live group exposure led by a therapist. All nine netCBT modules were completed by 62% of the subjects. Mean per-patient therapist time with netCBT totalled three hours over the nine weeks regarding administration and reading and answering emails. Unusually for social phobics, fully 69% were female and only 8% were unemployed. Subjects had not improved while on the nine-week waiting list, but after nine weeks of netCBT plus therapist email contact plus an online discussion group they improved significantly on social and general anxiety, depression

38   HANDS-ON HELP: COMPUTER-AIDED PSYCHOTHERAPY

and quality of life with an overall within-group effect size of 0.9. Gains consolidated by six-month follow-up (ES 1.3).

Discussion of Swedish net biblioCP systems for panic and social phobia

NetCP users improved in panic a bit less than did users of a net applied relaxation system which included exposure. The Swedish users had above average education, as was true for the Australian users of two internet systems for depression (Christensen et al., 2004a). Users of the Swedish system liked having self-help at home at convenient times, and higher ratings of treatment credibility associated with more improvement in the studies by Carlbring et al. (2005, 2006a), as in Osgood-Hynes et al. (1998) but not in the studies by Carlbring et al. (2001, 2003). The Swedish subjects felt pressured to work too fast through netCBT.

As the authors say, it is unclear how much less-educated subjects would improve with the Swedish workbook-type systems whose demands for emailed answers to multiple choice questions and/or essays resemble those of a college course (in contrast, *FearFighter*, *BTSteps* and *Cope* assume a reading age of 11). The Swedish open social phobia study is called 'Internet-based bibliotherapy with minimal therapist contact via e-mail', and three hours of therapist support time per patient is not negligible. Also unknown is how much compliance was boosted by the initial computer diagnostic screening having been followed by a live interview either face to face or by phone. Further Swedish studies with similar netbiblio systems are in train for spider phobia and snake phobia.

Individuals can buy access from Livanda to the Swedish netbiblio systems for anxiety (social, panic, generalized), depression, neck and back pain, stress, or sleep disorder at prices from 600 SEK (€65) to 2000 SEK (€220). The highest price allows unrestricted questions by email over six months. Many of the emailed questions and answers are made public on the site.

In brief, for Swedish net biblioCP overall panic disorder sufferers improved more than on a waitlist if they used netCP for panic/ agoraphobia. Gains were greater if they also had an online discussion group and email support and additional phone support, in which case gains were almost as good as with ftf CBT. In the two RCTs with the best outcome, therapist input totalled 3.7 or 2.5 hours – 70% to 50% less than the usual 8 hours of ftf therapist time. Net biblioCP for social phobia with email support for 3 hours plus an online discussion group plus 6 hours of live group exposure at a psychology department, led

> social phobics to improve up to 6–12 months follow-up. Social phobics improved even without live group exposure with netCP plus an online discussion group plus email support or with a total of 1.5 hours of phone support over 9 weeks. Such phone support seemed to reduce dropouts. Swedish netbiblio systems appear to be best for people with above-average education.

Australia: *Net Panic Online*

This net workbook system began as two modules (Klein & Richards, 2001) and was then modified slightly and reorganized into five modules (Richards & Alverenga, 2002). Both systems guided panic education, coping strategies, self-monitoring and cognitive restructuring and gave therapist support and quizzes at the end of self-assessment sections. After these two trials a full CBT website for panic disorder was developed called *Panic Online* (net*PO*). This password-protected system on a university website gave standard instructions and information that did not vary according to client input. It gave downloadable audio for relaxation, interoceptive and live exposure exercise instructions, slides for exposure, and links to other panic/anxiety websites. Users could enter weekly panic information online and/or email their therapist directly to obtain feedback.

RCT 1: 2-module system

A small Australian RCT (Klein & Richards, 2001) randomized 22 DSM-IV panic-disorder patients (86% women) to: (a) net-self-help (nature, effects and causes of panic and how to manage it including cognitive restructuring but no exposure); or (b) self-monitoring. Net self-help was accessed for one week from the patient's own terminal or at the research site. A therapist spent a mean of 3.5 hours per patient, including assessment time. Net-self-help's effect size 3 weeks after starting was just 0.2 to 0.5 but significantly greater than with self-monitoring, whose effect size was unspecified. There was no further follow-up.

Open trial: 5-module system

In this small Australian study (Richards & Alverenga, 2002), 9 of 14 DSM-IV panic-order patients completed it and improved in panic with an effect size of just 0.3, to 3 months post-treatment.

40   HANDS-ON HELP: COMPUTER-AIDED PSYCHOTHERAPY

RCT 2: Panic Online (netPO; Version 1)

Panic Online (net*PO*) was tested in a RCT in Australia (Klein, Richards, & Austin, 2006). A panic website yielded 130 self-referrals. In a 90-minute live phone interview a clinician screened and rated subjects who also self-rated online. Of the 55 panic disorder subjects enrolled, 82% had agoraphobia and 53% were on a psychotropic drug. They were randomized (concealed) to have six weeks of either: (a) net*PO* at home (n=19); or (b) therapist-aided CBT manual at home (*Mastery of Your Anxiety and Panic [MAP]*; Barlow & Craske, 2000; n=18); or (c) net-panic-information waitlist control (*Panic Resource*; n=18). Net*PO* and *MAP* each guided the same CBT tasks (controlled breathing, cognitive restructuring, interoceptive and situational exposure, relapse prevention), while a CBT therapist guided users through net*PO* by email with answers to queries within 24 hours. *MAP* subjects were posted a copy of the manual and a CBT therapist phoned weekly to monitor progress. Net-information controls were told to wait six weeks for CBT. Clinical psychology students phoned controls weekly to check their status. Assessments were not blind.

Of the 55 enrollees, 9 (16%) dropped out by week 6 (respectively 1, 3, 5). Analyses carried forward the last available observation. Compared to the net-information waitlist, at week 6 both net*PO* and *MAP* improved on every measure (panic, cognitions, anxiety and stress, number of GP visits, and physical health). Net*PO* was better than *MAP* in reducing clinician-rated agoraphobia and number of GP visits. At three months followup (20 weeks post-entry) both CBT groups maintained gains, with net*PO* being better on self-rated physical health and reduced GP visits. Subjects rated *PO* and *MAP* as equally credible and satisfying. Total psychologist time spent per client over the six-week study was appreciable: 5.5 hrs for *PO*, 4 hrs for *MAP*, 1 hr for controls. A psychologist sent a mean of 16 emails to *PO* clients and received a mean of 13 emails from them, and phoned *MAP* clients a mean of 8 times and controls a mean of 4 times. Total therapist-contact cost was A\$350 net*PO*, A\$379 *MAP*, A\$55 control. Subjects' number of days in the RCT was 46 net*PO*, 63 *MAP*, 40 control. The MAP manual had more content than the *PO* website and took longer to get through.

It is unclear how much the greater gains with net*PO* and with *MAP* reflected greater expectancies of change than in the control waitlist. The low dropout rate might reflect the 90-minute live phone screening interview and appreciable human contact during the RCT – the control waitlist had the least contact and the most dropouts.

That panic/agoraphobia improved with CBT comparably whether guided at home by net or manual plus appreciable remote support resembles a finding by Ghosh et al. (1988). In that RCT gains in panic/agoraphobia and other phobias were similar whether self-exposure was guided in a clinic either by a standalone computer or by the manual *Living With Fear* (or guided face to face by a therapist).

> *In brief*, improvement in the RCT of net*Panic Online* was similar whether CBT was guided by the net or by a manual with each also having substantial email or phone guidance. It is unclear how much their superiority to net-panic-information waitlist controls reflected a greater therapeutic expectancy.

RCT 3: 6-module netPO (Version 1) vs 13-module netPO + STRESS (Version 2; netPSO) vs information-only control WL

This small Australian RCT (Richards et al., 2006) tested net*PSO* which is net*PO* plus six more modules on coping with stress, time and anger management, tuning into one's thoughts, relaxation, and social connectedness. Net*PSO* took about 90 more minutes to read than net*PO*.

Of 68 self-referrals from an Australian panic website 63 were screened by 90-minute phone clinical interviews and online questionnaires; 32 met trial criteria including DSM-IV panic disorder. Entrants were randomized (concealed) to eight weeks of either: (a) net*PO* as in RCT 2 (n=12); (b) net*PSO* (n=11); or (c) net-panic-information waitlist control (n=9). Net*PO*, net*PSO* and netcontrol each had email support for respective means per participant of 376, 309 and about 52 minutes in all over eight weeks. Mean problem duration was 13 years, mean age was 37, and mean number of years of education was 13. Net*PSO* had more males than the other groups. Dropouts were 2 net*PO*, 1 net*PSO*, 2 control.

For missing data, analyses carried forward last observations. Net*PSO* was marginally better than net*PO* at week eight (post-treatment) but not at follow-up three months later. Net*PO* and net*PSO* were superior to the waitlist control on almost every measure.

> *In brief*, net*Panic Online* plus extra stress-management modules did not enduringly enhance the efficacy of net*PO*. This RCT is a fine example of how netCP facilitates dismantling research concerning which treatment ingredients are useful. It is unclear how much the superiority to the waitlist of net*PO* and net*PSO* reflected their better expectancies and far longer email durations of support.

42   HANDS-ON HELP: COMPUTER-AIDED PSYCHOTHERAPY

Canada: *Net Panic Program*

Panic Program offers 12 weekly sessions of netCBT self-help on a website (*Panic Center*) to promote interaction between panic sufferers and their healthcare professionals (Farvolden et al., 2005). The site's features include educational content, a nurse-moderated, bulletin-board support group, a screen for mood/anxiety disorders, a panic diary, and *Panic Program*. *Panic Program* is like a workbook on screens without much interaction. Site visitors register with it by completing a depression/anxiety screen, giving an anonymous email address and a screen name different from their own, their age, gender and country of residence, and information on their panic symptoms. They can then, for free, go through *Panic Program* at their own pace, download it, use the panic diary, and join the bulletin-board support group.

Open study

Over 18 months the *Panic Center* website had 485,000 visits and 115,000 page views from 100,000 visitors. Of 15,000 users who did the screening test, two-thirds were female. The screening diagnosis was (in 100s): GAD 60, panic disorder+agoraphobia 44, dysthymia 41, PTSD 37, agoraphobia but no panic 36, social phobia (non-generalized) 35, OCD 25, major depression 20, no diagnosis 19, panic disorder but no agoraphobia 3.

From the 1161 users who did session 1 of *Panic Program*, numbers dropped sharply over successive sessions (sessions 2, 3, 4, 5, 6 had respectively 525, 152, 145, 91, 46 users) and merely 12 (1%) users completed all 12 sessions. The 13% who did 3 or more sessions rated significant reductions in panics from weeks 1 to 2 to weeks 3, 6 or 8, interference with their daily lives decreased greatly, and the number meeting screening criteria for disorders which had been present at the start fell markedly over successive sessions. All 10 of the 12 completers of session 12 had used the support group and rated it as extremely helpful. Most support group users were passive visitors who did not post information.

Almost all the 1161 users (1159) downloaded the pdf version of *Panic Program* – a noteworthy minority of these said they were professionals. About 10% of users said they used *Panic Program* in collaboration with a healthcare professional. It is not known how many used and benefited from the printed version of *Panic Program* alone.

In brief, massive attrition over successive sessions cut the number of *Panic Program* completers to just 1% of the starters by session 12. The 13% who used it for ≥3 sessions improved, and 10% used it

> together with a healthcare professional. All but two users printed out the pdf version, and a small minority of these said they were healthcare professionals.

HANDHELD-DEVICE SYSTEMS

These are generally used to aid homework between ftf sessions (Table 2.3).

USA: Palmtop computer

For panic/agoraphobia

Australia: single-case study

A panic/agoraphobia patient used a palmtop computer to aid homework set during therapist-guided face-to-face (ftf) panic management (Newman, Kenardy, Herman, & Taylor, 1996). The palmtop had two modes for: (a) *diary* recording of anxiety and panic frequency; (b) *instruction* with feedback for cognitive restructuring, exposure, and breathing retraining. The number of panics per week fell from 8 to 0 by 12-weeks post-test.

Australia and California: RCT

This tested the above palmtop over 12 weeks in 20 patients who had DSM-III panic disorder (Newman et al., 1997a). Ten had ftf CBT for 12-hourly sessions plus the palmtop *diary* for homework, and 10 had ftf CBT for 4 sessions (total 6 hrs) with the palmtop *diary+instruction*. At 12 weeks post-entry, each group improved significantly and similarly in body symptoms, behavioural avoidance and panic cognitions. Patients who had 12-session ftf CBT plus a palmtop diary improved more clinically significantly at post-treatment but not at six-month follow-up.

Australia and Scotland: RCT

A two-site RCT (Australia/Scotland) tested the value of DSM-IV panic-disorder patients carrying the above palmtop between sessions to prompt and monitor relevant CBT homework (Kenardy et al., 2003a). Compared to Scottish patients, Australian ones were more educated and more often on benzodiazepines. The RCT randomized panic patients with (76%) or without (24%) agoraphobia to: (a) face-to-face (ftf) CBT in six sessions augmented by a palmtop computer; (b) six sessions of ftf CBT only; (c) 12 sessions of ftf CBT only; (d) waiting list. Of the 186 patients randomized, 23 did not start treatment and a further 23 began but dropped out before

TABLE 2.3
CP for **phobia/panic**: handheld devices aiding homework between ftf sessions

Study	Phobia/panic system	Design	Participants	Outcome
Newman et al. (1996, 1997a)	Palmtop computer to support panic management by ftf CBT.	1 case: 12w pre-post test; ftf CBT for 4 sess (total 6h) + palmtop diary and treatment.	Australia: 1 patient with **DSM-III panic disorder**.	Panics per week ↓ from 8 to 0 at post-test.
Newman et al. (1997b)	Palmtop computer to aid between-session homework in ftf CBT.	RCT, 12w: (1) ftf CBT for 12 1h sess + palmtop diary; (2) ftf CBT for 4 sess (total 6h) + palmtop diary + self-help.	Australia and California: 20 pts with DSM-III **panic disorder** (10 per condition), 18 completers (9 per condition).	Each treatment imp sig pre-post. 12 sess ftf CBT + palmtop had > clinically sig imp at wk 12, but at 6m fu = 4-session CBT + palmtop.
Kenardy et al. (2003a)	Palmtop computer to aid between-session homework in ftf CBT.	RCT over 12w: (1) 6 1h sess ftf CBT + palmtop n=39; (2) 12 1h sess ftf CBT n=41; (3) 6 1h sess ftf CBT n=42; (4) WL n=41. 6m fu.	Australia and Scotland (n per site unclear) 186 DSM-IV **panic disorder** +/− agoraphobia randomized, 107 completers.	12 sess ftf CBT ES 2.2 > 6 sess ftf CBT + palmptop ES 2.0 > 6 sess ftf CBT ES 1.5 > WL ES not given. Active treatments = at 6m fu.

Gruber et al. (2001)	Palmtop + ftf group CBT.	RCT over 12w: (1) 12 wkly 2.5h sess ftf group CBT; (2) 8 2.5h sess of ftf group CBT + palmtop; (3) waiting list. 6m fu.	California: 54 DSM-III-R **social phobia** pts, 18 per condition. Used palmtop mean of 20 times over 12w.	At post, 12 sess group CBT > 8 sess group CBT + palmtop > WL on most measures. At 6m fu, 12 sess = 8 sess CBT.
Przeworski & Newman (2004)	Palmtop to aid homework during ftf gp CBT.	1 case, 6 2h sess ftf group CBT + manual.	USA: 1 **social phobic** used palmtop >150 times.	Improved markedly.
Meuret et al. (2001)	Handheld capnometer → respiratory feedback + audiotape tones for breathing homework.	Case series: 5 80m sessions over 4w. 8w fu.	California: 4 patients with DSM-IV **panic disorder + agoraphobic** symptoms.	Sig imp including ↑ pCO_2; no panics and ↓ avoidance at post-treatment and 8w fu.
Meuret et al. (2006b)	Capnometer + audiotape as for Meuret et al. (2001).	RCT: (1) 5 ftf sess + 4w capnometer + audiotape-aided breathing homework vs (2) waitlist control.	California: 37 DSM-IV **panic/agora** pts: (1) Capnometer etc. n=20; (2) WL n=17.	Capnometer etc. > WL on symptoms, pCO_2 and respir. rate up to 1y fu. ES 2.2 to 0.80 – ↓ therapist time 37%.

session four (i.e. 46 [25%] gave no or inadequate change data), 107 (56%) were completers, and 93 (50% of the 186) reached nine months post-entry. The study included a power calculation, intent-to-treat and completer analyses, and reported means, standard deviations, effect sizes and clinically significant changes. All three CBT groups improved more than the waiting list. Improvement was greatest with 12-session ftf CBT, second most with six-session ftf CBT + palmtop computer, and third most with six-session ftf CBT without the palmtop (effect sizes respectively 2.2, 2.0 and 1.5, not given for WL). At six months follow-up the three treatment conditions were indistinguishable. It was unclear if the palmtop enhanced improvement with six ftf sessions enough to make its use more worthwhile than 12-session ftf without a palmtop. Cost-effectiveness analyses are in train.

For social phobia

California: RCT (Gruber, Moran, Roth, & Taylor, 2001)

Fifty-four DSM-III-R social phobics were assigned, 18 per condition, to: (a) 12 weekly 2.5 hr sessions of group CBT; or (b) eight 2.5 hr sessions over 12 weeks of group CBT + palmtop instructions intended to remind patients daily to do cognitive restructuring and exposure homework and check whether they'd done this and if not why not; or (c) a waiting list. Two psychologists using a manual led each group of six subjects. Dropouts from the three RCT conditions were respectively 4, 3 and 1 by post-treatment and 5 and 6 by six-month follow-up. Twelve-session group CBT was initially superior to eight-session group CBT + palmtop. By six-month follow-up, however, both group-CBT conditions were equally improved, though treatment cost was a bit less in the palmtop group due to slightly less use of therapist time. Both were superior to waiting list controls on most behavioural measures and social phobia symptoms. Each CBT patient used the ambulatory palmtop a mean of 20 times over 12 weeks.

USA: Single-case study

Far more frequent use of a palmtop (>150 times), together with five two-hour group ftf CBT sessions, was seen in a social phobic patient in the USA who improved markedly (Przeworski & Newman, 2004), despite the palmtop having been designed for use in GAD rather than social phobia. Similarly, social and specific phobics improved with *FearFighter* (Marks et al., 2004; Schneider et al., 2005), despite its design having been for use with agoraphobia/panic, spider and agoraphobics improved to some extent with *CAVE* even when their vicarious exposure concerned a lift (elevator) phobia (Harcourt, Kirkby, Daniels, & Montgomery, 1998; Smith, Kirkby, Montgomery, & Daniels, 1997), and flying phobics (Bornas et al., 2006).

Mixed phobics (Schneider et al., 2005) improved somewhat with non-exposure CBT. Such observations raise vital questions about how much anxiety reduction across CP studies reflected specific habituation, more general stress immunization and/or problem solving, and/or other mechanisms (Marks & Dar, 2000). Such questions go beyond our CP brief, but the CP observations during CP show its potential value as a tool to investigate mechanisms of improvement, quite apart from its value for the delivery of services.

California: Handheld capnometer to aid breathing control for panic/agoraphobia

Open study

Like some palmtop programs, this handheld-capnometer program gives users feedback based on their input, in this case to aid breathing therapy homework between sessions, and so can count as a simple CP device. In a thoughtful small study (Meuret et al., 2001; Meuret, Wilhelm, & Roth, 2004) four volunteers had DSM-IV panic disorder with agoraphobic symptoms. They had five 80-minute sessions over four weeks to learn that panic can be maintained by hyperventilation causing low CO_2 and to breathe slowly diaphragmatically. After session one they were given a capnometer to get immediate audiovisual feedback about CO_2 levels and respiratory rate during breathing exercises aimed at raising end-tidal pCO_2 and reducing breathing rate and instability. The sidestream capnometer sampled, through a nasal cannula, gas exhaled during breathing exercises, displayed measures on a monitor, and allowed data transfer to a computer. They were asked to do, in different settings, twice-daily 17-minute regular breathing exercises paced to tones on a pocket audiotape and to raise pCO_2 to 40mm Hg on the portable capnometer, and to rate symptoms and feelings in weekly diaries. Tapes for successive weeks were made to give respectively 13, 11, 9 and 6 tones per minute. Each exercise consisted of: (a) 2 mins sitting quietly; (b) 10 mins breathing paced to the taped tones while occasionally checking rate and pCO_2; (c) 5 mins breathing without pacing tones while maintaining subjects' previous rate and pCO_2. The subjects were compliant and very satisfied. They became panic-free and less avoidant, and raised their pCO_2 after four weeks treatment and at follow-up eight weeks later.

RCT

A RCT of use of the capnometer and an audiotape during breathing-therapy homework was run in 37 DSM-IV panic-disorder patients with (n=31) or without (n=6) agoraphobia (Meuret, Wilhelm, Ritz, & Roth, 2006a, 2006b)

48 HANDS-ON HELP: COMPUTER-AIDED PSYCHOTHERAPY

who included the four subjects of Meuret et al. (2001). After a ftf diagnostic interview, subjects were randomized (method unspecified) to four weeks of: (a) five hour-long sessions of capnometer-aided breathing therapy (n=20) (as in Meuret et al., 2001); or (b) a waitlist control group (n=17). For those 11/31 breathing-therapy subjects who began with normal pCO_2, focus was on breathing regularly. Mean duration of panic disorder was nine years. Most were well educated. All had respiratory monitoring for 24 hours before and after the end of the four-week trial – they had low pCO_2 at the start. Patients complied well and did 91% of the exercises advised. There were no dropouts during treatment and only 4 (12%) by 12-month follow-up. Breathing-therapy patients improved more than waitlist patients until 12-month follow-up on self-rated panic, agoraphobic avoidance and disability, as much as is usual after cognitive therapy or CBT, and pCO_2 and breathing rate normalized. On almost all measures between-group effect sizes were large, ranging from 2.2 to 0.8. The capnometer used cost $2500, and a competitor now costs $1295. Intriguing questions about mechanisms of improvement arise as gains occurred despite the absence of explicit exposure, cognitive restructuring or relaxation instructions, and baseline pCO_2 and respiratory symptoms did not predict outcome, while having a waitlist control left open how much improvement reflected a placebo effect. The total of 5 hours of therapist time per capnometer patient saved perhaps 37% of the mean of 8 ftfCBT hours per panic/agoraphobia outpatient in Marks's unit, or 62% of the 13 hours used by Barlow et al. (2000).

A smaller pilot trial (n=20) in Boston compared four weeks of handheld capnometer feedback during homework exercises to cognitive restructuring and homework exercises, with both groups then having three sessions of live exposure (Meuret et al., 2006b). Final results are awaited.

In brief, panic/agoraphobia patients improved when they used a handheld capnometer and an audiotape to guide breathing-retraining homework and it saved 37–62% of usual therapist time.

DISPLAY EXPOSURE SYSTEMS

Tasmania: PC indirect Computer-Aided Vicarious Exposure (*CAVE*)

CAVE (Table 2.4) is a computer game to teach users exposure therapy as they direct a supposedly phobic screen figure to approach and remain in

Study	Phobia system	Design	Participants	Outcome
Smith et al. (1997)	*Computer-Aided Vicarious Exposure (CAVE)* for spider phobia on standalone PC in clinic with a clinician present.	RCT 3 40-min sess over 6w: (1) relevant exposure + feedback; (2) relevant exposure without feedback; (3) irrelevant exposure + feedback. 9m fu.	Tasmania: 45 DSM-III-R **spider phobics**. Each group n=15.	All groups imp sig pre-post-9m fu. Outcome unaffected by relevance of exposure cues or by intermittent self-rating of anxiety.
Gilroy et al. (2000) and 33m fu by Gilroy et al. (2003)	*CAVE* as in Smith et al. (1997) above.	RCT of 3 45-min sess over 2w: (1) *CAVE*; (2) ftf-guided exposure; (3) relaxation. 33m fu.	Tasmania: 45 CIDI **spider phobics** n=15 per gp. 42 fu to 33m, by when had had further psychological therapy for problem (50 suitable/45 completers post-tr., 42 at 33m fu).	*CAVE* exposure imp sig = ftf exposure, > relaxation; ES 0.50–0.74 *CAVE*, 0.38–0.76 ftf exposure, 0.06–0.53 relaxation. At 33m fu sig gains kept, but not > relax which had had various other therapies.
Heading et al. (2001)	*CAVE* as in Smith et al. (1997) above.	RCT of 1 3h sess of: (1) *CAVE* (n=13); or (2) ftf-led exposure (n=14); or (3) waiting list (n=13). 4w fu.	Tasmania: 40 DSM-IV **spider phobics**.	*CAVE* < ftf-led exposure and = WL on all measures to 4w fu except SUDS. ES on FQ main phobia pre-post, pre-fu: *CAVE*: 1.1, 1.8; ftf exposure: 4, 4.1; WL = 0.3, 0.2.

continues overleaf

TABLE 2.4 Continued

Study	Phobia system	Design	Participants	Outcome
Fraser et al. (2001)	*CAVE* as in Smith et al. (1997).	RCT of 45-min sessions over 3w: (1) *CAVE* 3w sess; (2) *CAVE* 6 sess twice weekly. 4w fu.	Tasmania: 30 DSM-IV **spider phobics**, 15 per condition.	Sig imp pre-post and pre-fu for 3 and 6 sess. ES: FQ main phobia: 3-sess *CAVE*: 0.75 (pre-post), 2.25 (pre-fu); 6-sess *CAVE*: 2.3 pre-post and pre-fu.
Dewis et al. (2001)	*CAVE* as in Smith et al. (1997).	RCT: (1) 3 45-min sess over 3w or (2) live exposure, or (3) WL.	Tasmania: 28 **spider phobics** aged 10–17. Each cell n=9–10.	Up to 1m fu, *CAVE* > WL on ES but not sig, and sig < live exposure.
Harcourt et al. (1998); Kirkby et al. (1999)	*CAVE* as in Smith et al. (1997) above, except exposure cue was lift, not spider.	Open study of 3 × 45-min weekly sessions of *CAVE*. Ratings at end of session 3.	Tasmania: 18 DSM-III-R **agoraphobics** with or without panic, only one of whom had lift phobia.	Agora imp slightly. >; neuroticism r + with > exposure; > conscientiousness r + with harder exposure tasks, < agreeableness r + with > improvement.
Clark et al. (1998); Kirkby et al. (2000)	In Table 3.1 for OCD.	In Table 3.1 for OCD.	In Table 3.1 for OCD.	In Table 3.1 for OCD.

avoided feared situations shown on the screen until that figure's fear score drops. By pointing and clicking with *CAVE*'s computer mouse, users steer a 'phobic' screen figure through avoided discomforting scenes (e.g. spider phobic nearing a spider, agoraphobic leaving home, claustrophobic entering a lift, OCD washer touching garden soil) as that figure's supposed anxiety-thermometer score rises with each approach and then falls as the figure remains in the situation. The game gives and displays to users points for moving the figure towards exposure scenes, the aim being to score 2000 points. All mouse human–computer interactions are recorded for process analysis. A therapist is present as an observer who is not involved. *CAVE* was evaluated in five RCTs and two more explored the effect of personality on aspects of *CAVE* use.

Five RCTs of CAVE for spider phobia

RCT 1 (Smith et al., 1997) randomized 45 spider phobics to one of three *CAVE* treatments (each n=15): (a or b) relevant exposure (spider) either with or without the pictured person's assumed anxiety level displayed on-screen; (c) irrelevant *CAVE* exposure (lift) with anxiety ratings displayed. Phobias improved in all three groups by post-treatment and nine-month follow-up and gains were unaffected by relevance of the exposure cue or display on the screen of the figure's anxiety ratings.

RCT 2 (Gilroy et al., 2000, 2003) randomized 45 spider phobics to (each group n=15): (a) *CAVE*; (b) ftf live exposure; (c) audiotape-guided progressive muscle relaxation. Up to three-month follow-up *CAVE*'s effect size was small to medium and similar to that of therapist-delivered exposure but greater than that of relaxation. At 33-month follow-up (Gilroy et al., 2003), improvement was maintained for the 42/45 patients for whom data were available.

RCT 3 (Heading et al., 2001) randomized 40 spider phobics to: (a) one session of *CAVE*; (b) one session of ftf live exposure; (c) a waiting list control. Ratings were made a week after completing the session and at four weeks follow-up. *CAVE* was less effective than ftf live exposure and no better than the waiting list except on subjective units of distress. Effect sizes on the Fear Questionnaire (main problem) for pre-post and pre-1mfu for *CAVE* 1.1 and 1.8, for ftf exposure 4.0 and 4.1, and for waitlist 0.3 and 0.2.

RCT 4 (Fraser et al., 2001) randomized 30 spider phobics to: (a) three *CAVE* sessions or 2.6 *CAVE* sessions. Sessions were weekly for group one and twice-weekly for group two and were all completed within three weeks with follow-up four weeks later. Overall, three- and six-session *CAVE* improved significantly and similarly for pre-post and pre one-month follow-up, though at post-treatment effect sizes were larger and on more measures with six- than three-session *CAVE*. Effect sizes for FQ main problem at

52   HANDS-ON HELP: COMPUTER-AIDED PSYCHOTHERAPY

pre-post and at pre-follow-up were: three-session *CAVE* 0.8 and 2.3 and 6-session *CAVE* 2.3 for both.

RCT 5 was in 28 spider-phobic children and teenagers aged 10–17 (Dewis. Kirkby, Martin, Daniels, Gilroy, & Menzies, 2001). They were randomized to have three 45-minute sessions of *CAVE* or live exposure or be on a waitlist (each n=9 or 10). Up to one-month follow-up, across six measures *CAVE*'s effect size was smaller than with live exposure but mostly larger than in the waitlist group. The spider phobics improved no more significantly with *CAVE* than with being on a waitlist, and less than with live exposure and than with Gilroy et al.'s (2000) adult spider phobics who used *CAVE*. It was unclear how much this reflected *CAVE*'s screen person being an adult rather than a child or teenager. Neither study gave explicit exposure homework instructions.

Open study of CAVE for agoraphobia

In this open study (Harcourt et al., 1998; Kirkby, Daniels, Harcourt, & Romano, 1999) agoraphobic (DSM-III-R) volunteers used *CAVE* to move a supposedly lift-phobic figure they saw on a computer screen to enter and stay in a lift (elevator). This constituted irrelevant vicarious exposure as only one of the 18 subjects was lift-phobic. After three 45-minute weekly *CAVE* sessions they improved modestly (6–15%) on the three measures used. Surprisingly, more improvement related to low agreeableness (trust, straightforwardness, altruism, tender-mindedness) and low openness (open-mindedness, intellectual curiosity). More vicarious exposure done correlated positively with more neuroticism, and more difficult vicarious exposure tasks done related to more conscientiousness. Older subjects repeated the first stages of vicarious exposure longer before moving further up the hierarchy. Process measures did not correlate significantly with initial fear severity or outcome.

Open study of CAVE for OCD

See Clark et al. (1998) and Kirkby et al. (2000) in Chapter 3 and Table 3.1.

In brief, forms of *CAVE* on a PC have, across different RCTs, improved adult but not young spider phobics to varying extents and have in open studies improved agoraphobics slightly with irrelevant exposure and improved OCD slightly.

DIRECT NON-IMMERSIVE DISPLAY SYSTEMS

USA and UK: early PC systems

An early system in the USA comprised audiotaped relaxation training followed by computer-controlled desensitization for test anxiety (Table 2.5: Biglan, Vilwock, & Wick, 1979). In a psychology department, test-anxious students saw on a television screen 20 written items presented from a standard test-anxiety hierarchy. They were asked to imagine those items while relaxing and if they felt anxious to press a discomfort key which controlled computer instructions to relax and to repeatedly imagine scenes from the hierarchy written on the screen. Subjects had help from an assistant for a mean of two hours. Of 15 subjects who began, six dropped out and nine completed the program in a mean of four sessions and improved significantly on test anxiety.

A man with agoraphobia and obsessive ruminations used a second US system (Chandler, Burck, & Sampson, 1986; Chandler et al., 1988) to do systematic desensitization with repeated relaxation while seeing frightening pictures on a screen. The computer showed him how to do muscle relaxation and build a hierarchy of phobic stimuli. A counsellor reviewed his hierarchy to load relevant pictures into the computer. After the patient entered on the computer that he had relaxed with six neutral pictures, the computer displayed frightening hierarchy pictures for him to look at. If he felt anxious he pressed the spacebar to bring on a neutral scene and an instruction to relax. Once relaxed, he pressed the spacebar again to display a phobic scene. He was asked to practise between sessions relaxing while facing live situations he had seen as computer pictures. He became almost symptom free after 13 sessions and maintained his gains at eight months follow-up.

A UK display system for spider phobia was tested in a small RCT (Hassan, 1992). The 38 spider-phobic volunteers were randomized to either: (a) see a computer display of spider pictures up a hierarchy under their control in 40-minute sessions twice a week until they felt they could handle a real spider fearlessly (a therapist was present all the time); (b) do live exposure up a hierarchy in a therapist's presence; (c) do live exposure up a hierarchy in a therapist's presence after first seeing that therapist perform (model) each exposure task; (d) go on to a waitlist. All treatment sessions lasted 40 minutes. Across the three treatment groups mean number of sessions was four to five and mean total therapist time was three hours, so the computer condition saved no therapist time. The three treatment groups improved similarly and significantly and more than the waitlist group on their spider phobia (but not on tachycardia), and maintained their improvement for at least 45 days follow-up.

TABLE 2.5
CP for **phobia/panic disorder** – direct display systems

Study	Phobia system	Design	Participants	Outcome
Biglan et al. (1979)	Audiotaped relaxation + PDP15 desens. test anxiety + 2h support.	Open study, mean of 4 sess.	USA, Oregon: 15 **test-anxious** students began, 9 completed.	Test anxiety imp sig.
Chandler et al. (1986, 1988)	Screen display to desensitize agoraphobia.	1 case: 13 sess over 12w. Post-test 4w after session 13. 8m fu.	USA: 1 man with **agoraphobia** and **obsessive** ruminations.	Imp markedly on problem and FQ to post and 8m fu.
Hassan (1992)	Screen display for exposure in spider phobics.	RCT: (1) computer display; (2) and (3) live exposure without/with modelling; (4) waitlist.	UK: 38 **spider-phobic** volunteers.	Computer display and live exposure –/+ modelling imp =, > WL, until 45 days fu.
Nelissen et al. (1995)	Screen exposure display in spider phobia.	2 cases. 1h computer display, then 2h live exposure 1 sess only.	UK: 2 **spider-phobic** girls aged 9 and 10.	No imp after 1h display then much imp after 2h live exposure.
Coldwell et al. (1998, 2007)	*CARL* – screen display to aid exposure therapy for dental injection phobia.	RCT of *CARL* used with one dose of drug placebo or alprazolam 0.5mg or exposure 0.75mg.	USA RCT: 153 DSM-IV **dental injection** phobics used *CARL* with drug placebo or alprazolam 0.5 or 0.75 mg. 144 completers. 1y fu.	144 completed *CARL*, 143 had 1, and 92 had 2, dental injections. Almost half completed therapy with a hygienist in 1 sess. Imp continued to 1y fu.

Bornas et al. (2001a)	Screen display of flying photos + sounds.	Single case only: 8 sess over 4 w.	Majorca:1 **flying** phobic patient.	Improved.
Bornas et al. (2001b)	Screen display as in Bornas et al. (2001a).	RCT: (1) CAE (CP exposure) (n=15); (2) IRCAE (CAE + info + relaxation (n=18); (3) Waiting list (n=17) ?6w.	Majorca: 50 **flight phobics**: CAE = up to 6 50-min sess over 3w. Therapist attended all exposure sessions and end test flight.	CAE completed by 100% CAE, 72% IRCAE. Test flight at end completed by 93% CAE > 50% IRCAE > 12% WL. On flying fearCAE>IRCAE>WL.
Bornas et al. (2002)	Screen display as in Bornas et al. (2001a).	Open study of CAE: Majorca computer screen at airport (n=12), German univ clinic large screen (n=8).	Majorca and Germany: 20 **flight phobics**: inexperienced therapists, unlike Bornas et al. (2001a, 2001b). CAE 3.2h.	95% completed CAE and end-of-treatment flight, 90% showed fear reduction.
Bornas et al. (2006)	(1) CAE non-immersive display as in Bornas et al. (2001a). (2) MNE (multi-component 'non-exposure').	RCT: 6 50-min sess 2 × wk: (1) CAE mean 4.1 sess, no homework (n=19); (2) MNE including homework, mean ?? sessions (n=21). All pts paid €90. Blind clinician ratings.	Majorca: 40 pts with DSM-IV **fear of flying**. Completed 3w rx; 32 completed 6m fu (13/19 CAE, 2/21 MNE).	CAE and MNE imp = and sig and clinically. At 3w and 6m fu imp = CAE 42%, 44%; MNE 35%, 29%. ES at 3w, 6m fu CAE 3.6, 3.8; MNE 2.5, 2.0 on Fear of Flying Ques.

56 HANDS-ON HELP: COMPUTER-AIDED PSYCHOTHERAPY

A second UK display system for spider phobia (Whitby & Allcock, 1994) was used in two children aged 9 and 10 (Nelissen, Muris, & Merkelbach, 1995). Viewing the screen display for just one hour led to no improvement, but going on to two hours of live exposure led to marked improvement. The results are hard to interpret as the display's duration was only half that of live exposure and always preceded live exposure, so a potential order effect could not be excluded.

USA: PC system *CARL* (computer assisted relaxation learning) for dental-injection fear

CARL (computer assisted relaxation learning) is an ingenious PC display system in the USA (Coldwell, Getz, Milgrom, Prall, Spadafora, & Ramsay, 1998; Coldwell, Wilhelm, Milgrom, Prall, Getz, Spadafora et al., 2007; personal communications 14, 18, 19 July, 2005) which was effective and saved about 60% of therapist time in a RCT. *CARL* aids vicarious followed by live exposure therapy for fear of dental injections – such fear caused avoidance of dentistry in about 5% of University of Washington students and employees (Milgrom, Coldwell, Getz, Weinstein, & Ramsay, 1997). During vicarious exposure the patient reclines alone in a dental chair watching *CARL*'s computer-controlled video scenes on a Macintosh color screen mounted on a movable platform over the dental chair. The patient answers questions appearing on the screen using a movable keyboard sited under the monitor and a mouse on a mouse pad built into the arm of the dental chair. Early video scenes show a psychologist teaching a model patient (an actress) relaxation, paced breathing, and other coping strategies. *CARL* replays video scenes if the real patient's answers indicate more understanding is needed. *CARL* then plays seven two-minute video exposure scenes (steps) showing a hygienist explaining to the model patient the steps towards a dental injection, ending in giving that model patient an injection. If the real patient rates low anxiety after a step then *CARL* advances to the next video step up the hierarchy.

In the RCT below, after having rated low anxiety with every video step the real patient progressed, reclining in the dental chair, to have live exposure therapy with a dental hygienist who was cued by a teleprompt on a screen not seen by the real patient to give live exposure therapy following the vicarious exposure steps in *CARL*'s video. The hygienist's screen displayed the seven video exposure scenes with a model patient together with a line-by-line script and an arrow moving down it to pace her speed of doing live exposure with the real patient to match that in the scene with the model patient. If the hygienist fell behind she could pause the prompter. When she completed a live exposure step with the real patient like the vicarious step with the model patient, then the real patient saw an anxiety rating scale appear on the patient's screen and rated anxiety felt during that live exposure step. Depending on that rating, *CARL*'s computer moved the scene on the hygienist's screen one step back or forward. *CARL* also had further modules for research purposes.

Over 18 months, 52 dental-injection phobics completed *CARL*, of whom nine completed one-year follow-up, all of whom improved on their fear of injections and remained so at one-year follow-up (Coldwell et al., 1998). In a full RCT with *CARL* (Coldwell et al., 2007), 153 subjects with DSM-IV specific phobia of dental injections were randomized to have exposure therapy aided by *CARL* either together with a drug placebo or with an acute dose of 0.5 mg alprazolam or of 0.75 mg alprazolam. There was no non-netCP comparison group. The 144 subjects completed the RCT, at the end of which fully 143 (99%) had one dental injection (92 [64%] with low anxiety) and 134 (93%) had a second dental injection. Alprazolam conferred no advantage, and somewhat impaired benefits from exposure therapy. Improvement was maintained for at least a year. *CARL*'s results were promising. After spending a mean of about 85 minutes completing their viewing of *CARL*'s video, almost half the patients completed live exposure therapy with a hygienist in only one session of up to nine steps (mean time about 50 minutes) despite having been under no pressure and having been encouraged to repeat *CARL*'s steps as needed. Fainting occurred only a few times, perhaps reflecting the reclined position of the dental chair during exposure therapy.

CARL thus reduced dental-injection fear so at its end almost all users had a dental injection. It may be especially helpful where therapists are unavailable. *CARL* might save a mean of up to $250 per patient if patients completed its vicarious exposure phase using *CARL*'s computer-controlled video on their own before seeing a hygienist or dentist, e.g. if it becomes available on the internet. *CARL* is currently being evaluated in private practice dental offices. It is not yet available commercially.

In brief, unlike alprazolam, *CARL* was effective for fear of dental injections. It also saved much therapist time.

Majorca: Display system for fear of flying (Bornas et al., 2001a, 2001b, 2002; Bornas, Tortella-Feliu, & Llabrés, 2003, 2006)

Single case study (Bornas et al., 2001a)

This display system automatically configured a display of photos up the patient's fear hierarchy of flying situations (e.g. buying a ticket, being inside the aircraft, landing, having an aircraft accident) created from his answers to a fear of flying questionnaire integrated into the program. A flying-phobic man sitting in a dark room watched a computer's display on a 100×75 cm screen of frightening photos, plus matching audio cues, up his hierarchy. At intervals he gave fear ratings, and falls in these decided the next photos and sounds to be presented. A therapist sat close behind throughout treatment and gave occasional instructions, e.g. 'sit as if you're in an airplane'. The patient improved after eight sessions over a month and took a real flight with little discomfort.

RCT 1 (Bornas et al., 2001b)

Fifty flight-phobic volunteers who answered a newspaper ad were randomized to individual treatment by: (a) computer-aided exposure (CAE; n=15); or (b) one session of flight information and then four sessions of relaxation, then four CAE (IRCAE; n=18) sessions over 2.5 weeks; or (c) a waiting list (n=17) for three months, after which they had CAE. The CAE display was that of Bornas et al. (2001a). IRCAE subjects also saw a 40-minute video-taped interview with a pilot about flying and security and received a brochure about it, and were taught relaxation and asked to practise this as homework. Subjects had up to six (mean 3.1) 50-min CAE sessions twice a week over a mean total of three weeks in CAE or 2.5 weeks in IRCAE. A therapist attended all exposure sessions and a pre-planned end-of-treatment test flight.

By six weeks after trial entry, CAE was completed by all 15 CAE and 13/18 (72%) IRCAE subjects. The end-of-treatment flight was completed by significantly more CAE than IRCAE or waitlist subjects (respectively 93%, 50%, 12%). Fear of flying scores fell significantly more in CAE and IRCAE than waiting list subjects. This improvement continued to 6-month follow-up in the 48% of CAE and IRCAE subjects who gave information then.

IRCAE's added information about flying and doing relaxation did not enhance therapeutic benefit from CAE. CAE saved no therapist time as a therapist attended throughout. Whether CAE's results are better than those of imaginal exposure needing no equipment requires testing in a different RCT design. The same is true for whether self-administered CAE might be effective with far less therapist time.

Open study (Bornas et al., 2002)

Flight-phobic volunteers answered newspaper ads, of whom 12 had CAE using a computer screen in an office at an airport in Majorca and eight had CAE using a large screen in a German university clinic. As before, a therapist was present throughout CAE sessions and the test flight, but unlike in previous studies was inexperienced. Face-to-face screening lasted an hour. Mean total CAE exposure time was 3.2 hours. Of the 20 flight phobics, 19 completed CAE and a planned end-of-treatment flight, and 90% of subjects showed fear reduction.

RCT 2 (Bornas et al., 2006)

In a RCT in Majorca, 40 flying phobics were recruited by newspaper ads and randomized to one of two treatments in a university clinic, each designed for six 50-min sessions over three weeks by a therapist following a manual. Treatment one was an improved form of CAE (n=20) displaying flying-related pictures for a mean of 4.1 sessions. Treatment two was a non-exposure (NE) form of CBT given face to face (n=21) consisting of flying information, breathing and relaxation training, and challenging fearful thoughts, over six sessions. NE but not CAE patients had homework instructions. To control for use of a computer, NE subjects also saw two of the six CAE exposure pictures rather than non-exposure pictures. Total per-patient therapist time was 205 minutes in CAE and 300 minutes in NE.

The two groups had comparable scores at the start. Each treatment yielded significant and clinically meaningful improvement by the end of therapy, which was completed by all subjects bar one. Gains were maintained to six-month follow-up in the 65% of CAE and 90% of NE subjects who gave data then. Mean improvement was: after three weeks therapy, 42% CAE and 35% NE; at six-month follow up, 44% CAE and 29% NE. Effect sizes were large for fear of flying at three weeks and six-month follow-up, being respectively 3.5, 3.8 for CAE and 2.5, 2.0 for NE. At six-month follow-up CAE had significantly more recovered subjects (77% vs 44%), a finding resembling the superiority of exposure vs non-exposure CP at 1-month follow-up which was found by Schneider et al. (2005).

In brief, watching computer-aided displays of exposure cues improved flying phobics, though face-to-face therapy with minimal exposure but instead flying education, breathing and relaxation training and challenging fearful thoughts was almost as effective. This accords with findings in other studies that not only exposure but also certain non-exposure therapies can improve phobias (Marks & Dar, 2000; Schneider et al., 2005). A therapist was present throughout the displays, so CAE saved no therapist time. Whether having a therapist present for less time would impair outcome remains to be tested.

IMMERSIVE VIRTUAL REALITY (VR) SYSTEMS FOR ANXIETY DISORDERS

Many immersive VR systems have been developed as aids to exposure therapy (e.g. Rothbaum et al., 2000; Rothbaum, Hodges, Anderson, & Price, 2002). Their number is growing rapidly and the relevant literature is huge. With immersive VR systems, sufferers who are phobic of heights, flying or public speaking, or have PTSD, wear a display helmet on which they see phobia or stress-evoking scenes concerning their problem for up to an hour. Sufferers can thus gradually habituate and lose their fear. Exposure to VR scenes resembles various methods since the 1960s of doing exposure in imagination (in fantasy) or to photos, films or videos. At the time of writing such VR has not been shown to be superior to those earlier and far cheaper methods of exposure therapy. Just a single immersive VR system currently costs many thousands of dollars, though the price of VR can be expected to fall in years to come. VR is not yet available on the internet so patients travel to clinics to use it.

Immersive VR systems do not as yet make appreciable treatment decisions and so fall outside the remit of this review. That might alter if future VR systems come to tailor patients' progress through those systems according to the patients' responses. VR could then save therapist time in a way which it generally does not at present. Though it makes no treatment decisions, one ingenious VR system (*Snow World*) at an early phase of development is mentioned briefly in the section on pain in Chapter 8 (Hoffman, 2004).

CHAPTER THREE

CP for obsessive-compulsive disorder and post-traumatic stress disorder

---

CHAPTER SUMMARY

CP for **OCD** has only been studied in three systems. A USA palmtop/laptop system improved two patients. The USA–UK IVR *BTSteps* system was studied in 314 patients. Home use of *BTSteps* plus its workbook improved OCD in two open studies and two RCTs, is clinically efficacious as NICE recognized, and was cost-effective on several criteria. Scheduled brief support by phone enhanced improvement with *BTSteps*, which saves over 80% of clinician time. In its new internet form *BTSteps* is called *OCFighter*. An Australian *CAVE* system improved OCD in an open study in 13 volunteers.

With regard to CP for **PTSD**, too few details are available to properly gauge the value of a Dutch *Interapy* system for CP. It is unclear if it saves therapist time given apparently extensive time used for email support. A US system improved PTSD in a small waitlist-control RCT. VR systems are not detailed for reasons noted earlier.

TABLE 3.1
CP for **obsessive-compulsive disorder (OCD)** and **post-traumatic stress disorder (PTSD)**

Study	OCD system	Design	Participants	Outcome
Baer et al. (1987, 1988)	OCCheck on handheld (palmtop) computer + ftf ERP.	Open, 2 case reports.	USA: 2 **OCD** pts (2 others refused).	Imp for up to yr on using OCCheck, relapsed on stopping it.
Marks et al. (1998a); Greist et al. (1998) Bachofen et al. (1999); Nakagawa et al. (2000)	BTSteps (BTS) phone-IVR ERP guidance + workbook + live phone or ftf screening and rating. BTSteps as in Greist et al. (1998).	Open Study 1: 12w self-assessment and self-ERP: n=40. No fu. Open Study 2: n=23, as Study 1 above.	Study 1: 40 **OCD** (DSM-IV) pts – 25 in USA and 15 in UK. Study 2: 23 in UK **OCD** (ICD10) BTS pts vs 20 matched historical controls who had ftfERP.	Studies 1 and 2: >3/4 pts did self-assess: Just < half pts did >1 ERP sess, imp sig, esp if: > initial motivation, did >1 ERP sess – BTS = ftfERP controls, cut therapist time by 83%.
Greist et al. (2002); McCrone et al. (2006a)	BTSteps (BTS) as in Marks et al. (1998), Greist et al. (1998) above.	Multisite RCT over 12w: 2w self-assessment + 10w self-ERP; had 4 ftf evaluations (total 1h). Randomised: (1) BTS n=74 vs (2) ftfCBT n=69 vs (3) self-relaxat via audiotape n=75.	7 sites in USA, 1 in Canada: 218 DSM-IV **OCD** pts: 176 had at least 1 post-baseline evaluation: DOs: BTSteps 18%, ftfCBT 14%, relaxation 11%.	ftfCBT > BTS > relax on OCD and satisf; ES on YBOCS: BTS 0.8; ftfCBT 1.2, relaxation 0.4. BTS = ftfCBT in pts who did >1 ERP sess. DOs: BTS = ftfCBT, BTS > relax. 6m fu: only BTS imp >.
Marks et al. (2003); Kenwright et al. (2005)	BTSteps as Marks et al. (1998a), Greist et al. (1998).	Open study in CP self-help clinic.	W London **OCD** pts: 9/16 completers.	Imp sig, YBOCS ES 1.2 (40% reduction).

Kenwright et al. (2005)	*BTSteps* as in Marks et al. (1998a), Greist et al. (1998) above.	RCT for 17w using *BTSteps* plus support: (1) 9 *scheduled* calls from clinician (n=22), or (2) calls only *onrequest* from pt (n=22).	44 chronic **OCD** patients from round the UK using *BTSteps* via Maudsley Hospital or W. London clinic.	Scheduled vs onrequest had < DOs, > imp, 76 mins vs 16 mins support time per pt: scheduled imp > if did >1 ERP sess or liked *BTS* > ftfCBT.
Clark et al. (1998); Kirkby et al. (2000)	*CAVE* as in Table 2.4a, except exposure cue was dirt. No therapist support.	Open study: 3 45-min weekly sessions. Rated 1w pre and post *CAVE*.	Tasmania: (1) 13 **OCD** (DSM-III-R criteria) pts; (2) 10 non-OCD.	OCD pts imp sig, not clinically, esp if did > *CAVE* tasks and > intelligent. No ES or fu.
Lange et al. (2000a, 2002)	*Interapy*: net online standard writing tasks + email feedback/ support from clinical psychologists.	Open trial, pre-post 5w, 6w fu. 10 45-min writing sessions.	Dutch psychol students with **past trauma/grief**. No diagnosis. 36 applied/24 suitable/23 began/21post/ 20 fu.	Sig imp post and fu. Impact of Event Scale effect size 0.76.
Lange et al. (2003)	*Interapy*: as above + 11 hours therapist support.	RCT: 15 *Interapy* (2 DOs), 15 WL (3 DOs).	30 student volunteers ?	Interapy imp sig > WL. Effect size 1.5–2.0 for symptoms. fu?
Hirai & Clum (2005)	*Net Self-Help for Traumatic Consequences (SHTC)*.	RCT 2 8w: (1) net*SHTC* n=18; (2) waitlist n=18.	36 volunteers with **post-traumatic stress**: DOs 5 SHTC, 3 WL.	*SHTC* > WL on most measures, ESs large to moderate.

CP FOR OCD

USA: *OCCheck* on palmtop and laptop computers

Two OCD (DSM-III) patients with marked checking rituals who had not improved after much ftf guidance in exposure and ritual prevention improved when they were given *OCCheck* to use on a laptop computer at home and on a handheld (palmtop) computer carried outside the home in order to facilitate compliance (Table 3.1: Baer et al., 1987, 1988). They worsened when they did not use the computers and improved again on reinstating use of the computer. Two other patients refused to use *OCCheck*.

USA and UK: *BTSteps* (*BTS*) for OCD

This is an interactive-voice-response (IVR) system which OCD patients reach by phoning a toll-free number to a computer while looking at an accompanying workbook. The 800 or so voice files of *BTSteps* (*BTS*) guide users to set and monitor individually tailored self-exposure and ritual prevention (ERP) homework, keep a diary, make baseline and later ratings, get feedback on progress, deal with difficulties, and prevent relapse. *BTS* assumes an understanding/reading age of 11. *BTS* has been the subject of three open studies and two RCTs. Several studies were completed of *BTS*'s phone-IVR + workbook version in OCD patients in the UK, USA and Canada in varying proportions across different trials. An even more convenient internet version (*OCFighter*) using *BTS*'s phone-IVR algorithms will soon allow home access with no need for printed booklets and phone-IVR calls.

USA and UK: Open studies 1 and 2 of BTSTEPS self-assessment

These trials (Marks et al., 1998a) tested whether UK and USA referrals for OCD (to clinics at the Maudsley Hospital in London, Madison, WI, and Harvard University, MA) completed *BTS* self-assessment successfully prior to ERP self-help. All patients were given the *BTS* workbook and from home phoned the *BTS* computer in Madison to obtain IVR access to *BTS*'s Steps 1–4 of self-assessment. Each had Ethics Committee approval. The UK patients were already on a waiting list for ftfERP.

Altogether 63 patients took part (40 in Study 1: 15 UK, 25 USA; 23 in Study 2: all UK). A clinician diagnosed OCD in a ftf interview, spent 5 minutes explaining how to phone *BTS* and use its workbook, and gave subjects a PIN to access *BTS* and enter a personal password for further confidentiality. Of the UK patients 11 lived too far away to see their coordinator so they had a phone interview and were sent the workbook by post. The UK clinician phoned each UK subject at least once to deal with any technical problems.

Two-thirds of the patients who were offered self-assessment by *BTS* accepted and over three-quarters completed it at home including *BTS*'s IVR self-ratings of the YBOCS, HamD and WSA. *BTS* users had minimal time with a clinician. They completed self-assessment in three to four weeks after spending a mean total of an hour on IVR calls, mostly outside usual office hours. UK cases rated more severity than US subjects on the YBOCS, HamD and WSA. In Study 2, the five subjects who did not finish self-assessment with *BTS* also failed to finish subsequent ftfERP for which they were already on a waiting list. Completion of *BTS* self-assessment predicted later improvement with *BTS* or ftfERP.

BTSteps *outcome in Open Study 1 of Marks et al. (1998a)*

This examined outcome in the 40 UK/USA patients who began *BTS* self-assessment (Greist et al., 1998). Of the 25 who completed it, 17 patients went on to do >1 ERP sessions. They improved significantly on trigger discomfort, YBOCS and WSA, and 61% rated themselves much or very much improved on PGI. Greater gains related to > ERP sessions reported in *BTS* calls. *BTS*'s 30% improvement in YBOCS resembled that in multicentre trials of clomipramine, fluoxetine, fluvoxamine, sertraline and paroxetine. Most responders to a survey felt comfortable with and understood and followed *BTS*-IVR instructions.

BTSteps *outcome in Open Study 2 of Marks et al. (1998a)*

This evaluated outcome in the 23 UK patients markedly disabled by OCD who were on a waiting list for ftfERP (Bachofen et al., 1999; Nakagawa et al., 2000). Of these, 21 had enough time to use *BTS* for at least three weeks before they came off the waiting list to start ftfERP. They had a mean of 99 minutes of help from a coordinating psychiatrist during the mean of 67 days that they used *BTS*, spending a mean of 63 minutes on self-assessment calls and 253 minutes on ERP calls, 53% of all their IVR calls were made outside usual office hours.

The ten patients who went on to do ERP improved significantly on the YBOCS (33% drop) and the WSA, more so if they were more motivated at baseline and completed *BTS* self-assessment quickly. Patients who did <2 ERP sessions did not improve. Improvement and understanding ERP after using *BTS* resembled that of 20 matched historical controls who had ftfERP without prior *BTS*. After patients stopped using *BTS* to have ftfERP (having been on a waiting list for that) they made only marginal further gains but were more satisfied with ftfERP despite a high drop-out rate from it. Using *BTS* saved 83% of per-patient time spent in ftfERP – 99 vs 1118 mins, 11 vs 24 contacts. Outpatient *BTS* users needed less subsequent ftfERP than did their matched controls.

North America: Multisite RCT of BTSteps
(Greist et al., 2002)

This RCT compared the outcome in OCD with rituals of *BTS*-guided ERP, of behaviour therapist ftfERP, and of relaxation. It was conducted at seven US and one Canadian sites where none of the authors worked or held appointments. The RCT had local Ethics Committee approval, and patients gave written informed consent.

A power analysis determined sample size. Using masked randomization, 218 OCD patients (DSM-IV) were randomized to two assessment weeks followed by ten weeks of treatment by: (a) *BTS* (n=74); or (b) ftfERP (n=69); or (c) systematic relaxation guided by an audiotape and manual (n=75). Initial screening was by a clinician. Patients' OCD was initially severe (mean YBOCS 25) and very chronic (mean duration 22 years). All saw a clinician for 15 mins at baseline and at the end of weeks 2, 6 and 10 to evaluate gains and safety of participation; evaluation and ffCBT sessions were audiotaped for auditing. Outcome measures were self-rated. In a sub-sample of 90 patients self-ratings were compared with ratings of a clinician blind to treatment condition and did not differ significantly.

At baseline, the three treatment groups had comparable scores for YBOCS, WSA and HamD. Patients who had ≥1 evaluable post-week 0 visit (57 [*82%*] *BTS*, 55 [*86%*] ftfCBT, 67 [*89%*] relaxation) were included in end-point ITT analyses. By week 10, YBOCS improved significantly more after ftfCBT than *BTS* (mean drop 8.0 vs 5.6), each of which improved significantly more than did relaxation (drop 1.7), which was ineffective. YBOCS effect sizes were 0.84, 1.22 and 0.35 respectively for *BTS*, ftfCBT, and relaxation. The effect sizes of ftfERP and of *BTS* resembled those in other ERP trials and in SSRIs approved for OCD by the USA's FDA. The CGI too improved significantly more with ftfERP than *BTS* (60% vs 38% responders) and with each ERP group than with relaxation (14%). The same was true for PGI (responders 58% ftfERP, 38% *BTS*, 15% relaxation). FtfERP was not superior to *BTS* on the reduction in number of hours per day spent in rituals and in obsessions (3.4 hours fall with ftfERP and with *BTS*), with each condition being significantly better than relaxation (0.6 hours fall). On the WSA, ftfERP and *BTS* each improved significantly with no significant difference between them, and both improved significantly more than did relaxation.

FtfERP was not superior to *BTS* in completers of ≥1 ERP session (n=36, 65%). Thus, though more patients may have been motivated to do ERP with ftfERP than with *BTS*, once they began ERP they improved as much whether guided by either. Non-CBT clinicians who do not know exactly how to guide ERP might motivate patients to do ERP guided by *BTS*. In *BTS* and in ftfERP, patients who did >1 ERP session improved significantly more than those who did not. *BTS* patients who improved at week 10 improved slightly further at week 26 after continuing access to *BTS*, whereas ftfERP and relaxation responders at week 10 who then had no further treatment worsened slightly on their YBOCS at week 26. After week 10, *BTS* nonresponders who were then switched to ftfERP and relaxation nonresponders who were switched to *BTS* improved significantly by week 26, but ftfERP nonresponders who were switched to *BTS* did not.

At endpoint, satisfaction was greatest with ftfERP, next greatest with *BTS*, and least with relaxation. ftfERP and *BTS* patients were significantly more satisfied than relaxation patients. Satisfaction correlated significantly with improvement in each condition.

Mean call duration to *BTS* was 9 mins, 61% of calls being made outside office hours. Mean summed duration of all *BTS* calls was 140 mins. *BTS* patients improved more the longer they spent phoning *BTS* overall and doing ERP.

The *BTS* system tracked patients' detailed progress in therapy more easily than was possible in ftfERP regarding type of rituals for which patients did ERP, number of ERP sessions for each goal, and percentage of goals reported completed and associated drop in discomfort.

The RCT design could not address the potential effects of patients: (a) being selected face to face by a clinician before enrolment; (b) seeing a clinician for ratings at weeks –2, 0, 2, 6, 10 and 22 (though this did not make relaxation effective); (c) having a workbook; and (d) the value of *BTS* for patients who have obsessions but no overt rituals (all the RCT patients had overt rituals). *BTS* saved 85% of usual therapist time in ftfERP, the remaining 15% having been spent on initial screening.

In an economic analysis of the multicentre RCT (McCrone et al., 2006a), compared to relaxation, *BTSteps* had a lower cost per unit improvement on the YBOCS ($89) than did clinician-guided ERP ($168). *BTSteps* also had a lower cost per disability-adjusted life-year avoided ($4350 vs $9488). On these criteria *BTSteps* was thus a cost-effective alternative to clinician-guided ERP, though NICE disagreed on other criteria while recognizing the clinical efficacy of *BTSteps* (NICE Appeal Outcome letter, 15 February 2006).

UK: RCT of scheduled vs requested phone support for BTSteps (Kenwright et al., 2004)

This tested whether compliance and outcome with *BTS* was enhanced by brief proactively scheduled phone calls from a clinician. It studied 44 referrals with OCD from round the UK – 34 to the Maudsley Hospital in south London and a later 10 to a self-help clinic in west London (Marks et al., 2003). All but three were managed entirely by phone and never saw staff in person. All had masked randomized assignment to *BTS* for 17 weeks

68 HANDS-ON HELP: COMPUTER-AIDED PSYCHOTHERAPY

with brief live phone support by a clinician either (a) in nine *scheduled* clinician-initiated calls (n=22) or (b) only in *requested* calls from the patient (n=22). *Scheduled* patients had brief calls at weeks 1, 2, 4, 6, 8, 10, 12, 14 and 17 to briefly review progress, be praised for completing ERP tasks, be helped to work through *BTS* and potentiate ERP by facing feared consequences without avoidance, distraction or reassurance, agree at the end of most calls how to speed progress; e.g. reach another step in *BTS*, set a further ERP target before the next live support call, and, in the last call, be encouraged to follow *BTS*'s guidance to prevent relapse by anticipating problems and rehearsing how to deal with them. *Requested* patients were advised to phone (an answerphone was left on outside office hours) if they got stuck, upon which the therapist phoned them back. All patients received a *BTS* workbook, a PIN for IVR calls, and a helpline number, and during the first call chose their own four-digit password.

The patients' OCD was chronic (mean duration 16 years) and severe at baseline (YBOCS 26) with moderate depression (HamD 20), and 64% had failed with past ftfERP. Each group improved, but scheduled support patients had fewer dropouts, more completers of >2ERP sessions (95% vs 57%), more improvement on the YBOCS and WSA, and more time doing IVR calls (232 vs 178 mins). Apart from initial phone selection for 45 mins, mean total support time per patient over 17 weeks was 76 mins for scheduled and 16 mins for requested demand patients. Mean number of support calls was 7.5 for scheduled and 1.5 for on-demand patients. Better outcome was predicted by doing >1 ERP sessions and feeling comfortable using *BTS* and liking it more than ftfERP.

It is not known if scheduled support patients were more compliant because: (a) they were prompted to do daily individually tailored ERP and to complete the next *BTS* step before the next support call; or (b) just being scheduled to report progress motivated them to do more – for this motivating role a CBT therapist might be unnecessary. Compared to three past *BTS* trials (Bachofen et al., 1999; Greist et al., 1998, 2002), improvement in this RCT was similar with scheduled but less with requested support. Human contact in the scheduled group more resembled that in those three past trials than its smaller amount in the requested group. The effects of small differences in brief personal contact deserve further study.

UK: Open study of clinical effectiveness of BTSteps (Marks et al., 2003)

BTS was tested naturalistically in a primary care computer-aided self-help clinic for west London residents. Of 16 OCD patients offered the use of *BTS*, nine completed it and seven dropped out or gave no post-treatment data. The nine completers improved significantly on the YBOCS with an effect size of 1.2, the 40% reduction being more than in the previous studies above. They spent a mean total of four hours on *BTS* calls.

> *In brief*, home use of IVR-*BTSteps* plus its workbook was studied in 341 patients in all. In two open studies severe OCD cases who did exposure and ritual prevention with it improved like historical ftfERP controls. In a large multisite RCT with few dropouts it was more efficacious than relaxation and less efficacious than ftfERP on some but not other measures. In a second small RCT, scheduled brief support by phone enhanced *BTS* outcome. Improvement with *BTS* resembled that with clomipramine or SSRIs. *BTSteps* saved over 80% of clinician time, was cost-effective on several criteria, and can help OCD when therapist-guided ERP is unavailable.

Tasmania: Computer-aided vicarious exposure (CAVE) *for OCD*

CAVE for OCD is like *CAVE* for phobias (above and Table 2.4) except that it depicts a person, dirt cues and faucets at a sink (Clark et al., 1998; Kirkby et al., 2000). It asks patients to regard that person on a standalone PC screen as having contamination obsessions and washing rituals, and to guide them through exposure and ritual prevention (ERP). Users are unsupported by staff.

Open study

In this Tasmanian trial (Clark et al., 1998; Kirkby et al., 2000), 13 OCD (DSM-III-R) volunteers and 10 non-OCD controls with comparable age and education had three 45 mins weekly *CAVE* sessions and were rated one week before and one week after ending *CAVE*. OCD subjects improved significantly on the Padua Inventory and BDI and non-significantly on the YBOCS.

CP FOR PTSD

Netherlands: *Net Interapy*

This Dutch research (Lange et al., 2000a; Lange, van den Ven, Schrieken, Bredeweg, & Emmelkamp, 2000b; Lange, Schoutrop, Schrieken, & van den Ven, 2002; Lange, Rietdijk, Hudcovicova, van den Ven, Schrieken, &

Emmelkamp, 2003; Lange, van den Ven, Schrieken, & Smit, 2004) was with undergraduate psychology student volunteers who had post-trauma stress (not necessarily PTSD) or bereavement for a mean of five to six years. Therapists who gave email support to *Interapy* users were clinical psychology graduate students experienced in CBT. In an open study and two RCTs, users had five weeks of *Interapy*'s online standard guidance for self-help by CBT writing therapy (?unclear where users accessed *Interapy* and if no face-to-face contact with a therapist). They were given a manual (?unclear if by an administrator or posted), and a password. They did ten 45-minute sessions guided by *Interapy* to complete questionnaires, write two essays a week (ten in all) to ?email to their therapist, and read material before the next session. The first essays were to promote exposure by writing in the first person the trauma details and ensuing fears and thoughts. Later essays taught cognitive reappraisal via writing encouraging advice to a hypothetical friend who'd had the same trauma. In the final essay the students said goodbye to the trauma by writing a letter to someone close. Users ?self-rated progress online. ?Within two working days of receiving the essays by email, a therapist emailed feedback/support a total of three times. The mean total therapist time of 11 hours spent per patient in *Interapy* and in face-to-face trials of writing therapy seems comparable so *Interapy* may not save therapist time though it eases access to CBT guidance.

Open study (Lange et al., 2000a, 2000b)

Of 36 applicants, 24 were suitable, 23 began five weeks of *Interapy*, 21 completed it, and 20 reached subsequent six-week follow-up. From pre- to post- to follow-up the students improved significantly on the Impact of Event Scale (effect size 0.76), and improved similarly in depression, anxiety, insomnia and somatization. The percent of subjects scoring abnormally high fell from pre- to post-treatment to six-week follow-up (75–45–30% for avoidance, 80–35–30% for intrusion). Gains continued to 18-month follow-up (Lange et al., 2002). Of the 20 completers, nine found *Interapy*'s anonymity pleasant, eight found *Interapy* unpleasant, and three had no opinion. Outcome did not relate to internet experience.

RCT (Lange et al., 2003)

The 30 student volunteers were randomized (method unclear?) to *Interapy* or a waiting list (each n=15), from which respectively two and three dropped out. *Interapy* subjects improved more after *Interapy* than on the waiting list, effect sizes for PTSD avoidance being 2.0 and for intrusions 1.5. It is unclear if there is follow-up evidence.

USA: *NetCP Self-Help for Traumatic Consequences (SHTC)*

The netCP system *SHTC* (Hirai & Clum, 2005) was accessed by a password. Its modules taught breathing retraining, muscle and imagery-induced relaxation, cognitive restructuring, writing exposure, and mastery tests.

RCT

This concerned 42 young adults with subclinical post-traumatic stress who were recruited via ads, of whom 36 consented to enter an RCT (Hirai & Clum, 2005). They were randomized (concealed) to eight weeks of: (a) netCP self-help for traumatic consequences (*SHTC*) for post-traumatic stress (n=18) with therapist email prompts to do assessments and about the timeline (mean total therapist time per-patient was 20 minutes), or (b) waitlist control (n=18) (Hirai & Clum, 2005). There were 27 completers (13 *STHC*, 14 WL; 21 women, mean age 29, mean time since the trauma four years with onset in the last year in most). At post-treatment *SHTC* improved more than the WL on avoidance, intrusions, depression, anxiety and coping, with effect sizes ranging from large to moderate.

In brief, in a small RCT *SHTC* improved subclinical post-traumatic stress more than a waitlist given no expectation of improvement or control activity. The effect of *SHTC* per se thus remains unclear.

CHAPTER FOUR

CP for general anxiety and emotional problems

CHAPTER SUMMARY

For a variety of general anxiety and emotional problems we found 14 CP systems, from Australia (1), Sweden (2), UK (3) and USA (7). Only two were on the net. They were tested in a betatest, six open studies, one nonrandomized controlled study, and ten RCTs. The systems' functions ranged from simple teaching of relaxation to complex enhancement of counselling and stress management. Some of the systems might save therapist time. None has yet proved reliably valuable for general anxiety and emotional problems in the way which has been attained by certain CP systems for different clinical problems where effective therapy components have been better specified.

Especially in primary care, the differentiation of general anxiety from depression is often so arbitrary that ICD-10 introduced the diagnosis 'mixed anxiety/depression'. Reflecting this, CP systems for general anxiety some-times also reflect depression and vice versa. Systems mainly for depression are reviewed in Chapter 5. Further overlaps appear between general anxiety,

73

TABLE 4.1
CP for **general anxiety** and **emotional problems**

Study	Anxiety system	Design	Participants	Outcome
Baer & Surman (1985)	Relaxation system.	Open study, 2 sess, 40 mins all over 1w.	USA: 20 non-psychiatric volunteers.	Improved on anxiety, no fu.
Carlbring et al. (2003)	Net relaxation system.	RCT: (1) computer-relax; (2) ftf-relax; (3) surfing-net control.	Sweden: 60 student volunteers; 20 per condition.	Computer-guided = ftf-guided relaxation > surfing-net control.
Wagman & Kerber (1984)	*PLATO Dilemma Counselling System (DCS)*.	RCT: (1) *DCS* 2 sess in 1w (n=48) vs (2) no contact (n=62) 1m fu.	USA: students with troublesome psychological dilemmas.	*DCS* > controls at 1w, trend at 1m fu. ?*DCS* ↑ imp speed, not amount.
Slack & Slack (1972, 1977)	Computer-aided soliloquy: crossover RCT 1.	Crossover RCT: speak re emotional problems to: (1) computer vs (2) doctor.	USA: 32 paid volunteer men.	Pt-computer dialogue might ease later dialogue with doctor, soliloquy per se might help.
Slack et al. (1990)	Computer-aided soliloquy: crossover RCT 2.	RCT: (1) speak aloud vs (2) think quietly re emotional problems.	USA: 42 paid volunteer men.	Soliloquy, unlike thinking quietly, ↓ heart rate and state anx by end of interview.
Talley (1987)	*Therapeutic Learning Program (TLP)* Colby et al. (1989): goal oriented.	Open study of *TLP* users.	USA: 278/399 *TLP* users in employee benefits health plan.	Most < distressed, handled problem better, satisfied.

Dolezal-Wood et al. (1996)	Therapeutic Learning Program (TLP) of Colby et al. (1989).	RCT: (1) 10 wkly 1.5-hr sess of 35 mins TLP then ftf group CBT (n=53), or (2) ftf group CBT only (n=56).	California: 109 psychiatric outpts in stress management gp with mild/moderate depression and anxiety.	Both gps: depression imp = and satisfied to 6m fu, anxiety imp not sustained. TLP cut therapist time by 40%.
Jacobs et al. (2001)	Therapeutic Learning Program (TLP) of Colby et al. (1989).	RCT: 10 wkly 50-min sess individ: (1) TLP + 20 mins ftf help, or (2) ftf only.	California: 90 volunteers with mild/mod psychol problems.	To 6m fu, TLP ≤ ftf on various measures. TLP ↓ therapist time 40%.
Parkin et al. (1995)	Worrytel.	Open feasibility study, no outcome ratings.	London: 20 anxious primary care patients, 5 family doctors.	Patients and GPs found it easy to use, acceptable, empathic.
Newman et al. (1999)	Palm-top to aid homework during ftf group CBT + manual.	Open study over 8w to 6m fu.	3 USA pts with GAD.	Imp to 6m fu. Said to be cost effective.
Yates (1996b)	Balance on CD for PC: brief CBT advice.	Alternate allocation to (1) Balance (n=23) 1–2 sessions or (2) TAU/WL (n=22).	UK. Newcastle: 45 pts who GPs thought had anxiety or depression. DOs 2 Balance, 3 TAU.	At 1m: completers of 1.5 sessions – Balance imp > TAU/WL on anx and depression.
Marks et al. (2003)	Balance as Yates (1996b).	Open study.	W London: 69 ICD10 gen anx pts at stress self-help clinic – 12 refused, 23 DOs.	33 (48%) completers: imp on anxiety, depression, disability; ES 0.6, 0.6, 0.4.

continues overleaf

TABLE 4.1 Continued

Study	Anxiety system	Design	Participants	Outcome
White et al. (2000)	Interactive CD-ROM based on written *Stresspac* (White, 1998).	Open trial: 3 × 40-min sessions. Pre-post time unspecified. 6m fu after completion.	Glasgow: 38 DSM-IV anxiety disorder pts in clin psychol primary care service; 26 pts completed ≥2/3 sess.	20% at post and 50% at 6m fu had clinically sig improvement.
Jones et al. (2006)	*Stresspac (Sp)* touchscreen on PC + *Sp* manual 3 sess + relax tapes in 10 public libraries and 1 health centre.	RCT 1–3 sess, 6m fu: (1) *Sp* computer n=121, *vs* (2) *Sp* manual + 3 ftf apts n=24, *vs* (3) TAU n=25. ITT analysis, blind ratings.	Glasgow 170 patients scoring HADS >7 anxiety or mixed anxiety and depression.	119 patients gave post-measures at 6m. *Sp* computer < *Sp* manual, and = TAU. *Stresspac* manual > TAU.
Kenardy et al. (2003b)	Net-*Online Anxiety Prevention Program*, no therapist support.	RCT for 6w: (1) net n=43 or (2) waiting list n=40.	Queensland, Australia: 83 first-year psychology students Anxiety Sens. Index (ASI) > 23.	ASI sig drop but not sig >WL. ES for diff. measures 0.8–1.0 vs 0.2–0.4 for WL. No fu.
Zetterqvist et al. (2003)	Net-stress-management + scheduled therapist email support.	RCT over 6w. Completers: (1) Net self-help (n=23); (2) Waiting list (n=40).	Sweden: 100 subjects with perceived stress; 63 completers: 23 self-help, 40 waiting list.	Net > WL on completer, not ITT analysis. WL also improved significantly.

4. CP FOR GENERAL ANXIETY AND EMOTIONAL PROBLEMS 77

'stress', 'emotional or psychological problems', and 'adjustment disorder'. Such terminological fuzziness should be borne in mind in the overlap below of CP systems for general anxiety, stress and other emotional or psychological difficulties. Yet more fuzziness comes from some studies being in volunteers without obvious problems or with difficulties not amounting to formal syndromes.

NONCLINICAL STUDIES

USA: ELIZA

The classic ELIZA program in the USA (Weizenbaum, 1976) was designed to explore issues in artificial intelligence, not treatment. It simulated aspects of a Rogerian therapy conversation by displaying comments on a screen in response to sentences typed on a keyboard. Users felt comfortable disclosing personal details to the system.

USA: Computer-aided soliloquy

This early ingenious approach deserves to be better known (Table 4.1: Slack & Slack, 1977; Slack et al., 1990). Men not in therapy were paid to be interviewed about emotional problems by a computer which also encouraged them to speak about their problem for 10 minutes into a tape recorder's microphone beneath the computer screen. The computer controlled the tape recorder and monitored its microphone for the presence of speech, but was oblivious to the meaning of spoken words and the volunteers were so informed. The computer asked subjects about their anxiety when alone, with friends, strangers, in a crowd, at a party, at school, at work, and at home, and suggested they speak aloud: 'Now tell yourself how you feel when you are anxious. Speak out loud, into the (micro)phone. . . . Make a mental list of the circumstances most likely to make you anxious . . . now list them to yourself out loud.'

RCT 1

In an RCT (Slack & Slack, 1972, 1977) in 32 men who spoke about their emotional problems in random crossover order to (a) a doctor or (b) a computer, results suggested a patient–computer dialogue might ease later dialogue with a therapist and that soliloquy itself might be helpful.

RCT 2

In a second RCT (Slack et al., 1990), 42 healthy men used the computer system and the tape-recorded soliloquies first about anxiety-evoking situations, then about relaxation, and finally about their strategies for replacing anxiety with relaxation. In the random-order control crossover condition the computer encouraged subjects to think quietly about emotional situations instead of talking aloud about them. Soliloquy, unlike thinking quietly, decreased heart rate and state anxiety from the start to the end of the interview.

Other nonclinical systems

Another system taught students interpersonal skills (Campbell, Lison, Borsook, Hoover, & Arnold, 1995). In an RCT, 29 organizational development students learned in groups how to deal with uncooperative team members or with a domineering leader either by nine hours of human instruction including modelling and role play, or by only 4.5 hours of computer + video-based role play. Both groups acquired comparable skills, despite the second group having only half the time for human instruction. The relative contributions of the computer and video could not be separated.

Many clinical CP systems include a component of relaxation, which is often used for 'stress'. In a preliminary report, 20 non-psychiatric volunteers in the USA improved on anxiety after using a dedicated relaxation program for two sessions (Baer & Surman, 1985). In a RCT in 60 Swedish student volunteers, computer-guided and therapist-guided relaxation produced comparable relaxation which was greater than in students surfing the internet (Carlbring, Bjornstjerna, Bergstrom, Waara, & Andersson, 2006a).

In a semi-clinical study, students learned how to help people apply dilemma counselling principles to their own situation using the *Dilemma Counseling System* (*DCS*) (Wagman & Kerber, 1984). The *DCS* contained 69 unhappy life-choice problems and 400 solutions. In an RCT, 100 psychology undergraduates who had troublesome psychological dilemmas were randomized (method unspecified) to use *DCS* for two sessions over three hours (n=48) or to become no-contact controls (n=62). *DCS* users improved more in their problems than did controls after one week and a month later, though at one month only feeling more pleasant remained significantly better than in the controls. Many felt more at ease (40%) and independent (44%) on *DCS* than with a counsellor.

Clinical studies

Group therapy clients were helped to change their own behaviour by an early computer aid which facilitated their observing to one another the similarities and differences in their interpersonal interactions (Stone & Kristjanson, 1975).

DESKTOP AND PC SYSTEMS

USA: *Therapeutic Learning Program (TLP)*

Related ideas plus CBT were included in the goal-oriented *TLP* (Colby, Gould, & Aronson, 1989). Over five two-hour or ten one-hour sessions, groups of six to ten patients met with a human therapist and operated their own computer to display *TLP* text and menus over eight steps. These helped clients to identify interpersonal problems and suitable new behavior that might reduce them and to spot thinking errors and link them to past and present circumstances. Clients personalized each step on the computer, received a printout, and reported its content to the group. The computer generated between-sessions homework.

Open study

In an open *TLP* study of 399 users in a Cigna employee-benefits health plan, 278 reported data: 78% said their distress had dropped, 95% that they could handle their problem better, and 96% were satisfied, while 85% said *TLP* helped them to think more clearly and was easy to use. Past computer experience did not relate to these positive evaluations.

RCT 1 in USA

This was of 109 psychiatric outpatients in a stress management group with clinically significant depression (mild to moderate) and anxiety (Dolezal-Wood, Belar, & Snibbe, 1996). They were randomized (method unspecified) to either: (a) use *TLP* for 35 mins, each on their own computer in the group therapy room with the therapist present, followed by a 55 mins ftf group CBT session; or (b) ten weekly 1.5-hr ftf-only group CBT sessions. For all subjects, treatments involved ten 90 mins weekly sessions with the therapist in groups of eight to ten. Of 265 patients in the stress management group over two years, 109 (*TLP* n=53; ftf-only n=56) completed treatment and follow-up. *TLP* patients learned to operate the program easily. In both groups BDI depression improved similarly from moderate/mild to mild/none and continued this to six-month follow-up, though improvement in state anxiety was not sustained. Without loss of efficacy or satisfaction, *TLP* cut therapist time by 40%. During their saved time therapists did other work-related paperwork while being available to answer questions.

RCT 2 in USA

TLP's second RCT was in 90 volunteers who had mild to moderate psychological problems, probably less severe than in most outpatients (Jacobs, Christensen, Snibbe, Dolezal-Wood, Huber, & Polterok, 2001).

80   HANDS-ON HELP: COMPUTER-AIDED PSYCHOTHERAPY

After screening by phone and then two hours ftf, they were randomized (method unspecified) to have ten individual 50-minute sessions weekly of problem-focused psychotherapy in one of two conditions: (a) *TLP* – users could ask a therapist, who was not in the *TLP* room unless a question arose, about *TLP* use and to review post-session summary printouts and check them for signs of current crisis; users spent a per-session mean of 32 mins on *TLP* and 20 mins ftf with the therapist reviewing paperwork and housekeeping details (not like a therapy session except in a crisis); or (b) 50 mins ftf sessions. At post-treatment and six months later both groups improved similarly on most measures (not anxiety at six-month follow-up), but satisfaction and some aspects of improvement were less in *TLP* than ftf subjects. *TLP* saved about 40% of therapist time. In this RCT subjects began with less distress than in the previous one, and had individual rather than group therapy for 50 mins rather than 90 mins.

In brief, in both RCTs *Therapeutic Learning Program* saved 40% of the time of the therapist who though present throughout could do other paperwork most of the time. *TLP* produced gains lasting to six-month follow-up except on anxiety, but satisfaction and gains on some measures were slightly less with *TLP* than face-to-face care in the second RCT.

UK: *Worrytel*

This PC system was created for general anxiety sufferers in primary care (Parkin, Marks, & Higgs, 1995). They used a mouse and keyboard to go through screens, rate the 21-item General Health Questionnaire, choose from a list of phrases those that described their discomfort, and pick from a list of common anxiogenic problems those most like their own. Users could see vignettes of people describing those problems and how they dealt with them on CBT lines, and for problems like physical/sexual abuse, how to contact other agencies for help. *Worrytel* guided patients to devise their own self-treatment plan, rate their problems for distress and disability, and print out especially helpful screens and homework diaries for self-monitoring. They could return to *Worrytel* to rerate problems, get feedback, and choose other problems to work on.

Open study

In a pilot test, 20 anxious patients and five family doctors rated *Worrytel* as easy to use, acceptable and empathic. Patients felt less alone after seeing the

4. CP FOR GENERAL ANXIETY AND EMOTIONAL PROBLEMS   81

vignettes and that printouts were a useful adjunct to the screens. The doctors judged that patients' preliminary use of *Worrytel* gave clarity and focus to a consultation.

In brief, *Worrytel* requires further development before full clinical trials are mounted.

UK: *Balance*

The brief basic *Balance* system (Yates, 1996b) introduces patients to CBT with minimum interaction with them or data collection. It has been available in CD-ROM form.

Newcastle, UK: Controlled nonrandomized trial

This tested 45 consecutive patients in Newcastle whom GPs from five practices judged as having anxiety and/or related depression (Yates, 1996b). Subjects were allocated alternately to: (a) use *Balance* immediately (n=23) for one to two one-hour sessions; or (b) have GP treatment as usual (TAU) while on a waitlist to use *Balance* a month later (N=22). *Balance* patients used it on a CD on a PC, mostly in a research office or private room in a GP practice. A therapist helped patients start, checked them at 15-minute intervals, and let them decide whether to use *Balance* again. They completed a mean of just 1.5 sessions. One-month data were given by 20 subjects per condition (dropouts: 2 *Balance*, 3 TAU). Compared to TAU, *Balance* subjects improved more in anxiety and depression, but few applied its practical and CBT advice.

London: Open study

Balance on a CD was offered to 69 referrals to a computer-aided stress self-help clinic in west London who had general anxiety (Marks et al., 2003). Of these, 13 refused to use *Balance* and a further 23 dropped out or gave no post-treatment data. The 33 (48%) completers used *Balance* on a PC at the clinic (n=18), at home (n=13) or an internet café (n=2) over a mean of 40 days during which they had a mean of 43 mins ftf or phone support from a therapist. The completers improved significantly on anxiety, depression and disability, ES being respectively 0.6, 0.6 and 0.4.

In brief, the basic *Balance* system may require further development before having a RCT.

UK: *Stresspac*

Open study

An open trial in Glasgow (White et al., 2000) gave 38 DSM-IV anxiety-disordered patients PC touchscreen access to three 40-minute sessions of an anxiety management CD-ROM (based on the written CBT package *Stresspac* White, 1998). They used it in a clinical psychology primary care clinic at a health centre. Users also received eight written handouts. A science graduate without psychological experience was present in the room to help as needed. Computerized *Stresspac* included relaxation, panic control, sleep hygiene and coping strategies; 26/28 patients completed 2/3 sessions. Of these, 20% at post-test and 50% six months later had improved clinically significantly, i.e. close to normal ratings.

RCT

A RCT in Glasgow (Jones et al., 2006) tested *Stresspac* on a PC in 170 patients with anxiety or mixed anxiety and depression. *Stresspac* was accessed unsupported on a PC touchscreen for up to three sessions in ten public libraries and a health centre. Subjects were screened ftf, rated the Hospital Anxiety and Depression Scale (HADS) on a computer and if they scored eight or more the computer randomized them to: (a) PC *Stresspac* (n=121) unsupported; or (b) printed *Stresspac* (n=24) plus three ftf support sessions of unspecified duration; or (c) treatment as usual (TAU; n=25). Both *Stresspac* groups also had relaxation tapes. Printed *Stresspac* was stopped half-way as it increased GPs' work by requiring three GP appointments. There were 119 completers (PC-*Stresspac* 70%, printed *Stresspac* 71%, TAU 68%). Gains with PC-*Stresspac* were no more than with TAU. Some patients who improved markedly still did not consider PC-*Stresspac* helpful. The poorer results with PC *Stresspac* than previously might have reflected the PC sessions having no human support in the RCT. The authors refreshingly noted difficulties facing CP in primary care, e.g. rarity of sites for 'computer booths' in health centres, low numbers of patient referrals from GPs, GPs having no time to support patients, a psychology assistant having to travel between sites.

In brief, PC-*Stresspac* only had an effect when supported in an open study, but not when it was unsupported in a RCT.

NET SYSTEMS

Australia: *Net-Online Anxiety Prevention Program (OAPP)*

OAPP on the internet was based on earlier palmtop software (Newman et al., 1997a). It taught psychoeducation, relaxation, interoceptive exposure, cognitive restructuring and relapse prevention (Kenardy, McCafferty, & Rosa, 2003b). Each of its six sessions required users to cover the program material, practise a set of skills, and record progress daily. Subjects who did not continue through the modules received an email prompt (each taking 5 mins of human time) but no other human support was given.

RCT

Of 131 Australian psychology students who scored >23 on the Anxiety Sensitivity Index (mean score 31: 31–36 is the range in a clinical population), 83 (63%) accepted entry into a RCT (Kenardy et al., 2003b). Mean age was 20. They were randomized to net-accessed *OAPP* (n=43; 6 dropped out) or to a waitlist (n=40; 2 dropped out) for six weeks. At home or university they used net-*OAPP* for a total of 90 mins over eight occasions, using it longer if they accessed it at home rather than at the university. The *OAPP* group improved (not significantly) more than the waitlist. Effect size across measures was 0.8 to 1.0 for *OAPP* and 0.2 to 0.4 for the waitlist.

> *In brief, OAPP* subjects did not improve significantly more than a waitlist.

Sweden: *Net Stress Management System*

This net system (Zetterqvist, Maanmies, Ström, & Andersson, 2003) had an introductory module open on the net, and six treatment modules accessed by a password (sent by email) including applied relaxation, problem solving, time management, and cognitive/behavioural restructuring, plus further information on separate web pages. Sections could be skipped. Users emailed weekly registration forms of homework, and received confirmation of receipt and feedback and an email reminder if >2 weeks passed with no report from them. Users could email for extra email advice from a therapist.

RCT

Swedish subjects were recruited (Zetterqvist et al., 2003) via a web page and newspaper ads if they 'perceived no obstacles to participation'. Of 100 subjects randomized (unconcealed) to six weeks of: (a) netCBT on their own computer (n=23); or (b) a waitlist (n=40), 12 netCBT and 3 WL subjects withdrew before starting. Moreover, of 85 starters 15 dropped out of netCBT and 7 from the WL, leaving only 63 completers (23 netCBT, 40 WL). Dropouts and completers had similar features. Users completed a mean of 4.2 of the six treatment modules, and 12 users completed all homework and modules. Both netCBT and the WL improved significantly on perceived stress and on the HADS. NetCBT improved significantly more than WL on a completer analysis but not on an ITT analysis which assumed dropouts had not improved.

In brief, in this RCT netCBT for stress management had small effects in a sample whose clinical diagnosis was unclear.

USA: PALMTOP SYSTEM

An ambulatory palmtop system (Newman, Consoli, & Taylor, 1999) was used by three GAD patients who were also given a self-help manual and attended five to six two-hour group CBT sessions over eight weeks. Their anxiety improved gradually during treatment and continued to six months follow-up. The palmtop was estimated to save from \$630 to \$1058 per subject treatment episode in group or individual CBT. Subjects' reactions to using the palmtop were generally positive.

CHAPTER FIVE

CP for depression

CHAPTER SUMMARY

Since 1990 at least nine CP systems for depression were published from Australia, Sweden, UK (2), USA (4) and one jointly from the UK and USA. They include five PC systems, an IVR system, and three net systems. Interactivity of the systems ranged from limited in CP bibliotherapy with users who mostly had above average education, to complex interactivity of some other CP systems in less highly educated users. CP systems for depression were evaluated in at least 12 open studies, a nonrandomized controlled study, and nine RCTs. Subjects studied variously included inpatients, outpatients, primary care patients, and unscreened website visitors. NICE recently recommended the most published system, PC-based *Beating the Blues*, for managing depression in the English National Health Service, and it is in commercially licensed use around the UK. Across CP studies improvement of depression ranged from slight to large. Attrition was dramatic in net users who were unsupported (*ODIN*, 1 *MoodGYM* study). As expected, uptake and completion rates tended to be lower in field studies than in RCTs. Most waitlist and TAU RCT designs did not exclude potential placebo effects. Outcome was unimpaired when CP (*Good Days Ahead*) was given after ftfCBT with total therapist time cut from 450 to 250 minutes. It remains unclear what

TABLE 5.1
CP for **depression**

Study	Depression system	Design	Participants	Outcome
Selmi et al. (1990)	CBT for depression on PC giving education, instructions, case examples and clinical ratings.	RCT for 6w: (1) CP + mininimal therapist support n=12; (2) weekly ftfCBT (n=12); (3) WL (n=12).	USA: 36 volunteers with RDC non-suicidal mostly major depression.	Treatment groups imp sig = and >control; ES: (pre-post) on BDI: CP=0.9, ftfCBT=0.8; ES (pre-fu) on BDI PC=1.5; ftfCBT = 1.3.
Bowers et al. (1993)	*Overcoming Depression* (*OD*) on PC. Cognitive therapy but no behav. activation or individualized homework.	RCT: 8 daily sessions over 2w of: (1) *OD* (n=6) or (2) ftfCBT (n=8), or (3) inpatient care as usual incl drugs (n=8). No fu.	USA: 22 inpatients with marked major depression.	Mood imp with *OD*: < ftf CBT, but = inpt care as usual. Only ftfCBT had beh activ or individual. homework.
Whitfield et al. (2006); Hepburn (2004)	*Overcoming Depression 2* (*OD2*) CD-ROM.	Open study 6w: 6 50-min sess while on clinical psychol. service WL + 51 mins in all nurse support.	UK: 78 Glasgow referrals for dep/anx, 22 screened, 14 completed 6 *OD2* sess.	28% of WL invitees came for *OD2* screening (excess of males), imp after used *OD2*.
Osgood-Hynes et al. (1998)	*Cope*: phone-IVR self-help + manual + brief therapist phone or ftf screening and rating.	Open study: 12w pre to post-test.	USA and UK: 41 outpts with DSM-IV major depression and/or dysthymia.	Sig imp; 64% imp; US > UK patients for completion and imp. No fu.
Marks et al. (2003)	*Cope* phone-IVR as in Osgood-Hynes et al. (1998).	Open study: in self-help clinic.	UK: 56 depressed W London pts; 39/56 completed *Cope*.	Completers imp sig on BDI, HRSD and WSA; ES 1.2, 0.7, 0.9.

Wright et al. (2002)	*Good Days Ahead* (*GDA*) *for Cognitive Therapy*: (early version) at PC in clinic.	Open study + treatment as usual incl other concurrent treatment.	USA: 96 psychiatric inpts and outpts with anxiety-depressive disorders.	Sig symptom imp and ↑ in CBT knowledge, high satisfaction. No ES or fu reported.
Wright et al. (2003, 2005)	*GDA* modified version of Wright et al. (2002) + ftf screening + ftfCBT + ratings.	RCT 9 sess, 8w: (1) *GDA* + 25-min ftfCBT sess; (2) 50-min ftf CBT sessions; (3) WL. Each n=15.	USA: 45 outpts, drug-free mild-mod. major depression. DOs n= 2, 2, 1.	*GDA* + 25-min ftfCBT sessions = 50-min ftfCBT sess, both > WL. Gains continued to 6m fu.
Clarke et al. (2002)	*Overcoming Depression on InterNet* (*ODIN*) interactive cog therapy (CT). No live helpline.	RCT for 32 wks. Net CT (n=155) or WL (n=144).	USA: 299 HMO subscribers with depression.	NetCT no overall effect, small effect in cases mildly depressed at week 0.
Clarke et al. (2005)	*ODIN* as for Clarke et al. (2002) + phone or postcard reminders to return to netCT. No helpline.	RCT for 16w: (1) and (2) NetCT (75 postcard reminded, 80 phone reminded) or (3) TAU (n=100).	USA: 255 HMO subscribers with marked depressive symptoms.	Takeup rate only ?2% NetCT imp > TAU in mood, ES=0.28; no diff. of phone vs postcard reminders.
Christensen et al. (2004a); Griffiths et al. (2004)	net*MoodGYM* CBT. net*BluePages* depression education.	RCT for 6w: (1) *MoodGYM* n=182; (2) *BluePages* n=165; (3) control no website n=178. All gps also had 6 10-min phone calls by lay interviewer.	525 Australian mild-mod depressed, highly educated untreated subjects. Dropouts: (1) 25%; (2) 15% (1 vs 2 sig); (3) 11%.	*MoodGYM* CBT and *BluePages* education imp sig and =, and > controls, on mood and stigma. Imp continued to 12m fu.

continues overleaf

TABLE 5.1 *Continued*

Study	*Depression system*	*Design*	*Participants*	*Outcome*
Christensen et al. (2002)	net*MoodGYM*.	Open study of site use over 181 days.	465 site users who gave ≥2 self-ratings.	Mood imp sig with more site use.
Christensen et al. (2004b)	net*MoodGYM*.	Open study of site use by visitors v RCT subjects.	3176 visitors from 62 countries vs 182 RCT subjects from Canberra.	Mood imp sig and = in visitors vs RCT, but ≥4 times more attrition in visitors than in RCT.
O'Kearney et al. (2006)	net*MoodGYM*.	Nonrandomized nonmatched controlled study. (1) *MoodGYM* n=35. (2) Usual curriculum activities n=24.	Canberra schoolboys aged 15–16. Not necessarily depressed. 40% *MoodGYM* boys completed >half modules.	*MoodGYM* mostly no effect, except persistent very small superiority in self-esteem at 16w fu.
Andersson et al. (2004, 2005)	Swedish netCBT for depression + online discussion group + 2h email support by therapist.	RCT 10w: (1) net CBT n=57 vs (2) waitlist n=60; each + own online discussion gp.	117 Swedish depressed subjects. DOs 37% netCBT, 18% WL, DOs < educated than all subjects.	NetCBT > WL for depress (ES 0.9), not anx. Gains continued to 12m fu and no r to discussion gp postings.

> *GDA* might achieve with less substantial therapist time. In an especially instructive RCT, interactive CP (net*MoodGYM*) did no better than non-interactive information (net*BluePages*) with similar live phone support to a total of an hour. CP results were disappointing to modest where it gave cognitive restructuring but not behavioural activation instructions (*ODIN*, *OD1*). Some uncertainties about which aspects of CP per se are therapeutic for depression mirror our uncertainties about which aspects of ftf psychotherapy improve mood, given that diverse forms of brief ftf psychotherapy helped depression in RCTs (e.g. behavioural activation alone, CBT, interpersonal therapy, problem solving, mindfulness meditation).

STANDALONE COMPUTERS

USA: Desktop CP system (Selmi, Klein, Greist, Sorrell, & Erdman, 1990)

This self-help program gave individually tailored and text-based CBT self-help over six sessions. It guided cognitive restructuring and behavioural activation, tested the patient's understanding and gave feedback, suggested homework before the next session, and took clinical ratings. In a RCT (Table 5.1), 36 well-educated patients who had mild to moderate depression (RDC, mostly repeated major depressive disorder) were randomized to use the program at a PC in a clinic or have face-to-face (ftf) CBT or go on a waitlist (WL). A therapist phoned WL subjects during weeks 2–6 to assess depression and suicide risk. Program users could seek help from a therapist who was not in the room. Questions were mostly about computer procedures and contact was kept to a minimum. There were no dropouts. After treatment and two-month follow-up both treatment groups improved substantially and similarly, and significantly more than the waitlist. The value of CP for research was indicated by the RCT's finding that cognitive change accompanied but did not necessarily precede symptom improvement.

USA: *Overcoming Depression 1 (OD1)*

Overcoming Depression 1 (OD1) was a cognitive CP system which answered patients' key words and gave cognitive-therapy case scenarios, and at the end of each session patients could print out the dialogue and review this as homework (Colby & Colby, 1990; Colby, 1995). *OD1* did not teach behavioural activation or suggest behavioural or individualized homework.

RCT

In a small RCT (Bowers et al., 1993), 22 inpatients with marked major depression were randomized (method unspecified) to: (a) *OD1* use in eight daily inpatient sessions over two weeks (n=6); or (b) ftfCBT in eight daily inpatient sessions over two weeks (n=8); or (c) inpatient care as usual including antidepressant drugs (n=8). Mood improved with *OD1* less than with ftfCBT though about the same amount as with inpatient care as usual. The outcome is inconclusive as the design did not compare like with like: only the ftfCBT group had instructions for behavioural activation and for individualized homework.

UK: *Overcoming Depression 2*

A different system also bearing the name *Overcoming Depression* (henceforth called *OD2*) is a CD-ROM marketed by Calipso (www.calipso.com; Whitfield, Hinshelwood, Pashely, Campsie, & Williams, 2006). *OD2* offered six 50-minute weekly sessions at one of three sites (not at home). Its content includes text, cartoons, animations, interactive questions, sound and video.

Open study

This tested *OD2* in 78 consecutive referrals to a four-month waitlist of a Glasgow clinical psychology service where the referral letter noted depression as a major problem (Hepburn, 2004; Whitfield et al., 2006). Only 22 (28%) of the 78 invitees attended a 25-minute ftf screening by a psychologist. Males were twice more common among attenders than non-attenders (59% vs 27%) and mean age was 37. Attenders were given appointments to use the *OD2* CD-ROM weekly while on the waitlist. Users saw a nurse briefly at each session to assess risk, motivate them, and answer queries, to a total mean of 51 mins per user over the six weeks. Twenty patients came to at least one *OD2* session and 14 to all six *OD2* sessions; 15 returned ratings at three-month follow-up. Most were satisfied with *OD2* and preferred it to a book. *OD2* completers improved on depression and anxiety and continued their gains three months later, though most asked for further ftf help. The use of *OD2* did not cut the usual time spent in subsequent ftf care but seemed to reduce usual dropouts and enhance improvement.

The low uptake of CP by Scottish patients who were already on a waitlist for ftf care echoes a similar finding from four English waitlists for ftfCBT for depression/anxiety problems (Mataix-Cols, Cameron, Gega, Kenwright, & Marks, 2006). Patients may accept CP more if they are offered it as a first positive step in care and don't automatically expect ftf help from the start.

> *In brief*, in a small uncontrolled study of Calipso's *Overcoming Depression 2* offered to a clinical psychology service's waitlist, uptake was low but CP users improved and perhaps did better with subsequent ftf care.

UK: *Beating the Blues (BTB)*

Beating the Blues (BTB) is interactive CP recommended by NICE for depression. It is sold as two CDs which are loaded into a standalone computer. It has a 15-minute introductory video followed by eight 50-minute therapy sessions weekly. A clinical helper, usually a receptionist, secretary or nurse trained to use *BTB*, greets patients and settles them at the computer to work alone on *BTB*, and after the session checks the patient's progress report and books the next session. *BTB* helps patients identify and challenge automatic thoughts, thinking errors/distortions, core beliefs, and attributions, and to do activity scheduling, problem solving, exposure, task breakdown and sleep management, and homework between sessions. Session content and homework vary with patients' needs. Each session builds on the one before and its completion triggers printing of a progress report, and note of any suicidal intent, for the patient and referrer.

UK: Beta test

In an initial test of *BTB*'s functionality (Table 5.2: Proudfoot et al., 2003a) patients said it was helpful and easy to use and 11/20 completers improved non-significantly. *BTB* has had one major and one small RCT and five open trials in England.

UK: RCT 1

At seven GP surgeries (Proudfoot, Goldberg, Mann, Everitt, Marks, & Gray, 2003b) 310 referrals were screened on the 12-item General Health Questionnaire, and the GP assessed if they suited the inclusion criteria. Patients were asked to do the computerized Clinical Interview Schedule-Revised, which 100 (32%) refused; of the remaining 210 patients, 167 scored >12 and were randomized within each surgery to have either: (a) *BTB* + TAU (treatment as usual) from the GP (n=89); or (b) TAU only (n=78). TAU might include medication, discussion, social support and referral to other health professionals (not counselling/psychotherapy for *BTB*+TAU patients).

Randomization was stratified for prescription of antidepressant or anxiolytic medication (yes, no) and current illness duration ($\leq$6m, >6m).

TABLE 5.2
CP for **depression** *Beating the Blues* (BTB)

Study	Depression system	Design	Participants	Outcome
Proudfoot et al. (2003a)	*Beating the Blues* (*BTB*) on standalone PC in university office incl. video/audio.	Beta-test: 4w, no fu. 15-min video plus 8 50-min sessions twice weekly.	UK: 20 pts with mixed depression/anxiety. No concurrent psychol treatment.	Pts said *BTB* helpful, easy to use. 11 completers positive outcome but few sig gains.
Proudfoot et al. (2003b), and expanded sample (2004)	*BTB* on standalone PC in GP surgery + up to 10-mins nurse support per session if requested.	RCT over 8m: (1) *BTB* + TAU n=89/ expanded sample n=146 for 8 sess, vs (2) TAU-only n=78/ expanded sample n=128: drugs, GP and social support, onward referral.	UK: 167/(274 expanded sample) primary-care patients with CIS-R depression and/or anxiety.	DO: *BTB* + TAU = 35% (2003b)/ 29% (2004). Completers and non-completers: *BTB* + TAU imp >TAU at 2m post and 6m fu on depress, disability and attribution and > satisfied.
McCrone et al. (2004)	*BTB* on standalone PC in GP surgery + up to 10-mins nurse support per session if requested.	Costs 261 pts (*BTB* 139, TAU 123) Predictor analysis.		*BTB* + TAU cost £40 > TAU over 8m but > cost-effective.
Ryden (2005)	*BTB* on standalone PC in GP surgery + up to 10-mins nurse support per session if requested.			Nil predicted BDI-II.
Cavanagh et al. (2006b)	*BTB* on standalone PC in GP surgery, CMHT centre, or clin psychol service + brief support from staff (receptionist, nurse, psychologist).	Open trial 8w. 15-min video + 8 50-min sess (usually 1 per week) + TAU.	UK: n=219 primary- and secondary-care patients, with anxiety and/or depression, GHQ-12 ≥ 4.	219 pts began *BTB*, 135 (*62%*) completed, 104 (*47%*) rated post-*BTB*: imp CORE-OM in completer and ITT (ES 1.0 and 0.5) analyses, also imp on WSA.

Study				
Cavanagh et al. (2006a)		(as in Cavanagh et al., 2006b)		Pts said *BTB* credible, acceptable. Completers, esp women, post-*BTB* rated its features and experience positively. No r of pre-*BTB* ratings to DO or imp.
Grime (2003)	*BTB* on standalone PC in NHS occupational health department.	RCT over 12 weeks: (1) *BTB* + TAU n=24 for 8 sess *vs* (2) TAU-only n=24: incl drugs, GP and social support, onward referral.	UK: 48 public sector employees with stress-related absenteeism. DOs: 33% from *BTB*.	24 employees began BTB, 16 (67%) completed. ITT: *BTB* + TAU imp >TAU at 1m fu on depre, anx and attributional style.
Van den Berg et al. (2004)	As Cavanagh et al. (2005) but support by receptionist in community mh resource centre.	Open trial 8w. 15-min video + 8 50-min sessions (usually 1 per week) + TAU.	UK: 115 consecutive referrals CMHT rated likely to benefit from *BTB* + TAU began *BTB*. 52 (45%) DOs, 17 (15%) missing data.	115 pts began *BTB*; 46 (40%) completers imp in self-rated dep and anx. WL unchanged at 1y despite ↑ referrals.
Grundy (2004)	As Cavanagh et al. (2005) but brief support by trainee psycholog in clinical psycho service.	Open trial: *BTB* for 8w. 15-min video plus 8 50-min sessions (usually 1 per week).	UK: 8/15 *BTB* completers in clinical psychol service. No info on inclusion criteria.	Sig pre-post imp on anxiety and depression. Pts said *BTB* helpful and easy to use.
Fox et al. (2004)	As for Cavanagh et al. 2005 except support by asst psychologist in primary care.	Open trial 8w. 15-min video + 8 50-min sessions (usually 1 per week).	UK: referrals judged 'likely to benefit' from *BTB*.	39/56 (70%) referrals had ≥1 session, 27 (48%) completed *BTB*. No outcomes noted.
Kenwright et al. (2005)	As for Cavanagh et al. (2005) except brief support by CBT therapist in CBT service.	Preference trial 10w choice of: (1) *BTB* 8 sess in clinic + ftf support (mean 69 mins) n=22; or (2) workbook at home + scheduled phone support (mean 82 mins) n=36.	UK: 134 referrals to CBT clinic who had depression ±GAD, non-suicidal.	73 (54%) refused self-help. 58 had choice: 36 chose home workbook + phone support. 22 chose clinic *BTB* + ftf support, DOs 19% both gps. At 1m fu, BDI ES 1.2–1.3 both gps.
Hunt et al. (2006)	*BTB* on PC in GP surgery.	Open trial, 8 sess.	UK: 164 depressed/anxious pts, of whom 54 completed 8 sess.	Completers improved on BDI, GHQ and WSA.

94   HANDS-ON HELP: COMPUTER-AIDED PSYCHOTHERAPY

Randomly sorted cards naming *BTB*+TAU or TAU only were sealed in opaque numbered envelopes away from the surgery. Nurses opened them in numerical sequence, a process the researchers checked regularly. Unlike TAU-only patients, *BTB*+TAU patients had practice nurse support for up to 5 mins at the start and 5 mins at the end of each of eight weekly sessions. At each session's end the nurse checked patients had their printouts (summary, homework tasks, progress report) and booked the next session.

The 167 entrants had mild, moderate or severe depression (61), or mixed depression/anxiety (80), or an anxiety disorder only (24). *BTB* was not completed by 35% of patients. Taking into account data lost from 12 patients per group due to 'human error', post-treatment ratings were obtained for 50/77 (71%) *BTB*+TAU and 51/66 (77%) TAU-only patients. *BTB*+TAU patients (including the 35% *BTB* non-completers) improved significantly more than TAU-only on depression, anxiety and work and social adjustment (WSA) at two months (post-treatment) and kept their gains at six months follow-up.

The results largely continued when the RCT was expanded from the original 7 to 11 GP surgeries to test *BTB* interactions with clinical, demographic and setting variables (Proudfoot et al., 2004). From the expanded sample of over 406 patients screened (full total unknown as two practices gave no data) who met trial criteria, 274 patients (including the original 167) began the RCT (*BTB*+TAU n=146 of whom 29% dropped out from *BTB*; TAU-only n=128). In ITT analyses, *BTB*+TAU improved significantly more than TAU-only on depression (not anxiety), and on negative attributional style, and work and social adjustment, regardless of whether medication was prescribed and duration of previous or severity of current illness. *BTB*+TAU improved significantly more than TAU-only in patients with more initial anxiety and poorer positive attributional style. Patients were more satisfied with *BTB*+TAU than TAU-only. No predictors of BDI-II outcome were found in a study of the expanded sample (Ryden, 2005).

It is unclear how much the greater improvement of *BTB*+TAU than TAU-only patients reflected their use of *BTB* per se or their extra accompanying attention received of a total of up to 90 mins with non-therapist practice staff ($\leq$10 mins per *BTB* session) and of being scheduled to attend nine times over two months. In TAU-only, depressives tend to see GPs for 7 mins per consultation and to attend less often. Nor is it clear, without the results of a *BTB* vs ftfCBT RCT which is in progress, how much *BTB* saves CBT therapist time, though it could be appreciable.

An economic evaluation of *BTB*+TAU vs TAU in the expanded sample (McCrone et al., 2004) supported the cost-effectiveness of *BTB*+TAU: (a) it was clinically superior at negligible added cost; (b) at values of $\geq$£40 for a one-unit drop in depression (BDI-11), the probability of *BTB*+TAU being more cost-effective than TAU-only exceeded 80%; (c) *BTB*+TAU had a competitive cost-utility ratio of £5000 per quality-adjusted life year; (d) there were productivity gains from reduced lost employment costs. Mean service cost over eight months was £40 higher (not significant) with *BTB*+TAU than TAU-only.

UK: RCT 2

In a separate RCT, in an NHS occupational health department (Grime, 2003), 48 public sector employees with >10 days sickness absence due to stress, anxiety or depression in the past six months and a GHQ12 score ≥ 4 were randomized (concealment unclear) to 12 weeks of: (a) *BTB*+TAU (n=24); or (b) TAU-only (n=24). Numbers of dropouts and hours of support over the 12 weeks are unclear. Dropout numbers are unclear. In ITT analyses, *BTB*+TAU improved more than TAU-only on depression, anxiety, and negative attributions at week 12 (one-month follow-up) but not at three and six months post-treatment, by which times sample sizes were only 14 and 19.

Open trials of *Beating the Blues*

UK: Open study 1

An 11-site open trial (Cavanagh, Shapiro, Van den Berg, Swain, Barkham, & Proudfoot, 2006a, 2006b) checked whether the RCT outcomes generalized to naturalistic primary and secondary care settings. *BTB*+TAU was tested in 219 adults who had health-professional-identified depression and/or anxiety and a GHQ12 score of ≥ 4. Brief supervision was available from, usually, a receptionist or administrator. In completer and ITT analyses, patients improved significantly on the CORE-OM and WSA by post-treatment, and on self-reported depression and anxiety between sessions one and eight. Improvement continued in the 18% who gave six-month follow-up ratings. For completer (47% of starters) and ITT (all starters) analyses, on post-treatment ratings the uncontrolled ES was 1.0 (0.5) for CORE-OM and 0.5 (0.3) for WSA, and 0.8 (0.5) and 0.9 (0.6) respectively for self-rated depression and anxiety from sessions one to eight. Dropout rate was 38%, similar to that for primary care counselling/therapy services. At post-treatment most users, especially the women, said their experience of *BTB* was positive. Neither age nor pre-treatment ratings of acceptability and credibility of *BTB* related to completion or improvement.

UK: Open study 2

In a community mental health team clinic, 115 consecutive referrals whom the team rated as likely to benefit began *BTB*+TAU (Van den Berg,

96 HANDS-ON HELP: COMPUTER-AIDED PSYCHOTHERAPY

Shapiro, Bickerstaffe, & Cavanagh, 2004). Number of refusers is not reported. Of the 115 patients who began *BTB*, 63 (55%) completed it, 52 (45%) dropped out, data was missing for 17 (15%). Self-rated depression and anxiety improved in the 46 (40%) patients for whom ratings were available. Waiting times for CBT remained at one year despite increased referrals. Patients were satisfied with access to *BTB* and its ease of use.

UK: Open studies 3 and 4

In a clinical psychology service, 53% (8 of 15) of *BTB* users completed it, improved significantly on depression and anxiety, and found it helpful and easy to use (Grundy, 2004). In an assistant psychologist-led clinic in primary care, 70% (39 of 56 referrals) used *BTB* at least once (Fox, Acton, Wilding, & Corcoran, 2004) and 63% completed it. Satisfaction was good but clinical outcome was not reported.

UK: Open study 5

In a preference trial of self-help plus brief therapist support over ten weeks (Kenwright et al., 2006), of 191 new depression referrals to a CBT clinic, staff rated 134 as suitable for self-help, which 61 (46%) accepted. Of 58 patients given a choice, 36 preferred self-help by using a workbook at home with eight scheduled phone-support calls, while 22 preferred self-help by *BTB* in eight sessions in the clinic with face-to-face (ftf) therapist support. Patients said this mainly reflected their preference for doing self-help at home rather than in the clinic. Total mean duration of therapist support was 69 mins ftf for *BTB* users in the clinic and 82 mins on the phone for workbook users. About 18% dropped out from both groups. Both groups improved similarly from pre-treatment to 14 weeks (four-week follow-up) on depression, anxiety and WSA. Of self-help completers, about 19% from each group no longer needed ftf therapist treatment. In an uncontrolled comparison, the 47 patients who went on to have ftf therapist treatment had it for a mean of about five hours in both groups, vs 15 hours in the original refusers of self-help.

UK: Open study 6

BTB was set up on six standalone PCs spaced out in a room in one GP surgery, with an assistant psychologist available to answer queries ftf for five minutes and check the *BTB* printouts (Hunt, Howells, & Stapleton, 2006). Over 15 months, 164 clients used *BTB*, of whom 54 (33%) saw the introductory video and did all eight 50-minute sessions; 32 (21%) were still attending at the time of writing. The 54 completers improved on the BDI, GHQ and WSA, feedback tended to be positive, and some felt just a few sessions sufficed. The original plan to run BTB on standalone computers in all 32 GP surgeries in the area turned out to be impractical due to shortages of surgery space and staff to support users.

> *In brief*, in a big primary care RCT, *Beating The Blues* + treatment as usual (TAU) was efficacious for depression compared to TAU alone, at negligible added cost, and *BTB* users were satisfied. In a small RCT in an occupational health department gains were similar in the short but not long term. The RCTs' TAU design left open how much the gains were due to *BTB* per se and how much to the extra support and scheduled clinic visits *BTB* users had compared to TAU. *BTB* also improved in six open trials in primary and secondary care and had lower completion rates than in RCT entrants, as would be expected.

USA: *Good Days Ahead (GDA)*

GDA (Wright, Wright, & Beck, 2003) guides CBT with audio, video, graphics, checklists, self-help exercises, multiple choice questions and mood ratings, and assumes a reading age of 14. Used originally on a PC, a DVD version of *GDA* is now on sale.

Open study

A pilot trial of an early version (Wright et al., 2002) tested *GDA* in 96 psychiatric inpatients and outpatients who mostly had major depression and continued usual treatment while using *GDA* on a PC with a mouse and keyboard. *GDA* includes video and audio and has six modules: introduction, principles, changing automatic thoughts, taking action (e.g. pleasant events scheduling, graded live homework), changing schemas, and continuing progress. Seventy-five patients completed *GDA* and increased their knowledge of CBT. The trial did not aim at self-help.

RCT

In a RCT of *GDA*, medication-free outpatients were screened first by a nurse and then by a psychologist (interview durations unspecified). The patients had major depression of mild to moderate severity, BDI ≥ 14, and an age 14 reading ability (Wright, Wright, Albano, Basco, Raffield, & Otto, 2005). Number of refusers was not specified. The 45 trial entrants had a mean age of 41 and 15 years of education, and 75% were women. They were

98 HANDS-ON HELP: COMPUTER-AIDED PSYCHOTHERAPY

randomized (concealment unclear) to eight weeks of either: (a) one 50-minute (ftf) CBT session and then eight sessions comprising 25 mins with the therapist and then 25 mins use of *GDA* alone on a PC at the clinic; or (b) nine 50-minute ftfCBT sessions; or (c) a waitlist. Dropouts were two each for the CBT groups and one from the WL. Evaluators were blind though test of their actual blindness was not reported. The two CBT groups improved similarly and more than the waitlist, with 50% falls in the BDI attained by, respectively, 70%, 70% and 7%. Mean effect size was 1.1 for *GDA* + ftfCBT and 1.0 for ftfCBT alone. Gains continued to three and six months follow-up. *GDA* cut therapist time by 45% and yielded the most reduction in cognitive distortions and gain in CBT knowledge. *GDA* is sold by Mindstreet as a DVD for about US$50 to clinicians who give all the support and direction needed (J. Wright, email, 8 December 2004).

In brief, in an RCT in a clinic, mild to moderately depressed outpatients who had *Good Days Ahead* plus 45% less ftfCBT time than a ftfCBT-only group had comparable outcome to six months follow-up. Dropout rate was low – *GDA* patients had had two ftf screening interviews and then, before *GDA* sessions, ftfCBT to a total of over four hours over eight weeks. Shortening ftfCBT time from 450 to 250 minutes in all did not impair outcome. The question remains what *GDA* could achieve with just brief support rather than preceding ftfCBT.

INTERNET

USA: *ODIN* (*Overcoming Depression on the InterNet*) in a MHO

Unlike with most CP, *ODIN* users had no human support by phone, email or face to face.

RCT 1 (ODIN 1; Clarke et al., 2002)

This had sobering results (Table 5.1, pp. 86–88). The study used a private, nonprofit health maintenance organization's (HMO) electronic medical record to mail recruitment brochures to 13,990 adults, half of whom were already having treatment for depression and half (age/gender matched to the foregoing) were not; 526 replied. After giving online consent and mood ratings (mean 31 [=severe] on the Centre for Epidemiological Studies Depression Scale [CESD]), 299 adults self-selected and were immediately randomized to a link to: (a) an unattended cognitive therapy (CT) self-help website which taught cognitive restructuring in seven modules with interactive examples and practice (*ODIN*: www.feelbetter.org, n=144) without a live helpline; or to (b) a control website – that of the HMO which offered non-interactive information about health concerns, including depression (n=155). All were also free to obtain usual care. They were emailed reminders at weeks 0, 4, 8, 16 and 32 after entry to return to the website to self-rate progress, and were sent a $5 Amazon.com gift certificate for each completed assessment. Staff tried to phone subjects who did not answer two email reminders about a missing follow-up rating.

Of study entrants, 74% completed at least one post-entry assessment. Most subjects used the website infrequently (mean 2.6 sessions). The internet program had no post-treatment effect on the whole sample. It had a modest effect in those not severely depressed at week 0. Outcome did not relate to frequency of use of the website.

RCT 2 (ODIN 2; Clarke et al., 2005)

This had slightly better results. As with *ODIN* 1, the researchers again used HMO electronic medical records to recruit people with marked depressive symptoms. It mailed brochures in a plain envelope to 12,051 adults of whom half were already being treated for depression and half (age/gender matched to the former) who had no evidence of depression diagnosis or treatment in their medical chart. Of the 12,051, 255 people used the internet site, gave online consent and were randomized to have unlimited access to the unattended *ODIN* website with reminders at weeks 2, 8 and 13 to use *ODIN*: (a) either by postcard (n=75); or (b) by phone (n=80); or instead to have (c) control treatment as usual (TAU; n=100) with access not to *ODIN* but to a HMO health website giving information about depression without interactive skills training. *ODIN* subjects too were free to seek TAU. At weeks 0, 5, 10 and 16 all subjects were emailed for online self-ratings of the CESD and the SF12, staff phoned nonresponders to two email reminders for any rating, and all received Amazon.com $5–$20 gift certificates for completing ratings.

Of the 255 participants, 200 vs 55 respectively came from the depression-treated vs the untreated recruitment groups (3% vs 1% of those invited). Compared to nonrandomized subjects the 255 were older (64% vs 52% age 45 or older) and had slightly more females (77% vs 71%).

ODIN subjects used *ODIN* a mean of 3.5 times. Completion rates were 66% at 5–16 weeks, and 82% for at least one post-week-0 rating. Non-completers of at least one post-week-0 rating had higher initial depression and were older. More controls completed at least one post-week-0 rating (93%) than did phone- (76%) or postcard-reminded *ODIN* subjects (73%).

100 HANDS-ON HELP: COMPUTER-AIDED PSYCHOTHERAPY

ODIN subjects rated more improvement in depression than did controls (effect size was only 0.28 sds in the entire sample but 0.54 sds in those who had been most depressed at baseline). At week 16, 20% more *ODIN* than control subjects (44% vs 24%, p=0.02) were no longer at least moderately depressed. *ODIN* had no effect on the SF-12 or healthcare service use. Postcard- and phone-reminded *ODIN* subjects did not differ on outcome or frequency of return visits.

Unsurprisingly, of invitees already on depression treatment before the second RCT only 3% took up a postal offer of depression self-help with *ODIN*. It is sobering, however, that only 1% of invitees who had no evidence of depression diagnosis or treatment in their medical chart took up the *ODIN* offer, and that the effect size of improvement was modest though significant. How to raise take-up and subsequent gains is a major issue.

In brief, results were disappointing in the first *ODIN* RCT and better though still modest in its second RCT. It is unclear how much these reflected the overall samples having been (a) severely depressed or (b) never screened personally face to face or by phone or email and having no brief personal help by phone or email if they got stuck, or (c) the CP website having given instructions only about cognitive restructuring and none about behavioural activation (pleasant activities). The authors are piloting a more elaborate and interactive website that now includes both cognitive restructuring and behavioural activation.

Australia: *MoodGYM*

RCT (Christensen et al., 2004a; Griffiths, Christensen, Jorm, Evans, & Groves, 2004)

This careful RCT (Table 5.1, pp. 86–88) posted a questionnaire to 27,000 people aged 18–52 chosen randomly from the Canberra electoral roll; 23% (6122) returned it, of whom 752 agreed to participate, rated themselves as having moderate depressive symptoms, were not in psychological care, and had net access. Of the 752, 656 were posted consent forms and preRCT questionnaires. Of the 656, 525 completed the forms and were randomized. The 525 were 2% of all subjects sent the original questionnaire, 9% of those who completed and returned it, 69% of those eligible for the RCT, and 80% of the 656 who were sent consent forms and pre-RCT questionnaires. The 525 randomized were 71% female and had a mean age of 36 and more distress than all 6122 who returned the initial questionnaire. They were highly educated and over 90% had had marked past depression for which 64% had sought help. Mean duration of distress was not known. Mean CED-S depression was 22, appreciably less than the mean of 31 in Clarke et al.'s (2002) *ODIN* 1 RCT.

Randomization was to six weeks in one of three conditions, two of which were websites available free on the worldwide web: (a) *moodgym*.anu.edu.au (CBT for depression; n=182); or (b) *bluepages*.anu.edu.au (education about depression and its treatment, n=165); or (c) control weekly phone discussions with an interviewer (see below; n=178). *MoodGYM* guides users through five CBT modules including cognitive restructuring, pleasant activities and assertiveness training, a workbook with 29 exercises and assessments, printout summaries of module work, online quizzes, tailored suggestions for exercise type, and downloadable relaxation tapes. *Bluepages* gave information on effective treatments for depression. *MoodGYM* and *BluePages* subjects were posted detailed guides to use certain parts of their website each week. *MoodGYM* and *BluePages* did not overlap in what each delivered, except for shared depression assessment and relaxation downloads. Controls were not asked to use a website and were not posted weekly guides.

Lay interviewers using instruction booklets phoned *MoodGYM* and *BluePages* subjects weekly for ten minutes to direct use of their website. Lay interviewers phoned controls weekly for ten minutes to discuss lifestyle and environmental factors affecting mood: physical and artistic activities; education and hobbies; social, family and financial issues; physical health, medication and pain; nutrition and pain. For all three conditions each live phone call lasted about ten minutes, and participants had a total of 60 minutes of such phone contact over the six weeks.

The three groups had similar initial scores. *MoodGYM* had significantly more dropouts than *BluePages* (25% vs 15%; controls 11%); at week 0 dropouts vs completers had significantly more distress and knew more about psychotherapy. By six weeks, on intent-to-treat analyses (ITT), compared to controls *MoodGYM* and *BluePages* improved significantly more on depression (pre-post effect sizes respectively: ITT 0.1, 0.4, 0.4; completers 0.1, 0.6, 0.5; moderately-depressed >16 CEDS-D completers 0.3, 0.9, 0.8) and on stigma (−0.07, 0.11, 0.12; Griffiths et al., 2004). *MoodGYM* improved more on dysfunctional thinking and *BluePages* on knowledge of depression and its treatment. At 12-month follow-up gains remained. *MoodGYM* subjects completed a mean of half their exercises. This did not relate to change on CES-D, though improvement increased the more they used the site. The number of times that subjects accessed their site is unavailable for *MoodGYM* but was 4.5 for *BluePages*. Across the three trial conditions subjects were similarly satisfied with their experience of the trial.

Discussion of MoodGYM's *RCT*

Important questions arise from the RCT:

1. As is also asked of the Swedish netCBT systems, could the RCT results with the Australian *MoodGYM* system be replicated with less educated and more-severely depressed subjects?
2. How much did the two net groups do better because of: their net access per se; what they accessed; what they discussed with lay interviewers by phone; synergy of net access plus brief phone discussions? The unimproved controls had not been sent to a website, and had similar duration but not content of phone discussion with a lay interviewer.
3. Especially sobering, what were the RCT's effective therapy ingredients for depression? Improvement was similar whether website content + brief phone discussions concerned CBT for depression or just education about depression. *MoodGYM* subjects improving the more they used their site resembles findings with two other forms of CP:
   - OCD users of *BTSteps* who did ≥1 exposure and ritual prevention session improved more than those who didn't in an open study (Greist et al., 1998) and in a RCT (Greist et al., 2002) and in the RCT improved as much as patients who had therapist-guided CBT.
   - depressed users of *Cope* in an open trial (Osgood-Hynes et al., 1998) improved more if they used more CBT modules. Moreover, improvement did not relate to whether those modules concerned behavioural activation, or cognitive restructuring, or assertive communication. This accords with findings from a large face-to-face RCT that depression improved as much with the component of behavioural activation alone as with full CBT (Gortner, Gollan, Dobson, & Jacobson, 1998; Jacobson et al., 1996). If CP such as *MoodGYM*, *BluePages* and *Cope* has modular components this can greatly speed the running and analysis of dismantling trials compared to face-to-face trials. Accelerating the dismantling of effective therapy ingredients is crucial given the growing number of types of brief psychotherapy that were effective in RCTs, an issue which takes us beyond the scope of this review.
4. Did *MoodGYM* have more dropouts than *BluePages* (25% vs 15%; 11% control) because it was more interactive? Phobia/panic patients seemed to discontinue treatment with *FearFighter* early more often when asked to do more self-help tasks (Schneider et al., 2005).
5. What background and training do lay interviewers need to give phone support to subjects doing CP? This affects the organization and funding of net-accessed self-help services on a regional, national and international basis.

> *In brief,* mood improved similarly in highly educated subjects with mild or moderate depression who were directed to either CBT (*MoodGYM*) or depression education (*BluePages*) on the net plus live phone support for an hour in all over six weeks with a lay interviewer. They improved more than randomized subjects who were not directed to a website but had live phone discussions with a lay interviewer differing in content from that of the phone discussions with CBT or depression education subjects.

Worldwide visitors: Two open studies of *MoodGYM*-site visitors worldwide

Open study 1

The first open study (Christensen, Griffiths, & Korten, 2002) examined *MoodGYM* use over 181 days by site visitors, including 2909 registrants of whom 1503 made at least one online assessment and, separately, 71 psychology students who visited the site for training. The site had hardly any direct marketing, yet had over 800,000 hits with over 297,000 page views and 17,600 sessions of which 63% were casual (<6 page views, <6 mins) and 20% lasted >15 mins. Its visitors came from over 62 countries, including 35% from the USA and 33% from Australia. Mean age was 36, and 60% were female. Users could use any module/s and self-rate as desired. Users who completed ≥1 rating of depression (n=1503) or anxiety (n=1049) rated more ill than the students or than a Canberra young-adult sample. Females rated more ill than males. Visitors' depression and anxiety improved significantly where they rated ≥2 assessments (depression n=465; anxiety n=223) while going through the modules.

Open study 2

The second open study (Christensen et al., 2004b) compared the improvement in depression and anxiety of: (a) 19,607 visitors to the *MoodGYM* site from >62 countries who enrolled by 2003 by agreeing to research on data entered and giving a name and password, thus creating a record in the database; and (b) the 182 RCT subjects from Canberra who had been randomized to *MoodGYM* in the above RCT (Christensen et al., 2004a). A small proportion of the visitors and their data were in the first study. Post-registration attrition was greater among visitors than RCT subjects: fewer visitors self-rated depression and anxiety ≥once (62% vs 86%) and far fewer rated these ≥twice (16% vs 67%), but RCT subjects had many chances to be

104 HANDS-ON HELP: COMPUTER-AIDED PSYCHOTHERAPY

excluded or drop out before randomization and registration. The 3176 visitors giving some self-ratings resembled the 182 RCT subjects in age, gender, and high baseline depression (higher than is usual in community surveys), and visitors who completed >1 module began with more depression. The visitors and the RCT subjects improved similarly in depression and anxiety as they went through *MoodGYM*, though the visitors did fewer ratings. Depression but not anxiety improved more as the number of modules completed rose from 2 to 4 but not 5 (n=3055, ?, 138 respectively). Importantly, *BluePages* visitors improved at least as much as did *MoodGYM* visitors (H. Christensen, email 17 April 2005). Visitors of neither site had supporting phone calls, unlike the RCT participants.

There was a very marked increase in attrition after registration. Only 16% of the visitors rated depression ≥twice compared to 67% of the RCT subjects, and <5% of visitors who completed module 1 also completed final module 5. Marked attrition as visitors went through modules was also noted with the ODIN unassisted self-help site for depression in the USA (Clarke et al., 2002), though attrition was reduced by email or postcard reminders (Clarke et al., 2005). Comparable massive attrition was also seen among visitors going through a Canadian *Panic Program* (Farvolden et al., 2005). Among UK users of the IVR form of *BTSteps* for OCD, compliance and improvement were greater when a therapist scheduled a few brief phone calls with patients than when they were just asked to phone for help when they wanted it (Kenwright, Marks, Graham, Franses, & Mataix-Cols, 2005). The general point is that subjects use net- or IVR-accessed self-help sites better if they are briefly reminded to do so in various ways. Such reminders only need a small fraction of the resources used for face-to-face therapy.

In brief, it is encouraging that depression improved in *MoodGYM* website visitors, and as much as in the RCT, as unlike in the RCT no one contacted site visitors by phone or email to complete *MoodGYM* or ratings. Crucially, visitors to *BluePages* improved at least as much. It is not known if the visitors had concurrent professional help. Less encouraging is the striking rise in attrition after registration.

Canberra: Controlled nonrandomized nonmatched study of *MoodGYM* in adolescent males

This study asked an interesting question, whether *MoodGYM* could reduce depression or vulnerability to it in schoolboys aged 15–16 who were unselected for either feature (O'Kearney, Gibson, Christensen, & Griffiths,

2006). It allocated 78 Canberra boys aged 15–16 from six school tutor groups to either: (a) five sessions of *MoodGYM* (n=35 from three groups whose tutors agreed to supervise *MoodGYM* users); or to (b) a control group doing standard personal development activities in the school curriculum (n=24 from three other groups). It was not feasible to match the tutor groups or randomize youths to the *MoodGYM* or control condition. At baseline, vulnerability to depression was greater in *MoodGYM* than control boys. Only 40% (14/35) of *MoodGYM* starters completed half or more of its modules. At the end and 16 weeks later the two groups did not differ on an ITT analysis. *MoodGYM* boys who finished ≥3/5 modules were superior to controls through to 16-week follow-up only on self-esteem, but this gain was very small, and reduction in vulnerability to depression was not sustained to that point. *MoodGYM* youths in the present, unlike past studies, had not sought participation, nor were they necessarily distressed, nor were they encouraged to use *MoodGYM* outside tutor group time, nor had *MoodGYM* content been adapted to their age group. Despite the sample's having more self-rated symptoms than established cut-offs (25% depressed, 33% vulnerable to depression) it was too small to detect any prevention.

Net Swedish system

This systematic RCT for depression (Andersson, Bergstrom, Hollandare, Ekselius, & Carlbring, 2004; Andersson, Bergstrom, Hollandare, Carlbring, Kaldo, & Ekselius, 2005) resembled that of Swedish RCTs for panic (Carlbring et al., 2001, 2003, 2005) in its (a) recruitment by advertisements; (b) online screening of referrals from answers to website questions (short CIDI, MADRS and personal details in this RCT); (c) net system's workbook format: subjects went through successive modules presented after their answers to each end-of-module's quiz were automatically emailed to a therapist whose name and photo appeared on the website, and who emailed them individually tailored feedback and access to the next module; (d) web-based self-ratings. The depression workbook system presented CBT in 89 text pages over five modules, seen consecutively pending progress: introduction, behavioural activation, cognitive restructuring, sleep and physical health, relapse prevention and future goals. Subjects rated the MADRS at each use of the website if ≥1 week had passed since last use. They came from different regions in Sweden (55% not in a city) and were not asked to attend the research clinic. At the time 70% of Swedes had internet access.

Of 343 subjects with mild-moderate major depression who answered ads by sending website inclusion forms, 117 had concealed randomization to: (a) netCBT (n=57); or to (b) a waitlist (WL, n=60) pending netCBT. Each group could access its own monitored online discussion group. Topics included CBT content in netCBT, and sick leave and being depressed in the

WL. Mean time in the trial phase was ten weeks. Most netCBT users reached module 4 and 65% completed all modules; completion of more modules related weakly to better mood at post-treatment. At the end of the trial 36/57 netCBT and 49/60 WL subjects completed ratings. Twice more patients dropped out of netCBT than from the WL (37% vs 18%), mainly because treatment seemed too demanding. University education was less common among dropouts than among all subjects (50% vs 62%), and the overall educational level was above average. NetCBT improved significantly more than WL on BDI and MADRS (but not BAI), between-group ESs being respectively 0.9, 0.8 and 0.5, and these gains continued to six months. At month 6, ex-WL patients had had netCBT and improved; 36 netCBT and 35 ex-WL patients self-rated then, and 68% no longer had clinical depression.

Outcome was better in those who had initially fewer depressive episodes, less depression and anxiety and better quality of life, but did not relate to medication use. Total therapist time spent per netCBT patient was two hours, including screening, answering emails, and monitoring the discussion group. The therapist emailed 506 messages in all, most of which were to netCBT patients. Outcome did not relate to medication or the number of postings to the online discussion group. Total postings were 233 for netCBT – mainly about treatment – and 842 for the WL – mainly about subjects' problems. Because more netCBT than waitlist subjects discussed CBT material and had email contact with a therapist, it is unclear how much the netCBT group's superiority reflected those two extra treatment ingredients. It is also unclear how much the netCBT would benefit a less educated sample, given that the whole sample had an above average education while dropouts were less educated than completers and there were some comments that the text and homework were too demanding.

In brief, in a careful RCT in people with above average education, Swedish netCP was better than a waitlist at persistently improving depression. It had twice more dropouts. The design could not detect how much the netCP group's superiority came from its online discussion of CBT and extra email contact with a therapist and the waitlist's not expecting to improve.

PHONE-INTERACTIVE VOICE RESPONSE (IVR)

USA and UK: *Cope*

Cope (Osgood-Hynes et al., 1998) is a CBT self-help system with modules for assertiveness training, constructive thinking, pleasant activities, and maintaining gains. It assumes an understanding/reading age of 11. In *Cope*'s phone-IVR version, users were, after screening, given an ID number and personal password to obtain free 24/7 phone-IVR access to *Cope* from home, and *Cope* booklets to read before making 11 phone calls to the *Cope* computer in Wisconsin. At each call, *Cope* checked for suicidal plans. If patients admitted to any, then *Cope* asked them to stop and see a clinician instead, while staff monitoring *Cope*'s computer phoned or faxed the responsible clinic. *Cope* asked questions and, depending on patients' answers, gave customized feedback regarding progress and made treatment suggestions. *Cope* has had two open studies of its IVR version and no RCTs. An even more convenient internet version (*netCope*) using *Cope*'s phone-IVR algorithms allows home access with no need for printed booklets and phone-IVR calls.

USA–UK: Open trial

An open study of *Cope* concerned 41 US and UK patients who had DSM-IV major depression and/or dysthymia and were moderately disabled but not suicidal (Osgood-Hynes et al., 1998). Mean problem duration was five years. After face-to-face or live-phone screening at their research site, patients were given an ID and personal password for free access to *Cope*, and *Cope* booklets to use before and during phone calls to *Cope* from home. Patients visited their research site again at week 12 to complete end-of-treatment ratings of the HamD and the WSA. They phoned *Cope* mostly outside office hours, for a mean total of 2.5 hrs over 13 calls; 68% completed *Cope* and felt comfortable using it. In ITT analyses, by the end of treatment patients improved significantly (64% by ≥half) on mood, and also on disability. HamD and WSA scores dropped from moderate to mild. Of the completers, 75% felt *Cope* had improved their quality of life.

Cope users improved the more they used *Cope* and the more logical they had rated it initially. Some UK patients had asked to use *Cope* if their GP was not told of this. Fewer UK than US patients completed *Cope* and improved. They were less familiar at that time with IVR and had more dysthymia, initial work impairment, and desire for personal communication. No follow-up was reported. Completers' improvement resembled that in depressed outpatients who had CBT, interpersonal therapy or imipramine in a US multisite RCT for depression, and exceeded that in the RCT's waiting list (Elkin et al., 1989). That study's response criterion of HamD <7 at post-treatment was met by 54% of the *Cope* patients. Moreover, in ITT meta-analyses from the US Agency for Health Care Policy and Research (Clinical Practice Guidelines for Depression), the estimated percentage of adult outpatients responding was 54% to antidepressant/SSRI drugs and 50% to psychotherapy – and to *Cope* was 49%. The 32% *Cope*

108 HANDS-ON HELP: COMPUTER-AIDED PSYCHOTHERAPY

non-completion rate mirrored the mean 40% non-completion rate (range 4–90%) for ftfCBT and antidepressant drugs.

UK: Open trial in west London

Cope's second open study was of referrals to a primary care stress self-help clinic for west London residents who had ICD-10 depression or mixed depression/anxiety (Marks et al., 2003). They were more severely ill and had more comorbid anxiety disorders than those in Osgood-Hynes et al.'s (1998) trial. After phone or ftf screening by a therapist and obtaining an ID, personal password and *Cope* booklets, patients called *Cope*-IVR from home. Of 56 patients offered *Cope*, 1 refused and 16 dropped out or gave no post-treatment data. By post-treatment the 39 completers improved in mood (BDI, HamD) and disability (WSA), ES being 1.2, 0.7 and 0.9 respectively, pre-post severity dropping from moderate-to-severe to mild-to-moderate. Users had phoned *Cope* for a total mean of two hours over a mean of 65 days, during which they had a mean of 46 minutes of therapist live-phone support. Of the 39 patients, 3 had suicidal plans at pre-treatment yet were given access to *Cope* as they were highly motivated for self-help, and they improved. More pre-treatment severity associated with more post-treatment improvement.

In brief, in two open trials of 80 completers in all, IVR-*Cope* used at home together with workbooks improved mood and social adjustment even when there was comorbidity. It will shortly be tested on the internet. *Cope* has had no RCT.

CHAPTER SIX

CP for eating problems

CHAPTER SUMMARY

We traced 13 CP systems for diverse eating problems, 9 from the USA and 1 each from Australia, Germany, Sweden and the UK. The systems were evaluated in at least 30 studies, including 18 RCTs and 5 non-RCT group comparisons. They were variously designed to just monitor eating behaviour or to cut therapist time or to prevent, improve or maintain benefits regarding eating disorders. Study durations ranged from a mere six days to five years, but most lasted about two months and reported short-term outcome. System types and aims varied hugely. At the simple end were wristwatch or hand-held computers or a scale linked to a PDA or semi-automated phone SMSs in order to prompt users to rate eating behaviour on site and perhaps to exercise or do other CP homework or to eat at a normal rate. At the more complex end were multisession, multimedia, interactive standalone or net systems offering brief education about eating attitudes and behaviour in high school girls or college women or overweight adults and a CD-ROM guiding eight interactive CBT sessions in a clinic for bulimia. Computer-aided monitoring alone did not improve eating disordered behaviours. Some CP studies reported benefits for eating problems. Even when significant, effects seemed fairly modest, take-up was low and dropout rates were high. The

---

109

TABLE 6.1
CP for **eating problems** on desktop, PC, handheld computers and other devices

Study	CP system	Design	Participants	Outcome
Witschi et al. (1976)	Desktop-aided dietary counselling.	Pilot in 17 women, 8 men.	Mass., USA: 25 interested volunteers.	Comments used in program development.
Slack et al. (1976)	Desktop-aided dietary counselling.	RCT: (1) interviewed by computer then 2w later by nutritionist, or (2) reverse order.	Mass., USA: 64 overweight volunteers (32 men, 32 women).	Nutritionist took 17% less time with men who'd already had computer interview.
Andrewes et al. (1995)	PC: *DIET* used in research clinic.	RCT for 1 sess: (1) *DIET* for 45 mins (n=25) vs (2) *ELIZA* PC psychotherapy simulation, for 10 mins (n=25).	Melbourne, Australia: 50 female nonclinical volunteers (mean age 24).	*DIET* > *ELIZA* on knowledge of dieting and eating disorders, but not on + attitudes to eating and body image.
Andrewes et al. (1996)	PC: *DIET* used in research clinic.	RCT 1w, 2 sess: (1) *DIET* (n=27); (2) PC *ELIZA* simulation of nondirective counselling (n=27).	Melbourne, Australia: 54 women with DSM-III-R anorexia (28), anorexia with bulimia (8) or bulimia (18).	*DIET* > *ELIZA* on knowledge and positive attitudes to eating. *DIET* rated as easy to use and helpful.
Burnett et al. (1985)	Handheld *CADET – Computer-Assisted Diet and Exercise Training*.	Matched gps 8w + 8m fu: (1) *CADET* + ftf CBT re weight loss (n=6) vs (2) same ftf CBT, no *CADET*, n=6.	California, USA: 12 ≥35% overweight women aged 30–50.	*CADET* + ftf > ftf only on weight loss at 8w (8lb vs 3lb), and at 8m post treatment (18lb vs 2lb).
Agras et al. (1990)	Handheld *CADET*.	RCT for 12w + 1y fu: (1) 1 gp introd session + *CADET*; (2) as (1) + 4 ftf gp CBT sess; (3) 10 ftf gpCBT sess, no *CADET*.	California, USA: 90 women mild-to-mod. obese (BMI 25–35), without bulimia. Completers (n=?23).	*CADET* only = *CADET* + 4 gpCBT sess = 10 ftf gp CBT sessions (mean 5lb) to 12 wks and 1y fu.

Burnett et al. (1992)	Handheld *CADET-II*.	RCT 12w: (1) *CADET-II* alone 4d/w; (2) *CADET-II* alone 7d/w; (3) *CADET-II* 4d wk + biwkly ftf support gp. Completers = 6, 7, 10.	Wisconsin, USA: 40 mild-to-mod. obese women aged 20–50. Nos. randomized N.A. 43% DOs, no diffs between conditions.	Completers weight loss: *CADET-II* 7d alone 8lb > *CADET-II* 4d alone 1lb but = *CADET-II* 4d + ftf support gp 3lb. No fu.
Greeno et al. (2000)	Handheld computer-aided immediate on-site assessment of binge eating.	Weight and age-matched group comparison for 6d.	Pennsylvania, USA: women: (1) 41 with binge-eating disorder; (2) 38 weight- and age-matched without such disorder.	Binging preceded by poor mood, low alertness, sense of poor eating control, craving for sweets. Nondisordered women also binged often.
LeGrange et al. (2001)	Wristwatch computer-aided immediate on-site assessment of binge eating ('ecological momentary assessment').	Group comparison of overweight women over 2w.	New York, USA: women age 18–65, BMI>27.3 with (1) DSM-IV BED (n=22), or (2) nonBED (n=20). 4/22 BED and 3/20 NBED dropped out.	BED=NBED binge episodes and negative affect, restraint and low positive affect as antecedents for both gps. BED>NBED in stress and binge desire before both normal and binge-eating episodes.
LeGrange et al. (2002)	Wristwatch computer-aided immediate on-site recording (IOSR) of binge-eating behaviour.	RCT over 2w + 1y fu: (1) group CBT + IOSR (n=19) vs (2) gp CBT only (n=22). Randomization stratified for weight.	New York, USA: women aged 18–65, BMI>27 with DSM-IV BED. via local ads. 6/22 gp CBT and 7/19 gp CBT + IOSR dropped out.	Completer analysis: group CBT + immediate on-site recording = group CBT only.
Farchaus-Stein & Corte (2003)	Palmtop computer-aided immediate on-site assessment of binge eating.	Within-group study over 4w, data for weeks 1 + 2 vs 3 + 4 (n=16).	Michigan, USA: 16 women with SCID anorexia or bulimia (purging type). 3 DOs. Participants got $50 for study completion.	Eating-disordered behaviours did not drop from weeks 1–2 to weeks 2–4.

continues overleaf

TABLE 6.1 *Continued*

Study	CP system	Design	Participants	Outcome
Bergh et al. (2002)	*Mandometer* food-weighing scale during lunch + display of eating rate and satiety ratings.	Pragmatic RCT over 5–27m + 5-yr fu: (1) immediate trtment incl *Mandometer* (n=16: 12 outpts and 4 inpts); (2) WL, treatment deferred 7–22m (n=16).	Sweden: consecutive referrals with anorexia or bulimia. 4 WL patients DOs: 1 withdrew consent, 3 with worsening symptoms.	14/16 treated pts imp in 5–27m imp in eating rate, BMI, psychopathology, medical status and social adjustment. 1/16 controls imp to 22m.
Delichatsios et al. (2001)	*Telephone-Linked Communications-Eat* (*TLC-Eat*) interactive voice response (IVR) system to improve adults' eating habits.	RCT for 6 months: (1) IVR *TLC-Eat* calls wkly for 26 weeks (5–7 mins per call) (n=148); (2) IVR *TLC-Exercise* calls to ↑ physical activity (n=150).	Mass., USA: 298 sedentary adults with poor diets. Pre ratings: 78% IVR, 76% counseling; 6m fu: 41% IVR, 35% counselling.	Completers: *TLC-Eat* > *TLC-Exercise*: fruit intake, imp global diet, ↑ diet fibre, ↓ saturated fat. ITT: *TLC-Eat* > *TLC-Exercise* on fruit intake.
Bauer et al. (2003)	SMS semi-automated direct phone-based programme for bulimia aftercare.	Case reports: after inpt care 2 pts sent SMS for 13w to report progress wkly. Could also send free text, get wkly edited personalized feedback.	Germany: 2 young bulimic women.	SMS weekly reports of improved symptoms but low body satisfaction.

most evaluated system, net*Student Bodies*, improved eating attitudes but evidence for improved behaviour was more tentative. In a big RCT (n=480) with a waitlist design, net*SB* plus online discussion groups was followed by less onset of eating problems in certain at-risk students, but the role of net*SB* per se remains unclear. The RCTs usually had control/contrast groups lacking an expectation of improvement (e.g. on a waitlist) or lacking the bulletin board, email, phone or other face-to-face support which often accompanied CP, thus precluding conclusions about the value of CP per se as opposed to differential support and/or expectations of improvement across groups. Adding online discussion groups or email guidance seemed to add value to such CP. In contrast, one hour of ftf therapist support did not add value when CD-ROM guidance was given in a clinic.

DESKTOP AND PC

USA: Computer-aided dietary counselling

This desktop system (Table 6.1: Witschi, Porter, Vogel, Buxbaum, Stare, & Slack, 1976) had 375 questions and explanations in an interview about diet history, food intake on a usual day, diet and menu planner. It suggested how to lessen caloric intake, control eating, and increase activity. It gave calorie tabulations for each food reported, each meal, and the total day. It helped users plan meal-by-meal menus for one or more days within the recommended caloric range (1200–1700 kcals per day).

Beta test

Volunteers (17 women, 8 men) interested in the program tried it before it was used with overweight patients (Witschi et al., 1976). It gave a critical commentary to uncover defects such as obscure, poorly worded or unclear questions or instructions and illogical or other unsuitable interviewing strategies. Answers led to the program's adaptation for an experimental study of computer-aided dietary counselling (Slack, Porter, Witschi, Sullivan, Buxbaum, & Stare, 1976).

RCT

The 64 overweight volunteers (half men) aged 20–60 were randomized (concealment unclear) to be interviewed either by a computer and then two weeks later by a nutritionist for about an hour (n=32), or in the reverse order (n=32). When a nutritionist's interview preceded the computer interview she was given the computer session printout to use as she wished. The computer interviews took about 90 mins and the nutritionist's interview about an hour. Fifty-six subjects (88%) returned three months later for repeat interviews with the computer and the nutritionist, plus a weight check. The nutritionists spent 17% less time with those men who had already been interviewed by computer. The volunteers found the computer interview helpful.

Australia: *DIET* educational program about bulimia and anorexia

DIET was a health information program for eating disorders used on a PC (Andrewes, Sat, & McLennan, 1995; Andrewes et al., 1996). It gave a case vignette and information about diet, exercise, nutrition and risk factors for eating disorders, and quizzed users about their knowledge and reviewed information where incorrect answers were given.

RCT 1

Fifty young Australian women without eating disorders, recruited through posters and fliers on a university campus and in a shopping mall, were randomized (alternate allocation, concealment not clear) to use: (a) *DIET* (n=25); or (b) the *ELIZA* placebo program (n=25; Weizenbaum, 1976) for one session in a research clinic (Andrewes et al., 1995). Compared to the *ELIZA* placebo, *DIET* increased knowledge but not global dysfunctional attitudes towards eating and body image.

RCT 2

Fifty-four Australian women with DSM-III-R anorexia (28), anorexia with bulimia (8), or bulimia (18), recruited from eating disorder clinics, were randomized (concealment unclear) to use: (a) *DIET* (n=27); or (b) a PC interactive simulation of non-directive counselling (Pivee, 1990; n=27), on two occasions over a single week in the research clinic (Andrewes et al., 1996). Using *DIET* improved knowledge and positive attitudes to eating more than the placebo. Users rated *DIET* as easy to use and helpful. No dropouts or follow-up data are reported.

In brief, in two small RCTs, in a comparison with the *ELIZA* placebo program, after using *DIET* for one or two sessions young women without eating disorders improved their dieting and eating disorder knowledge, and those who had an eating disorder also improved

> eating and body image attitudes. The two RCTs were unusual in including a CP placebo (as in the studies of Marks et al., 2004; Schneider et al., 2005) to control for the effects of CP per se.

HANDHELD COMPUTERS

USA: Handheld *CADET* (*Computer-Assisted Diet and Exercise Training*) for obesity

Developed in California (Burnett, Taylor, & Agras, 1985), the handheld *CADET* promoted CBT for gradual and modest weight loss. It beeped at intervals to prompt users to set daily goals of food intake and exercise and to record compliance with these. *CADET* also suggested meal plans, made motivational statements, fed back reported exercise taken and calories consumed, praised targets achieved, and showed graphs of progress.

Pilot matched-comparison study

Among 12 adult women in California who were ≥35% overweight, 6 who had ftfCBT weight-loss instruction and also used *CADET* for 8 weeks lost a mean of 8 lb vs 3 lb in 6 matched women who had similar ftfCBT instruction without *CADET* (Burnett et al., 1985). At 8 months post-treatment, mean weight loss continued more in ftf+*CADET* than ftf-only subjects (18 vs 2 lb).

RCT 1

This tested (Agras, Taylor, Feldman, Losch, & Burnett, 1990) whether *CADET* could enhance CBT for women who had mild-to-moderate obesity (Body Mass Index [BMI] 25–35) but not bulimia. In California, 90 such women were randomized to: (a) *CADET* with an introductory group session on its use, treatment rationale and manual, and a calorie book; or (b) same as (a) plus four group CBT sessions with a therapist; or (c) ten group ftfCBT sessions with a therapist. Completers (n=23) numbered respectively only 6, 7 and 10. All three groups lost weight similarly by week 12 (but less than half that expected: 5 lb overall) and maintained similar weight loss to one year follow-up. The authors suggested that cost-effectiveness was greater for the *CADET* groups.

RCT 2

The same group (Burnett, Taylor, & Agras, 1992) recruited by newspaper ads 40 mild-to-moderately obese women in Wisconsin whose BMI was

116   HANDS-ON HELP: COMPUTER-AIDED PSYCHOTHERAPY

25–35 and BDI ≤15 and who were in good health and not pregnant or planning to become so. They were randomized to 12 weeks of: (a) or (b) *CADET-II* (enhanced memory capacity) only for either: (a) four days per week; or (b) seven days per week; or (c) *CADET-II* four days per week plus a biweekly hour-long therapist-led support group. *CADET-II* for seven days and *CADET-II* for four days plus a ftf support group lost weight significantly over the 12 weeks. Weight loss was greater in users of *CADET-II* alone for seven days a week than for four days a week (8 lb vs 1 lb), but not than in *CADET-II* used for four days a week with a ftf support group (3 lb). More weight loss related to more days of *CADET-II* use and more self-monitoring. The 12-week completion rate was 58%, with similar attrition across the three conditions at a level said to be usual for behaviour therapy for obesity which emphasized exercise and gave no incentives to stay in treatment. No follow-up was reported.

> *In brief*, in one small matched trial and two small RCTs, *CADET* led to more weight loss than in an education-only control and similar weight loss to that with *CADET* plus ftf group CBT or with ftf group CBT only. Weight loss continued to one year in the minority of completers in the RCT reporting this.

USA: Handheld computers

Matched-comparison trial (Greeno, Wing, & Shiffman, 2000)

Binge-eating-disordered women without depression (n=41) presenting for weight-loss treatment (BMI 30–45) and weight- and age-matched women without that disorder (n=38) used handheld computers ('self-monitoring companion') for six days to monitor appetite, eating and its site, and mood for eating and randomly prompted (every 30–125 minutes) non-eating episodes. Pre-trial, binge episodes were preceded by poor mood, low alertness, sense of poor eating control and sweets craving. The non-disordered women also binged often, and their binges did not differ in frequency, calorie or nutrition content from those in the BED women.

USA: Wristwatch computer

These were used to prompt 'ecological momentary assessment' – immediate pen-and-paper-diary monitoring of eating, feelings and behaviours before all eating episodes, after binges and at random times, to try to enhance treatment outcome in binge-eating disorder (LeGrange, Gorin, Catley, & Stone, 2001; LeGrange, Gorin, Dymek, & Stone, 2002).

Group-comparison trial

In New York, overweight women (BMI$\geq$27) with (n=22) and without (n=20) binge-eating disorder (BED) were recruited through newspaper advertisements (LeGrange et al., 2001). Prompted by the wristwatch computer the women recorded, wherever they happened to be, eating, feelings and behaviour prior to eating, after bingeing and at random times for 14 days. Four (18%) of the women with BED and three (15%) of those without BED dropped out of the study. Prior to normal eating and to binges, women with binge-eating disorder had more stress and desire to binge than non-BED women but did not differ on binge antecedents, frequency or duration.

RCT

A short RCT in New York (LeGrange et al., 2002) recruited, via local newspaper ads for free treatment, 41 women (aged 25–63, 93% white, mean duration since bingeing onset = 28 years) meeting DSM-IV criteria for binge-eating disorder. They had two weeks of: (a) group CBT plus the wristwatch computer (n=19); or (b) group CBT only (n=22). The CBT was based on a manual by Telch and Agras (1992). Randomization was stratified by weight (details unclear). Six (27%) of the group CBT women and seven (37%) of the group CBT plus wristwatch computer women dropped out of treatment. On intent-to-treat analysis remission from bingeing and frequency of binge episodes was similar across the two groups after two weeks and at one-year follow-up (LeGrange et al., 2002).

> *In brief*, outcome was not enhanced by two weeks' use during group CBT of a wristwatch computer system to prompt on-site monitoring of eating feelings and behaviours.

USA: Palmtop

This system (Farchaus-Stein & Corte, 2003) could record on-site vomiting, laxative use, diuretic use, exercising and binge eating immediately each of those eating-disorder behaviours occurred. It was carried everywhere for four weeks by 16 volunteers who had SCID threshold or subthreshold bulimia or purging-type anorexia. They were recruited by community ads. Mean age was 23, and 88% were white and 12% Asian. They proactively recorded details of episodes of eating-disorder behaviour on the palmtop computer. A research assistant downloaded subjects' entries weekly. Of 16 starters, 3 dropped out and 13 (81%) recorded a mean total of 25 (SD 30) episodes of eating-disordered behaviour. Participants said they failed to record a mean of two episodes over the four weeks. Data for the first and last two weeks were similar, so recording the behaviours immediately on site did not reduce them.

> *In brief*, in this small study computer-aided on-site recording of eating behaviours did not reduce eating disordered behaviours.

Sweden: *Mandometer* to train eating and recognizing satiety in eating disorders

The *Mandometer* (Bergh et al., 2002) consists of a personal digital assistant (PDA) connected to a food-weighing scale. It is used once daily to record and train eating rate and satiety in people with eating disorders. The patient eats warm food from a plate on the scale and rates (via the PDA) satiety at one-minute intervals. Results are displayed onscreen on a training curve for eating rate and satiety (up to 350 g in 10–15 mins). The curve is adjusted up for anorexia and down for bulimia.

RCT

Thirty-two consecutively-referred patients who had anorexia (n=19) or bulimia (n=13), but not unspecified eating disorders or anorexia needing immediate medical care (Bergh et al., 2002), were randomized (concealment unclear) to: (a) treatment including use of the *Mandometer* (n=16; 12 outpatients, 4 inpatients); or (b) a waitlist (n=16). After a median of 14 months (range 5–27), remission was seen in 14 of the 16 patients who had immediate treatment including the *Mandometer* but in only 1 of the 16 on the waitlist. Patients in the RCT formed a small minority of 168 patients at the clinic over seven years whose treatment included use of the *Mandometer*. Estimated remission rate was 75% over 15 months with 93% of these continuing in remission for one year.

> *In brief*, a Swedish clinic claimed good outcome with eating disorders after a complex treatment including eating and satiety training with the *Mandometer*. The research was not designed to identify the *Mandometer*'s contribution to patient outcome.

USA: *Telephone-Linked Communications-Eat* (*TLC-Eat*) IVR system to improve adults' eating habits

The *TLC-Eat* interactive voice response (IVR) system (Chapters 1, 3, 7) helped people monitor their diet and gave educational feedback, advice and behavioural counselling in weekly calls lasting five to seven minutes (Delichatsios et al., 2001).

RCT

This RCT (Delichatsios et al., 2001) was in 298 adults (aged >25, 72% women) who were sedentary and on a suboptimal diet. They were recruited via screening in a multisite multispecialty group healthcare practice. Mean age was 50, with 45% being white and 45% African-American. They were randomized (concealment unclear) to six months of: (a) weekly totally-automated IVR calls to *TLC-Eat* to encourage changes in diet (n=148); or (b) weekly totally-automated IVR calls to *TLC-Exercise* to encourage physical activity (but not changes in diet; n=150). Food-frequency ratings were completed at the start by 78% of *TLC-Eat* and 76% of *TLC-Exercise* entrants, and six months later by 41% of *TLC-Eat* and 35% of *TLC-Exercise* subjects. Of *TLC-Eat* subjects, 76% had phoned the system at least once and 18% phoned 21 or more times over the six months. On completer analysis, *TLC-Eat* compared to *TLC-Exercise* subjects: raised fruit intake by 1.1 servings more per day; improved global diet quality by 9% more, raised dietary fibre intake more by 4.0 grams/day, and cut saturated fat by 1.7% of total energy intake. On intent-to-treat analysis, fruit intake rose more in *TLC-Eat* than *TLC-Exercise* subjects.

> *In brief*, in an RCT of sedentary adults on suboptimal diets, access to IVR *TLC-Eat* improved diet more than did access to IVR *TLC-Exercise* in the minority who gave six months data.

Germany: Semi-automated short text-messaging (SMS) for bulimia aftercare

A short-text messaging service (SMS) was offered to bulimic patients for six months after discharge from inpatient psychotherapy (Bauer, Percevic, Okon, Meermann, & Kordy, 2003). Patients sent weekly SMSs about their bulimic symptoms and received weekly SMS feedback text generated by the SMS program according to their text but edited by clinicians for plausibility

120   HANDS-ON HELP: COMPUTER-AIDED PSYCHOTHERAPY

and further individual patient information. Two three-month case examples were reported out of 30 patients in a SMS study whose outcomes are not yet available.

CD-ROM SYSTEMS (TABLE 6.2)

UK: *Overcoming Bulimia (OB)*

Overcoming Bulimia (OB) (Bara-Carril et al., 2004) is marketed by Calipso on a CD-ROM. Its eight interactive consecutive modules guide cognitive-behavioural, motivational and educational strategies. Each module takes about 45 minutes at a computer in the research clinic and gives a workbook task to complete. Users are asked to complete one or two modules a week. A researcher introduces them to *OB* for 20 minutes and books their appointment sessions (as in *Beating the Blues*). Users have no clinician contact.

Open study 1 of OB

London, UK patients came from a waitlist or consecutive referrals to a local eating disorders unit. Of 60 who had DSM-IV bulimia or unspecified eating disorder and were offered *OB*, 47 (78%) used it in the unit. Of these 47 (94% female), 2 withdrew from *OB*, 19/45 (42%) starters completed all eight sessions, and 26/45 (58%) did fewer sessions. At two months 39/45 (87%) gave data and noted reduced bingeing, vomiting and laxative/diuretic use (all significant) and exercise (non-significant). At least 40% of the patients were on antidepressant drugs at entry, which may have helped improvement. The authors said uptake resembled that for ftf care in the unit, dropout rates resembled those for unselected bulimics, and compared to ftf care, falls in vomiting and purging were similar with *OB* but somewhat less for bingeing.

The same research group (Murray et al., 2003) looked for predictors of *OB* uptake. Of consecutive referrals offered *OB* in two specialist NHS eating disorders services, 81 patients (78 women, 76% British, mean age 29 and BMI 23) completed baseline measures. (It is unclear how many participated in the Bara-Carril et al., 2004; Murray et al., 2007, studies.) Compared to the 60 (74%) who began *OB*, the 21 who did not start *OB* expected it to be less useful for themselves (but not others) and had a range of concerns and misunderstandings.

Open study 2 of OB: first OB cohort vs new cohort having OB + brief therapist support

Outcome of the first *OB* cohort (Bara-Carril et al., 2004) was compared with that of a fresh London cohort (Murray et al., 2007) of consecutively

TABLE 6.2
CP for **eating problems** on CD-ROM and internet

Study	CP system	Design	Participants	Outcome
Bara-Carril et al. (2004)	*Overcoming Bulimia (OB)* CD-ROM in an eating disorders unit.	Open trial 1: pre-post 4–8w + 2m fu: 8 × 45-min interactive *OB* sess guiding cog-beh, motivational and educational strategies (n=47).	London: 57 new referrals with bulimia or unspecified eating disorder. 45/57 (*79%*) began *OB*, 19/57 (*33%*) completed all 8 sess.	At 2m fu: sig ↓ bingeing, vomiting, purging vs *OB* users, non*OB* users had binged and vomited > often and been ill <long.
Murray et al. (2007)	*Overcoming Bulimia (OB)* CD-ROM as in Bara-Carril et al. (2004), but with added 1h total of therapist support over 8w.	Open trial 2: (1) *OB* cohort of Bara-Carril et al. (2004) (n=57) vs (2) new cohort had *OB* + 3 × 20-min ftf therapist help at wks 1, 3, 8 (n=50).	London: 50 new referrals with bulimia or unspecified eating disorder. 39/50 (*78%*) began *OB* and 17/50 (*34%*) did all 8 sess.	Both groups imp sig pre-post and at 2m fu with small diffs between them. 1h in all of therapist support gave no major benefit.
Murray et al. (2003)	*Overcoming Bulimia (OB)* CD-ROM in an eating disorders unit.	Predictors-of-uptake study: 81 pts offered *OB* did baseline assessments.	London: 81 pts with bulimia or other eating disorder. 60 (*74%*) had ≥1 session of *OB*.	Pts who did not take up *OB* had < expectation of OB's helpfulness for themselves, but not for others.
Shapiro et al. (2005)	*Empowerment Solution for Permanent Weight Control (ESPWC)*: CD-ROM CBT for binge-eating disorder (BED) and obesity.	RCT 10w + 2m fu: (1) CDROM CBT, 10 sess (on any computer, n=22); (2) manualized ftf gp (5–10 per gp) CBT, 10 90-min sess (n=22); (3) waitlist for 10w (n=22), then at week 10 given choice of CD-ROM or ftf gpCBT.	North Carolina, USA: 66 enrolled, with DSM-IV BED (70%) or bingeing recruited via newspaper ads, flyers, univ listserve for free treatment. DOs: CDROM 7 (*32%*), ftf gpCBT 9 (*41%*), WL 2 (*9%*). 48 (*73%*) gave ≥1 post-wk0 assessment.	At 2m fu (19w post-entry) ftf gpCBT > CDROM = WL on EDI, ftf gp CBT = CDROM > WL on ↓ binge days. At 10w and 2m fu: ftf gpCBT = CDROM on BES, binge days, intake of fast food, fruit, veg, breakfast and BMI. At 10w, *75%* of WL chose CDROM over ftfCBT.

continues overleaf

TABLE 6.2 Continued

Study	CP system	Design	Participants	Outcome
Winzelberg et al. (1998)	CD-ROM *Student Bodies* (*SB*) used on any computer with a CD drive.	RCT for 8w + 3m fu: (1) *SB* + email support gp + reading/writing assignments (n=27); (2) WL control (n=30).	California, USA: 57 women undergraduates with BMI>19 and no eating disorder. DOs 7/27 *SB*, 5/30 WL.	3m fu: *SB* > WL Body Shape Quest between-gp ES 0.6, not other measures. < than on similar ftf therapy.
Winzelberg et al. (2000)	net*Student Bodies* (*SB*) used on any computer with internet access.	RCT for 8w + 3m fu: (1) net*SB* + online disc gp + reading/writing assignments (n=31); (2) WL control (n=29).	California, USA: 60 women students wanting to imp body image satisfaction. BMI ≥18. Ads. DOs to 3m fu: 23% *SB*, 31% WL.	ITT analysis: *SB* imp > WL on body image (BSQ ES = 0.3) and EDI drive for thinness, bulimia subscales at 3m fu.
Celio et al. (2000)	net*Student Bodies* (*SB*) used on any computer with internet access.	RCT 8w + 4m fu: (1) *SB* + online disc gp + 3 1–2 hr ftf gp sess + reading/writing homework (n=27); (2) *Body Traps* 8 wkly 2-hr lectures + gp disc + homework as in (1) (n=25); (3) WL (n=24).	California, USA: women students via campus ads. At 4m fu: DOs = 24%: 3 *Student Bodies*, 10 *Body Traps*, 5 WL.	At 4m fu ITT analysis: *SB* imp >WL on weight/shape concerns (ES=0.6), eating concerns (ES=0.4), restraint (ES=0.7) and drive for thinness (ES=0.7). *Body Traps* did not differ sig from *SB* or WL.
Zabinski et al. (2001)	net*Student Bodies* (*SB*) used on any computer with internet access.	RCT for 8w, 10w fu: (1) *SBodies* + moderated bulletin board (n=31) or (2) waitlist (n=31).	California, USA: 62 women students at risk of eating disorder, none past or current. 6 DOs.	At 10w fu all students improved, but *Student Bodies* = WL.

Bruning-Brown et al. (2004)	High-school girls aged 15: net *Student Bodies* (*SB*) during class; their parents: net *Student Bodies parent program* (*SBpp*) on any net-linked PC.	Gp comparison for 8w + 4m fu: Girls: (1) *SB* 1h a wk in class + online discu. bullet. board (n=102). (2) Usual health class (n=51). Parents of net*SB* girls: (1) *SBpp* 4w (n=22) inc online disc gp; (2) WL (n=27); Parents of regular health class girls WL (n=20).	California, USA: 153 girls age 15 on school health course + their parents. Students: Parents 96% mothers. 60% refused. Only 11 used *SBpp*.	At 8w but not 4m fu, *Student Bodies* imp > regular classes on Eating Restraint (ES=0.3) and on content knowledge. At 4w parents sig ↓ critical attitudes to weight and shape (pre-post ES=0.5, 0.6 on various measures).
Abascal et al. (2003)	net *Student Bodies* + online group discuss, in 1 of 3 conditions formed so that baseline eating disorder risk and motivation of peer users were only high or only low or mixed.	Gp comparison I: over 6w of 3 girls' classes formed so that peer users' baseline risk and motivation were: (1) high only (n=22); (2) low only (n=30); (3) mixed (n=23).	California, USA: 78 high-school girls aged 15 in mandatory phys. educat/ health course who had high or low eating-disorder risk & motivation. 3 refusers.	All classes ↑ knowledge pre-post. High imp on Shape & Weight Concerns (pre-post ESs=0.5). Low imp Shape concerns (pre-post ES=0.3). High girls in mixed class imp on Restraint (pre-post ES=0.5), Shape concern pre-post ES= 0.8 and Thinness Drive pre-post ES=0.8.
Luce et al. (2005)	net*Student Bodies* (*SB*) + core health curriculum + online discussion gp (chc+odg) *Student Bodies* and odg tailored to particular risk gp.	Gp comparison II: over 8w of gps at risk of: (1) eating disorder n=36; (2) overweight n=16; (3) both risks n=5; (4) neither risk n=111. All gps had chc + odg. Gps 1, 2, 3 also had *SB* + odg for their risk gp. Gp 4 chc + odg only.	California, USA: 188 girls age 15 on high-school health course at risk of eating disorder and/or overweight or neither. 12 refused, 2 DOs.	Completers of *Student Bodies* + odg (42%) improved sig on weight (pre-post ES=0.8), shape (pre-post ES=0.6) and eating concerns (pre-post ES=0.5), and restraint (pre-post ES=0.4).

continues overleaf

TABLE 6.2 *Continued*

Study	*CP system*	*Design*	*Participants*	*Outcome*
Low et al. (2006)	*netStudent Bodies* plus online discussion groups.	RCT 8w + 8m fu: (1) *SB* + clinically moderated online discussion group (14 completed); (2) *SB* + unmoderated disc. gp (19 completed); (3) *SB* only (14 completed); (4) assessment-only control (never accessed SB; 14 completed).	North East USA: 72 undergrad women without eating disorder via email ads. 92% white. 7/72 (10%) never logged on to *SB*. 64% logged on ≥8 times. 61 (*85%*) completed and were paid $40 to do so.	Completers: At 8w and 8m fu: *All SB gps* > control on Drive for Thinness, Body Dissatisfaction and weight and shape concerns. At 8m fu: *SB* + unmoderated disc gp > control on body dissatisfaction and weight and shape concerns. 8m fu ITT: net*SB* > control on Drive for Thinness only.
Taylor et al. (2006)	Net*Student Bodies* (net*SB*) plus moderated online discussion group.	RCT over 8w + booster session net*SB* for 2w at 9m fu, 2y fu and 3y fu: (1) net*SB* plus clinically moderated online discussion group (n=244), each group n=14–24; (2) waitlist control (n=236).	San Diego and San Francisco Bay, USA: women age 18–30 liable to develop eating disorder, with BMI ≥18<32, recruited by flyers in academic institutions, campus mail and media. 480 randomized, 59 (*14%*) no fu. 28 (*11%*) of net*SB* never logged on.	Completers at 8w and 1y fu: net*SB* > WL on Weight and Shape Concerns (ES: 8w, 0.8; 1y fu, 0.4) and on Global EDE-Q and Drive for Thinness. At 3y fu: eating-disorders onset no ↓ overall but did ↓ in those with baseline: (a) compensatory behav and (b) BMI ≥ 25.
Jacobi et al. (2005)	net*Student Bodies* (*SB*) + asynchronous moderated discussion group + reminders 2 × weekly by email.	RCT 8w: (1) *SB* (n=50) + discussion gp 2 × wkly + reminders by email if not used vs (2) waitlist control (WL).	Trier and Gottingen, Germany: 100 women students without eating disorder via ads. Drop-outs 3 *SB*, 0 WL.	At 8w, *SB* improved > WL on several risk scales especially in the 22% of women at high risk (10 *SB*, 12 WL).

Tate et al. (2001)	Net*Behavior Therapy for Weight Loss* (*BTWL*) wkly self-monitoring via e-diary on website + clinician email feedback + online bulletin board + info website accessed on workplace intranet.	RCT 6m: (1) Net*BTWL* weekly (n=46) + ?wkly clinician emails + online bulletin board; (2) net-control info website (n=45). All had 1 gp intro session incl. 1h instruct on beh weight control. Got $10 for 3m fu, $25 for 6m fu.	US eastern seaboard: 91 (81% women) overweight hospital employees linked to email and net. Did not complete 3m or 6m fu: 28% net*BTWL*, 29% net-education.	Completers at 3 and 6m: net*BTWL* > control on weight loss, ↓ waist circumfer., and logins, and at 6m > lost ≥5% initial weight. ITT similar outcome. – > weight loss in each gp if > login frequency.
Tate et al. (2003)	Net*Behavior Therapy for Weight Loss* (*BTWL*) as in Tate et al. (2001) + same wkly clinician emails + online bulletin board.	RCT 12m: (1) net*BTWL* wkly (n=46) vs (2) control info. website (n=46). All + 1h gp intro sess, web tutorial on wt loss, links to > wt loss sites, wkly emails of wt loss info/reminder.	Rhode Island, USA: 92 overweight adults (BMI=27 to 40) at risk for Type II diabetes (1 or more additional risk factors). 84% rated at 1y fu.	ITT at 12m: net*BTWL* > net-info on ↓ weight, % ↓ body weight, ↓ BMI and waist circumference. – > weight loss each gp if > login frequency.

referred patients who were offered not only eight weekly sessions of *OB* in the unit but also, at the ends of *OB* sessions 1, 3 and 8, three 20-minute therapist support periods to encourage completion of *OB* and homework and clarify *OB* information. Of 50 eligible clients, 39 (78%) began therapist-supported *OB*. The first unsuppported and the second supported cohort improved similarly pre-post on binge frequency, vomiting and laxative/diuretic use though supported patients used laxatives more. A similar proportion attended all eight *OB* sessions. At subsequent two-month follow-up more of the supported cohort had ceased excessive exercise. The authors concluded that therapist support had not conferred major benefit on *OB* uptake or completion or on improvement.

In brief, in two open studies a third of patients who were offered *Overcoming Bulimia* in a specialist eating disorders clinic used it there for eight weeks. They improved, and 3 × 20-min spells of ftf therapist support did not enhance gains, on which point an RCT would aid a definitive conclusion.

USA: RCT of *ESPWC* CD-ROM for binge-eating disorder and obesity

This USA CD-ROM for binge-eating disorder (BED) and obesity is sold as *Empowerment Solution for Permanent Weight Control CD* (*ESPWC*; www.empower-plan.com) for $50. It is based on one of the authors' cognitive-behavioural manual for healthy weight control (Bulik, 1997). It has illustrations, photos, videoclips and interactive exercises and six characters whose personal stories guide users through a ten-week program and model exercises.

RCT

A RCT in North Carolina, USA (Shapiro, Reba, Dymek-Valentine, Hamer, & Bulik, 2005) recruited, via local newspaper ads, community flyers and university campus lists, 66 adults with DSM-IV BED or subthreshold frequency of binge eating. They were randomized (concealment unclear) to ten weeks of: (a) *ESPWC* CD-ROM used on any computer (n=22); or (b) ftf group CBT plus a manual (n=22 in groups of 5–10) for 90 minutes weekly; or (c) waitlist, to be offered at week 10 a choice of ftf group CBT or the CD-ROM. Dropouts were *ESPWC* CD-ROM 7 (32%), group CBT 9 (41%), and waitlist 2 (9%). The 48 (73%) who gave post-week 0 ratings were 96% women, mean age 40, 69% white, mean BMI 36, of whom 70% had DSM-IV

BED. All patients were analysed within the group to which they had been randomized if they had at least one post-week-0 assessment, and WL scores at ten weeks were carried forward to two months. Among the 48 completers, at two-month follow-up (19 weeks post-entry), group CBT improved more on the EDI than CD-ROM and WL, both CD-ROM and group CBT had fewer binge days than the WL. There were no differences across the three groups on other outcome measures (BES, number binge days, consumption of fast food, fruit and vegetables, breakfast, BMI). At week 10, 15/20 (75%) waitlist subjects chose to have the CD-ROM over ftf group CBT.

In brief, ESPWC CD-ROM improved less than ftf group CBT plus a manual on some but not other measures up to two months after treatment, and improved more than a waitlist on some measures. CD-ROM and ftf CBT each had more dropouts than the waitlist. At week 10 more waitlist subjects chose the CD-ROM than ftf CBT.

INTERNET

USA: *Student Bodies* eating disorders prevention program

A Stanford, California group developed *Student Bodies* (*SB*; Winzelberg, Taylor, Sharpe, Eldredge, Dev, & Constantinou, 1998) and later modified it. The *SB* program is based on *The Road to Recovery* self-help book (Davis et al., 1989), on CBT (Cash, 1991), and on good practice guidelines. It covers eating disorders, healthy weight regulation, nutrition and exercise, helps users assess their attitudes and behaviour about weight and shape, gives personalized feedback on risk of developing an eating disorder, asks users to keep a journal about their concerns and pressures towards a too thin body image, helps them identify their body image and factors producing this, and focuses on regular eating, nutrition and exercise for young women and misconceptions about these. *Student Bodies* includes audio and video documentaries, personalized feedback, self-quizzes, self-monitoring, goal setting, weekly reading and writing tasks in a set order, and is accompanied by a moderated online discussion group. All *SB* studies were in the USA bar one in Germany.

RCT 1 of Student Bodies (SB) on CD-ROM

An RCT in California (Winzelberg et al., 1998) recruited, through campus ads, 57 women students who had no current eating disorder and had a

128   HANDS-ON HELP: COMPUTER-AIDED PSYCHOTHERAPY

normal BMI$\geq$19. They were randomized (concealment unclear) to eight weeks of either: (a) *Student Bodies* used on a CD-ROM accessed on any computer, plus an email support group plus reading and writing homework (n=27); or (b) a waitlist (n=30). They were paid $10 for participation. Ethnic origin included 54% Caucasian and 20% Asian-American. Users could freely 'graze' the *SB* CD-ROM on any computer. Of study entrants, 7 (26%) *SB* and 5 (17%) waitlist subjects dropped out or were not followed up. Over eight weeks treatment and three months follow-up, compared to the waitlist the *SB* students improved significantly more on body image but not on eating attitudes and behaviours. At three months follow-up, between-group effect sizes were a medium 0.6 for *SB* on the Body Shape Questionnaire and 0.5 down to 0.3 on other measures, being a half to a third as effective as in the face-to-face therapies on which *SB* is modelled.

RCT 2 of Student Bodies (first on net)

This RCT in California (Winzelberg et al., 2000) evaluated eight weeks access to net *SB* by 60 women students recruited via campus ads who wanted to improve their body image satisfaction despite having a normal BMI$\geq$18. They were randomized (concealment unclear) to either: (a) a net version of *SB* plus an online discussion group both accessed on any internet-enabled computer (n=31); or (b) a waitlist (n=29), and were paid $25 for participation. Ethnic origin included 53% Caucasian and 35% Hispanic. Dropout rate to three-month follow-up was 23% *SB* and 31% waitlist. On intent-to-treat analysis the two groups did not differ at week 8 but at three-month follow-up *SB* improved more on the Body Shape Questionnaire (ES=0.3), Drive for Thinness, and Bulimia subscales of the Eating Disorder Inventory.

RCT 3 of Student Bodies (second on net)

A third RCT in California by the same group (Celio et al., 2000) recruited, via campus ads, 76 women who had high body dissatisfaction but no current eating disorder or BMI$\leq$17.5. They were randomized (concealment unclear) to eight weeks of: (a) net *SB* plus an online discussion group via any net-enabled computer, plus three face-to-face one to two hour group sessions, plus reading and writing assignments (n=27); or (b) a *Body Traps* classroom course of eight weekly two-hour group educational sessions about body image which were moderated, plus reading and writing assignments (n=25); or (c) a waitlist (n=24). Entrants were 67% Caucasian and gained two academic credits for participation. At four-month follow-up 76% gave data (n=58) and 24% dropped out. On ITT analysis immediately post-treatment, *SB* improved significantly more than the waitlist on weight/ shape concerns (ES=0.6) and disordered eating attitudes (ES=0.4 to 0.7)

6. CP FOR EATING PROBLEMS 129

and maintained their gains to four-month follow-up. *Body Traps* did not differ significantly from either *SB* or the waitlist.

Compliance in the above *Student Bodies* studies was rated as percentage of screens read per number of screens assigned (Celio, Winzelberg, Dev, & Taylor, 2002). *SB* had significantly more compliance when it used (a) a more structured approach to complete it, (b) phone or email reminders, and (c) financial or course incentives. More compliance related significantly to more improvement.

RCT 4 of SB (third on net), in students at risk

San Diego researchers working with the Stanford group tested net*SB* in California among 62 women students at risk for an eating disorder (Zabinski, Celio, Wilfley, & Taylor, 2001). They had a high Body Shape Questionnaire score ($\geq$110) but a normal BMI>19 and no past or current eating disorder, agreed to take part, and did baseline assessment. They received course credit and $25 for participation. Mean age was 19 and pretreatment BMI 25. Ethnic origin included 66% Caucasian, 27% Latin/Hispanic. The students were randomized (concealment unclear) to either: (a) *SB* plus a moderated online bulletin board both accessed on any net-enabled computer (n=31); or (b) a waiting list (n=31). Ten-week follow-up was completed by 90% (27 *SB*, 29 waitlist). All participants improved on eating disorder measures. *SB* did not do significantly better than the waitlist.

RCT 5, of netSB in women students with no eating disorder

This RCT from a related team (Low et al., 2006) tested the effect of eight weeks of access to net*SB* on any net-linked computer in 72 women undergraduates without an eating disorder who were recruited in the northeast USA by an email ad; 92% were Caucasian. They were randomized (concealment and n per cell unclear) to eight weeks of: (a) net*SB* plus a clinically moderated online discussion group (14 completers); or (b) net*SB* plus an unmoderated online discussion group (19 completers); or (c) net*SB* alone with no discussion group (14 completers); or (d) assessment-only control without access to *SB* or expectation of that later (14 completers). They were paid $40 for completion. In the three net*SB* groups, 64% used net*SB* at least eight times for a mean of four hours in all over eight weeks. Presence or type of online discussion group did not affect net*SB* use but the sample was small. At eight weeks net*SB* completers improved more than controls on Weight and Shape Concerns, Drive for Thinness, and Body Dissatisfaction, and to eight months follow-up (85% gave ratings) remained superior to controls on those measures except on Body Dissatisfaction. On ITT analysis at eight months follow-up net*SB* was superior to controls only

130 HANDS-ON HELP: COMPUTER-AIDED PSYCHOTHERAPY

on Drive for Thinness. Net*SB* users logged on for a mean of four hours in all over eight weeks. The three net*SB* groups had similar numbers and total durations of log-ins.

In brief, in a small RCT, compared to assessment-only controls, at eight weeks and eight months net*SB* use by women undergraduates associated with drop in some risk factors for eating disorders. Net*SB* plus an unmoderated online discussion tended to fare best. It is hard to tell the effects of net*SB* per se as the controls were small in number and had no non*SB* activity apart from assessment.

RCT 6, netSB to prevent eating disorder in high-risk women students

This RCT (Taylor et al., 2006) recruited, via campus emails, posters and mass media, 480 Californian women aged 18–30 at risk of developing eating disorder (weight and shape concerns ≥50, BMI ≥18 and ≤32). Of other respondents 157 were excluded (incomplete baseline assessments 89, refusal after initial interest 15, did not meet inclusion criteria 30, other 23). Enrollees included 60% white, 17% Asian and 10% Hispanic. Mean age was 21. Subjects received \$25 for each completed follow-up assessment. The women were randomized (interviewers blind to group assignment) to either: (a) eight weeks access to net*SB* plus a moderated online discussion group (14–24 women each) plus booster access to net*SB* for two weeks at four months post-treatment (n=244); or (b) waitlist with an offer to complete net*SB* (n=236). Of the netSB group 28 (11%) never logged on; the rest viewed a mean 79% of assigned *SB* web pages and 97 (40%) logged onto ≥1 booster session though this did not predict outcome. Outcome was rated immediately post-intervention, and at one, two and three years follow-up. Follow-up data was not given by 59 (14%; 38 net*SB*, 21 WL). Number of log-ons and their duration were not reported.

Net*SB* had lower Weight and Shape Concerns than the waitlist at about two months (ES=0.8) and one year post-enrolment (ES=0.4), and was also superior to the waitlist on Global EDE-Q (post-treatment ES=0.70, 1yrfu ES=0.4) and Drive for Thinness (post-treatment ES=0.6, 1yrfu ES=0.4), but not on the EDI-bulimia subscale, BMI or depression. At three-year follow-up onset of eating disorders did not decline overall but did drop in those who had had baseline compensatory behaviours such as self-induced vomiting, use of laxatives, diuretics and diet pills, and driven exercise (below threshold for ED diagnosis) and b. BMI≥25.

> *In brief*, among young women with high weight and shape concerns, access to net*SB* plus a moderated discussion group associated with fewer such concerns up to one year post-entry. For net*SB*, women with baseline BMI≥25 and compensatory eating behaviours had less onset of subclinical and clinical eating disorders over three years. The waitlist design could not tell how much the risk reduction was due to net*SB* per se, to the accompanying moderated online discussion group, or to an attention-placebo effect.

RCT 7, netSB to prevent eating disorder in German women students

This RCT (Jacobi, Morris, Bronisch-Holtze, Winter, Winzelberg, & Taylor, 2005) in two German universities (Trier and Gottingen) advertised for female students without a current or recent eating disorder. Of 143 emailed a screening questionnaire, 118 completed and returned it and also had a phone-screening interview, of whom 12 did not meet criteria. One hundred were randomized (concealment unclear) to eight weeks of: (a) a German adaptation of net*SB* (n=50) used on any computer plus participation in a moderated asynchronous group discussion board, together with twice-weekly reminders by email if they failed to log on or visit the session's main pages or post messages to the group discussion board; or (b) a waitlist control (n=50). Subjects were paid for completing all assessments (net*SB* €30 + a small gift, controls €40). Dropouts were 3 net*SB*, 0 waitlist. At week 8, among the 97 completers net*SB* was better than the waitlist control on attitudes/behaviours concerning disturbed eating and the knowledge test. Effect sizes were higher for reducing risk in those 22 women (10 netSB, 12 control) who began with a higher risk (Weight Concerns Scale score ≥42) of developing an eating disorder. The waitlist design could not say how much the risk reduction was due to the use of net*SB* per se or the attendant online discussion group with their expectancy or attention-placebo effects. Results at three-month follow-up await publication.

Group comparison 1, of netSB used with peers having either similar or mixed risk/motivation

At a private all girls high school, 78 girls age 15 in three physical education/health classes were offered the use of *SB* (Abascal, Bruning-Brown, Winzelberg, Dev, & Taylor, 2003) in one of three conditions. These conditions depended on baseline scores for weight and shape concerns and motivation. Within the three classes the students were in one of three

132   HANDS-ON HELP: COMPUTER-AIDED PSYCHOTHERAPY

conditions: (a) high risk/high motivation; (b) lower risk and/or lower motivation; and (c) mixed risk/motivation. Ethnic origin included Caucasian 55%, Asian 14%, Hispanic/Latina 12%. During their 45-minute class periods, users logged on to net*SB* one day a week for six weeks; three girls refused to join. Knowledge rose significantly in all classes. The high risk/high motivation class improved in shape and weight concerns (ESs 0.5) and made fewer negative and more positive comments during online group discussion than high risk/high motivation girls in the mixed class. No other between-class differences were found. High girls in the mixed class improved on Restraint (ES=0.5), Shape concerns (ES=0.8) and Drive for Thinness (ES=0.8). Analysis of online discussion group content suggested that high risk/high motivation students in their segregated group were less likely to make negative comments (about the program, people with weight and shape issues or themselves) and more likely to make positive comments (ditto) than high risk/high motivation students in the mixed group. The authors concluded that high-risk motivated girls might benefit most from SB if they used it in a class with similar high-risk motivated peers.

Group comparison 2, of netSB suited to risk type

Of 15-year-old girls enrolled in high school health classes (Luce et al., 2005), 188 were assessed online for risk of eating disorder and/or weight gain via self-reported weight and height (Killen et al., 1994); 174 agreed to take part – 57% were Caucasian. The girls were assigned to one of four groups according to their risk of: (a) eating disorder (n=36); (b) overweight (n=16); (c) both (n=5); (d) neither (n=111). All had core health curriculum teaching for eight hours with homework on healthy eating, physical activity, appearance concerns and eating disorders awareness, and an online discussion group about such topics. The 36 at risk of eating disorders were also offered a form of *SB* targeting body-image enhancement, the 16 at risk of being overweight were also offered a form of *SB* targeting weight management, and the 5 at risk of both could use both forms of *SB*. The 111 girls at risk of neither problem were only offered the universal curriculum of *SB*. All groups improved pre-post in weight and shape concerns (core curriculum group pre-post ES=0.3; body image enhancement group pre-post ES=0.8).

Group comparison of netSB in unselected high school girls and of netSB for their parents

Bruning-Brown, Winzelberg, Abascal, and Taylor (2004) tested in unselected Californian schoolgirls age 15 and their parents the net *SB* eating disorder prevention program and online discussion group together with an unstructured net *Student Bodies parent program* (*SBpp*) designed to be used over four weeks with an online discussion group (odg). *SBpp* encouraged parents to accept variations in weight and shape, discouraged criticism of daughters, gave exercises and education to show if parents might be reinforcing unhealthy attitudes to weight and shape and to recognize unhealthy eating, showed relevant behaviours and their implications, helped parents decide if their daughters needed to diet, and taught parents to discuss with them their weight and shape.

Of schoolgirls age 15, 153 were assigned by classroom to eight weeks of either: (a) net*SB* including a moderated online bulletin board (n=102) for an hour a week during health classes, plus reading and writing homework; or (b) regular high school health classes (n=51), based on their class schedules. The girls' ethnic mix was 56% white, 16% Asian, 11% Hispanic, 17% other. At eight weeks but not at four months, *SB* girls had significantly but slightly reduced eating restraint (ES=0.3) and greater increases in knowledge (ES=0.5), compared to girls in regular classes.

Only 69 (40%) of the 153 eligible parents agreed to take part in the study. Parents of net*SB* girls were randomized (concealment unclear) to either: (a) four weeks of *SBpp* from any net-linked computer (n=22); or (b) a waitlist (n=27). Parents of girls in regular health classes were all assigned to a waitlist (n=20). Parental uptake of *SBpp* was small. Just 11 *SBpp* parents (all but one were mothers) logged on to *SBpp* (37% of those randomized, 14% of those eligible) though this small minority significantly reduced their critical attitudes to weight and shape at four weeks. Follow-up data is not reported.

In brief, in unselected schoolgirls of whom only some were at risk of developing eating disorders, *Student Bodies* cut eating restraint slightly at eight weeks but not at four months. The small minority of parents who used *SBpp* lessened their critical attitudes to their daughters' weight and shape at four weeks.

In brief overall, in seven RCTs and three group-comparison studies of *Student Bodies* (all in the USA except one in Germany, all but the first RCT on the internet), college and high school females using it improved their attitudes (longest follow-up to one year) towards eating, weight and shape, more than a waitlist or a standard high school health class, and as much as 16 hours of education about

134 HANDS-ON HELP: COMPUTER-AIDED PSYCHOTHERAPY

eating, weight and exercise. Take-up was often low. In a large RCT, net*SB* and a moderated online discussion group were followed by reduced onset of eating disorders in at-risk students with baseline BMI≥25 and compensatory behaviours. Net*SB* was usually offered with nonCP features such as online discussion groups or ftf group CBT, making it hard to judge the contribution of *SB* per se.

USA: *NetBehaviour Therapy for Weight Loss* (net*BTWL*)

Net*BTWL* is an individually tailored CP program (Tate, Wing, & Winett, 2001) on a website encouraging weekly self-monitoring reports via an electronic diary, plus weekly email counselling with a clinician, access to a bulletin board and an information website, and an introductory group session giving an hour of behavioural instruction on weight control.

RCT 1

This studied hospital employees (81 women, 10 men) who were healthy but overweight (mean BMI 29) and in no other weight-loss programs for a year (Tate et al., 2001). All 91 (81 women) employees had one ftf group session guiding them how to lose weight and were then randomized (concealment unclear) to 24 weeks of either: (a) net*BT* (n=46) on a website also giving access to an online bulletin board, requesting self-monitoring and home-work weekly, and giving them weekly clinician feedback by email; or (b) an information-only website (n=45) without clinician feedback or an online bulletin board. Of the 91 randomized, 72% (33 net*BTWL*; net information 32) completed all three ratings. Net*BTWL* completers had, compared to net information, more weight loss (4 vs 2 kg), reduction in waist circumference (7 vs 3 cm) and logins (19 vs 9 times) at three months. Weight loss and reduction in waist circumference were retained to six months in both groups. More of the net*BTWL* subjects achieved the target 5% weight loss (45% vs 22%) at six months. More log-in frequency related to more weight loss in both groups.

RCT 2

The same group (Tate, Jackvony, & Wing, 2003) screened 237 adults answering newspaper ads or on a waitlist at the author's research centre. Of these, 92 (6 men, 82 women) were overweight (BMI mean 33, mean age 49) and at risk for type 2 diabetes. They were randomized to a year of either: (a) net*BTWL* (n=46) plus e-counselling (email support); or (b) net*BTWL*

6. CP FOR EATING PROBLEMS   135

only (n=46) without clinician feedback. Each group also had one initial ftf counselling session, had a weekly email reminder to email their weight weekly, and received weight loss information. At one year about 84% per group came; on intent to treat analysis net*BTWL* had, compared to the control website, more loss of weight (4 vs 2 kg; 5% vs 2% of initial weight), fall in BMI (1.6 vs 0.8) and slimmer waists (7 cm vs 4 cm), and had logged on to the website more often. In both groups more frequent log-ins related to more weight loss, as in RCT 1. Therapist time per client was not noted.

In brief, in two RCTs in the USA, at 6–12 months net*BTWL* plus weekly email clinician feedback improved weight loss in overweight hospital employees and in adults at risk of diabetes more than net*BTWL* alone. The design did not allow conclusions about the impact of net*BTWL* alone without weekly clinician emails and online bulletin board participation.

CHAPTER SEVEN

CP for substance misuse

CHAPTER SUMMARY

Seven **stop-smoking** CP systems were evaluated in ten studies including five RCTs. Of the seven systems, five were from the USA, one was from the UK and Ireland, and one was in French from Switzerland. A phone-IVR system recruited via worksite and media ads. The other systems were net-based and invited website visitors to register with stop-smoking sites giving tailored information, education, email prompts and support and in some cases an online discussion group and other peer support. The systems were tested in four RCTs and four non-RCTs. Subjects mostly enrolled without a diagnostic screen and most dropped out prematurely. How to retain a higher proportion is still unclear. Study durations ranged from 1 to 12 months. In two RCTs having computer-information controls, smoking fell more by three months with CP, though only a small minority were abstinent. Huge numbers of smokers can access net stop-smoking systems. As only a small minority of all smokers actually use such systems, formal cost-effectiveness studies are needed to judge the overall value of the gains achieved.

Seven CP systems to lower **alcohol intake**, mostly for non-heavy drinkers, were evaluated in 11 studies including seven RCTs. Of the nine systems, five were from the USA and one each from Canada,

137

Netherlands, New Zealand and UK; five were on a PC, three on the net, and one on both. Study participants ranged from unscreened health clinic attenders to seekers of help for problem drinking, to schoolgirls and youths at community sites. Study sites included a student health centre, a research clinic, an inpatient clinic, schools, community sites, and netsites whose visitors were invited to complete drinking questionnaires and get tailored feedback or, in more complex systems, CBT self-help with decision-making tools and advice, monitoring and relapse prevention. System use ranged from a mere five minutes to eight weekly 15–45 minute sessions. Except in a RCT which recruited netsite browsers, most enrolling participants tended to complete the studies, unlike CP stop-smoking studies, where most dropped out. Compared to a waitlist, after an eight-week CP system or a one-off 90-minute system drinking dropped to one year follow-up. Compared to an information leaflet only, a ten-minute CP system plus leaflet for known bingeing students found less alcohol use at six weeks, but in students not screened for bingeing an expanded version of that system did not reduce drinking. Adding a self-help book enhanced a five-minute CP system which was minimally effective. In a big prevention RCT, at community sites where youths had used *SODAS* on a PC, over four years the youths reported less 30-day use of alcohol, tobacco and marijuana than youths at sites where *SODAS* had not been offered, especially if *SODAS* had been offered together with parent help. In a RCT of problem-drinking volunteers with above-average socioeconomic status, education and motivation, net*Drinking Less* plus a minimally moderated online discussion board cut drinking more than net information without a discussion board. The effects are unclear of *DL* per se vs an online discussion board. Cost-effectiveness studies were not found of CP for alcohol reduction.

Three USA CP systems for **drug misuse** were reported, in one RCT and one two-schools comparison in young people, and in a betatest, one open study and two RCTs in poor undereducated USA women who used it just once postpartum in an obstetric hospital. The young people studies found short-term changes in attitude so far. In the postpartum women, at four-month follow-up, self-rated drug misuse supported by urinalysis was less in women who had been randomized to use the full system than to use only its assessment part (64% vs 84%).

TABLE 7.1
CP to reduce **smoking**

Study	System	Design	Participants	Outcome
Schneider (1986)	*Go Nosmoke* as below.	Open study.	USA: 28 smokers.	7/28 abstinent at 3m fu.
Schneider et al. (1990)	*Go Nosmoke* behavioural stop-smoking program on any networked PC.	RCT for ≤6 months: (1) full *Go Nosmoke* only; (2) full *Go Nosmoke* + stop-smoking forum; (3) control *Go Nosmoke* only; (4) control *Go Nosmoke* + stop-smoking forum.	USA based but available worldwide: 1158 smokers (age ≥18) subscribing to CompuServe Information System (networked). Recruited via print and electronic media.	62% did ≥1 sess, > with full *Go Nosmoke*. Access: Forum=no Forum; ITT analysis Abstinence: Full > control *Go Nosmoke* at 3 and 6m fu (ns) Nonabstinent people sig ↓ smoking at 1, 3, and 6m fu.
Schneider et al. (1995a)	Toll-free phone-IVR stop-smoking system (*Ted*).	Open trial over 12 months (n=571).	USA: 936 smokers age ≥18 via worksite health promotion, print media and radio in New York, Connecticut and North Carolina. 365 consented but did not start *Ted* and 571 began *Ted*.	571 starters: 35% quit smoking during *Ted*, 14% abstinent 6m after call 1. 83% phoned ≥2×, 46% ≥5× >abstinence at 6m if no quit history, low nicotine dependence, > and longer IVR calls. ns: user's manual, *Ted* reminders.

continues overleaf

TABLE 7.1 Continued

Study	System	Design	Participants	Outcome
Strecher et al. (2005)	Net *Committed Quitters*™ *Stop-smoking Plan* (*CQ*).	RCT 12w: (1) net-based *CQ*, 3 tailored net newsletters, email support messages to enrollee and supporter (n=1991) vs (2) net-control without tailored content, newsletters or support messages (n=1980). £20 worth of oral care products on completing surveys in wks 6 and 12, or £5 worth on completing wk 6 or 12 survey.	UK and Ireland: 3971 adult smoking nicotine-gum buyers using net. Of 5171 invited enrollees, 77% agreed to start and 470 never did, 31 DOs by 6w. At 6w 1850 (53%) rated, 37 not read materials, 552 used > quit aids or programs. 15 > DOs. At 12w: 1491 (43%) rated, 45 not read materials, 471 used > quit aids or programs. Response rates: *CQ* = control.	ITT quit rates: net*CQ* > net-control at 6 wks (4-week abstinence) and 12 wks (10-week abstinence).
Etter (2005)	Net*StopTabac* (net*ST*) questionnaire on website. From replies *ST* shows stage-of-change-matched booklet to print out and tailors personalized 6–9 page counselling emails including cartoons and graphs.	RCT 11w: at start: (1) net-*ST* (n=5966), or (2) net-modified system (< tailoring questions, > info re nicotine replac.) (n=6003). Both gps: + emails at 11w, + > counselling email letters at 1 and 2m, + access to info, discuss forums, + chat rooms on website.	Website in French, researcher in Switzerland. Over 15m, 11,969 (2% of) website visitors agreed to data being stored and registered just once, were randomized. 7732 (65%) DOs did not answer emails for data at 11w.	At 11w, 7-day abstinence rate net*ST* >net-modified system ITT 15% vs 11%, completers 37% vs 34% especially if already contemplating quitting and if heavier smoker (>11 per day). No follow-up.

Feil et al. (2003)	*QuitSmokingNetwork* (*QSN*): net guidance to stop smoking, interpersonal support by peer and expert bulletin boards and library of cessation resources and links.	RCT: smokers randomized to get: (1) $10 or (2) $20 (n's unclear) for 3m ratings. Nonresponders to email prompts also randomized to > prompts by (1) email or (2) USmail (n?).	Researchers in Oregon, USA: USA and Canada smokers (n=606) aged ≥ 18 at least contemplating quitting, 161 (*44%*) did not reply to 3m assessment.	ITT: 7-day abstinence rate at 3m = 18%.
Cobb et al. (2005)	*QuitNet* (*QN*) tailors info, + forums/chatrooms (asynchronous/synchronous messaging), internal emails, online expert counselling (ask-an-expert forum) + recommendations + supports FDA-approved stop-smoking drugs.	Email survey at 3m post-registration: 1501 emails sent, 185 (*12%*) bounced. Of 1316 delivered, 385 (*29%*) completed. 181 (*47%*) without reward, 128 (*33%*) with $20 reward and 76 (*20%*) with $40 reward.	Researchers in Mass. and Rhode Island, USA: worldwide (81% USA, 8% Canada, 4% UK) consecutive *QN* registrants during a 14-day window.	ITT analysis of smokers at registration: 7-day abstinence rate at 3m = 7% (rate for responders 30%).

continues overleaf

TABLE 7.1 *Continued*

Study	System	Design	Participants	Outcome
Lenert et al. (2003)	Net*StopSmoking* system for one-time use.	Open survey at least 30 days after registration (no charge) on the website.	Of 49 USA smokers (recruited by email to 1048 smokers who had completed online smokers' survey), 9 did not start, 40 (*82%*) set quit date within 30d and sent baseline data, 10 (*25%*) did all 8 modules. 1m fu of 26/49 (*53%*) enrollees.	ITT analysis: 18% enrollees abstinent for 7d at 30d post-quit date. 8 (*16%*) > enrollees ↓ cigarettes ≥50%. 78% of respondents said site had ↑ intention to quit and 94% felt it had helped their quit efforts.
Lenert et al. (2004)	Net*StopSmoking* (*SS*) for one-time use.	Quasi-experimental trial: 2 consecutive groups used (1) *StopSmoking* alone (n=199) or (2) *Stop Smoking* plus automated individually timed educational messages (*ITEMS*; n=286).	485 *web using* smokers (*location unclear*) recruited via search engine activity and web browsing. > *SS*-only than *SS + ITEMS* (35% vs 26%) gave data at 30 days post quit date.	ITT analysis: 14% of *SS + ITEMS* gp had 7d abstinence at 30d post-quit date. *SS + ITEMS* imp odds of successful quitting 2.5 times. Quit effort: *SS + ITEMS* > *SS*-only (83% vs 54%).

SMOKING REDUCTION

USA: *Go Nosmoke* PC stop-smoking system

Pilot USA study

A behavioural stop-smoking program (*Go Nosmoke*) was made available 24 hours a day, for use by any CompuServe Information System (CIS) subscriber on any networked PC, and linked to an electronic bulletin board used by fellow smokers and a psychiatrist, psychologist, and lay ex-smoker (Schneider, 1986). Users were taught to recognize feelings and activities triggering smoking, make smoking an ordeal, break the link between urges to smoke and lighting up, and keep a smoking diary. Advice was tailored to each smoker's answers and progress toward quitting smoking. At three months post-treatment 7 of 28 users were nonsmokers, similar to results from face-to-face programs.

RCT

A RCT (Table 7.1: Schneider, Walter, & O'Donnell, 1990) randomized 1158 smokers (84% men) from North America and elsewhere to up to six months of: (a) or (b) full *Go Nosmoke* either with or without a stop-smoking forum; or (c) or (d) a control *Go Nosmoke* version either with or without a stop-smoking forum. Subjects typed *Go Nosmoke* into a CIS-networked PC to complete study consent screens. It explained the rationale, described how to keep a smoking diary, and asked questions about users' smoking history and attitude and reasons for smoking. Users chose a quit date and went to the main menu for unlimited use at any time. Full *Go Nosmoke*'s menu offered personalized smoking-cessation instructions, a smoking diary, urge-stoppers, problems-while-quitting guidance, and a progress graph, and relapse prevention methods available indefinitely. Control *Go Nosmoke*'s menu offered just two sets of instructions broadly outlining behavioural methods which were neither interactive nor personalised. A stop-smoking forum was a further menu choice for a random half of participants, allowing them to read and join discussions about quitting.

Of all 1158 users, 62% used *Go Nosmoke* at least twice, more so with full than control *Go Nosmoke* (65% vs 59%) and (non-significantly) more with than without the forum (63% vs 59%). Full versus control *Go Nosmoke* subjects reported non-significantly more abstinence at follow-up (1 month 7% vs 5%; 3 months 7% vs 4%; 6 months 11% vs 8%). Control *Go Nosmoke* subjects who had no access to the forum reported less abstinence than the rest at one- and three-month follow-up. Non-abstinent subjects in all groups reported smoking less at one month (uncontrolled pre-post ES=0.54) and at six months (uncontrolled pre-post ES=0.32) than at enrolment.

144 HANDS-ON HELP: COMPUTER-AIDED PSYCHOTHERAPY

> *In brief*, full compared to control *Go Nosmoke* subjects called more often and tended to be more abstinent, but effects were small. Abstinence was least in control *Go Nosmoke* subjects without access to a stop-smoking forum.

USA-based: *Ted* phone-IVR stop-smoking system

Open USA trial

A sophisticated interactive-voice-response (IVR) stop-smoking system (*Ted*) was offered via workplace health promotion, print media and radio in New York, Connecticut, Tennessee, and North Carolina, USA (Schneider et al., 1995a). It was toll-free. IVR callers were posted consent forms. Those who returned a signed form pressed their touch-tone phone keypad to choose options from *Ted*'s successive menus (see p. 64 and p. 107 for IVR use of *BTSteps* and *Cope*). Users could call 24/7 as much as they liked. *Ted* described preparation, quitting and maintenance stages, asked questions to decide user's stage and personalize *Ted*'s later aspects. *Ted*'s preparation stage explained behavioural methods of avoiding cigarettes in interactive conversational messages three to five minutes long and repeatedly emphasized user's characteristics, progress in *Ted*, and reasons for quitting. Users set a quit date, and during a ten-day quit phase heard messages tailored to days before, on, and after that date, were asked to keep a diary, were praised for success, were told the money they had saved so far, and were urged to call if there were slip-ups or smoking urges. The maintenance phase lasted as long as users wished, with continuing praise of nonsmoking and encouragement of nonsmoking after slip-ups, plus techniques to remain abstinent.

Signed consent forms were posted back by 975 smokers, of whom 571 (59%) called at least once after receiving an information sheet, the toll-free number to call, and an ID number for access. Over a year, *Ted* was called twice or more by 473 (83%), and five or more times by 262 (46%). Of all 571 starters, 35% quit smoking while using *Ted* and 14% were abstinent six months after their first call. Better outcome at six months (abstinence) related to no past history of quitting and to low nicotine dependence, and (as with *BTSteps* and *Cope*) more frequent and longer calls. Of those who called ≥5 times 68% quit and 22% were abstinent six months after call 1. Of callers, 72% chose at least one urge-stopper message, and 52% chose to keep a smoking diary. Again as with *BTSteps* and *Cope*, few (9%) left any voicemail messages for staff. In nested RCTs, there was no effect of receiving an extra user's manual or *Ted* reminders.

7. CP FOR SUBSTANCE MISUSE 145

In the early 1990s the authors licensed *Ted* for some years to Johnson & Johnson Health Management, Inc., which made *Ted* part of its "Live for Life" health promotion site and offered it at IBM's and other clients' worksites (Schneider, email, personal communication, 9 November 2005).

> *In brief*, over one-third of callers quit smoking in the short term after starting IVR-*Ted*, but only 14% remained abstinent six months later. Quit rates were at least as high as in other media-based programs, but, except among those who called ≥ 5 times, lower than in face-to-face programs. Those who quit smoking while using *Ted* were far more likely than the rest to be abstinent at one-month follow-up. Those abstinent at six months had tended to make more use of *Ted* than did those still smoking.

UK: net*Committed Quitters*™ (*CQ*)

The net-based *Committed Quitters*™ *Stop-Smoking Plan* (*CQ*; Strecher, Shiffman, & West, 2005) individually tailors CBT stop-smoking and relapse-prevention guidance over ten weeks for smokers buying *NiQuitin CQ 21* (nicotine-replacement-therapy gum for smokers of >10 cigarettes a day). *CQ* content depends on answers to enrolment questions on the net about demographics, smoking history, motives for quitting, and expected difficulties quitting and challenges. *CQ* content includes stimulus control, raising self-efficacy, coping suggestions, and encouragement of compliance with nicotine replacement therapy.

RCT

CQ was tested in a large RCT over 12 weeks against a standard behavioural smoking-cessation program (Strecher et al., 2005). Smokers aged ≥ 18 who bought *NiQuitin CQ 21* for >10 a cigarettes a day in the UK or Ireland, were given a password to access a website on any net-linked computer to start free behavioural support. For those connecting, study-inclusion criteria were: set a target quit date within seven days of enrolling, valid email address and net access for ten weeks, agreement to follow-up. Of nearly 5171 invited enrollees (n=3971, 77%) agreed to take part. They were randomized (method unclear) to either: (a) net-based *CQ*, three sequential tailored net newsletters, emailed behavioural-support messages to the enrollee and to an identified supporter; or (b) a net-based control with a similar graphic design, navigational structure and some CBT concepts from the *CQ* but without tailored materials, the three newsletters, or a chance to

146   HANDS-ON HELP: COMPUTER-AIDED PSYCHOTHERAPY

find a supporter for helpful advice. Subjects were sent oral care products worth £20 for completing both a 6- and 12-week survey or £5 for completing one survey. Of the 3971 enrollees, 470 (12%) never logged onto the program, 31 (1%) dropped out by week 6, 1850 (53%) answered the six-week net survey, 37 (2%) said they had not yet read the materials, and 552 (30%) had used further quit aids or programs. In the remaining 1228 (31% of those randomized), at six weeks post-enrolment, quit rates (abstinent for past 28 days) were higher in *CQ* than controls (54% vs 47%; ITT 26% vs 21%). From 6 to 12 weeks, 15 more dropped out. Of 1491 (43%) who answered the 12-week net survey, 45 (3%) had not yet read the materials and 471 (32%) had used further quit aids or programs. Among the remaining 864 (22% of the original 3971), at 12 weeks the quit rate (abstinent for past 70 days) was higher in *CQ* than controls (55% vs 43%; ITT 20% vs 16%). *CQ* and controls did not differ in response rates at 6 and 12 weeks. Initial smoking had been less among improved than unimproved subjects. The authors estimated that *CQ* could be disseminated at less than $1 (about €0.80, or £0.60) per smoker for large populations.

In brief, among adult smokers using nicotine replacement gum who enrolled for net*CQ*, the 22% who replied at week 12 were more likely to be abstinent (55% vs 43%) after support by the individually-tailored net*CQ* than by an untailored net control with fewer elements, though on ITT analysis benefit from individually tailored net*CQ* was marginal.

France and Switzerland: *Stop-Tabac*

Net *Stop-Tabac* (*ST*) (Etter, 2005) was in French on the *Stop-Tabac.Ch* website (listed first in Google.fr if searched with 'arrêter de fumer', 'fumer' or 'tabac'). Net*ST* gave a questionnaire to assess demographics, smoking status, stage of change, tobacco dependence and attitudes, self-efficacy, use of self-change strategies and coping methods, and intention to use nicotine replacement therapy. Based on the replies *ST* gave a stage-of-change-matched booklet to print out, and emailed a personally tailored six- to nine-page counselling letter including cartoons and graphs.

RCT

ST was tested in a large RCT (Etter, 2005) which over 15 months recruited visitors to the *Stop-Tabac.Ch* website who chose to use a computer-tailored stop-smoking system (mean age 34, 39% male, mean 19 cigarettes per day).

The 11,969 (2% of all) visitors who agreed to their data being stored and who registered only once (74% were current smokers) had a randomized presentation of one of the two net systems over 11 weeks, i.e. either: (a) net*ST* (n=5966); or (b) a net modified system (n=6003) having fewer individually tailored questions, more general information about nicotine replacement therapy, and no stage-of-change-matched booklet. Each group could also access information, printable leaflets, discussion forums and chat rooms on the *Stop-Tabac.Ch* website. Both groups were emailed further counselling letters at one and two months post-wk 0 (16% had two or more counselling letters during the 11-week program).

At week 11, replies to an email and three reminder emails about seven-day abstinence were not received from 7732 (65%) i.e. dropouts (n's for *ST* and for modified system are unclear). At 11 weeks, the seven-day abstinence rate was slightly better with *ST* than the modified system (ITT 15% vs 11%; completers 37% vs 34%) and was better with subjects who had been contemplating quitting and smoking >11 cigarettes per day (both ITT and completers). Running the website including both computer-tailored systems cost US$60,000 per annum (2005) for 8000 users of the systems and over 500,000 other visitors who used other aspects of the website, resembling, the authors said, the cost of running a small stop-smoking clinic for 50 people per month.

In brief, among the 35% of enrollees in the RCT who gave data at 11 weeks, slightly more quit smoking with *Stop-Tabac* than with a less individually tailored version of it. It is unclear whether the less tailored version was better than nothing at all, and no follow-up was reported.

USA and Canada: *QuitSmokingNetwork*

The *QuitSmokingNetwork* (*QSN*) (Feil, Noell, Lichtenstein, Boles, & McKay, 2003) net-based stop-smoking program emphasizes quitting benefits, guides craving avoidance, dealing with craving and getting social support, and gives self-efficacy messages. Users also have an ask-an-expert email option and a moderated peer forum introduced by email from a paraprofessional ex-smoker.

North America: RCT

QSN was evaluated (Feil et al., 2003) in adult smokers in the USA and Canada who were recruited by registration with major search engines,

148 HANDS-ON HELP: COMPUTER-AIDED PSYCHOTHERAPY

banner ads, posting on internet discussion groups, radio and print ads and features, and brochures sent to healthcare settings. Of 606 smokers registered on the *QSN* website and completing baseline questionnaires, 72% were women, 81% white, 85% aged 25–54, and 77% smoked ≥ 16 cigarettes per day. They were randomized to get either: (a) $10 (n unclear); or (b) $20 (n unclear) for three-month ratings. The authors said participants tended to use *QSN* more immediately after baseline rating and at weekends. Of *QSN* elements, the moderated peer forum was used most frequently.

Eighty-three days after baseline rating, a subsample of 370 (61%) of those registered (they had completed a three-month pilot) were emailed a '1-week until assessment' reminder. Only 56 (15%) emails were returned as addresses were invalid or the service was disrupted. The rest (n=314) were posted a three-month assessment and sent a second email at 90 days saying the three-month follow-up assessment was ready at the *QSN* website, which 169 (54%) completed. Of those who did not rate after prompts, 68 (47%) were sent an assessment by: (a) email (n=22); or (b) post (n=46). In all 209 (56%) completed three-month ratings of whom 67 (32%) noted seven-day abstinence (ITT 18%); 132 (63%) rated *QSN* as 'very easy' or 'easy' to use. Smokers recruited via the internet quit more than did those recruited by other methods. Completion rates were similar among those offered $10 (55%) vs $20 (60%) and those contacted by email (55%) vs US mail (50%).

In brief, three months after enrolment in *QuitSmokingNetwork*, just over half the subjects self-rated, of whom one-third reported seven-day abstinence (18% ITT), and two-thirds found *QSN* easy to use. Reply rates did not vary with small differences in monetary rewards or with mode of contact (email/mail).

USA: *QuitNet (QN)*

The *QuitNet (QN)* internet stop-smoking program (Cobb, Graham, Bock, Papandonatos, & Abrams, 2005) interactively tailors information and a quitting-guide partly based on users' stages of change, helps them set a quit date, gives a quit calendar with coping strategies for the quitting stage, a quitting counter of money and 'life' saved by quitting, plus tailored next steps suggested each time users log on. *QN* also recommends and supports FDA-approved stop-smoking drugs and a user forum (asynchronous messaging), and internal email system and chat rooms (synchronous messaging), and 'ask-an-expert' email and forum options.

7. CP FOR SUBSTANCE MISUSE   149

Worldwide email survey

QN was evaluated (Cobb et al., 2005) in website users who registered during a 14-day window. The 1501 registrants smoked a mean of 21 cigarettes per day at registration, 71% were women, 91% non-Hispanic white, 48% had a college degree or higher, and mean age was 38 (range 16–81). Of the registrants, two-thirds visited the site more than once. At three months post-registration, 1501 email questionnaires were sent, each with an encrypted identifier embedded in the clickable link tying the follow-up survey to the user's *QN* record; 1316 (88%) were delivered successfully and 185 (12%) bounced. Of delivered emails, 385 (29%) were completed, 181 (47%) without incentive, and 128 (33%) after \$20, and 76 (20%) after \$40, were offered two and six days respectively after the first email.

ITT analysis excluded never-smokers (n=27) and ex-smokers (n=450). At three months post-enrolment the 7-day quit rate was 7% and 30-day quit rate was 6%. For repliers the 7-day quit rate was 30%. Those still smoking at three-months were smoking less (7 fewer cigarettes per day; uncontrolled pre-post ES=0.65). Quitters used *QN* more often and for a longer total time, viewed more pages, and were more likely to use *QN*'s social support elements (emails, asynchronous and synchronous messaging). Although 57% had used quit-smoking drugs with *QN* and 28% had used another form of therapy (e.g. counselling, acupuncture), such extra help did not predict quitting at three months. Repliers spent nine hours (+/–31hours) on *QN*. Methodological problems included whether to count as users registrants with bounced email addresses and one-time-only website visitors.

> *In brief*, at three months post-*QuitNet* registration, an email survey was answered by just under a third of *QN* enrollees, of whom 30% noted seven-day abstinence (ITT 7%).

USA: *StopSmoking* website (*SS*)

Net*StopSmoking* (*SS*; Lenert et al., 2003) is an unmoderated website for one-time use. It gives standard educational materials and others tailored to user's answers to an online questionnaire showing their stage of change (precontemplation, contemplation, preparation, action, maintenance, relapse), beliefs, attitudes and intentions, and an interactive calendar to set a quit date within the next 30 days.

150 HANDS-ON HELP: COMPUTER-AIDED PSYCHOTHERAPY

Pilot study

A pilot study (Lenert et al., 2003) invited 1048 USA smokers to enrol by email (how identified is unclear), of whom 49 (5% of invitees) were recruited (mean age 46, mean 19 cigarettes per day, 78% female, 84% white, 75% some college education). Of the 49, 9 (20%) did not start, 40 (82%) set a quit-smoking date within 30 days and returned online baseline data, 10 completed all eight system modules, and 26 (53%) gave one-month data. On ITT analysis, 9 (18%) enrollees had been abstinent for 7 days at day 30, 8 (16%) more had a $\geq$50% drop in cigarette use, 78% said the site had increased their intention to quit, and 94% felt it had helped their quit efforts.

Quasi-experimental trial

This trial (Lenert, Munoz, Perez, & Banson, 2004) recruited USA smokers who visited the *SS* website via search engine activity or browsing (mean 21 cigarettes per day, mean age 39, 60% female, 60% college education, 73% white). It assigned two consecutive groups to have either: (a) Net*SS* alone (n=199), or (b) Net*SS+ITEMS* (automated individually-timed educational messages; n=286). On ITT analysis 14% of *SS+ITEMS* subjects had 7-day abstinence 30 days after the quit date. After controlling for differences in demographics and risk factors for relapse between the two groups, *SS+ITEMS* improved the odds of successful quitting 2.5 times. More *SS+ITEMS* than *SS*-alone subjects undertook a quit effort by 30 days after the quit date (83% vs 54%).

In brief, in an open pilot some net*StopSmoking* users had quit smoking at 30 days post-quit date. Users reduced smoking still more if they also had individually timed educational messages.

ALCOHOL PROBLEMS

UK: *Computer-Aided Relapse Management for Alcohol Problems* (CARM)

CARM (Table 7.2: Yates, 1996b; cited by Marks et al., 1998b; Marks, 1999) was used by 11 inpatients over one and a half hours and compared with a session of human-guided relapse prevention in nine inpatients. It was said to add value in care and to be in regular use in some UK clinics. Further details are not available.

TABLE 7.2
CP for **alcohol** misuse

Study	System	Design	Participants	Outcome
Yates (1996a, 1996b)	PC relapse management (*CARM*) for alcohol dependence.	Case-control study: one 1.5h sess: (1) *CARM*; (2) ftf-guided.	UK alcohol-dependent inpatients. 11 *CARM*, 9 ftf-guided.	'Added value' of *CARM*.
Hester & Delaney (1997)	PC *Behavioural Self-Control Program for Windows* (*BSCPWIN*) in research site offices.	RCT 10 weeks + 1y fu: (1) immediate *BSCPWIN* for 8 wkly sessions over 10 wks (15–45 mins per session) + self-monitoring of between-session drinking (n=20); (2) WL control (delayed-*BSCPW* as in (1), but from week 10 (n=20).	New Mexico, USA: 40 non-severely dependent adult drinkers scoring ≥8 on the AUDIT. Ss w/ MAST >19 were screened out of the study) as MAST ≥19 = treatment with abstinence goal.	At 10w, immediate *BSCPW* ↓ drinking by 61%, WL did not ↓ drinking until used *BSCPW* from 10w, after which ↓ drinking similarly. Imp continued to 1y fu. Outcome like that with ftf delivery of same protocol (meta-analysis).
Squires & Hester (2002)	PC *Drinker's Check-Up* (*DCU*).	5 focus groups (n=51) saw 1h demo of *DCU* prototype, completed survey and discussion.	New Mexico, USA: Drinkers (AUDIT ≥8) and panel of brief-treatment experts.	*DCU* was rated 'feasible' on 20/22 survey items by drinkers and 12/12 survey items by expert panel.
Squires & Hester (2004)	PC *DCU* as in Squires & Hester (2002).	3 case illustrations from Hester et al. (2005).	New Mexico, USA: see above.	3 cases detailed from above.
Hester et al. (2005)	PC *DCU* as in Squires & Hester (2002) in research site offices.	RCT over 4 wks, 1y fu: (1) immediate-*DCU* (n=35); (2) WL for 4 weeks, then delayed *DCU* (n=26). Drinkers/ significant others paid $40/$20 per assessment.	New Mexico, USA: 61 drinkers aged ≥21, scoring ≥8 on the AUDIT, with significant other willing to corroborate self-reported drinking. 18% dropout.	Immediate-*DCU* ↓ drinking by wk 4 (ES=0.9) > WL (ES=0.2). Delayed-*DCU* ↓ drinking non-sig within 4 wks. At 1y, each group 50% ↓ in drinking quantity/frequency and imp in alcohol-related consequences and dependence.

continues overleaf

TABLE 7.2 Continued

Study	System	Design	Participants	Outcome
Schinke et al. (2004a, 2005, 2006)	*SODAS* City Adventure* CD-ROM on PC for youths to think, **not drink.** *Stop, options, decide, act, self-praise.	RCT of 43 community sites (514 youths), 10w + booster sessions at 18m and 30m, annual fu to 4 years: (1) *SODAS* 10 × 45-min sess completed alone (13 sites, n=190); vs (2) *SODAS* as (1) + parent help (13 sites, n=161); vs (3) no-help control (17 sites, n=163).	NY, NJ, Delaware USA: 514 economically disadvantaged youths age 10–12 (mean 11.5) sought via ads by community agencies. Youths and parents given coupons for completing study aspects. DOs: at 1y fu 1 user, at 2y fu 68, at 3y fu 45, at 4y fu 42 (8%).	Completers at 3y fu: ↑ in alcohol, tobacco and marijuana use: < in *SODAS* and *SODAS* + parent help than in control, and *SODAS* + parent help < *SODAS* only < control; for family involvement in alcohol-use prevention, *SODAS* + parent help > *SODAS* only > control. 4y fu: outcomes similar.
Schinke et al. (2004b)	*TC Live* CD-ROM on PC for young people. (*TC* = *Totally Cool* to **avoid violence and not take drugs**).	RCT by site, 1 sess, post-test straight after: (1) *TC Live* 1 20-min individ sess + staff support and instruc. (4 sites; n=64) vs (2) usual ftf prevent. (incl. roleplay, help by site staff + workbook exercises) (4 sites; n=65) vs (3) no-prevention control (4 sites, n=60).	NY, USA: at 12 community sites 189 economically deprived youths aged 7–15 (mean 9.6, 50% girls). 54% African American, 18% Carribean American, 19% Hispanic. No drop-outs reported.	Completers: *TC Live* = usual prevention > no-prevention control on strategies to avoid violence and < control on regarding drug users as 'cool'. Usual prevent. > *TC Live* = control on reported ability to say no to drug-use offers.
Schinke & Schwinn (2005)	*Girls and Stress gender specific intervention (GSI)* on CD-ROM on PC at school to **reduce stress, cigarettes, alcohol and drugs.**	Two schools compared re 1 sess and 2w fu: (1) *GSI* 1 25-min individ. sess (n=47) vs (2) *Keep a Clear Mind* (*KCM*) 1 40-min classroom drug abuse prevention lesson from teachers (n=44).	NY, USA: two schools: 91 girls aged 12–13. Parental consent rate = 95%. No drop-outs reported.	Completers: *GSI* > *KCM* re more stress-reduction methods and identification of unhealthy stress-reduction methods. *GSI* < *KCM* in approval of, likely use and plans to use cigarettes, alcohol and drugs.

Study	Intervention	Sample	Results
Kypri et al. (2004)	Net *Screening and Brief Intervention* (*SBI*) used on PC in student health centre.	RCT: (1) *SBI*: 10–15-min self-assessment + personal feedback on drinking + alcohol leaflet (n=51). (2) Same leaflet, no *SBI* (n=53). At 6w/6m email/fu + lunch reward.	Otago, New Zealand: 112 binge-drinking attenders at student health centre invited to RCT, 8 refused, 104 began. 84 (81%) did 6w fu, 94 (90%) 6m fu.	*SBI* + leaflet imp. > leaflet-only: at 6w on drinking, bingeing and personal problems, at 6m on personal and academic problems but not on drinking.
Kypri & McAnally (2005)	Net *Screening and Brief Intervention* (*SBI*) extended re exercise and fruit and veg intake, used on PC in student health centre.	RCT + 6w fu: (1) full *SBI*: 10–15-min self-assess + feedback on drinking/smoking, exercise, fruit/veg intake (n=72) or (2) *SBI* assess only (n=74), or (3) no assess or feedback (n=72). At 6w: email fu + cheap pen reward.	Otago, New Zealand: 277 attenders at student health centre invited to join study. 59 did not take part, of whom 43 (16%) refused. 218 completed randomized intervention. 187 (86%) replied to fu (similar both gps).	*SBI* assessment + feedback gp met recommendations for daily fruit and veg intake and physical activity vs no *e-SBI* gp. No differences in hazardous drinking prevalence were found. No differences in smoking were predicted.
Cunningham et al. (2005)	Net assessment and personalized feedback for problem drinking (*NAPFD*) for one-time use.	RCT 1 5-min sess then 3m fu: (1) *NAPFD* < 5 mins (n=29); (2) *NAPFD* < 5 mins + self-help book *DrinkWise* posted immediately?:OK (n=19).	Researchers in Ontario, Canada. Worldwide users of site (recruitment methods unclear). Repliers (% of users unclear): 75% Canada, 23% USA. 69% women. 35 > completers agreed but no 3m fu.	3m after net*NAPFD*, net*NAPFD*-only ↓ drinking. Net*NAPFD* + book > net*NAPFD*-only on ↓ drinking and alcohol-related consequences. Repliers drank less at start than nonrepliers.
Riper et al. (2007)	Net *Drinking Less* (*DL*) + briefly moderated online discussion forum (odf). Password access.	RCT: 6m and 1y fu: (1) net*DL* + odf n=134 vs (2) net info only n=134. At 6m fu email: 110 DOs (41%: *DL* = info only).	Netherlands: 268 problem drinkers via newspaper ads, website consent form posted, website screening.	At 6m: *DL* + odf > info only on all 5 alcohol measures: Between-gp ES=0.37 for weekly drinking at 6m, 0.03 at 12 months.

154   HANDS-ON HELP: COMPUTER-AIDED PSYCHOTHERAPY

USA: PC *Behavioural Self-Control Program for Windows (BSCPW)*

The PC *Behavioural Self-Control Program for Windows* (*BSCPW*; Hester & Delaney, 1997) teaches non-severely dependent drinkers to drink moderately (based on Miller & Munoz, 1982). It has eight modules: goal setting; self-motivation; rate control; setting rewards and penalties; developing alternatives; identifying high risk situations; relapse prevention; final progress review and feedback. Users enter self-monitoring data each time they use *BSCPW* to get feedback on consumption relative to their goals. They could access *BSCPW* for eight weekly sessions, each lasting 15–45 minutes.

RCT

In a RCT (Hester & Delaney, 1997) in New Mexico, USA of *BSCPW* used for free, 40 non-severe drinkers (Alcohol-Use Disorders Identification Test [AUDIT] ≥8) who wanted to drink less were recruited via local health providers, driving-under-influence screening, and radio, print, electronic media and shop flyers. Inclusion criteria were: age ≥21, ≥age 14 reading ability, named ≥2 significant others to verify self-reports. Exclusion criteria were: ≥19 Michigan Alcohol Screening Test (scores of ≥19 indicate poor long-term outcomes (Miller, Leckman, Delaney, & Tinkcom, 1992), psychosis, cognitive impairment or severe affective disorder impairing comprehension, medical contraindications to further drinking (e.g. pregnancy). Subjects were randomized (concealment unclear) to ten weeks of either: (a) immediate-*BSCPW* (n=20) in eight 15–45 minute sessions in research-site offices plus self-monitoring of drinking between sessions (usually by pen and paper but could be on a diskette for home-PC users); or (b) waitlist (n=20) followed at week 10 by *BSCPW* as (a). The sample was 70% Anglo and 28% Hispanic. There were three dropouts – one at ten weeks and two more by one year.

From weeks 0 to 10, immediate *BSCPW* subjects (*waitlist week 0–10 ratings in italics in brackets*) improved weekly mean drinking (standard ethanol units – SEUs) from 35 (*42*) to 14 (*34*), peak blood alcohol concentration (BAC) from 180 mg% (*158*) to 60 mg% (*131*), and drinking days per week from 4.7 (*5.5*) to 3.7 (*4.8*). Ex-waitlist subjects who began *BSCPW* at week 10 then also improved significantly on all measures, with a mean week-20 SEU of 21, peak BAC of 74 mg% and drinking days per week of 4.1. At one-year follow-up, 37/40 starters completed ratings and continued significantly reduced weekly SEU, peak BAC, and drinking days. Significant others verified self-reported reduction in drinking. From week 0 to one-year follow-up, the at-risk-% of subjects (>14 SEU per week) dropped from 95% to 65%. After *BSCPW*, on each drinking day mean drinking halved from six to three beers. Outcome was like that with ftf delivery of the same protocol as calculated by the authors in their meta-analysis of studies by Miller et al. (Hester & Delaney, 1997).

> *In brief*, in non-severely-dependent drinkers, ten weeks of *BSCPW* was followed by impressively reduced drinking compared to a waitlist with consumption cut by half, and benefits continuing to one-year follow-up. The waitlist design could not tell how much of the improvement was an attention-placebo effect.

USA: *Drinker's Check-Up (DCU)*

The PC and net *DCU* is from New Mexico, USA (Squires & Hester, 2002). It offers CP for drinkers on standalone PCs or the net in English and Spanish. For individual users, after self-registration *DCU* offers integrated assessment, feedback and decision-making modules taking about 90 minutes in all to complete. It assesses users' drinking, risk factors, alcohol-related problems, dependence and motivation, and gives personalized feedback to users. Users then say how ready they are to change: if 'not at all ready to change', they can print out their feedback and an *Alcohol and You* pamphlet; if 'unsure', *DCU* offers a decisional-balance exercise; if 'really ready', *DCU* helps users to set goals and develop a plan of change. A *DCU therapist* version allows professionals to tailor assessments for clients and manage client records, and a *DCU Follow-up Drinker's Check-up* module offers outcome reports.

Feasibility study

DCU's feasibility was evaluated by drinker focus groups and an expert panel of judges (Squires & Hester, 2002); 51 adult drinkers (≥ 8 AUDIT) recruited by a market research company in New Mexico rated *DCU* as 'feasible' on 20/22 survey questions, the only two questions not endorsed being about their own motivation to quit drinking after seeing a *DCU* demonstration. Four experts rated *DCU* as feasible on 12/12 survey questions.

RCT

DCU's effectiveness when used without charge was tested in a RCT in adults seeking help for problem drinking in an urban area of New Mexico (Hester, Squires, & Delaney, 2005). Drinkers (AUDIT ≥ 8) were recruited through media ads. Inclusion criteria were: age ≥ 21, reading level >7th grade, had significant others willing to verify consumption, no other treatment for alcohol problems or medical conditions benefiting (e.g. pregnancy)

156　HANDS-ON HELP: COMPUTER-AIDED PSYCHOTHERAPY

from abstinence. Of 141 screened by phone, 83 drinkers completed face-to-face screening of whom 7 were ineligible and 15 did not attend baseline ratings after randomization (13 from WL). The 61 trial entrants were 52% male, 79% Caucasian and 13% Hispanic. They were randomized (concealment unclear) to: (a) immediate-*DCU* (n=35), one 90-minute session completed in the research office; or (b) a waitlist for four weeks (n=26) followed by delayed-*DCU* in the research office. At baseline and later ratings entrants were paid $40 and significant others $20. Six dropped out, and five were lost at one year (17% immediate-*DCU*; 19% delayed-*DCU*). By week 4, drinking fell with immediate-*DCU* (ES=0.9) but only slightly and non-significantly in the waitlist (ES=0.2). At one year, drinking quantity and frequency had improved by 50% with immediate-*DCU* and delayed-*DCU* (ex-WL), and alcohol-related consequences and dependence were also improved. Gains were faster with immediate- than delayed-*DCU*. Three cases from this RCT were detailed by Squires and Hester (2004).

In brief, immediate-*Drinker's Check-Up* reduced drinking over four weeks compared to a waitlist (delayed-*DCU*), and drinking was halved by one year. Improvement was similar to that with the same brief protocol delivered face-to-face (effect size 1.0 for *DCU* vs 1.1 ftf in studies of Miller, Wilbourne, and Hettema (2003). The waitlist design could not exclude an attention-placebo effect.

USA: *SODAS* City CD-ROM for young adolescents to think, not drink

The *SODAS* acronym means Stop, Options, Decide, Act and Self-praise to think, not drink. This interactive alcohol-use prevention CD-ROM from New York (Schinke et al., 2004a; Schinke, Schwinn, & Ozanian, 2005) is for young adolescents to use alone on a PC wearing headphones at an after-school agency, home or elsewhere. Each weekly 45-minute session is navigated through problem-solving steps in a computerized urban landscape. It takes about 7.5 hours in all over ten weeks to complete goal setting, coping, peer pressure, refusal skills, norm correcting, self-efficacy, decision making, effective communication, and time management. The youths also do 30-minute booster sessions at about 18 and 30 months post-entry. Parents can see, in English or Spanish, a 30-minute videotape and written material including two newsletters about alcohol-use prevention. In follow-up years 2 and 3, parents could also attend a two-hour workshop about *SODAS* and interactive exercises to complete with their child, and return a postcard to report completion.

RCT by site (Schinke et al., 2004a, 2005, 2006)

The 514 children age 10–12 (mean 11.5; 51% girls; 54% Black, 30% Hispanic, 11% White) were recruited via ads by community agencies offering recreation, after-school programs and social services for economically disadvantaged youth at 43 community sites in New York, New Jersey and Delaware. Those sites (not youths) were randomized to have either: (a) *SODAS* CD-ROM only, over ten 45-minute sessions weekly and 30-minute booster sessions at about 18 and 30 months post-start (13 sites; n=190); or (b) *SODAS* as (a) plus parent help (13 sites; n=160); or (c) no-help controls (17 sites; n=163) (Schinke et al., 2004a, 2005). All ten *SODAS* sessions plus the booster sessions at 18- and 30-month follow-up were completed by 95% of *SODAS*-only and 91% of *SODAS*+parent help. In the child+parent arm 83% of the parents watched the videotape, 67% attended a workshop at about 18 months post-entry and 79% of the parents completed interactive *SODAS* exercises with their child. Alcohol, tobacco and marijuana use in the last 30 days were self-rated for four years. Dropouts at three-year follow-up were just 8% of *SODAS* only, 12% of *SODAS*+parent help, and 7% of controls, and at four years were 42 (8%) overall. Reported alcohol, cigarette and marijuana use were low at baseline (in each group a mean of less than '1 or 2 instances' of use over the past 30 days).

Completers in all three groups increased alcohol, tobacco and marijuana use over time, but less so in the two *SODAS* groups than in controls; effect sizes were large (>0.8) for all three substances. At three years, the lowest alcohol use was in *SODAS*+parent, though *SODAS*-only also drank less than controls, and in accord with this, family involvement in alcohol-use prevention was greatest in *SODAS*+parent and least in controls. At four years (Schinke et al., 2006), dropouts were just 8%; tobacco, alcohol, and marijuana use were less in the *SODAS*+parent arm than in the *SODAS*-only arm, and less in both *SODAS* arms than in controls. Problem-solving skills, peer drinking behaviour and family involvement all mediated outcomes at four years. Though *SODAS* aimed to reduce early use of alcohol, it also lowered youths' use of cigarettes and marijuana.

In brief, in a large prevention RCT with few dropouts, at sites where youths had used *SODAS* with or without parent help, over four years those youths reported less 30-day use of alcohol, tobacco and marijuana than youths at sites where they had not been offered *SODAS*. Substance use was least where *SODAS* was offered together with parent help. Effects were large though clinical significance is hard to interpret given the ordinal measure of substance use. Checks on self-ratings would aid understanding of *SODAS*'s impact.

158   HANDS-ON HELP: COMPUTER-AIDED PSYCHOTHERAPY

New Zealand: *Net Screening and Brief Intervention (SBI)* for hazardous drinking

The New Zealand net*SBI* system recorded students' weight and a 14-day retrospective diary of drinking, and then gave personalized feedback on screen comparing users' drinking to recommended upper limits and to university and national norms, and told users their risk status and estimated BAC for heaviest binges in the last four weeks.

RCT 1

Net*SBI* was tested (Kypri et al., 2004) in a university student health centre in Otago, New Zealand. In its reception area, 178 students aged 17–26 visiting the centre during a nine-day research window were invited to do, on a net-linked PC, a three-minute Alcohol Use Disorders Identification Test (AUDIT) of drinking. Of 167 who completed it, 112 (67%) scored ≥8 and drank ≥4 (women) or ≥6 (men) standard drinks in a row at least once in the last four weeks. The 112 were invited to join the RCT, of whom 8 refused and 104 were randomized (concealed from research staff and participants) to either: (a) free password-protected access to *SBI* on a PC in the health centre for 10–15 minutes in all, plus an *Alcohol Facts and Effects* leaflet (n=51); or (b) get the leaflet only (n=53). At six weeks, the 104 students were emailed a net-survey and were sent a NZ$4.95 lunch voucher; at six months they were posted a pen-and-paper survey, a NZ$4.95 lunch voucher and an invitation to an interview about research for which they would get a NZ$15 music voucher. Non-responders were sent email, phone and postal reminders to complete each survey. In the 84 (81%) giving data at six weeks, *SBI*+leaflet vs leaflet-only students noted less total drinking, bingeing and personal problems. In the 94 (90%; no group differences) giving six-month data, *SBI*+leaflet vs leaflet-only students noted fewer personal and academic problems, but no differences in drinking. *SBI* was accessed entirely online, with a research assistant only obtaining research consent in the waiting room. The design could not exclude an attention-placebo contribution to effects.

RCT 2

In the same student health centre a RCT tested an *extended* form of net*SBI* incorporating assessment and feedback on not only drinking but also exercise, fruit and vegetable intake and smoking (Kypri & McAnally, 2005). In the centre's reception area, 277 unscreened students (49% female, mean age 20, 75% white) were invited to complete a confidential computerised survey in the waiting area, followed by a net survey six weeks later. Of 277 invitees, 59 (22%) did not complete the study (43 of whom refused); 218

(78%) agreed and were randomized (concealed) to either: (a) full *SBI*: 10–15 mins self-assessment + personal feedback on drinking, exercise, fruit and vegetable intake, and smoking (n=72); or (b) SBI-assessment module only (n=74); or (c) no assessment or feedback (n=72). At six weeks the students were emailed a link to a web-based questionnaire and were sent a pen worth US$0.50. In the 187 *(86%)* giving data at six weeks, compared to SBI-assessment-only, full *SBI* did not differ on alcohol but was more likely to do healthy amounts of exercise and eat enough fruit and vegetables.

In brief, six weeks after prompted use of net*SBI* in a health centre, drinking fell in bingeing students in one study but not in a second study of *extended* net*SBI* in students previously unscreened for alcohol intake, though after using *extended* net*SBI* students did exercise and eat more healthily. Net*SBI*'s value used unprompted at home remains to be explored.

Canada: *Net assessment and personalized feedback for problem drinking (NAPFD)*

This Canadian net program (*NAPFD*) (Cunningham, Humphreys, & Koski-James, 2000) offers a one-time, 21-tem assessment of drinking and its consequences which takes <5', and a page of personalized feedback based on the answers.

RCT

Net*NAPFD* (Cunningham et al., 2005) was tested in a RCT which recruited subjects worldwide who registered while browsing on the Centre for Addiction and Mental Health's webpage. Over two years people who accessed net*NAPFD* on the website (about 500 per month, total n=about 12,000) were asked immediately after using *NAPFD* for consent, via the site's 'hotlink' button, to be followed up three months after using it. Compared to non-repliers, consenting repliers had at the start drunk less (AUDIT) with fewer alcohol-related consequences. Of the *NAPFD* users whose consent was sought (n unclear), 83 agreed and were randomized, blind to condition, to: (a) not be sent (n=42); or (b) be posted (n=41; when posted unclear) the self-help book *DrinkWise* (Sanchez-Craig, 1997). Of the 89, 49 *(58%;* 69% women) replied at three months – 29 had only used net*NAPFD* and 19 had used net*NAPFD* and been posted *DrinkWise*. Net*NAPFD*-only users noted a drop in drinking from baseline (AUDIT 16→13) but not of standard drinks in a typical week or alcohol-related consequences.

> *In brief*, compared to non-repliers, the tiny minority of consenters to follow-up had drunk less at the start than non-repliers, while the even smaller minority who gave three-month data were atypical drinkers in being mainly female. The effect of net*NAPFD* used for five minutes is hard to judge without a net-non*NAPFD* control. In the minority of net*NAPFD* users who were randomized, sending a self-help book was therapeutic.

Netherlands: *Drinking Less* (DL)

Net *Drinking Less* (*DL*; Riper, Kramer, Conyn, Cuijpers, & Schipper, 2007) is in Dutch (MinderDrinken). It guides CBT self-help for mild to moderate problem drinkers to cut alcohol consumption down to a sensible limit (not total abstinence). Net*DL* access was password protected, and the only human support was from an online discussion board.

RCT

Dutch problem drinkers were recruited via newspaper ads referring interested readers to the study website where they could download an informed consent form. Posted signed consent was received from 335 people of whom 305 completed an online screening questionnaire. Of these, 268 completed a pre-treatment questionnaire and were suitable; 90% were contemplating reducing their drinking soon and did not aim at abstinence, 88% said they had never had professional help for their alcohol problem and 65% said they did not need that, though only 3% were drinking within guideline limits for sensible drinking. Fully half were women though usually only a fifth of problem drinkers are female. They had above average socio-economic status and education and most had a paid job. Most saw themselves as very experienced net users and half thought they could help their alcohol problem via the net. The 268 subjects had concealed randomization to password-protected net access to: (a) *DL* (n=134) plus access to a minimally moderated online discussion forum; or (b) net alcohol information (info; n=134) without a discussion forum. Numbers giving ratings were, respectively at six months, one year: *DL* 74, 75 (info 84, 94). Dropout rates resembled those in other studies of self-help for problem drinking, and at 6 and 12 months were: *DL* 45%, 44%; info controls 37%, 30%. Dropouts and completers had similar baseline features.

Moderating the discussion board took two hours weekly in all of a junior researcher's time. Of the 62% (n=165) of subjects answering the question, 83% (*DL* = info) used their assigned net system, but only 66% of

DL respondents (53/80) used *DL* beyond its home page. Results were analysed with multiple-imputation to compensate for subjects lost to follow-up. At six months (*and 12 months in italics*) both groups had cut alcohol consumption, and *DL* improved clinically and statistically more than information only: on both primary measures – not exceeding the weekly guideline limit (31% vs 8%; *23% vs 12%*) and not drinking hazardously (42% vs 20%; *36% vs 18%*), and on secondary measures – were no longer problem drinkers (20% vs 5%; *16% vs 5%*), cut weekly drinking from 43 units by more (to 39 vs 29 units; *35 vs 31 units*; between-group effect size in favour of *DL* = 0.37, *0.03 at 12 months*). Outcome compared favourably with that of other brief treatments, self-help, and GPs' brief help to reduce drinking. It is worth testing what proportion of all problem drinkers in the community might take up and benefit from an offer to use net*DL*, and how much an RCT's consent, screening and rating procedures affect that proportion, but ethical committees may not permit such tests.

In brief, in a RCT of problem-drinking volunteers with above average socioeconomic status, education and motivation, net*Drinking Less* plus a minimally moderated online discussion board reduced drinking more than net-information without a discussion board. It is unclear how much the effect reflected *DL* per se relative to online discussion.

DRUG MISUSE

USA: *TC (Totally Cool) Live* CD-ROM for drug abuse, anger and violence prevention

The *TC Live* interactive drug abuse and violence prevention CD-ROM from New York (Table 7.3: Schinke, Di Noia, & Glassman, 2004b) is for young people to use on a PC, aided by community site staff. *TC Live* teaches drug-abuse prevention and anger control in four problem-solving steps through prompts, options and branches.

RCT by site (Schinke et al., 2004b)

In New York City at 12 community sites (after-school agencies, neighborhood clubs, centres, outreach, recreation), 189 economically deprived young people aged 7–15 (mean 9.6; 50% girls) were recruited. The sites were randomized to offer drug-abuse and violence prevention education as either:

TABLE 7.3
CP for **drug** misuse

Study	System	Design	Participants	Outcome
Ondersma et al. (2005, Study 1: betatest)	Tablet PC with touchscreen *Motivational Enhancement System* (*MES*) for perinatal drug use for 1h in private room in obstetric hospital.	Betatest of *MES*'s assessment and intervention sections.	Detroit, USA: 47 women (30 postpartum from urban obstetric hospital, 10 mothers on substance-abuse treatment, 7 women on methadone maintenance).	Postpartum and drug-using women found *MES* acceptable, feasible, easy to use, respectful, humorous, interesting. 23/25 preferred touchscreen to touchpad navigation.
Ondersma et al. (2005, Study 2: open)	Tablet PC with touchscreen *Motivational Enhancement System* (*MES*) for perinatal drug use, used in private room in obstetric hospital.	Open study: self-rated treatment motivation pre-*MES* and after using each of its 3 intervention components (counterbalanced; n=40).	Detroit, USA: 40 postpartum women assigned to *MES* from pilot RCT (Study 3 below) and larger trial (Ondersma et al., 2006 below).	*MES* use was followed by 61% rise in motivation to change drug misuse.
Ondersma et al. (2005, Study 3: pilot RCT)	Tablet PC with touchscreen *Motivational Enhancement System* (*MES*) for perinatal drug use, used in a private room in an obstetric hospital.	Study 3. RCT 1h session then mean 6w follow-up: (1) *MES* assessment + *MES* brief intervention (n=15) vs (2) *MES* assessment only (n=15).	Detroit: 30 postpartum women in urban obstetric hospital had used illicit drug in pre-pregnancy month. 8 more refused. DOs at 6w: 5 intervention, 3 assess only.	6w after *MES* session: just 1 woman per condition said used drug in past 14 days. *MES* assess. + intervention > motivat to change vs *MES* assess only but ES 0.49 ns.

Ondersma et al. (2006, Study 4: RCT)	Tablet PC with touchscreen *Motivational Enhancement System* (*MES*) for perinatal drug use used in a private room in an urban obstetric hospital.	RCT 1 1h sess then 4m fu: (1) *MES* assess + *MES* intervention (n=55) + 2 posted mother and baby health brochures 4w and 9w later + offered taxi fare + $20 to have drug-use evaluation at local clinic (**0** took this up) vs (2) *MES* assess only n=52.	Detroit: 107 poor postpartum women at obstetric hospital who used illicit drugs in pre-pregnancy month. 76 (37 assess + intervention, 39 assess-only) gave 4m fu data, 31 (29%) DO. All had gift vouchers: $30 at baseline and $60 at fu.	Completers: *MES* assess + *MES* intervention + brochures imp > *MES* assess-only in urinalysis-validated self-report of any drug use at 4m fu and any except marijuana but not marijuana alone. **0** accepted > treatment.

164   HANDS-ON HELP: COMPUTER-AIDED PSYCHOTHERAPY

(a) *TC Live* CD-ROM, for four 40-minute sessions on a PC aided by community site staff (*4 sites;* n=64); or (b) usual prevention of drug abuse and violence including role plays, workbook exercises and guidance from same staff (4 sites; n=65); or (c) no intervention control (4 sites; n=60). There were no dropouts. On self-ratings immediately after their session, compared to controls, *TC Live* and usual prevention youths said they found people who use drugs less 'cool' and recognized more the value of strategies to avoid anger and violence. Usual prevention subjects also felt more able than non-intervention controls to 'say no' to drug offers.

In brief, in an RCT by site in economically disadvantaged young people at 12 community sites, attitudes to drug use, anger and violence control improved immediately as much after on-site use of *Totally Cool Live* for four 40-minute sessions as after comparable usual prevention teaching, and improved more than after no intervention. *TC Live* still needs follow-up and measures of behaviour.

USA: *Girls and Stress gender-specific intervention* (*GSI*) CD-ROM to prevent drug abuse

The *GSI* interactive drug-abuse-prevention CD-ROM from New York (Schinke & Schwinn, 2005) is for girls aged 12–13 to use alone once for 25 minutes on a school's PC while wearing headphones. *GSI* covers 'what is stress?', 'drugs and stress', 'dealing with stress' and 'stress-reducing techniques'. It uses video and narration education about stress and substance use, and guides relaxation training.

Two-school comparison study

The 91 girls aged 12–13 (ethnicity unreported) were recruited in two schools in New York City after parental consent was given (withheld in only 5%). The schools were randomized to offer drug-abuse prevention education as either: (a) *GSI* CD-ROM, one 25-minute session completed alone (n=47); or (b) Classroom *Keep a Clear Mind* prevention taught by teachers in one 40-minute session (n=44). Two weeks later no dropouts were reported. On self-ratings, compared to *KCM* girls, *GSI* girls said they: were more likely to use more stress-reduction methods; approved less of and had fewer plans to use cigarettes, alcohol and drugs; were less likely to use cigarettes or beer if offered those by a best friend.

> *In brief,* girls reported healthier attitudes to using cigarettes, alcohol and drugs to reduce stress two weeks after a *GSI* session than after a classroom drug-abuse prevention lesson. Actual substance use was measured but did not change.

Detroit, USA: tablet PC with touchscreen *Motivational Enhancement System (MES)* for perinatal drug use

MES from Detroit, USA is accessed on a touchscreen computer with headphones. It has assessment and intervention sections with changing graphics to maintain interest. A 3D cartoon character reads the words onscreen aloud (user does not need to read) to guide users through *MES* like a therapist in a ftf motivational interviewing session. The assessment section takes 40 minutes and asks about current drug use and readiness to change. The intervention section takes 20 minutes concerning: (a) feedback about the bad effects of the drug use reported, readiness to change, and how reported drug use compares with adult women's norms; (b) pros and cons of drug use and related change; (c) a summary and query about user's interest in change plus optional goal setting regarding drug use.

Betatest of MES's acceptability and feasibility (Ondersma, Chase, Svikis, & Schuster, 2005; Study 1)

In Detroit 47 women (30 postpartum from an urban obstetric hospital, 10 mothers on substance-abuse treatment, 7 women on methadone maintenance) consented to consult on the development of *MES* by reviewing an early version in a single one-hour session in a private room in an obstetric hospital. They found *MES* acceptable, feasible, easy to use, respectful, appropriately humorous, and interesting.

Open study (Ondersma et al., 2005; Study 2)

In Detroit, self-reported treatment motivation was assessed before using *MES* and again after using each of its three intervention components in 40 postpartum women aged 18–45 who had used drugs before pregnancy, had slept since giving birth, and had no narcotic pain medication in the last three hours. *MES* use was followed by significant rises in motivation to avoid and/or change drug use.

RCT 1 *(Ondersma et al., 2005; Study 3)*

This tested 30 Detroit postpartum women (29 African American, mean age 23, 27 low income, 11 daily or almost daily drug use in their three pre-pregnancy months) who gave birth in an urban obstetric hospital, reported illicit drug use in their pre-pregnancy month, had slept since birth, and had no recent narcotic pain medication. They were randomized (research assistant blind to condition) to complete in a private room in the hospital a single session of: (a) *MES* assessment + intervention sections (n=15); or (b) *MES* assessment only (n=15). At a mean of six weeks later, 22 women (10 assessment + intervention, 12 assessment only) gave data. Only one per condition reported drug use in the previous 14 days, and the two groups did not differ significantly on motivation to change, though *MES* assessment + intervention subjects tended to report more motivation to avoid and/or change drug use (between-group ES=0.49).

RCT 2 *(Ondersma, Svikis, & Schuster, 2006)*

RCT 2 recruited 107 Detroit postpartum women (104 African-American, mean age 25, mean IQ 87, 44 below high school education, 95 had public assistance in last year) who had used an illicit drug in their pre-pregnancy month, had slept since birth, and had no recent narcotic pain medication or grief due to birth outcome. They were randomized (research assistant blind to condition) to a single session of either: (a) *MES* assessment + *MES* intervention (n=55) plus two mother-and-baby health brochures posted to home four and nine weeks later, plus offer of a taxi fare plus a $20 gift voucher to attend a local clinic for substance use evaluation (none took up this offer); or (b) *MES* assessment only (n=52). *MES* was used in a private room in the hospital. Of the 107 women 76 (71%; 37 *MES* assessment + intervention, 39 *MES* assessment only) gave follow-up data four months later. On completer analysis then, compared to *MES* assessment only *MES* assessment + *MES* intervention plus mailed brochures reported significantly lower drug use at follow-up for all substances (between-groups ES=0.46) and all substances except marijuana (ES=0.40), but not for marijuana alone (ES=0.39). At four months on urinary tests and self-reports drug misuse was found in 67% of *MES* assessment + intervention women and 84% of *MES* assessment-only women (between-groups Logit *d* .50; not significant). *None* took up an offer of further help, fitting the fact that 87% of drug misusers neither get nor want help, and 75% of those who reduce drug misuse do so without professional help; only 9% of the women had been treated for drug misuse before the study (Ondersma, personal communication, 10 April 2006).

In brief, poor undereducated women with pre-pregnancy drug misuse used *MES* in an obstetric hospital for an hour, found it acceptable and feasible, and increased in motivation to avoid/and or change drug misuse. In a RCT, four months after prompted postpartum use of *MES* assessment + *MES* intervention for one session in an obstetric hospital followed by receipt of two posted mother-and-baby health brochures, self-reported drug misuse (except marijuana) fell slightly to moderately compared to postpartum women who did *MES* assessment only.

CHAPTER EIGHT

CP for miscellaneous adult problems: pain, tinnitus distress, insomnia, sexual problems, schizophrenia

CHAPTER SUMMARY

We sourced 19 studies, including 15 RCTs, of nine CP systems for a range of adult problems not otherwise included in this review. The problems included pain (headache, back pain, pain during burn-wound dressings), tinnitus, insomnia, jetlag, sexual problems, and schizophrenia. A Swedish netCP system improved users' **headaches** in two RCTs; attrition rates were not cut by adding email support and therapist-initiated phone calls. A USA RCT improved **headache** modestly in the third of users who rated at two-month follow-up. **Back pain** improved similarly with Swedish netCP and a waitlist, though netCP reduced catastrophizing more. A USA virtual reality system to reduce **pain during burn-wound dressings** needs more research. For **tinnitus distress**, Swedish netCP plus email support was more effective than a waitlist and as effective as group CBT to one-year follow-up after having required less therapist time per patient. Compared to a waitlist, Swedish netCP plus email therapist support improved **insomnia** more on only one of nine sleep measures. A USA CP system reduced self-rated **jet lag** in a beta study. **Couples** reported positive engagement and improved **sexual knowledge and behaviour** one to two weeks after using the Canadian *Sexpert* CP prototype for a single session in four RCTs. In **schizophrenia** sufferers a USA-based

169

TABLE 8.1
CP for **pain, tinnitus distress, insomnia, jetlag**

Study	System	Design	Participants	Outcome
Ström et al. (2000)	Swedish netCP for recurrent **headache**.	RCT for 6w: (1) netCP + email support 40 mins vs (2) WL. All monitored symptoms.	102 Swedish pts with recurrent headache. DOs ?netCP, ?WL/45 completers: 20 netCP and 25 waitlist.	netCP self-help > waiting list for headache. No fu. > time-efficient than usual clinic treatment.
Andersson et al. (2003)	Swedish netCP for recurrent **headache** as above, but upgraded.	RCT 6w: (1) netCP + email support 40 mins + phone support 60 mins (n=24) vs (2) as gp 1, but no phone support.	44 Swedish pts with recurrent headache. DOs 29% with, 23% without, phone support.	Adding 1h of phone support to email support did not sig ↑ imp or adherence. Imp 50% < than in RCT 1.
Devineni & Blanchard (2004)	USA *netCP* for chronic **headache**.	RCT: 2w baseline + 4w netCP + 2m fu: (1) NetCP musc relax + cog stress management (if tension headaches) or autogenic training + biofeedback (if migraine or mixed headaches), vs (2) WL (had netCBT as in (1) after 4w).	New York, USA-based study: 139 worldwide adults with chronic tension/migraine headache for $\geq 1y$, recruited from websites inc. ads. 83% US, 12% Canada and W Europe, 5% other. 38% treatment DO. 65% lost to 2m fu.	NetCP > WL on ↓ headache (ES=0.54). 39% netCP imp clinic sig on headache, ↑ to 47% at 2m fu. NetCP imp headache and related disability, 35% ↓ medication, > time-efficient than usual clinic treatment.

Buhrman et al. (2004)	Swedish netCP for chronic **backpain** management.	RCT: 1w baseline: (1) 6w netCP (22 completers) vs (2) 6w WL (29 completers) then netCP. Rated 1w post- and 3m.	56 Swedish chronic backpain volunteers. 51 completers after 5 DOs (3netCP, 2WL).	51 completers: netCP = WL?, both gps improved equally?.
Hoffman (2004)	USA: *Snow World* VR distraction during **painful** burns dressings.	Awaiting RCTs.	Unclear.	Unclear.
Andersson et al. (2003)	Swedish netCP for **tinnitus distress**.	RCT for 6 weeks: (1) netCP (n=53) vs (2) WL 6w (n= 64) then netCP.	117 Swedish adults with tinnitus 6m or longer for which had seen doctor. DOs 51% netCP, 0%WL. At 1y 46 netCP, 50 exWL.	At 6w, netCP > WL on tinnitus. At 1y fu 31% of all patients (28% netCP, 34% WL → netCP imp sig on tinnitus.
Kaldo et al. (2006)	Swedish netCP for **tinnitis distress**.	See page 177.	See page 177.	See page 177.
Ström et al. (2004)	netCP for **insomnia** + email (rarely phone) helpline to and prompts from therapist.	RCT over 5w: (1) netCP n=54 vs (2) WL 2m then netCP n=55.	109 Swedish patients with DSM-IV chronic primary insomnia. 28 DOs (24 netCP, 4 WL).	At post-treatment both gps imp; net CP > WL on only 1 of 9 sleep measures.
Lieberman (2003)	Net self-help for **jetlag** personalized advice re timing of natural-light exposure.	Beta open study.	Washington, DC study base, 20 volunteers worldwide returned ratings.	> self-rated compliance related sig to less jetlag on day 3 after travel.

> CP system to improve cognitive skills found some gains in three RCTs but did not control for placebo effects, while a Scottish psychoeducation system had no effect. The waitlist design used in many of the CP studies could not rule out attention-placebo effects. The Swedish netCP systems used netbiblioCBT whose efficacy needs to be tested in less well educated subjects.

PAIN: HEADACHE IN ADULTS

For pediatric headache, see Chapter 9 including Table 9.1 (Connelly, Rapoff, Thompson, & Connelly, 2006).

Internet

CP for headache has been subject to at least three RCTs on the internet, two with a Swedish system and one with a USA system. The Swedish netCP workbook system (Table 8.1: Andersson et al., 2003; Ström et al., 2000) gave six weeks of guidance on applied relaxation, autogenic training and problem solving, and asked subjects to record daily headache intensity and duration and medication, and weekly frequency of relaxation practice. Subjects reported results weekly, and each week were emailed a fresh part of the netCP system. The USA netCP system (Devineni & Blanchard, 2004) gave four weeks of netCP consisting of: for tension headache, progressive muscle relaxation and cognitive stress coping, and for migraine or mixed headache, autogenic training plus progressive muscle relaxation.

Sweden: RCT 1

Through newspaper, magazine and web ads a Swedish RCT (Ström et al., 2000) recruited 102 adult volunteers who had recurrent primary benign headaches at least once a week over at least six months. After screening via forms sent on the net, subjects were randomized (unconcealed) to six weeks of either: (a) netCP at home (n=20); or (b) a waitlist (n=25). All subjects were asked to monitor symptoms. Therapist time was a mean of 40 minutes per patient to email information and training modules and confirm diaries from subjects. Dropouts were 56% (rate per group unspecified) and compared to completers tended to be younger with headaches of shorter duration. Merely two subjects phoned with personal questions despite having an opportunity to do this. Among completers, by six weeks, netCP compared to the waitlist led to significantly fewer headaches (31% vs 3%) and more patients whose headaches reduced by 50% or more without increasing medication, and more clinically significant improvement (50% vs 4% of subjects). Cost-efficiency measured as % improvement/therapist time was calculated as being 12 times greater than with usual clinical treatment. Caution is needed in interpreting the results due to the 56% dropout rate, the absence of follow-up, and the waitlist's having no attention placebo though it did monitor symptoms. The authors said users of self-help material require at least 12 years of schooling (reading age 17–18), which might apply to their netCP, but *FearFighter*, *BTSteps* and *Cope* assume a reading age of 11.

Sweden: RCT 2

This small RCT (Andersson et al., 2003) of the Swedish netCP system (in upgraded form) for headache tested the effect of adding weekly therapist-initiated phone calls to users. Headache sufferers were again recruited via newspaper and net articles and screened via the net. The 44 suitable subjects were randomized (concealment unclear) to six weeks of either: (a) netCP with email support of unspecified duration plus weekly therapist-initiated phone calls for a mean of ten minutes to foster treatment adherence; or to (b) net CP plus only email not phone support. The phone support did not significantly enhance improvement of the headache index (29% vs 23%) or completion rate (71% vs 65%). Gains were only about 50% of those in the first Swedish RCT, though subjects also improved on disability, depression, maladaptive coping and perceived stress.

In brief, headaches improved in users of the Swedish netCP system, more than on a waitlist with symptom monitoring but no attention placebo, and more in the first than the second RCT. The dropout rate was not cut significantly by adding to an unspecified duration of email support an hour in all of therapist-initiated phone calls.

USA: netCP for chronic headache

RCT

This USA-based netCP for chronic tension or migraine headache of ≥ 1 yr duration was tested in a worldwide RCT (Devineni & Blanchard, 2004). Recruitment was via net hyperlink exchanges with headache and chronic pain websites, ads on health and wellness websites, registration with major search engines, and headache newsgroups. Homepage visitors who read about it and completed a consent form were emailed individual log-in

174   HANDS-ON HELP: COMPUTER-AIDED PSYCHOTHERAPY

details for entry to netCP at the right point on later visits. A researcher screened form data and sent eligible subjects treatment manuals, rating forms and project materials as web pages. They were asked to print these as hard copy and to keep a daily headache diary for a two-week baseline (and during treatment), and were emailed reminders of missed entries. Two different headache-type groups were then each randomized (concealment unclear) to four weeks of: (a) immediate netCP; or (b) a waitlist with further symptom monitoring for two more weeks and then start treatment. Tension headache sufferers were trained in progressive muscular relaxation and cognitive strategies to lessen stress. Sufferers who had migraine (with or without aura) or mixed headaches had autogenic training plus limited biofeedback of hand temperature instead of cognitive strategies.

NetCP was offered to 156 people of whom 139 began it – 83% in the USA, 12% in Canada and western Europe. Post-treatment dropouts were 43% netCP and 34% waitlist. Ratings came from only 49 (35%) subjects at two-month follow-up. Compared to completers, dropouts had less severe headaches at baseline, reported less perceived benefit from netCP, and had less computing experience. Headache type did not affect outcome. Immediate netCP and waitlist both improved significantly by week 4, with immediate netCP improving significantly more than the waitlist on Headache Index (ES=0.54), Symptoms (ES=0.59) and Disability (ES=0.54). By two-month follow-up, headache had improved significantly further in completers as a whole. Clinically significant gains ($\geq$50% drop in headaches without a rise in medication) were made at week 4 by 39% of netCP and 6% of waitlist subjects, and at two months by 47% of all participants, all of whom had had netCP by then. Headache worsened in 12% and 2% respectively of netCP completers at four weeks and two months. NetCP completers used medication significantly less at four weeks and two months, though differences between immediate netCP and the waitlist were small at week 4 (p=0.08, ES=0.23).

Mean therapist time per participant was 1.3 hours including sending information, giving feedback, confirming data integrity, tracking status, and troubleshooting. Participant time spent doing netCP was not reported. Cost-outcome estimation (completers' mean % drop on the Headache Index divided by therapist time in minutes) was 0.3, about six times better than with usual clinic treatment and similar to other home-based RCTs of chronic headache (Haddock et al., 1997).

In brief, in this USA-based RCT chronic headache improved modestly in the 35% of netCP users who rated at two-month follow-up.

8. CP FOR MISCELLANEOUS ADULT PROBLEMS   175

PAIN: CHRONIC BACK PAIN

Internet

Swedish system

This netCP workbook (Buhrman, Faltenhag, Ström, & Andersson, 2004) guided self-management of chronic back pain by education, applied relaxation, exercise and stretching, activity pacing, cognitive restructuring, generalization and maintenance. Subjects were asked to keep a daily pain diary and email this weekly. If not sent they were emailed a reminder a week later.

RCT

Subjects were recruited by newspaper and net ads over 18 days in 2001 (Buhrman et al., 2004). After screening from self-reports on the web, 56 chronic back pain sufferers were randomized using dice (concealment unclear) to a week of self-monitoring followed by six weeks of either: (a) netCP pain management plus weekly therapist-initiated 10-minute phone support calls; or (b) a waitlist, and a week later subjects emailed self-ratings. Five (8%) dropped out (3 netCP, 2 WL), leaving 51 completers (22 netCP, 29 WL) of whom 35 were women. At a week post-treatment both groups improved similarly on pain ratings with netCP being superior on catastrophizing. Some improvement continued at three-month follow-up, by when waitlist subjects too had had netCP.

In brief, netCP improved similarly to the waitlist on back pain but more on a catastrophizing scale.

PAIN DURING BURN WOUND DRESSINGS

Virtual Reality

USA: Snow World *distraction system*

The VR glacial *Snow World* aims to distract burns patients from the fire of painful daily dressings to their burns (Hoffman, 2004). During those dressings, patients don a VR helmet to view scenes of flying through an icy canyon, river and waterfall as snowflakes drift down, and shoot snowballs into the scene and hear them splash into the river. RCTs of *Snow World* in burns patients are needed.

TINNITUS DISTRESS

Internet

Swedish netCP system

This netCP workbook system (Andersson et al., 2002) guided six weeks of applied relaxation, cognitive restructuring for negative thoughts/beliefs about tinnitus, positive imagery, sound enrichment, hearing tactics, advice on noise sensitivity, concentration exercises, sleep management, physical activities, and relapse prevention. All modules included homework assignments and weekly reports on a report web page for weekly submission, together with any questions, after which they received an encouraging email with an instruction to go to the next module.

RCT

Via Swedish newspaper and web ads, this RCT (Andersson et al., 2002) recruited 117 adults who had tinnitus distress of over six months duration for which they had seen a doctor. Subjects were randomized (unconcealed) to either: (a) netCP (n=53) via the net for six weeks; or (b) a waitlist (n=64) with an offer of netCP after the six-week wait. Dropouts by week 6 were 51% netCP (most at its start) and 0% waitlist. Some dropouts felt the system went too fast. Total therapist time per patient was not monitored. On a completer analysis (26 netCP, 64 WL), at six weeks improvement of >50% occurred in significantly more subjects after netCP than after being on a waitlist. At one year post-entry, the proportion of patients whose tinnitus distress was >50% improved was 31% (27/86) of completers and 13% (27/117) of all entrants if the 51% of netCP dropouts were counted as unimproved. The waitlist design precluded judgement of how much the superiority of netCP subjects' gains was due to netCP per se rather than to the accompanying therapist contact by email and attention placebo which waitlist subjects did not have.

Open study

This concerned 77 Swedish tinnitus-distress sufferers who were referred for CBT from an audiology or ENT clinic and preferred netCP to weekly ftf CBT individually or in a group (Kaldo-Sandström, Larsen, & Andersson, 2004). NetCP was revised slightly from that used by Andersson et al. (2002). It was given in six modules over six to ten weeks. Emailed reports of completion of each module and its diary allowed progress to the next module. If a therapist had not heard from a patient within two weeks s/he sent an email encouraging contact. Dropouts were 30% (23/77). Very few patients took up an offer of one to three extra face-to-face sessions with the therapist. Patients improved on tinnitus distress, depression, anxiety and insomnia. Improvement was clinically significant in completers (*in bracketed italics, all cases counting those without ratings as unimproved*) for 39% (*27%*) at post-treatment and 33% (*23%*) three months later. Better outcome associated with more compliance.

RCT 2

This study (Kaldo, Levin, Widarsson, Buhrman, Larsen, & Andersson, 2006) tested the modified netCBT system used by Kaldo-Sandström et al. (2004). After being screened by a 15-minute phone and 60-minute face-to-face interview, 51 Swedish tinnitus sufferers rated distress daily for a week. They then had concealed randomization to have six weeks of either: (a) password-accessed netCBT (n=26) plus a total of two hours email support per client by a CBT therapist; or (b) ftfCBT (n=25) over seven weekly two-hour sessions in a group with six or seven members. There was then a further week of daily distress ratings. The sample had a mean age of 46 and 15 years education. Full treatment was completed by 62% of netCBT and 76% of ftfCBT subjects. NetCBT patients completed a mean of 4/6 diaries, and ftfCBT patients a mean of 5/7 ftf sessions. Only two people gave no week 8 ratings and seven no one-year ratings. Clinically significant improvement was greater than in RCT 1 (Andersson et al., 2002), being attained in netCBT (*and in ftfCBT in bracketed italics*) by 38% (*44%*) of subjects at week 8 and 35% (*44%*) at one year. Pre-post effect size was 0.7 netCBT and 0.6 ftfCBT. A unit of improvement took 41% less therapist time per patient with netCBT than with group ftfCBT. Satisfaction was similar across the two conditions. Having no attention-placebo control meant the effect of attention rather than CP per se could not be excluded.

In brief, in Swedish subjects tinnitus distress improved in the short term more with net biblioCBT plus email therapist contact than in waitlist subjects. Improvement to one-year follow-up was similar with netCBT plus email support to that with group ftfCBT, though netCBT took less therapist time per patient. Neither design could exclude an attention-placebo rather than CBT effect. The efficacy of net biblioCBT in less well educated subjects remains to be tested.

INSOMNIA

Internet

Swedish netCP system

This netCP workbook system for insomnia (Ström et al., 2004) guided sleep restriction, stimulus control, cognitive restructuring, applied relaxation, and

178 HANDS-ON HELP: COMPUTER-AIDED PSYCHOTHERAPY

medication withdrawal. Subjects were emailed a password to start and prompts to email sleep diaries weekly, and reminder emails if diaries were a week late.

RCT

In this RCT (Ström et al., 2004), via newspaper and web ads 109 adults were recruited who reported DSM-IV chronic primary insomnia at web-based screening. Mean duration was 11 years and 61% were women. They were randomized (unconcealed) to either: (a) five weeks of netCP (preceded and also followed by two weeks of self-monitoring) plus email therapist contact for a total of ?minutes over nine weeks; or (b) a waitlist for nine weeks followed by netCP. Completers received a cinema ticket as a gift. Dropouts were 24/54 (44%) from netCP and 4/55 (7%) from the waitlist, and had less severe sleep problems than the completers. By week 9 both groups improved. NetCP plus email contact improved significantly more than the waitlist on only one of nine sleep measures (on dysfunctional sleep beliefs and attitudes; between-groups ES=0.8). At nine-month follow-up after immediate netCP in 13/54 (24%) starters and six-month follow-up of 25/55 (45%) ex-waitlist subjects who had delayed netCP, some improvement continued in the minority who gave data.

> *In brief*, insomniac completers of netCP plus email therapist contact improved significantly more than waitlist completers on only one of nine sleep measures, and the waitlist design did not allow differentiation of netCP from potential attention-placebo effects. NetCP had many dropouts.

JETLAG

Internet

USA: Net self-help for jetlag

Based on six pieces of trip information entered on a website by users, this automated self-help system (Lieberman, 2003; www.mentalperformance.com) devised a personalized schedule of natural-light exposure and avoidance.

Beta study

In this preliminary study (Lieberman, 2003), 20 volunteers, mostly invited by the author, returned completed surveys after a total of 30 aeroplane

8. CP FOR MISCELLANEOUS ADULT PROBLEMS   179

trips. After controlling for number of time zones crossed, more self-rated treatment compliance related significantly to less jetlag on day three of the trip.

SEXUAL PROBLEMS

PC system

Canada: Sexpert

Sexpert was a prototype PC expert system for couples or individuals seeking information or advice about their sexual relationship. It asked questions (multiple choice, yes/no, quantitative) in a session usually lasting about 50 minutes and helped couples negotiate a treatment plan. Further intended, but never developed, sessions consisted of prescription and review of sexual and communication homework assignments. *Sexpert* gathered information about background and any sexual dysfunction including historical antecedents and potential misconceptions about sexuality, and explored users' sexual repertoire (initiation, foreplay, intercourse positions, afterplay, etc.) and non-sexual aspects of their relationship. It simulated a 'therapeutic dialogue'. *Sexpert* elements were tested for engagement, acceptability and behaviour change in one open study and four RCTs from 1988 to 1993. *Sexpert* remained incomplete as funds ran out. Granting agencies were uninterested and software companies only wanted to commercialize a finished product (Binik, Ochs, & Meana, 1996).

The absence of other CP systems for sexual problems mirrors the rarity of RCTs of CBT for sexual difficulties over the last 30 years. Their paucity is astonishing given how common and distressing they are and the deep attention they get in everyday life, the media and the courts.

Open study

Ten couples (personal acquaintances and sex therapy clinic patients) with varied computer experience and educational backgrounds had a *Sexpert* session on a PC to study its feasibility and acceptability (Table 8.2: Binik, Servan-Schreiber, Freiwald, & Hall, 1988). After the researcher briefly introduced them to *Sexpert*, couples were left to use it. The couples said *Sexpert*'s dialogue was logical, appropriate and intelligent and their interactions with it resembled traditional therapist sessions.

RCT 1

Thirty-two undergraduate students (mean age 21, 12 male) answered an offer of $? to take part in a study (Binik, Westbury, & Servan-Schreiber,

180

TABLE 8.2

CP for sexual dysfunction

Study	System	Design	Participants	Outcome
Binik et al. (1988)	*Sexpert* PC prototype: 2200 rules, 200 pages of dialogue.	Open trial – no duration reported. Used in sexual therapy clinic.	Montreal, Canada: 10 couple volunteers and sex therapy clinic patients.	*Sexpert* dialogue experienced as logical, appropriate and intelligent by couples.
Binik et al. (1989)	*Sexpert* on PC as above, 500-rule subset.	RCT1: 1 session: (1) 20 mins PC *Sexpert* (n=8); (2) 20 mins modified PC *Sexpert* (n=8); (3) Paper + pencil *Sexpert* (n=8); (4) 20-min control PC program (n=8).	Montreal, Canada: 32 undergraduate students (20 female). Paid $? to participate.	Attitudes to PC (but not paper and pencil) *Sexpert* improved after using it. PC *Sexpert* very easy to use.
Binik et al. (1994)	*Sexpert* on PC as above, introduction and repertoire modules.	RCT2: 1 45-min sess + 2w fu: (1) PC *Sexpert* (18 couples) vs (2) paper and pencil *Sexpert* 16 couples vs (3) comp. game no sex content (16 couples).	Montreal, Canada: 50 heterosexual couples answered campus ads. 12 > couples did not attend and 4 > couples dropped out. *?paid.*	Attitudes to *Sexpert* imp with use, retained to 2w fu. No diffs in sex behav over 2w fu but foreplay and sexual communication ↑ after *Sexpert* vs paper-and-pencil gp.

Ochs et al. (1993, 1994)	*Sexpert* on PC as above, introduction and repertoire modules.	RCT3: 1 50-min sess + 2w fu: (1) PC *Sexpert* 50 mins (21 couples) vs (2) 50-min sex-info video (20 couples); vs (3) 50-min read/discus sex info book (20 couples) vs (4) 50-min crossword nonsexual (20 couples).	Montreal, Canada: 81 heterosexual couples answered ads on campus and community newspaper. 33 other couples did not attend and 4 > DO. Couples paid $80 to take part.	Attitude to *Sexpert* imp after use (unlike to sex-info video) to 2w fu. No change in sex beh. *Sexpert* = video = book > crossword on sex behav, comm and learning at 2w fu.
Ochs & Binik (1998)	*Sexpert* on PC as above, introduction and repertoire modules.	RCT4 1 50-min sess + 1w fu: (1) *Sexpert* vs (2) sex-info video vs (3) ftf therapist vs (4) crossword with no sex content (all n's unclear).	Montreal, Canada: 77 heterosexual couples via campus and community newspapers. 39 > couples did not attend sess 1. DOs 3 > couples. Couples paid $30.	Completers: Attitudes to *Sexpert* imp to 1w fu. *Sexpert* and therapist rated as similarly engaging. *Sexpert* < therapist for learning about sex, reported imp?? in relationship at 1w fu.

182 HANDS-ON HELP: COMPUTER-AIDED PSYCHOTHERAPY

1989) of attitudes to sex therapy. They were randomized to: (a) 20-minute dialogue with *Sexpert* (n=8); or (b) 20-minute dialogue with modified *Sexpert*, not in the first person (n=8); or (c) paper-and-pencil answers to the same questions as those asked by *Sexpert* (n=8); or (d) 20 minutes using a control non-sexual program (n=8). Results with standard and modified *Sexpert* were similar, so the two groups were pooled for analysis. Subjects rated both *Sexpert* and the control program as very easy to use. Their initial attitudes to *Sexpert* were negative but improved significantly as they used it, which was not found in subjects answering the same questions in a paper-and-pencil format.

RCT 2

Fifty heterosexual couples (mean age 23) answered ads on campus and in the university newspaper. They were randomized (Binik, Meana, & Sand, 1994) to: (a) *Sexpert* for 45 minutes (18 couples); or (b) paper-and-pencil answers to the same questions as those asked by *Sexpert* (16 couples); or (c) interaction with a text-based computer game with no sexual content (16 couples). Subjects first disliked *Sexpert* but came to like it more on rating it two weeks after they used it. In contrast, couples who answered the same questions in a paper-and pencil format disliked this all the time. No differences were found within or between groups on sexual behaviour monitored daily over the two weeks after their session. At two weeks, foreplay and sexual communication was said to have increased significantly by the PC *Sexpert* group compared to the paper-and-pencil 'Sexpert' group. Twelve other couples who volunteered did not attend and four others dropped out during the study.

RCT 3

Eighty-one heterosexual couples (mean age 26) answered ads on campus and in university and city newspapers. They were randomized (Ochs, Meana, Pare, Mah, & Binik, 1994) to 50 minutes of: (a) *Sexpert* (21 couples); or (b) a sex information video (20 couples); or (c) a sex information book – reading and discussing (20 couples); or (d) working on a crossword with no sexual content (20 couples). Couples were paid $80 for participation. Before the session, attitude to *Sexpert* as a source of information was negative and to the book was positive. Attitude to *Sexpert* changed significantly to positive after using it and remained so to two-week follow-up, and was not found in couples who watched the sex-information video. Attitude did not relate to previous experience of computing. Thirty-three other volunteer couples did not attend, and four more dropped out. The study did not report what couples actually learned from the various information sources or how the sources impacted on sexual behaviour.

8. CP FOR MISCELLANEOUS ADULT PROBLEMS   183

RCT 4

Seventy-seven heterosexual couples (mean age 27) answered ads in campus and community newspapers. They were randomized (Ochs & Binik, 1998) to 50 minutes of: (a) *Sexpert* (n unclear); or (b) a sex information video on practical knowledge of sex (n unclear); or (c) face-to-face therapy with Dr Binik (n unclear); or (d) working together on a crossword puzzle with no sex content (n unclear). Attitudes to *Sexpert* became positive after using it and remained so one week later. The couples rated *Sexpert* and the ftf human therapist as similarly engaging, but rated *Sexpert* as less good than the ftf session for learning about sex and changing sexual behaviour. They were paid $30 for participation. Thirty-nine other couples did not attend the session, and three more dropped out during the study.

In brief, in four RCTs couples using the *Sexpert* prototype for a single session came to like it as a way of learning about sex and sexual problems, and reported improved sexual behaviour one or two weeks later. They rated *Sexpert* as similarly engaging to a human therapist, but learned and improved sexual behaviour more with face-to-face human therapy. *Sexpert*'s early results seem to justify more work to nudge it towards becoming a routine clinical tool.

SCHIZOPHRENIA

USA: *Captain's Log Cognitive System (CLCS)* for cognitive rehabilitation in schizophrenia and schizoaffective disorder

Three USA RCTs tested the computerized *Captain's Log Cognitive System* (*CLCS*; Sandford & Browne, 1988) for cognitive rehabilitation in schizophrenia and schizoaffective disorder. *CLCS* has five modules, each with three to eight cognitive training tasks for attention, concentration, memory, visuospatial and visuomotor skills, and conceptualization. Various modules were selected for each of the three RCTs.

RCT 1

This RCT (Burda, Starkey, Dominguez, & Vera, 1994) at a Miami VA Medical Center tested the value of CLCS for 69 inpatients (67 male) with chronic schizophrenia or schizoaffective disorder who were on neuroleptic and/or mood stabilizing medication. They were randomized (concealment

TABLE 8.3
CP for **schizophrenia**

Study	System	Design	Participants	Outcome
Burda et al. (1994)	PC: *Captain's Log Cognitive System* (*CLCS*)	RCT for 8w: (1) *CLCS* in 24 30-min sessions + TAU (n=40) vs (2) TAU only (n=40).	Miami, USA: 69 VA inpts with chronic schizophrenia or schizoaffective disorder. DOs 0 *CLCS*, 28% controls.	Completers: *CLCS* + TAU imp on memory, cogn complaints; TAU-only did not improve.
Bell et al. (2001)	Neurocognitive enhancement therapy (*NET*) i.e. *CLCS* as in Burda et al. (1994), used alone up to 5h/wk + bi-wkly cognitive feedback/ support gps + wkly social processing gps.	RCT 20w: (1) *NET* + work therapy (n=31) vs (2) work therapy only (n=34).	Two Connecticut, USA clinics: 65 outpatients with schizophrenia or schizoaffective disorder. DOs not reported.	ITT: *NET* + work therapy > work-therapy-only on executive function, working memory, affect recognition.
Bellucci et al. (2002)	*CLCS* as in Burda et al. (1994).	RCT for 8w: (1) *CLCS* in 16 half-hr sessions with trainers (n=17) vs (2) WL (delayed access to *CLCS*, n=17); no trainers.	New Jersey, USA: 34 day-centre clients with schizophrenia or schizoaffective disorder. All but one on antipsychotics.	*CLCS* > WL on cognitive functioning (verbal memory, attention) and negative symptoms.
Jones et al. (2001)	PC education via touchscreen in resource centre for community services.	RCT 5 'sessions', no. of wks not reported. PC time self-paced, total median 69 mins: (1) PC + support by research assist; (2) PC + nurse (1h per sess); (3) nurse only (1h per session).	Glasgow, Scotland: 112 schizophrenia outpts ICD10 randomized/ completed/3m fu 1.56/34/ 33; 2.28/20/20; 3.28/13/12.	ITT and completers: Pre-post-3m fu: no between- or within-group differences in knowledge or mental state.

unclear) to eight weeks of either: (a) *CLCS* (n=40) in 24 half-hour computer sessions in a computer lab within the hospital + treatment as usual (TAU); or to (b) TAU only (n=29). Dropouts were 0 from *CLCS* + TAU and 11/40 (28%) from TAU only. At eight weeks, unlike TAU-only, *CLCS* + TAU improved on most memory tests, the Trailmaking Test, and cognitive complaints. *CLCS* subjects also often asked for further unscheduled computer sessions. It is unclear how much their short-term improvement reflected an attention-placebo rather than *CLCS* effect. No follow-up was reported.

RCT 2

This second RCT (Bell, Bryson, Greig, Cocoran, & Wexler, 2001) included *CLCS* attention, memory, executive function and dichotic listening modules) in neurocognitive enhancement therapy (NET). The RCT was in two Connecticut clinics over 20 weeks in 65 outpatients with schizophrenia or schizoaffective disorder. Almost all were on antipsychotic drugs, mean age was 41, and 74% were men. In the RCT NET consisted of: (a) *CLCS* used alone for up to 5 hours a week in 2–3 sessions (maximum = 20 weeks × 5 hrs = up to 100 hrs); plus (b) biweekly feedback from a functional-cognitive-assessment/support group of unspecified duration plus a weekly social-processing group of unspecified duration; plus (c) work therapy consisting of up to 15 hours a week of paid entry-level medical centre work plus individual and group support and job coaching (n=31). Patients were stratified by cognitive functioning and randomized (concealment unclear) to five months of either: (a) *CLCS* + NET + work therapy 15 hours a week (n=31); or to (b) work therapy alone for up to 20 hours a week. Dropouts were not reported. Over the 20 weeks NET + work therapy patients spent a mean 59 hours in NET (time on CLCS not reported) and a mean of 216 hours in work therapy (vs 247 hours in the work therapy only group). On ITT analysis post-treatment at five months, NET + work therapy was superior to work therapy only on executive functioning, working memory and affect recognition.

RCT 3

The third RCT was in New Jersey, USA over eight weeks in 34 day-centre attendees with schizophrenia or schizoaffective disorder. Mean age was 42, and 47% were men. Subjects were randomized (concealment unclear) to either: (a) *CLCS* for 16 half-hour sessions with trainers giving reinforcement and encouragement (n=17); or (b) a waitlist with delayed access to *CLCS* (n=17). All participants also took part in the day centre's regular therapy activities. Raters were blind to treatment condition. At eight weeks,

186 HANDS-ON HELP: COMPUTER-AIDED PSYCHOTHERAPY

compared to the waitlist, *CLCS* + trainers improved more in cognitive function (verbal memory, attention) and negative symptoms (ESs 0.3–0.4).

Glasgow: Touchscreen computer-aided education in schizophrenia

RCT

In a Scottish RCT (Jones et al., 2001), of 230 eligible outpatients with schizophrenia in a community services resource centre, 118 (51%) refused to participate. The remaining 112 (aged 18–65, 67% male) were randomized to five sessions (sessions/course durations not reported) of either: (a) computer education – general and personal information from the viewing patient's medical record and questionnaires plus feedback displays, and if requested a personalized printout at the end of the session, via a touchscreen, plus 'minimal' (duration unreported) support from a research assistant (n=56); or (b) education sessions with a community psychiatric nurse, giving the same information as the computer, plus a generic information leaflet (n=28); or (c) both (n=28). Median total time spent on the computer was 69 minutes. Dropout rates were 39% computer, 54% nurse, 29% both combined (not significant). At post-treatment and three-month follow-up there was no within or between group difference in knowledge and mental state.

In brief, each of the three *CLCS* RCTs reported some cognitive gains but none controlled for placebo effects from the attention received by *CLCS* users but not by the contrast groups, so the value of *CLCS* per se remains unknown. The Scottish study found no effect. CP for schizophrenia has thus not yet yielded obvious benefits as yet.

CHAPTER 9

CP for problems in children and teenagers

CHAPTER SUMMARY

CP for childhood phobias, anxiety, depression, headache, brain injury, autism, encopresis was developed in at least seven systems in Australia (1), UK (2) and USA (4). They were tested in at least three open studies and five RCTs lasting from just one session to 35 weeks. The systems ranged widely from simple presentation of a set of stimuli with progress to another level if answers were correct, through to multi-module, multimedia CD-ROM and net systems guiding a broad range of therapy tasks. Some CP systems were implemented as enhancements of TAU while others were part of joint CP plus live therapy either ftf or by videoconferencing. In various RCTs CP allowed ftf therapy time to be cut without impairing anxiety or headache reduction, and improved encopresis, parents' management of brain-injured progeny's behaviour, and taught autistic children to recognize emotions in cartoons and stories. The results seem promising for the use of CP to help a variety of mental health problems in children. (For prevention of substance misuse and violence in young adolescents, see *SODAS*, *DAVP* and *GSI* in Chapter 7 and Tables 7.1 and 7.2.)

Of six children's interactive **asthma-education systems** (none on the net), five were from the USA and one from the UK. They used personal or case vignettes and games. All had an RCT and one a pilot

---

187

> study too. Of the RCTs, five were in asthma clinics and one in ordinary school classes. Comparisons were with usual care, non-asthma computer games, or educational booklets. The systems generally increased asthma knowledge in children and parents, improved asthma management and, where measured, cost savings from fewer emergency room visits. Children and parents were generally satisfied with the systems. Overall, CP for managing childhood asthma had encouraging results.

PHOBIAS AND ANXIETY

PC display systems

Open study

Chapter 2 described one spider-display system used by two spider-phobic children (Nelissen et al., 1995) and another in an RCT in spider-phobic children and teenagers (Dewis et al., 2001).

Internet

Australia: BRAVE NetCP for childhood anxiety

The *BRAVE* netCP system for childhood anxiety is from Queensland, Australia (Table 9.1: Spence et al., 2006). *BRAVE* stands for Body signs, Relax, Activate helpful thoughts, Victory over fears, Enjoy yourself. *BRAVE* on the net has 20–30 web pages with colour animations, noises, rollover images, pop-up messages, self-assessment quizzes and personalized feedback. It guards security and confidentiality by passwords, security software and firewalls. Commercial access costs A$100.

RCT

BRAVE was tested in a RCT in 42 boys and 30 girls who at a parent interview had a main DSM-IV anxiety diagnosis with a clinician severity score ≥4/8. They were attending mental health clinics and school counsellors and were aged 7–14 (mean 10). The children were randomized to one of three conditions: *Condition 1* (n=27): 50% net*BRAVE* – half the ten weekly child sessions and half the six weekly concurrent parent sessions were net*BRAVE* at home, while half the face-to-face (ftf) CBT sessions were at a clinic in one-hour groups of three to nine children and separately at the same time of their parents with a therapist. They were also given a *BRAVE* manual and workbook in which to record home tasks between sessions. Before starting net*BRAVE* at home the children and parents had a

TABLE 9.1
Problems in **children** and **teenagers** – **phobias, anxiety, headache, brain injury, autism, encopresis** (for **asthma** see Table 9.2 on page 199)

Study	Problem	Design	Participants	Outcome
Nelissen et al. (1995)	PC display of spiders.	Open study: 1 1h sess.	UK, 2 spider phobics.	No improvement.
Dewis et al. (2001)	*CAVE* for spiderphobia.	See Table 2.5.	See Table 2.5.	See Table 2.5.
Spence et al. (2006)	*BRAVE*: Net-aided CBT for childhood **anxiety**.	RCT 10w: (1) 50% net CBT at home by child and parents + 50%ftf gp CBT in clinic as in (2) below (n=27) vs (2) 100%ftfgpCBT in 2h sess at clinic: child (10 sess + 2 booster 1h sess); parent (6 sess + 2 booster 1h sess) (n=22) vs (3) WL (n=23).	Queensland, Australia: 72 children age 7–14 with anxiety diagnosis score ≥4/8 on clinician severity at parent interview. Drop outs: 15% 50%netCBT, 14% 100%ftfCBT, 0% waitlist.	50%netCBT=100%ftfCBT >WL. % kids no anx disorder post-trtment 56/65/13 on clinician severity and 55/45/9 on Beh Checklist. 50%netCBT > 100%ftfCBT =WL on Anx. 50%net CP >WL on Depress. 50%netCP = 100%ftf CBT satisf. Gains OK to 1y fu.
Connelly et al. (2006)	*Headstrong*: CD-ROM for recurrent **headache** in children aged 7–12.	RCT 4 wks + 3m fu (uncontrolled): (1) *Headstrong* (n=17) vs (2) WL (n=20). Each + TAU + headache diaries Families received $50 on completing assessments.	Kansas, USA: 37 children age 7–12 with recurrent migraine headache; 9 refusers, 6 DOs, 17 completers, n=14 at 3m fu.	ITT child and carer ratings: *Headstrong* > WL in ↓ headache frequency, duration and intensity; = WL on related disability. In completers saved 60% of therapist time.

continues overleaf

TABLE 9.1 *Continued*

Study	Problem	Design	Participants	Outcome
Wade et al. (2005a, 2005b, 2006)	*Family Problem Solving* (*FPS*) for **brain-injured** children.	Open pilot ≤35 weeks using *FPS* self-guided web-exercises + videoconferencing (6 families inc 8 parents, 6 brain-injured children and 5 siblings).	Ohio, USA: 8 families inc. child aged 5–16 who had moderate to severe brain injury >15 months earlier, no medication or treatment for attentional or behavioural problems Living at home, spoke English, no evidence of child abuse.	Parents imp on stress, family burden, SCL90, depress., not anxiety. Children imp on antisocial behav, not in executive functioning or depression. Family rated *FPS* moder. to vs easy to use, vs helpful. Therapist prep. and contact time bit > ftf due to technical issues.
Wade et al. (2006)	*Family Problem Solving* (*FPS*) for **brain-injured** children.	Family RCT ≤35 wks: (1) *FPS* (n=24) ≤12 net sessions (8 core + 4/6 supplem) + 2 start home visits (1 by res assist, 1 by therapist) + ≤12 videoconfer family therapy session with therapist + TAU. (2) Internet resources comparison (IRC, n=20). TAU + high-speed net access, brain-injury homepage + links, no *FPS* content.	Ohio, USA: 45 families inc. child age 5–16 who had moderate to severe brain injury <2 years previously. 2 (8%) *FPS* dropped out before treatment ended, 1 (4%) completed treatment but not outcome measures. 0 IRC dropped out.	Completer analysis: *FPS*>IRC on parent-rated depression, anxiety and general psychiatric symptoms.

Silver & Oakes (2001)	*Emotion Trainer*: PC program to teach children aged 12–18 with **autism** spectrum disorders to recognize and predict emotions in others.	RCT for 2 weeks: (1) 10 half-hour sessions on *Emotion Trainer* in school vs (2) usual classes.	UK: 12 age, gender and school class matched pairs of children with autistic spectrum disorders. Children aged 10–18, with British Picture Vocabulary Scale reading age of >7.	Emotion trainer group > usual classes group post-treatment on emotion-recognition cartoons task and strange stories. NS differences in a facial expression photographs task.
Ritterband et al. (2003a)	Net *U-Can-Poop-Too* (*UCPT*) enhanced toilet training program as adjunctive therapy for childhood **encopresis**.	RCT over 3 weeks: (1) *UCPT* + TAU from primary care physician (n=12). (2) TAU from primary care physician only (n=12).	Virginia, USA: Children age 6–12 soiling ≥once a week, no diagnosis to explain it.	*UCPT* + TAU > TAU on soilings, bowel movements in toilet, >unprompted trips to toilet. Both gps imp knowledge, toileting behav. Rated *UCPT* easy, understandable, enjoyable, implementable.

192 HANDS-ON HELP: COMPUTER-AIDED PSYCHOTHERAPY

one-hour group computer tutorial. After treatment ended they also had two booster sessions, one month later in the clinic, and three months later by computer at home. Net*BRAVE* users could email a therapist if they had queries. *Condition 2* (n=22): 100% ftfCBT at the clinic in a group for children (ten sessions) and parents (six sessions) as for Condition 1 including the *BRAVE* manual and workbook, but with no net*BRAVE*. *Condition 3* (n=23): a waitlist, rated at weeks 0 and 10.

Dropout rates were low – 14–15% in the CBT conditions, 0% in the waitlist. Records of therapist activities across conditions, including email contact with families, suggested a 43% reduction in total therapist time for 50% netCBT compared to 100% ftfCBT. On completer analyses, by the end of treatment the percentage of children no longer having a primary (*or any*) anxiety diagnosis was 56 (*45*) for 50% netCBT, 65 (*55*) for 100% ftfCBT, and 13 (*9*) for the waitlist. The 50% netCBT children improved more than the 100% ftfCBT or waitlist children on self-rated anxiety, but not on parent ratings of the child's anxiety, clinician severity ratings, or internalizing behaviours on which both CBT groups improved similarly and significantly more than the waitlist. The 50% netCBT condition improved significantly more than the waitlist in depression, but not more than the 100% ftfCBT condition. At one-year follow-up both CBT groups maintained therapy gains or improved further, with 100% ftfCBT tending to be superior. Both CBT conditions rated similar high satisfaction with treatment. Net compliance was good in children and parents: they spent a mean of 46 minutes per internet session, viewed 96% of treatment pages, and completed 91% of homework forms and quizzes of the treatment pages during the ten-week child and six-week parent treatment phase. Just over half the children and parents did the three-month netCBT booster session.

In brief, in a small RCT 50% net*BRAVE* + 50% ftf group CBT was an acceptable and efficacious treatment for childhood anxiety which saved just under half therapist time.

DEPRESSION

Internet

MoodGYM *used at school*

A controlled nonrandomized study aiming to prevent depression in 15- to 16-year-old males (O'Kearney et al., 2006) is described in Chapter 5 along with other *MoodGYM* studies.

9. CP FOR PROBLEMS IN CHILDREN AND TEENAGERS   193

HEADACHE

CD-ROM

USA: Headstrong

Headstrong (Connelly et al., 2006) is a CD-ROM pain-management program for recurrent headache in children aged 7–12. It has four modules (education, relaxation, thought changing, pain behaviour modification), each with 3–6 ten-minute 'lessons' plus homework (e.g. relaxation diaries) to be completed one per week.

RCT

An RCT (Connelly et al., 2006) tested *Headstrong* against a waitlist in 19 boys and 18 girls aged 7–12 who attended a pediatric neurology outpatient clinic for recurrent headache. They had a mean age of 10 and were mostly white (86%) and on prophylactic medication (65%). Nine other families refused to participate. After keeping 14-day baseline diaries, 37 children were randomized (concealed; stratified by age 7–9 or 10–12) to four weeks of either: (a) *Headstrong* used at home (n=17); or (b) a waitlist with a *Headstrong* start date two months later (n=20). All 37 were also asked to continue treatment as usual by following the advice of their neurologist, who was kept blind to the randomization condition. Families were offered $50 ($10 per assessment pack) to complete the study.

The *Headstrong* and waitlist groups did not differ at baseline. Four weeks after randomization, three per condition gave no data. Using last-observation-carried-forward imputation for missing data, at the end of week 4, compared to the waitlist, *Headstrong* children and their carers reported significantly less headache frequency, duration and intensity, but not less disability. Clinically significant reduction in headache was reported for 53% of the treatment group (20% of the waitlist) post-treatment. Gains endured to three-month follow-up in the *Headstrong* group (ITT analysis). *Headstrong* was thought to save 60% of the usual ten hours of therapist time taken by most headache treatment programs (M. Rapoff, personal communication, 23 August 2005) in the 38% of randomized subjects who reached three-month follow-up.

In brief, in a small RCT *Headstrong* enhanced TAU in reducing children's headache in the minority of starters who reached three-month follow-up, and saved 60% of therapist time.

BRAIN INJURY

Internet

USA: Net Family Problem Solving (FPS) to reduce parental distress after a child's brain injury

Family Problem Solving (*FPS*) from Ohio, USA integrates self-guided net material with videoconferencing of a therapist and family with a brain-injured child (Wade, Wolfe, Maines Brown, & Pestian, 2005a; Wade, Wolfe, Pestian, & Brown, 2005b). The website's self-guided part can be used by several family members sitting together round the computer. It guides 12 sessions – eight for all families about problem-solving, communication and brain injury behaviour management, and four supplemental for a given family's concerns with anger, pain and stress management, work with the child's school, siblings, and marital communication. Each net session teaches problem solving and other skills, shows video clips of families modelling skills, and gives interactive exercises with animations and graphics to practise them. Completing answers to each website question allows progress to the next section. A research assistant visited the family to install a computer with a high-speed internet connection and a web camera and to train them to use *FPS* and complete baseline ratings. The therapist did a structured interview of the family at home about current problems and goals, and then scheduled weekly or biweekly videoconference interviews to review completed exercises and start the family working on a problem or goal they identified.

Open pilot study

In a pilot study of 8 parents, 6 children (2 girls, 4 boys) with moderate to severe brain injury of 15–29 months duration whose mean age was 9 years (range 7–16), and 5 siblings, families completed a mean of 10 web sessions and 10 videoconferences over 26–35 weeks (Wade et al., 2005a, 2005b). Improvement was significant on parental stress, family burden, depression and other symptoms, and on children's antisocial behaviour, but not on parental anxiety or child's depression or global behaviour (Wade et al., 2005a, 2005b). Family members rated the self-guided aspects of *FPS* as moderately to very easy to use and very helpful (Wade et al., 2005a, 2005b). For a videoconferencing novice therapist the time spent preparing and running *FPS* sessions resembled that during therapy without *FPS*, though troubleshooting technical problems increased time spent per family.

RCT

In an RCT, 45 families were recruited from the trauma registry of an urban children's hospital who had a child aged 5–16 with moderate to severe brain injury of <2 years duration living in the family home, spoke English, and had no evidence of child abuse (Wade et al., 2005). The families were randomized (unmasked: aware of assignment) to ≤35 weeks of: (a) net*FPS* (n=24); or to (b) an Internet Resources Comparison (IRC) group (n=20) who continued preRCT care (TAU) and received a computer with high-speed internet access to a home page of brain-injury resources and links (same as the *FPS* homepage), but no access to *FPS* session content. The children (17 girls, 28 boys; mean age 11) were injured a mean of 14 months pre-entry, severely so in 25% of *FPS* and 35% of IRC subjects; 76% were Caucasian and 24% African-American. Only two *FPS* (8%) and no IRC families dropped out before treatment ended ≤35 weeks, and one more completed *FPS* but gave no end-of-treatment follow-up measures. The 24 *FPS* families completed a mean of ten computer modules and ten videoconference sessions. At week 0, *FPS* and IRC did not differ on outcome or other measures. At the end of treatment (≤35 weeks), on completer analyses *FPS* parents had significantly less depression, anxiety and general psychiatric symptoms than did IRC parents, but had similar problem-solving skills. All the parents said they would recommend *FPS* to others and 94% found the self-guided *FPS* website moderately to extremely easy to use, though 33% said they would prefer to see a therapist in person. *FPS* did not save therapist time compared to usual care and may even have needed extra therapist time solving IT issues, but in the same time topics were covered in more depth, with videoconferencing building on material from the website (Wade, personal communication, 30 November 2005).

In brief, net*FPS* teaches problem-solving skills to families of children with brain injury. It offers up to 12 interactive computer modules, each supported by a videoconferenced family therapy session delivered in real time by a therapist. Compared to TAU controls who also had non-interactive internet information, parents using net*FPS* improved more in depression, anxiety and other psychiatric symptoms but not in problem solving. As net*FPS* was accompanied by videoconferencing family sessions the unique impact of net*FPS* is hard to judge.

AUTISM SPECTRUM DISORDER

Personal computer system

UK: Emotion Trainer PC program to teach young people with autism or Asperger syndrome to recognise and predict emotions in others

The *Emotion Trainer* PC program from the UK (Silver & Oakes, 2001) teaches young people with autistic spectrum disorders to better recognize and predict emotional responses in others from photos of facial expressions, photos and descriptions of events, happy outcomes when you get what you want and sad when you don't, thoughts, and pleasure and disappointment. Correct answers bring up a 'well done' animated pop-up screen. Wrong answers bring on 'try again' with a hint and then a direct cue to the correct answer. Completing 20 items correctly in a section allows progression to the next section.

RCT

A RCT tested *Emotion Trainer* in 12 age-, gender- and school-class-matched pairs of children with autistic spectrum disorders who were aged 10–18 and had a reading age of ≤ 7. During ten lunchtime or after-school sessions over two to three weeks, one member per pair was randomized (concealment unclear) to use *Emotion Trainer*, and the other control child attended normal lessons only. *Emotion Trainer* children used it a mean of eight times; two children did not complete it and one child's data was lost. *Emotion Trainer* users improved significantly more than the other children on emotion-recognition cartoons and on strange stories, but not on facial-expression photographs. More use of *Emotion Trainer* predicted more improvement on emotion recognition and strange stories. No follow-up data was presented. *Emotion Trainer* requires ten hours of professional time; without the computer the faces would be shown on flash cards (M. Silver, personal communication, 24 August 2005).

In brief, in a small RCT *Emotion Trainer* used over ≤ 3 weeks produced short-term improvement in emotion recognition in young people with autism spectrum disorders.

9. CP FOR PROBLEMS IN CHILDREN AND TEENAGERS 197

ENCOPRESIS

Internet

USA: NetU-Can-Poop-Too for childhood encopresis

U-Can-Poop-Too (*UCPT*) from Virginia, USA gives parents and children net-guided, child-focused toilet training for encopresis (Ritterband et al., 2003a; www.ucanpooptoo.com). Child and carer can use it together at home. Its 200+ web pages have illustrations, interactive components, animated tutorials and reward quizzes to teach: spontaneous use of the toilet and clean underwear, how to strain well by increasing intra-abdominal pressure while relaxing the external anal sphincter, use laxatives to keep the colon fairly empty and have regular bowel movements, explanation of overflow incontinence. The initial three core modules take 60–90 minutes to complete on ≥one occasion. One and two weeks thereafter follow-up sessions are completed including brief assessments, answers to which yield suggestions to use further treatment modules out of 27 such modules focusing on fears of toilet use, social isolation, diet, hygiene and other issues. Each module takes 5–10 minutes to complete. Therapist time to construct and complete each child's individually tailored behavioural contract with the help of *UPCT* varies across families and has not been measured.

Pilot RCT

In a pilot RCT (Ritterband et al., 2003a), through flyer posting and direct physician referral, 24 families were recruited who had a child age 6–12 who soiled at least once a week and had no diagnosis other than constipation to explain the encopresis. At baseline, 19 boys and 5 girls (mean age 8) soiled about once a day. Most parents said their child had finished toilet training, and 16 (67%) were on a laxative (mean duration 19 months). The children were randomized (unmasked, participants aware of group assignment) to receive: (a) *UCPT* at home + treatment as usual (TAU) from their primary care physician; or (b) TAU alone. The two groups were similar at baseline. *UCPT* families were given a computer and printer linked to the net. A research assistant visited all families at home at the start of the study and phoned several times during it to answer concerns.

UCPT+TAU parents reported a pre-post mean drop in weekly soiling accidents from 6 to 0.5 with no post-treatment soiling in 70% of *UCPT*+TAU versus 45% of TAU children. From pre- to post-treatment *UCPT* children significantly increased their number of bowel movements in and unprompted trips to the toilet, while both groups improved in knowledge and toileting behaviour. Users accessed *UCPT* a mean of 14 times over the three treatment weeks. Post-treatment, *UCPT* users rated it as easy

198 HANDS-ON HELP: COMPUTER-AIDED PSYCHOTHERAPY

to use, understandable, useful, implementable, and enjoyable for the children. Therapist time savings from *UCPT* were not tracked. A larger multisite RCT is underway.

In brief, in a pilot RCT *U-Can-Poop-Too* enhanced the outcome of TAU for children with encopresis. Whether it saves therapist time is not known.

CHILDHOOD ASTHMA

Childhood asthma is included here as psychogenic triggers are often said to play an appreciable role with self-help being needed to take them into account. At least six CP systems for childhood asthma have been reported, five of them largely in game format.

CD-ROM

USA: IMPACT (Interactive Multimedia Program for Asthma Control and Tracking)

IMPACT (*Interactive Multimedia Program for Asthma Control and Tracking*) from Missouri is a net-enabled CD-ROM whose movies and animation files are copied to the hard drive to speed loading while responses and data go to the server using the net (Table 9.2: Krishna, Francisco, Bala, Konig, Graff, & Masden, 2003). It discusses asthma mechanisms, triggers and medication, and strategies to manage asthma. *IMPACT* includes animated lessons in self-management and activities teaching children to accurately describe their symptoms and medication use.

RCT

IMPACT was tested in a RCT in 228 Missouri children aged <18 at a pediatric pulmonary and allergy clinic who had asthma without chronic lung disease (Krishna et al., 2003). They were randomized (unclear if concealed) to: (a) use *IMPACT* (n=107) during routine clinic visits as well as have treatment as usual (TAU = standard care); or (b) TAU only (n=121). For TAU, children had an individual action plan with daily details on self-management, 8 generic and ≥ 4 child-specific instruction sheets (e.g. about prescribed medication and a device), and 1.5 hours education and training by a nurse practitioner over three clinic visits plus 15-minute subsequent monitoring sessions.

TABLE 9.2
Problems in **children** and **teenagers** – **asthma**

Study	Problem	Design	Participants	Outcome
Krishna et al. (2003)	*IMPACT (Interactive Multimedia Program for Asthma Control and Tracking)* net-enabled CD-ROM used at lung and allergy clinic.	RCT over 12m: (1) *IMPACT* + TAU (n=107). (2) control TAU asthma education instruction sheets + nurse education (n=121).	Missouri, USA: 228 children aged <18 who had asthma without chronic lung disease. 21 others excluded. Dropouts by 12 months: 61% *IMPACT* and 64% control.	Completers at 1yr: kids and carers: *IMPACT* > control on ↑ knowledge, ↓ per-yr asthma days and visits to emergency room and daily dose of inhaled steroids. Not sig in lung function or quality of life.
Rubin et al. (1986)	*Asthma Command (AC)* PC game on **asthma** clinic PC to improve asthma self-management vicariously.	RCT 10m ± 6 sess of: (1) *AC* + 5-min review of printout with staff + TAU (n=32) vs (2) Control computer game + 5–10 mins instruct. on asthma management + TAU = regular clinic visits (n=33).	Connecticut, USA: 65 children age 7–12 with asthma and ≥3 acute visits in past year. 21 other eligible kids not contactable, refused, or did not attend sess 1. DOs 3 *(10%)* from *AC*, 8 *(24%)* from control.	*AC* + TAU > control game + TAU on asthma knowledge and management, but not on acute visits, hospital days or school absence.
Bartholomew et al. (2000)	*Watch, Discover, Think and Act (WDTA)* PC game to improve **asthma** self-management vicariously.	RCT ≤16 months (mean 8): (1) *WDTA* + TAU (n=70). (2) TAU = regular clinic visits preceded by phone-call reminders (n=63).	Texas, USA: Children aged 6–17 who had asthma without other chronic disease, mostly on Medicaid. 38 more eligible children refused or were not contactable at the start of the study.	*WDTA* + TAU > TAU only on parent report of asthma ??treatment. *WDTA* ↓ admissions of younger kids, ↓ symptoms for kids with milder asthma, and imp function if *WDTA* was used for longer.

continues overleaf

TABLE 9.2 Continued

Study	Problem	Design	Participants	Outcome
Homer et al. (2000)	*Asthma Control: (ACont)* PC interactive **educational** game to teach children **asthma** management.	RCT 10m: pts were asked to return 3 times to asthma clinic to play: (1) *Asthma Control* (n=76) vs (2) control game + educational material (n=61).	Boston, USA: Of parents of 471 children aged 3–12 with asthma, 334 (71%) refused entry of 137 entrants, DOs 25% *AC*, 20% control.	*ACont* > control only on asthma knowledge; both gps imp = on healthcare use, asthma severity, parental time, peak flow availability.
McPherson et al. (2002a)	*Asthma Files (AF)*: PC **asthma education** game.	Pilot study, 1 sess: After demo, child used *Asthma Files* alone at home (n=10).	Nottingham, UK: 10 boys age 7–14 with asthma at outpt clinic. 21 other ineligible kids.	*AF* ↑ knowledge of asthma triggers and management immediately after use.
McPherson et al. (2006)	*Asthma Files (AF)* PC **educational** game for **asthma**.	RCT, 1 sess: (1) *Asthma Files* used at home on laptop during one visit by researcher; the 82% with access to a computer kept a copy of AF, plus asthma information booklet (n=51). (2) Booklet alone (n=50). 1m and 6m fu.	Nottingham, UK: 101 7–14 year olds attending hospital asthma clinics. 4% study drop out at 1m, 12% drop out at 6m fu.	ITT at 1m: *AF* + booklet >booklet alone on asthma knowledge and control. No diffs in parental knowledge or lung function. *AF* + booklet >booklet alone on days off school and oral steroid use at 6m fu. 95% *AF* gp agreed it was a good way to learn about asthma.
Yawn et al. (2000)	*Air Academy (AA): The Quest for Airtopia* CD-ROM game for **asthma education.**	Nonclinical class-level RCT 6w + 4w fu: (1) or (2) *AA* played in health and science classes for 20 mins 3 × w for 6w with or without 30 mins physician's asthma talk vs (3) regular classes with no *AA*, (all n's unclear).	Minnesota, USA: 87 students in 3 fourth grade classes. Age 9–10, only 10/87 with asthma.	*Air Academy* > regular classes on asthma knowledge at wk 6, benefits retained to 4w fu thereafter. Physician's talk no effect

A year after the first visit a minority of subjects (39% *IMPACT*+TAU, 36% TAU-only) gave outcome data. The authors suggest that the dropout rate reflects the mild asthma of some participants and the limited nature of insurance cover for specialist services (S. Krishna, personal communication, 25 August 2005). *IMPACT*+TAU improved more than TAU on increased knowledge about asthma, reductions in asthma days per year, schooldays missed, activity limitation, emergency room visits per year, and mean daily dose of inhaled corticosteroids, but not in lung function nor in child or caregiver quality of life scores. *IMPACT* users said they found it easy to use and navigate, interesting and enjoyable and completed 40–100% of the program; 61% said they would use *IMPACT* again, but ranked it second to the physician as an asthma information source. Teenage children found it the least enjoyable.

Reduction in annual emergency room visits translated into savings of $900 per child in the *IMPACT* group (compared to $300 in the controls who received printed and verbal asthma education).

> *In brief*, though adding *IMPACT* somewhat enhanced gains from usual care, outcome data were from too small a proportion of subjects to judge generalizability of its value.

Personal computer games about asthma

USA: Asthma Command (AC): PC game 1 to enhance asthma self-management

Asthma Command (*AC*) is an interactive PC game from Connecticut (Rubin et al., 1986) to teach children how to manage asthma by recognizing symptoms and allergens, using medications and emergency room and physician visits appropriately, and attending school. *AC* aims to help children learn to manage asthma vicariously at asthma clinic visits by playing an adventure game on a clinic PC for about 40 minutes to manage a game character's asthma (*CAVE* in Chapter 2 is another vicarious system, for exposure for adult anxiety disorders). The game ends by giving the child a printout about asthma management based on game performance. The child, parent and clinic staff review this for five minutes.

RCT

AC was tested in Connecticut in a ten-month RCT at regular asthma clinic visits by 35 boys and 30 girls aged 7–12 (66% white) who had at least three acute visits for asthma in the past year (Rubin et al., 1986). They were randomized (children were asked not to reveal condition; physicians were kept blind to the study) to: (a) *Asthma Command* + TAU (n=32); versus (b) a control non-asthma related computer game + TAU (5–10 mins advice on asthma management; (n=33)). TAU involved clinic visits about every six weeks (mean total = 6, range 3–7). Twenty-one more eligible children refused entry, were uncontactable or did not attend at the start. Dropouts were 3 (10%) from *AC* + TAU, 8 (24%) from the control + TAU. At post-test, compared to the control +TAU, *AC* +TAU had improved more on asthma knowledge and behaviour, but not in acute visits, hospital time or school absence. *Asthma Command* did not seem to reduce staff time.

In brief, adding a game of *Asthma Command* to about six asthma clinic visits over ten months yielded more improvement in asthma knowledge and management than did usual care plus a computer-game placebo.

USA: Watch, Discover, Think, and Act (WDTA): PC game 2 to enhance asthma self-management

Watch, Discover, Think and Act (*WDTA*) is a PC game from Texas (Bartholomew et al., 2000). It aims to help children learn in an asthma clinic to manage asthma vicariously by playing an adventure game to manage the game character's asthma. *WDTA* is accessed on a clinic PC at the end of regular clinic visits. At the game's end the child and carer each get two game printouts with rewarding messages, a reminder of the self-regulatory process taught, and a discussion of the game scores with clinic staff, while the child gets an asthma action plan from the physician or research assistant.

RCT

WDTA was tested in Texan inner-city clinics in 86 boys and 47 girls aged 6–17 who had moderate to severe asthma without other chronic disease (Bartholomew et al., 2000). Most were on Medicaid. All were English speaking, and 46% were Hispanic and 50% African-American. Thirty-eight more eligible children refused entry or were uncontactable at the start. They were randomized (unclear if randomization concealed) to: (a) *WDTA* + TAU (n=70); or to (b) TAU only (n=63). TAU involved regular clinic appointments preceded by a phoned reminder. The overall dropout rate (% unclear) was similar across the two groups. Participation lasted 4–16 months (mean 8), and *WDTA*+TAU attended the clinic more for scheduled visits. At post-test, compared to TAU only *WDTA*+TAU had fewer admissions in younger children (but not fewer emergency room visits overall), fewer symptoms for children with mild asthma, and improved behavioural repertoires for children participating for longer. Parents in the intervention group reported better asthma management than in the control group on the 'asthma treatment' scale of the Parent Asthma Management Interview at post-treatment. Of the *WDTA* children 97% said they would tell their best friend that the game was fun and educational. *WDTA* did not appear to reduce staff time.

In brief, in inner-city children *WDTA* enhanced asthma management compared to usual care in the short term, but did not seem to reduce staff time.

USA: Asthma Control PC game 3 to enhance asthma self-management

Asthma Control (*ACont*) PC program in Boston, USA is a computer game (as are *Asthma Command* and *WDTA* above) including a superhero with asthma who simulates daily events and teaches: symptom recognition and monitoring; allergen identification; sound use of medication and health services; continuing normal activity. The player uses knowledge of asthma to complete six levels of *ACont* reflecting different types of exposure or environmental challenge (e.g cockroaches, outdoor play, morning medication).

RCT

In an RCT of *ACont* in Boston (Homer et al., 2000), the parents of 471 asthmatic children aged 3–12 were offered inclusion at an asthma clinic, of whom 137 (29%, 61% of these black; mean child's age 8) consented and did baseline ratings. The 137 children were stratified by age, asked to return for three clinic visits, and randomized (concealment unclear) to play during those visits either: (a) *Asthma Control* (n=76); or (b) a control non-educational computer game and also read age-appropriate asthma leaflets (n=61). Return for ≥ 1 study clinic visits was made by 63% of *ACont* and 57% of control children. All three sessions were attended by 32% of *ACont* and 21% control children. Staff phoned parents monthly eight times to collect data. At ten months, the percentage of 137 sets of parents completing the exit questionnaire was 75% *ACont*, 80% controls.

Asthma Control children improved significantly more than controls only on asthma knowledge, not on emergency department and unscheduled office visits, asthma severity, impact of asthma on parental personal time, child behaviour, or use of peak flow meters. On all measures both groups improved in the year after compared to the year before entering the study. All *AC* children said they enjoyed the game (unlike their parents), mean time to complete it being 30 to 60 minutes.

In brief, in an asthma clinic only 29% of parents agreed to join a study of *Asthma Control*. Child users, compared to appropriate controls, improved on asthma knowledge but not severity or other measures.

UK: Asthma Files (AF): PC game 4 to enhance asthma self-management

Asthma Files (AF) is an interactive, educational program from Nottingham, UK (McPherson et al., 2002a, 2002b), used on a PC to improve children's knowledge of asthma triggers and management through games and entering personal information (peak flow and triggers) which become part of a printable self-management plan.

Pilot study

AF was evaluated in an small open study of ten boys aged 7–14 (median = 11) who had asthma and had been attending an outpatient clinic for up to 12 years (median = 6.5). Twenty-one other eligible children did not take part in the study. Following a demonstration of *AF* the child explored *AF* alone at home. After use of *AF*, knowledge about asthma triggers rose significantly.

RCT

A RCT in Nottingham, UK (McPherson et al., 2006) was done in 101 children aged 7–14 who were attending hospital asthma clinics. They were randomized (not concealed) to: (a) *Asthma Files* used at home on a laptop during a single visit from a researcher (n=51), of whom 41 had access to a computer and kept a copy of *AF* on a CD-ROM plus an asthma-information booklet; or (b) the same asthma information booklet only (received by post) without *AF* (n=50). Of the 101 starters, 96% completed one-month follow-up and 88% six-month follow-up. In an intention-to-treat analysis at one month, in the *AF* group the children had better asthma knowledge and

9. CP FOR PROBLEMS IN CHILDREN AND TEENAGERS 205

perceived control but not lung function, and parental knowledge was no better, than in the booklet-only group. At six months, the *AF* group reported fewer days off school and less oral steroid use than the booklet-only group. Of the *AF* children 95% agreed *AF* was a good way to learn about asthma.

> *In brief, Asthma Files* improved asthmatic children's knowledge and perceived control of asthma one month after use. They had fewer days off school and used less steroids at six months than information booklet-only controls.

USA: Air Academy: Quest for Airtopia CD-ROM game 5 for asthma education

Air Academy: Quest for Airtopia from the USA (Yawn et al., 2000) is a fourth computer game asthma education tool (as are *Asthma Control, Asthma Command* and *WDTA* above), used by children aged 6–12 on a CD-ROM. It presents asthma disease knowledge and management skills, with motivating tools to reward these skills.

QuasiRCT

In a nonclinical RCT where school classes (not children) were randomized, 87 children (only 10 with asthma) from three classes aged 9–10 were tested over six weeks of: (a) *Air Academy* alone vs (b) *Air Academy* + a 30-minute physician's asthma talk during a four-week follow-up, vs (c) no intervention (Yawn et al., 2000). After 20 mins technical instruction in health and science classes, children from two classes were allowed to play *Air Academy* as desired for the last 20 mins of computer labs held three times a week over six weeks. Numbers of children per condition were unclear. Both *Air Academy* groups gained asthma-related knowledge and retained it over the subsequent four weeks. Neither the physician's asthma talk nor longer playing times altered outcome.

> *In brief, Air Academy* improved asthma-related knowledge in children who mostly had no asthma.

CHAPTER TEN

Synthesis

SCOPE OF CP STUDIES

We found 175 studies covering 97 CP systems from at least nine countries (Table 10.1). Almost half came from the USA and a fair number from the UK, Sweden and Australia. Almost a third of the CP systems were net-based. The most frequent type of study was an RCT. The RCTs most often had waitlist or care-as-usual controls, confounding interpretation of results as we discussed in Chapter 1. Placebo-attention controls are not yet as common in CP as in drug-therapy research.

Surprisingly few systems came in computer-game format except for childhood asthma, though one might expect that attractive therapy games could have wide appeal. Designs of the first motor cars closely mimicked those of their forebears (horse-drawn carriages) and it took decades for radically different car designs to evolve into machines sharing little with animal transport beyond having four round wheels. Similarly, CP systems often mimic much of their forebears – traditional CBT and bibliotherapy – but in time may exploit more of the avenues opening up with new technologies.

The commonest CP systems concerned phobic/panic disorder, followed by eating problems and problems of childhood and adolescence, and then general anxiety/emotional problems and depression. Quite a few guided self-help for alcohol and smoking problems. Few dealt with OCD, drug misuse, PTSD or schizophrenia. Hardly any dealt mainly with insomnia,

207

TABLE 10.1
Number of CP systems by clinical problem, system type, country of origin/testing, type of study

	Number of CP systems
Clinical problem	
Phobia/panic	18
Eating problems	13
Children and adolescents	12
• Childhood asthma	6
General anxiety/emotional problems	10
Depression	9
Physical problems:	8
• Pain	4
• Tinnitus distress	1
• Insomnia	1
• Jetlag	1
• Sexual problems	1
Alcohol problems	7
Smoking	6
OCD	3
Drug misuse	3
• Anger and violence prevention	1
PTSD	2
Schizophrenia	2
Nonclinical or semi-clinical	4
Total	**97**
CP system type	
Internet	31
Desktop PC	27
Handheld device	11
CD-ROM	10
Computer game	8
Non-immersive virtual reality	5
IVR	4
Virtual reality	1
Total	**97**
Country of origin and/or testing	
USA	45
UK	15
Sweden	10
Australia	9
Multinational	7
Canada	3
Unknown	3
Netherlands	2
New Zealand	1
Germany	1
Spain	1
Total	**97**

TABLE 10.1 *Continued*

Type of study	No. of studies
RCT	103
Open	45
Beta	9
Cases	6
Other	12
Total	**175**

anger and sexual difficulties. None dealt with enuresis, stammering, epilepsy, bipolar or personality disorders. Such omissions are noteworthy given that CBT is of some value for anger management, enuresis, insomnia, stammering, and several sexual difficulties.

MENTAL HEALTH PROBLEMS CP HAS HELPED

Research into computer-aided psychotherapy (CP) has generated ingenious and diverse ways of helping a variety of disorders, with studies ranging from brief beta tests and pilots to full multicentre RCTs with follow-up. No CP system is a panacea, just as no form of ftf psychotherapy is a cure-all. Most CP systems sensibly targeted a sliver of conditions from the broad spectrum of mental health problems.

Encouragingly better therapy results with CP than contrasting approaches together with over 50% cut in therapist time, were found, among others, for phobia/panic disorder (*FF*, Swedish netbiblioCP), OCD (*BTSteps*), depression (*BtB*), obesity (*BTWL*), problem drinking (*DL*), and childhood anxiety (*BRAVE*), encopresis (*UCPT*) and asthma (*IMPACT, AC, AF*). NICE now recommends one therapy system for phobia/panic (*FearFighter*) and another (*Beating the Blues*) for depression. Prevention CP reduced risk factors for developing eating problems (*SB*) and problem drinking in youths (*SODAS*). Definitive CP help for PTSD, general anxiety and emotional problems, smoking and drug misuse awaits further development. We found just one system (*Sexpert*) for sexual dysfunction, now defunct despite its early promise. CP for psychoses has yet to bear ripe fruit. No systems were found for nightmares, tics or compulsive gambling. Even where outcome was hopeful, reservations remain regarding those therapy CP systems where the RCTs only had controls on a waitlist or usual care and so could not exclude expectancy/placebo effects.

Many mental health clinics receive referrals with a broad range of problems, e.g. phobias, panic, general anxiety, OCD, PTSD and depression, and/or eating disorders like anorexia and bulimia. No single existing CP system can help all comers. Broad-spectrum clinics can offer a broad spectrum of CP systems, one for each type of problem referred. A start on this path was made in a London primary-care clinic for anxiety and depressive disorders (Marks et al., 2003). It devised a screening questionnaire (Gega, Kenwright, Mataix-Cols, Cameron, & Marks, 2005) to filter referrals who might have any such disorder, and offered suitable phobia/panic patients *FF*, general anxiety clients *Balance*, OCD subjects *BTSteps*, and depressed sufferers *Cope*. PTSD patients were offered *FF* for their phobia/panic symptoms and *Cope* for their depressive symptoms, thus managing most features of PTSD. In an open study CP users improved encouragingly and significantly, especially if they had been referred by GPs or self-referred (Mataix-Cols et al., 2006). GPs who could refer their patients for immediate CP at the clinic over a year cut by 80% their referrals to more costly secondary mental health care. Once the CP clinic closed, the GPs could no longer refer their patients for CP and their referrals to secondary mental health care rose back to the original level.

VIRTUAL CLINICS?

Effective CP systems are coming on stream for a growing range of mental health difficulties. This allows clinics to offer an expanding range of CP systems to a widening range of referrals with varying problems. Now that many CP systems can be used on the net, a small administrative base can offer netCP on a large scale, together with brief support by phone, email or SMS, to anyone in reach of a net-linked computer and a phone. In this way a clinic can change its presence from being mainly physical to largely 'virtual'. This happened with the above London clinic (Marks et al., 2003) once patients obtained remote access not only to IVR*BTSteps* and IVR*Cope* but also to *netFF*. In the clinic's final phase *netFF* users actually had their brief phone support from Switzerland after the psychiatrist supporting them moved from London to Basle. The number of patients' personal visits to the clinic dropped sharply despite a rise in the numbers of people being treated. The clinic's interview rooms and computers and printers in them were used less and less.

Virtual clinics which patients don't have to attend physically benefit clients by reducing their travel, stigma, and scheduling of appointments for CP sessions. By becoming virtual, clinics themselves gain from reduced costs of space (fewer interview rooms) and need for fewer computers and printers.

SCREENING SUITABILITY FOR CP

Studies have varied hugely in their methods of determining suitability for CP. Some did no, or hardly any, screening, as in certain netCP trials. Others gave password-protected access to CP on the net, IVR, or other computers only after screening patients in diverse ways. Screening often employed DSM-IV, ICD-10 or other criteria via net or other computer interviews, or by email, phone or face-to-face (ftf) interviews with a clinician. Certain clinics asked referrals to complete paper-and-pencil questionnaires which clinicians then scanned quickly to filter initial referrals prior to a ftf or phone interview (e.g. Gega et al., 2005) lasting from a few minutes to an hour or longer depending on the study.

What was screened for depended on which CP system/s patients were to use. Criteria of suitability for CP tended to reflect criteria of suitability for clinician-led therapy. Recruits were often asked to complete standard rating scales for anxiety, depression, eating disorders, drinking, etc. Exclusion might be due to suicidal plans, drug/alcohol misuse, psychosis or other comorbid problems, learning disability, and insufficient literacy to use a given CP system. Occasionally screening tested motivation to do CBT and CP, and asked for age and place of residence if the CP was for a restricted age group or community. Ability to pay was not a big issue for investigators recruiting referrals for research, but payment is becoming a constraint as demand grows for CP on a routine basis outside research trials.

The aims of screening were rarely discussed. If CP users have no problem suitable for self-help by a given CP system then their use of that system wastes their time but does not deny more suitable sufferers access to that system if it is available on the net or IVR for an unlimited number of sufferers. However, unsuitable patients doing CP do deny help to more suitable patients if in the process they also consume an associated finite resource, e.g. brief live support by phone, email or ftf, or time on a computer in a clinic, or a slot on a licence limited to a specified maximum number of users.

Harmful effects from not screening?

Little is said about potentially harmful effects of CP for unsuitable patients. Some wonder if failure to improve with CP may make patients refractory to subsequent ftf care from which they might have benefited had they had ftf care first. Evidence of that happening after CP any more than after failure with ftf care or being on a waitlist is hard to find. There is limited evidence to the contrary. Outpatients who used CP while on a waitlist for ftf CBT subsequently required less-than-usual ftf time with a therapist (Nakagawa et al., 2000).

Might suicide risk be better detected and managed in human than computer interviews? Close scrutiny did not find this. Suicide risk was predicted better in a computer interview than a clinician interview (Greist, Gustafson, Stauss, Rowse, Laughren, & Chiles, 1973). In a computer interview of patients in the waiting room of an emergency service, suicide plans had been disclosed by 31 patients, in 25 of whom the plans had been

212 HANDS-ON HELP: COMPUTER-AIDED PSYCHOTHERAPY

undetected in a ftf consultation; within 45 days four patients returned after a suicide attempt (Claassen & Larkin, 2005). In another study, three patients who had severe depression and active suicidal ideas did well with *Cope* and only brief therapist support (Gega et al., 2004; Marks et al., 2003). However, even if further research confirms that suitably designed CP can manage suicide risk, courts seem unlikely to accept that any time soon. Few clinicians would be keen to pioneer this delicate task.

WHAT IS CP?

In addition to the range of computer interfaces, amount and type of human support and other implementation issues reviewed in this monograph, the content of various CP systems ranged widely across different aspects of CBT. Most systems gave educational information – generally generic and occasionally also tailored to individual users. Users might see and perhaps hear information on screen and/or or print it out in leaflets and/or get manuals to use together with the CP. Many systems helped users assess current problems with feedback on functioning and change over time on repeated measures. Often they guided clients through steps to set themselves action plans and goals and to consider resistances to overcome in order to enhance motivation. They might suggest 'change techniques' such as behavioural activation, exposure, changing of negative thoughts to positive ones, and relapse prevention. Some CP systems used a 'narrator' or 'therapist' character guiding users through self-help. They frequently showed vignettes of sufferers who had the client's sort of problem and how they overcame it step by step, with written, pictorial, animated and/or video information to bring these features to life. Many systems helped users work out homework (generic or tailored) as part of self-treatment.

HUMAN SUPPORT OF CP USERS

Support duration, frequency and content

Some human support is usual during CP and self-help (Newman, Erickson, Przeworski, & Dzus, 2003) and increases adherence to CP. As with screening, trials differed greatly in the duration and type of human support they gave CP users. A handful gave none (e.g. 1 *MoodGYM* study, *ODIN 1*, *Panic Program, Stresspac*). Most gave at least some human support either ftf or by phone or email. Contact durations ranged from just a few minutes (*CARL*) to about an hour in all over three months (e.g. *BtB, FF, MoodGYM's* RCT, *Overcoming Bulimia*), to three to four hours (e.g. *GDA, PO*, Swedish netbiblio systems), to as long as is usual without CP (e.g. *Interapy*, VR systems) so saving no therapist time. NetCP systems commonly gave access to online group discussions and bulletin boards (e.g.

QuitNet, QuitSmokingNetwork, Student Bodies), sometimes moderated, sometimes not. Users might be given printed workbooks or leaflets with the CP (e.g. IVR*BTSteps*, IVR*Cope*, *NAPFD*, *SBI*).

Though a certain amount of human support for CP users may increase adherence, it also increases cost. Cost-effectiveness studies are needed of differential amounts of support of various CP systems in order to find crossover points beyond which further human support no longer pays by increasing improvement with CP.

Frequency of contact also differed considerably across studies. Where patients used standalone CP systems in a clinic, a supporter often saw them for a few minutes at the start and end of each CP session (e.g. *BtB*, standalone*FF* [not *netFF*]). Many Swedish netCP users had weekly email contact, sometimes personalized by a display of the therapist's name and photograph on the net, and sometimes supplemented by live phone calls. *NetFF, MoodGYM* (RCT) and many Swedish bibliotherapy CP users had scheduled brief phone calls or email contact every week or two. NetCP systems commonly offer online discussion groups for support (e.g. *DL*).

Content of human support for CP users spanned brief technical help only to checking of and praising progress, rating of outcome and self-help tips, to videoconferences, counselling, or brief or usual CBT. *FF* users often needed a few minutes of help to decide on exposure goals and homework.

Scheduled vs requested support

One RCT compared, in OCD users of *BTSteps*, support calls which were either scheduled and therapist initiated, or requested by patients when they thought they needed help (Kenwright et al., 2005). Adherence and improvement were better with scheduled than requested calls, and very few patients sought help on their own initiative. The superiority of scheduled calls might reflect a deadline effect – knowing that someone will call at a fixed time is an incentive to complete homework before then. It might also reflect users' diffidence in contacting a therapist. In other studies users rarely grasped opportunities to contact the therapist by voicemail (e.g. Greist et al., 2002; Osgood-Hynes et al., 1998) or direct phone (Andersson et al., 2003; Ström et al., 2000). In keeping with this, nightmare sufferers who were posted self-help material hardly ever phoned a helpline number they were given (Burgess, Gill, & Marks, 1998).

The scheduled vs requested support issue deserves further RCTs as it affects how CP support services might be run. Since NICE recommended *FearFighter* to manage phobia/panic in the NHS and requires Trusts to implement this guidance, *netFF* licences have been bought by Trusts for sufferers from catchment area populations of millions in all across England and Wales. It might make sense to organize regional helpline services to make scheduled calls to users that will be more numerous than the fewer requested calls expected to be made. An incidental problem to solve in a sizeable CP-helpline service is how to arrange that the minority of users who initiate calls speak to their previous supporter whenever possible rather than have to start with someone new each time.

Channel of support

The channel for giving support in different studies might be by post, ftf, phone, SMS, voicemail, email or the internet. The last four could be synchronous or delayed.

Background and training of supporters

In most studies supporters were psychiatrists, psychologists, nurses or GPs who were qualified or at various stages of training, or graduate mental health workers with no clinical background. Supporters working with IMM had gone through each CP system they were supporting as pretend patients and then been trained for two days how to answer questions asked frequently by users. A few administrators (non-clinicians) working with IMM also became helpful supporters after similar brief training. Little is known about the best short training to give brief support to users of different CP systems.

TIME USERS SPEND ON CP

At one end of a range, subjects spent just five minutes on a single occasion answering a form on a computer screen about problem drinking and getting computerized feedback tailored to their input (e.g. *NAPFD*; Cunningham et al., 2005). Such systems are called CP because the advice given was partly tailored according to input. At the other extreme are complex CP systems which mimic many more aspects of the therapy process (e.g. *BtB*, *BTSteps*, *Cope*, *FF*), and need correspondingly longer time from users – as much as eight hours over up to three months. Certain CP systems ask for fewer contact hours but are available for even longer periods for continuing monitoring and relapse prevention (e.g. online smoking cessation programs).

A second time issue is the pace at which users go through more complex CP systems. Some required users to go through them at a prescribed rate over six or more weeks, as in some of the Swedish and Australian netbiblio systems and in *BtB*. Swedish netbiblio users frequently felt the pace was too fast. Other systems give subjects more latitude about their speed of work, as with *netFF*, *BTSteps* and *Cope* which could be used mostly for up to ten weeks. Before proceeding to certain *FF* steps, users are asked to leave enough days on which to do exposure homework, and are cautioned against too frequent CP 'visits' at that stage.

EDUCATION AND AGE OF USERS

Information about these is often absent. Subjects using workbook-type CP with net*MoodGYM* and Swedish netCP were more educated than the general population. Completers of Swedish netbiblioCP for depression were more educated than dropouts (Andersson et al., 2005). *FF, BTSteps* and *Cope* assumed a reading age of 11 and were not structured like college texts. Except where the CP was targeted at children or teenagers, CP users were generally aged 16–65 as in most CBT. CP aimed at the elderly is under development. Certain studies mentioned the successful use of CP by people aged over 70.

LIVE THERAPIST VS CP

The scepticism of many patients and professionals about CP stems in part from a long-held belief that improvement with psychotherapy requires a relationship or other major involvement with a therapist. That may be true for some patients, but is not upheld in the thousands of people who improved when guided in CP studies with only brief human contact. Brief support for a few minutes at a time to a total of an hour or so over two or three months is not much of a relationship or major therapist involvement. Such brief support, however, can strongly motivate people to follow CP guidance. Its role resembles that of a helpline to get us over teething problems when starting to use a new computer program or other technology – a few seconds or minutes of appropriate advice helps us over hurdles so we don't throw up our hands in despair and give up. A CP system's efficacy relies on users' adherence to its instructions. Carers who know little about CBT can nevertheless motivate patients to do self-help with the aid of CP. In a *BTSteps* RCT once patients began to do exposure homework they improved as much when this was guided by the computer as by a face-to-face behaviour therapist (Greist et al., 2002).

Just as patients may become overdependent in ftf therapy so they can get overattached to CP. A few OCD cases began to use *BTSteps* in a ritualistic mechanical manner and had to be dissuaded from too frequent contact, just to use CP to guide properly-done exposure/ritual prevention homework.

CP's advent without agreed quality standards brought criticism that its content is inferior to that of therapist-led CBT. Content depends on the authors of the system, who vary in orientation and training. As noted, depression improved little with CP when the CP omitted behavioural activation advice. Phobia/panic is less likely to improve with CP which omits exposure instructions. This issue with CP is the same as with the content of

216 HANDS-ON HELP: COMPUTER-AIDED PSYCHOTHERAPY

ftf therapy. Some CP systems give basic CBT education or guide only fragments of CBT such as VR giving exposure scenes or palmtops prompting homework. Others take over far more of a therapist's tasks to also help users plan and implement therapy, monitor outcome and prevent relapse as in full CBT (e.g. *BtB*, *Cope*, *BTSteps*, *FF*).

CONSTRAINTS AND PATIENTS' PREFERENCES

Therapists cannot work round the clock. Their appointments being limited to certain hours constrains access to help. This constraint is not eased by CP systems which are available only on standalone computers in clinics with usual working hours. The constraint is eased by making CP systems accessible at home on the net or by phone or a handheld device. These allow round-the-clock access to self-help guidance, though associated brief support from a professional will remain restricted to office hours until 24-hour call centre support becomes economically viable. Other limits imposed by research study designs cut flexibility for patients, e.g. having to give ratings at scheduled times which might have been a chore, though this may have concentrated their minds on doing required homework in time for a rating deadline. More study is needed of patients' preference for being screened and subsequently supported face to face or by phone or by email, of how to access CP (handheld devices, standalone or net-linked computer in a clinic, at home or elsewhere, touchscreen or tablet PCs, IVR), which system to use for a given problem (choice is limited at present), and between CP or manual self-help each with brief therapist support. Providing CBT services that fit patients' preferences could give them more sense of control and enhance satisfaction and engagement.

CP EFFECT ON SYMPTOMS AND FUNCTIONING

RCTs have evaluated CP against the 'gold standard' of therapist-led treatment (e.g. Greist et al., 2002; Kenardy et al., 2003a, 2003b; Marks et al., 2004), against a manual with similar content (Ghosh et al., 1988; Jones et al., 2006), against psychological placebos (e.g. relaxation in Carlbring et al., 2003; Marks et al., 2004; self-monitoring in Klein & Richards, 2001), against treatment as usual without the extra support and scheduled visits given to the CP group (e.g. Proudfoot et al., 2003b), or against a waiting list with neither an expectation of improvement nor placebo attention (e.g. Carlbring et al., 2001). Open studies had no comparison groups and had confounds such as receipt of other concurrent help (e.g. medication, psychotherapy), and inferred the effectiveness of CP from effect sizes (Cohen's d) and clinical significance of outcome.

A common rule of thumb is that an effect size of 0.2 or below denotes ineffectiveness, 0.2–0.4 a small effect, 0.4–0.8 a moderate effect, and 0.8 or more a large effect. CP systems had effect sizes ranging from tiny (0.2, for a palmtop system – Kenardy et al., 2003b) to as great as 4.3 for Main Problem with *FF* (Marks et al., 2004). Another rough rule is that change is clinically significant if >50% of patients score above a given cut-off point. Applying such rules should take into account the often markedly disparate amounts of improvement across measures of change even within studies. Different studies differed greatly in what was measured (e.g. symptoms, disability, knowledge of treatment principles, risk factors) and in the measures' validity.

CP UPTAKE, COMPLETION AND ATTRITION RATES

These rates give some indication of CP's acceptability though their meaning is not always obvious. One review of attrition covered 46 papers relating to 36 research studies (Waller & Gilbody, 2006).

The rate of uptake is the proportion of people offered CP who then go on to actually use it. This proportion is almost impossible to gauge accurately for open-access netCP systems (e.g. *MoodGYM*, stop-smoking programs) where the potential client pool round the world may number many millions (e.g. all depressed people or smokers who use the internet). It may be easier to estimate where clear referral pathways to a CP system are established and those offered CP are monitored for system use. In research trials as opposed to service use, CP uptake is confounded by research uptake. This is especially true in RCTs, where potential users may be discouraged if they don't draw randomization to active CP, are subjected to tediously repeated measurement, and/or have to follow strict protocols. In an RCT of *BTB* (Proudfoot et al., 2004), 132 of 406 clients meeting screening criteria (by GP and computerized diagnostic interview) refused to take part in the RCT.

Completion rate is the proportion of people who use a CP system for a given number of sessions or length of time previously agreed between therapist and patient. Ironically, on this definition the highest 'completion' rates tend to be in control waitlist or other groups – that doesn't mean such control 'procedures' are a good way to help one's problem. The definition is also problematic as users vary in the speed with which they can digest and implement CP guidance. Moreover, it is easier to identify the last session for completion in sequential self-help systems consisting of steps in a chain (e.g. *FF*, *BTSteps*, Swedish netbiblio systems) than in CP systems with several optional modules (e.g. *Cope*). With this caveat, the completion rates across different studies ranged from as high as 86% (e.g. *OAPP*) down to 1% with several unsupported websites (e.g. *ODIN*, *Panic Program*, 1 *MoodGYM* study). With such a huge spread many reasons for attrition can be expected with different types of CP. Dropouts had higher baseline scores (Kenardy et al., 2003b), lower satisfaction (Wright et al., 2002) and lower improvement (Greist et al., 2002). Reasons for dropout include disliking the CP system used, change of personal circumstances, and not wanting to return post-treatment ratings (Richards & Alvarenga, 2002), which reluctance complicates accurate judgement of actual improvement. Some users say they learn what to do from early CP guidance and thereafter do successful self-help on their own. With such cases imputing last-available ratings forward (so-called 'intent-to-treat' analyses) assuming that clinical state froze since the last rating may underestimate improvement.

More needs to be known about which and why certain patients don't take up or drop out prematurely from different types of CP, including demographic, linguistic and other cultural influences. There is evidence that attrition is cut by offering CP as an early rather than late step on the path to care (Mataix-Cols et al., 2006), and by giving brief scheduled clinician support (Kenwright et al., 2005).

COST, COST EFFECTIVENESS, AND CP'S PLACE IN HEALTHCARE PROVISION

Some CP is sold in the form of CD-ROMs or passwords for net access, e.g. *BRAVE, BTB, ESPWC, GDA, FF,* Swedish netbiblio systems. Prices differ widely depending on whether they are for individual users or for health authorities or insurers with differently sized catchment-area populations. The costs of ftf care are also problematic. Bold assumptions that don't always reflect reality closely were made in some cost-effectiveness comparisons of CP with ftf care (e.g. NICE, 2006).

What economic analysis should be used for CP vs current care depends on the questions being asked. If the aim is to effectively treat more patients at the lowest possible cost, a cost-minimization analysis could decide which type of CP or current care treats more patients well for the same money. If the aim is to cut down costs in the current provision of services, then a cost-effectiveness analysis could work out the cheapest of CP and current care options of equal efficacy. For unequal efficacy of different treatment options, a cost-benefit analysis could examine how much treatment outcome per patient would be affected if more patients were treated at the same cost. It is too early for an agreed consensus to have emerged on how to evaluate CP's cost and cost-effectiveness.

CP developers commonly expect their new system will be profitable. Hard experience suggests otherwise. It costs millions of dollars to develop and clinically test CP systems to the stage of obtaining national regulatory approval. This cost may be far less than the reputed hundreds of millions of dollars needed to develop drugs to the same stage, but it is still daunting for

10. SYNTHESIS   219

developers. Open studies take less time and money than do RCTs, but yield less recognition. Regulatory approval demands RCTs which are usually very expensive and take years to run, analyse and publish. Moreover, getting regulatory approval is no guarantee that the relevant healthcare service, insurance companies or other providers will fund the approved CP system. The least expensive way of funding CP might be for central bodies to fund national licences for particular CP systems, but that has yet to be achieved. As funders wake up to the benefits flowing from funding CP, CP might become as commercially viable as drugs and other healthcare devices.

It is too early to know how CP systems which improve clinical problems effectively or reduce the risk of getting them fit best into countries' diverse healthcare and educational systems. Though some CP is on sale to individuals or organizations, perverse incentives to eschew it abound in insurance and governmental arrangements for health care. To take an example, a European professor was so impressed by seeing *FearFighter* and the fact that it could quadruple the number of phobia/panic patients his clinic could treat without hiring more therapists that he contacted the relevant health insurer to arrange payment to his clinic for a *FF* licence. Back came the reply that annual payment to his clinic would remain the same whether it treated its usual 100 patients a year face to face or 400 patients a year with *FF*. His insurer's funding rules meant his clinic would lose money by paying for and using CP even though patient throughput could shoot up without impairing outcome. Such disincentives bedevil every land. Changing them is a nontrivial task.

Lecturers round the world who present encouraging results with CP are besieged by audience members seeking CP for their patients. Interest melts away on learning that payment is needed for most CP as it is for a new drug or other healthcare device. Even where CP is several times more cost-effective than ftf care, funders are not used to paying for CP in the way they are used to funding expensive medication or pacemakers or surgery.

As yet we lack conclusive information about the cost implications and impact of CP on health service provision and utilization. Researchers and service providers need to identify what exactly they want to achieve by introducing CP into a health service and then explore the costs of different implementation models.

CHAPTER 11

Conclusion

Answering the question 'Does CP work?' is like answering the query 'Do drugs work?'. Reply to the latter depends, among others, on the medication and how it is given, the problem it is intended to help, and the outcome measure and when it is measured. Similarly, answers about the efficacy of CP depend, among others, on the particular CP system used, where and for what it is used and with what human screening and support, and the outcome measures and when they are rated. The present review dealt separately with different clinical problems. Results from the literature about the clinical effectiveness of CP are encouraging but not uniformly conclusive because of the variability of participants, settings, modes of delivery, comparators and outcome measures across different studies. In addition, many questions about how to implement CP in everyday clinical practice have yet to be answered definitively, e.g. patient preferences, how best to support CP users, and the cost implications of various implementation models. This literature review found that:

1 Screening before allowing access to CP was by net, phone or face-to-face interview with a clinician mostly using tools for diagnosis rather for CP suitability per se.
2 Criteria for suitability for CP were commonly like those for clinician-led CBT. An exception is high suicidal risk usually leading to exclusion. Another exception is risk-reduction studies requiring subjects to be non-clinical or subclinical at risk of developing depression or eating problems.

3 Exceptionally high attrition rates after starting CP occurred in some net systems accessed by unscreened users. In studies which did screening (the bulk of reports) much of the 'attrition' was before starting CP by excluding subjects who didn't meet trial criteria. As in any treatment, the more 'suitable' that subjects were for CP the fewer they were but the more they were likely to improve.

4 More attrition with CP was variously associated with more severity, less satisfaction, less improvement, absence of ftf screening or support, and change in personal circumstances. The lowest attritions were often found with control procedures requiring patients to do little.

5 For a growing list of problems (at present including phobia/panic, OCD, depression, bulimia, problem drinking, childhood asthma – see start of this chapter) some CP systems were as or more effective than clinician-guided CBT on some measures in some studies and each was more effective than psychological placebo or a waiting list. CP reduced apparent risk for developing eating disorders.

6 Effect sizes varied hugely across CP systems from very large (4.3) to very small (0.2) or none depending on the system, syndrome and outcome measure.

7 In RCTs 'control' groups ranged from waiting lists to computerized information or placebo attention to ftfCBT. Inevitably each type of control group answered particular questions and begged others.

8 We need to learn far more about which aspects of CP systems actually help users and which are redundant or even inimical. Much of this knowledge will be guided by maturation of what we know about the same issues in face-to-face psychotherapies. Other elements may be unique to CP, e.g. whether 'bells and whistle' multimedia interactivity enhances improvement compared to similar guidance offered more simply and cheaply.

9 More needs to be known about the best type, frequency, duration and site of human support for CP users, and what type of training and supervision is needed to become a supporter.

10 More also needs to be known of patient preference for screening and for support face to face vs phone vs email, for using CP at home vs a clinic or elsewhere, for PC vs phone-IVR vs palmtop, for touchscreen vs usual screen vs tablet PC.

Across the world numerous studies are in train concerning many of the CP systems reviewed above and quite a few newer systems. It is too early to mention them here. The work reviewed in this monograph shows that computer-aided psychotherapy is coming of age regarding its efficacy for an expanding list of difficulties. In contrast, its adoption in everyday practice lags behind. This could change rapidly just as other technologies transformed healthcare with scans, joint replacements and a host of other now routine procedures undreamt of by earlier generations. This monograph is a snapshot of escalating developments auguring well for sufferers from many mental health problems.

APPENDIX I

Search method

We searched for English-language studies of any computer-aided psychotherapy for adults with any mental health problem. It covered studies from 1999 (inclusive) onwards and any earlier studies not reviewed by Marks (1998a, 1998b, 1999), whether they were randomized controlled trials (RCTs), cohort studies, or surveys and case studies/reports, with no quality threshold. It extracted all reported outcomes including patient preference, improvement in symptoms and disability, predictors of outcome, therapist time involved, cost, acceptability, satisfaction, service utilization, and others.

Searches were made of the Cochrane Library, Cinahl, Medline, PsychInfo, Social Sciences Citation Index and Embase using a combination of terms (with Boolean ANDs and ORs) for each aspect of the review, so that each term reflected either a synonym or a different concept relating to a specific aspect. Search terms were: for '*disorders*', anxiety, depression, trauma*, PTSD, obsess*, compulsi*, OCD, phobia*, panic, general* anxiety, stress; for '*interventions*', CBT, cognitive, behavio*, therapy, self?help, treat*; for '*computer*', computer*, internet, informatics, multimedia, virtual reality, online, biofeedback, interactive, technology. An asterisk* denotes truncated words to include different derivatives. A question mark ? denotes different spellings, e.g. behavio* includes behavio(u)r(al) and behavio(u)rs; self?help captures both self help and self-help.

Known experts in CP and members of the International Society for Research on Internet Interventions were emailed invitations to send relevant manuscripts under review or in press, conference papers, and dissertations, and were asked if they knew any other work in the field.

The programs and abstracts of many conferences and the reference lists of further relevant papers were scanned to find studies which met this review's

226 HANDS-ON HELP: COMPUTER-AIDED PSYCHOTHERAPY

inclusion criteria. Key relevant journals (e.g. *International Journal of Human-Computer Interaction, Computers in Human Behavior, CyberPsychology and Behaviour*) were also hand-searched for grey literature which may not appear in medical databases. All the foregoing led to a snowball effect. Searches were closed in May 2006.

DATA EXTRACTION PROCESS, QUALITY ASSESSMENT, SYNTHESIS

Information from each study was extracted under four headings into a data extraction form (see below):

1. *CP system*: name, technology used, content and structure of system, site/setting of access, human support (background, training, content, means, procedure).
2. *Method*: study design, outcome measures, comparison groups, confounding variables.
3. *Participants*: main problem, population pool, recruitment, screening and assessment procedures, inclusion/exclusion criteria, sample size per condition and features (age, gender, severity, ethnicity, class, geographical region, other).
4. *Results*:
   - use of CP (rates of uptake, completion and dropouts), number and duration of computer sessions, therapist support (time supporting patients and type of support)
   - effect on symptoms, disability, distress and other
   - patient preference for different modes of CP use
   - acceptability to and satisfaction of patients and professionals
   - cost implications and impact on service provision and utilization.

Each study was evaluated (Khan et al., 2001) for its methodological rigour (sample size guided by a power calculation and representative of the population studied, clear randomization and blinding procedures, reasonable interpretation of the results given previous work in the field) and its importance for CP in general (addressed questions not previously examined).

DATA EXTRACTION FORM

General information

- Author
- Title
- Source (*publication details, conference proceedings, personal communication, etc.*)
- Contact details of corresponding author.

CP system under study

- Name of system
- Technology used (e.g. *software, web pages, Interactive Voice Response*, etc.)

APPENDIX I: SEARCH METHOD   227

- Content and structure (*exposure, cognitive restructuring, breathing retraining* etc.)
- Site/setting of access (*clinic, home, GP surgery*, etc.)
- Human support: background (e.g. *nurse, psychologist, technician*, etc.)
- Training required (e.g. *in CBT, computers*, etc.)
- Content (e.g. *administration, treatment advice*, etc.)
- Means (e.g. *face to face, telephone, email*)
- Procedure (e.g. *on request, scheduled*, etc.)
- Duration (*in minutes/hours and as % of total treatment time*).

Methods

- Study design (e.g. *RCT, case study, observational, cohort*, etc.)
- Outcome measures
- Comparators (e.g. *'golden standard', psychological placebo, controls*, etc.)
- Confounding variables (e.g. *concurrent treatments, demographic variables*)
- Duration of follow-up.

Subjects

- Main problem (e.g. *phobias, depression, undifferentiated anxiety*, etc.)
- Population pool (e.g. *general population, inpatients, outpatients, students*, etc.)
- Recruitment procedures (e.g. *advertisement, GP referrals*, etc.)
- Rate of uptake
- Screening and assessment procedures (e.g. *who did the screening, specific tools used*)
- Inclusion and exclusion criteria
- Sample size (*in each condition if applicable*)
- Sample characteristics (*age, gender, ethnicity, class, geographical region, other*).

Results

- Use of CP: rates of uptake and completion (*or dropouts*)
- Number and duration of computer sessions
- Therapist support given (*time spent supporting patients and type of support*)
- Effect (*symptoms, disability, distress, other*)
- Patient preference for different modes of CP use (*if relevant*)
- Acceptability and satisfaction by patients and professionals
- Cost implications and impact on service provision and utilization.

APPENDIX II

Availability and contacts for CP systems reviewed

?UA = Unclear if available, but reference given, and website and an author's email contact if known.

Air Academy: The Quest for Airtopia. PC game for children to manage asthma (Yawn et al., 2000). ?UA. icaxan.com site link is down.

Asthma Command. PC game for children to manage asthma (Rubin et al., 1986) ?UA.

Asthma Control. PC game for children to manage asthma (Krishna et al., 2003). ?UA.

Asthma Files. CD-ROM game to help children to manage asthma. ?UA. amy.mcpherson@nottingham.ac.uk.

Balance. CD-ROM for general anxiety. Available commercially Mental Health Foundation (www.mhf.org.uk).

Beating the Blues. PC CP for depression. Available commercially Ultrasis plc (www.ultrasis.com).

Behavioural Self-Control Program for Windows. PC CP for problem drinking. Available commercially in English and French. www.behaviortherapy.com/software.htm.

BRAVE netCP for childhood anxiety (Spence et al., 2006). brave@psy.uq.edu.au.

BTSteps for OCD. IVR version ?UA, but net version available commercially as *OCFighter* from CCBT Ltd. stuart@fearfighter.com, www.ccbt.co.uk.

CADET diet and exercise training (Burnett et al., 1985, 1992). ?UA. kburnett@miami.edu.

CAE for flying phobia (Bornas et al., 2001a, 2001b). ?UA. Xavier Bornas, Majorca.

229

230   HANDS-ON HELP: COMPUTER-AIDED PSYCHOTHERAPY

Captain's Log Cognitive System. PC CP for cognitive training. Available commercially info@braintrain.com, www.braintrain.com.

CARL for dental and injection phobia (Coldwell et al., 2007). ?UA. nacrohd@u.washington.edu.

Committed Quitters™ Stop-Smoking Plan. netCP for smoking cessation. Available free http://committedquitters.quit.com.

Computer-aided education in schizophrenia PC Touch-screen (Jones et al., 2001). ?UA.

Computer aid to facilitate observing interpersonal interaction (Stone & Kristjanson, 1975). ?UA.

Computer-aided muscle relaxation and desensitisation (Chandler et al., 1986). ?UA.

Computer display system for spider phobia (Hassan, 1992). ?UA.

Computer display system for spider phobia (Nelissen et al., 1995; Whitby & Allcock, 1994). ?UA.

Computer-aided dietary counseling (Witschi et al., 1976). ?UA. wslack@caregroup. harvard.edu.

Computer-aided exposure (see *CAE*) for flying phobia (Bornas et al., 2001a, 2001b). ?UA. Xavier Bornas, Majorca.

Computer-Aided Relapse Management for Alcohol Problems (CARM) (Yates, 1996b). ?UA.

Computer-aided soliloquy. ?UA. wslack@caregroup.harvard.edu.

Computer-aided vicarious exposure (CAVE) for phobias and for OCD. ?UA. Ken.Kirkby@utas.edu.au.

Computer-Assisted Diet and Exercise Training (see *CADET*) (Burnett et al., 1985, 1992). ?UA. kburnett@miami.edu.

Computer-Assisted Relaxation Learning (see *CARL*) for dental and injection phobia (Coldwell et al., 2007). ?UA. nacrohd@u.washington.edu.

Computer-controlled desensitization for test anxiety (Biglan et al., 1979). ?UA.

Cope for depression. IVR version ?UA, but *Cope*'s netCP version is available commercially from CCBT Ltd. stuart@fearfighter.com, www.ccbt.co.uk.

Desktop CP system for depression (Selmi et al., 1990). ?UA. docselmi@ extremezone.com.

DIET educational program about bulimia and anorexia (Andrewes et al., 1995, 1996). ?UA.

Drinker's Check-Up for alcohol problems. Available commercially reidhester@ lobo.net, www.drinkerscheckup.com/.

Drinking Less netCP for problem drinking (Riper et al., 2007). ?UA. hriper@trimbos.nl.

ELIZA simulates a Rogerian therapist. Available free on net, e.g. at www. manifestation.com/neurotoys/eliza.php3.

Emotion Trainer on PC for young people with autism/Asperger's to recognize/ predict emotions in others. Available commercially at msilver@emotiontrainer. co.uk, www.emotiontrainer.co.uk/intro.htm.

Empowerment Solution for Permanent Weight Control. CD available commercially www.empower-plan.com.

APPENDIX II: AVAILABILITY OF CP SYSTEMS   231

Family Problem Solving (*Putting the Pieces Together*) netCP to reduce parental distress after a child's brain injury (Wade et al., 2005a, 2005b). ?UA. Password-protected site. shari.wade@cchmc.org.

FearFighter CP for phobia/panic. Available commercially CCBT Ltd, stuart@fearfighter.com, www.fearfighter.com.

Girls and Stress gender-specific intervention (*GSI*) CD-ROM to prevent drug abuse among teenage girls (Schinke & Schwinn, 2005). ?UA. schinke@columbia.edu.

Go Nosmoke PC stop-smoking CP (Schneider et al., 1990). ?UA.

Good Days Ahead DVD CP for depression and anxiety. Available commercially www.mindstreet.com/.

Handheld capnometer to aid breathing control for panic/agoraphobia (Meuret et al., 2001, 2004, 2006a, 2006b). ?UA. ameuret@bu.edu, ameuret@smu.edu.

Headstrong CD-ROM pain management for recurrent headache in children (Connelly et al., 2006). Being tested in a NIH R01 trial, not available for general use. mrapoff@kumc.edu.

Interactive Multimedia Program for Asthma Control and Tracking (*IMPACT*) (Krishna et al., 2003). ?UA. santoshkri2003@yahoo.com, Krishnas@slu.edu, impactasthma.missouri.edu.

Interapy for PTSD, depression and burn-out (Lange et al., 2000a, 2000b). ?UA. In Dutch. www.interapy.nl.

Interpersonal skills system for students (Campbell et al., 1995). ?UA.

Managing Anxiety (Schneider et al., 2005). ?UA. a.j.schneider@bluewin.ch.

Mandometer to train eating and recognize satiety in eating disorders. Available commercially www.mandometer.us.

Mobile computers for ecological momentary assessment of eating, feelings and behaviours (Legrange et al., 2001, 2002). ?UA. legrange@uchicago.edu.

Mobile computers for immediate on-site recording of eating-disordered behaviours (Greeno et al., 2000). ?UA.

MoodGym for depression. Free training to detect and prevent depression and anxiety. Available free at www.moodgym.anu.edu.au. Sister website www.bluepages.anu.edu.au.

Motivational Enhancement System (*MES*) tablet PC with touchscreen for perinatal drug use (Ondersma et al., 2005, 2006). ?UA.

Net assessment and personalized feedback for problem drinking (*NAPFD*) (Cunningham et al., 2000, 2005). ?UA.

NetCP for chronic headache (Devineni & Blanchard, 2004). ?UA.

Net self-help for jetlag. Available free www.mentalperformance.com.

NetBehaviour Therapy (*netBT*) *for Weight Loss* (Tate et al., 2001, 2003). ?UA. DeborahTate@brown.edu.

OCFighter netCP version of *BTSteps*. Available commercially CCBT Ltd, stuart@fearfighter.com, www.ccbt.co.uk.

OCCheck for OCD on palmtop and laptop (Baer et al., 1987, 1988). ?UA. lbaer@partners.org.

ODIN for depression. Available free at www.feelbetter.org.

Online Anxiety Prevention Project (*OAPP*) NetCP. Available free at www2.psy.uq.edu.au/~jkweb.

232 HANDS-ON HELP: COMPUTER-AIDED PSYCHOTHERAPY

Overcoming Bulimia CD-ROM. Available commercially Calipso, www.calipso. co.uk.

Overcoming Depression 1 (Bowers et al., 1993). ?UA.

Overcoming Depression on the Internet (see *ODIN*). Available free at www.feelbetter. org.

Overcoming Depression 2 CD-ROM. Available commercially Calipso, www.calipso. co.uk.

Palmtop CP for general anxiety (Newman et al., 1999). ?UA. mgn1@psu.edu.

Palmtop CP for panic and agoraphobia (Newman et al., 1996, 1997a, 1997b). ?UA. mgn1@psu.edu.

Palmtop CP for social phobia (Gruber et al., 2001; Przeworski & Newman, 2004). ?UA. btaylor@leland.stanford.edu, mgn1@psu.edu.

Palmtop CP for on-site recording of eating-disorder behaviours (Farchaus-Stein & Corte, 2003). ?UA.

Panic Online. NetCP (Klein et al., 2006). ?UA. www.med.monash.edu.au/ mentalhealth/paniconline/.

Panic Program. NetCP. Available free www.paniccenter.net.

PLATO Dilemma Counselling System PC CP (Wagman & Kerber, 1984). ?UA.

Putting the Pieces Together: see *Family Problem Solving*, shari.wade@cchmc.org.

QuitNet (QN) internet stop-smoking program. Available free www.quitnet.com.

QuitSmokingNetwork (QSN) (Feil et al., 2003). ?UA.

Screening and Brief Intervention (SBI) NetCP for hazardous drinking (Kypri et al., 2004). ?UA. kypri@tpg.com.au.

Sexpert PC self-help for sexual and relationship problems (Binik et al., 1988, 1994, 1996). Not available. binik@ego.psych.mcgill.ca.

Short text-messaging (SMS) semi-automated for bulimia aftercare (Bauer, Percevic, Okon, Meermann, & Kordy, 2003). ?UA.

Snow World VR for distraction from pain (Hoffman, 2004). ?UA. hunter@hitL. washington.edu, www.hitl.washington.edu/projects/vrpain.

SODAS CD-ROM to prevent drug and alcohol abuse in young adolescents (Schinke et al., 2004a, 2004b, 2005). ?UA. schinke@columbia.edu.

StopSmoking NetCP (Lenert et al., 2003, 2004). Available free llenert@ucsd.edu, www.stopsmokingcenter.net.

Stop-Tabac NetCP. Available free www.stop-tabac.ch/en/welcome.html.

Stresspac PC CP for managing anxiety. Available commercially www.harcourt-uk. com/.

Student Bodies NetCP eating disorders prevention program. ?UA. bml.stanford.edu/ multimedia_lab/.

Swedish netCP bibliosystems for anxiety (social, panic, generalized), depression, neck and back pain, stress, and sleep disorder). Available commercially Livanda, www.livanda.se.

Ted stop-smoking phone-IVR CP (Schneider et al., 1990). Not available.

Telephone-Linked Care-Eat (TLC-Eat). IVR CP, part of *TLC* for health promotion (diet, physical activity, cigarette smoking, alcohol use, disease screening) and chronic disease management and self-care (hypertension, CHF, CAD, DM,

APPENDIX II: AVAILABILITY OF CP SYSTEMS   233

COPD, asthma, depression, and combinations of these). (Delichatsios et al., 2001). ?UA. rfriedma@bu.edu.

Therapeutic Learning Program (TLP) PC CP (Colby, 1995; Colby and Colby, 1990). ?UA.

Totally Cool (TC) CD-ROM to prevent violence and drug abuse among urban youth (Schinke et al., 2004b). ?UA. schinke@columbia.edu.

U-Can-Poop-Too NetCP for childhood encopresis. ?UA. info@ucanpooptoo.com, www.ucanpooptoo.com.

Watch, Discover, Think and Act (WDTA) CD-ROM/PC game for asthma self-management (Bartholomew et al., 2000). ?UA. lkb@sph.uth.tmc.edu.

Worrytel PC CP for general anxiety (Parkin et al., 1995). Not available.

APPENDIX III

CP references by clinical problem

CHILDHOOD AND ADOLESCENCE PROBLEMS

Bartholomew et al. (2000); Clarke (unpublished); Clarke (unpublished); Connelly et al. (2006); Cunningham (unpublished); Glazebrook, McPherson, Forster, James, Crook, and Smyth (2004); Homer et al. (2000); Krishna et al. (2003); McPherson, Forster, Glazebrook, and Smyth (2002a); McPherson, Glazebrook, and Smyth (2002b, 2003); McPherson, Glazebrook, Forster, James, and Smyth (2006); Palermo (unpublished); Richards, Cannon, and Scott (unpublished – a,b); Ritterband et al. (2003a); Robinson et al. (unpublished); Rubin et al. (1986); Silver and Oakes (2001); Spence et al. (2006); Wade, Carey, and Wolfe (2006); Wade et al. (2005a, 2005b); Wade, Wolfe, and Pestian (2004); Yawn et al. (2000).

DEPRESSION WITH OR WITHOUT ANXIETY

Andersson et al. (2004, 2005); Bowers et al. (1993); Cavanagh et al. (2006a, 2006b); Christensen and Griffiths (2002); Christensen et al. (2002, 2004a, 2004b); Clarke et al. (2002, 2005); Colby (1995); Colby and Colby (1990); Fox, Acton, Wilding, and Corcoran (2004); Griffiths et al. (2004); Grime (2003); Grundy (2004); Hepburn (2004); Hunt, Howells, and Stapleton (2006); Jacobs et al. (2001); Kenwright et al. (2006); McCrone et al. (2004); O'Kearney et al. (2006); Osgood-Hynes et al. (1998); Proudfoot et al. (2003a); Proudfoot et al. (2003b, 2004); Ryden (2005); Selmi et al. (1990); Slack and Slack (1972, 1977); Slack et al. (1990); Talley (1987); Van den Berg et al. (2004); Wright et al. (2002, 2003, 2005).

235

236 HANDS-ON HELP: COMPUTER-AIDED PSYCHOTHERAPY

EATING DISORDERS

Abascal et al. (2003); Agras et al. (1990); Andrewes et al. (1995, 1996); Bara-Carril et al. (2004); Bauer et al. (2003); Bergh et al. (2002); Bruning-Brown et al. (2004); Burnett et al. (1985, 1992); Cash (1991); Celio et al. (2000, 2002); Davis et al. (1989); Delichatsios et al. (2001); Farchaus-Stein and Corte (2003); Greeno et al. (2000); Jacobi et al. (2005); LeGrange et al. (2001, 2002); Low et al. (2006); Luce et al. (2005); Murray et al. (2003, 2007); Norton, Wonderlich, Myers, Mitchell, and Crosby (2003); Rifas-Shiman, Willett, Lobb, Kotch, Dart, and Gillman (2001); Rimm et al. (2002); Shapiro et al. (2005); Slack et al. (1976); Tate et al. (2001, 2003); Taylor, Agras, Losch, and Plante (1991); Taylor et al. (2006); Telch and Agras (1992); Winzelberg et al. (1998, 2000); Witschi et al. (1976); Zabinski et al. (2001, 2003).

GENERAL ANXIETY/EMOTIONAL PROBLEMS

Baer and Surman (1985); Campbell et al. (1995); Colby et al. (1989); Dolezal-Wood et al. (1996); Jones et al. (2006); Kenardy et al. (2003b); Marks et al. (2003); McGarry, Jones, Cowan, and White (1998); Newman et al. (1999); Parkin et al. (1995); Stone and Kristjanson (1975); Wagman and Kerber (1984); Weizenbaum (1976); White et al. (2000); Whitfield et al. (2006); Yates (1996a, 1996b, 1996c); Zarr (1984); Zetterqvist et al. (2003).

OBSESSIVE-COMPULSIVE DISORDER

Bachofen et al. (1999); Baer et al. (1987); Baer et al. (1988); Clark et al. (1998); Greist et al. (1998, 2002); Kirkby et al. (2000); Marks et al. (1998a); McCrone et al. (2006a); Nakagawa et al. (2000).

PAIN, TINNITUS DISTRESS, INSOMNIA, JETLAG

Andersson et al. (2002, 2003); Buhrman et al. (2004); Devenini and Blanchard (2004); Hoffman (2004); Kaldo et al. (2006); Kaldo-Sandström et al. (2004); Lieberman (2003); Ström et al. (2000, 2004).

PHOBIA/PANIC DISORDER

Andersson et al. (2006); Biglan et al. (1979); Bornas et al. (2001a, 2001b, 2002, 2003, 2006); Botella, Villa, Banos, Perpina, and Garcia-Palacios (1999); Carlbring (2004); Carlbring et al. (2001, 2003, 2005, 2006a, 2006b, 2007a, 2007b); Carlin, Hoffman, and Weghorst (1997); Carr et al. (1988); Chandler et al. (1986, 1988); Choi (2005); Coldwell et al. (1998, 2007); Dewis et al. (2001); Farvolden et al. (2005); Fraser et al. (2001); Fullana and Tortella-Feliu (2001); Garcia-Palacios et al. (2001); Gega et al. (2005, 2007); Ghosh et al. (1984, 1988); Ghosh and Marks (1987); Gilroy et al. (2000, 2003); Gruber et al. (2001); Harcourt et al. (1998); Hassan (1992); Heading et al. (2001); Kenardy et al. (2003a); Kenwright et al. (2001, 2004); Kirkby et al. (1999); Klein and Richards (2001); Klein et al. (2006); Maltby, Kirsch, Mayers, and Allen (2002); Marks et al. (2004); Mataix-Cols et al. (2006); Matthews, Kirkby, and

APPENDIX III: CP REFERENCES BY CLINICAL PROBLEM   237

Martin (2002); McCrone et al. (2006a); Meuret et al. (2001, 2004, 2006a, 2006b); Mühlberger, Herrmann, Wiedemann, Ellgring, and Pauli (2002); Nelissen et al. (1995); Newman et al. (1996, 1997a, 1997b, 1999, 2003); Palmer, Bor, and Josse (2000); Przeworski and Newman (2004); Richards and Alvarenga (2002); Richards, Klein, and Carlbring (2003); Richards, Klein, and Austin (2006); Riva, Molinari, and Vincelli (2001); Rothbaum et al. (1999b, 1999c, 2000, 2002); Schneider et al. (2005); Shaw et al. (1999); Smith et al. (1997); Smith, Rothbaum, and Hodges (1999); Whitby and Allcock (1994); Wiederhold and Wiederhold (2000).

POST-TRAUMATIC STRESS DISORDER

Difede and Hoffman (2002); Hirai and Clum (2005); Jager, Emmelkamp, and Lange (2004); Lange et al. (2000a, 2000b, 2002, 2003, 2004); Lange, van den Ven, Schrieken, and Emmelkamp (2001); Ready, Rothbaum, and Hodges (2001); Rothbaum et al. (1999a, 2001).

SCHIZOPHRENIA

Bell et al. (2001); Bellucci, Glaberman, and Haslam (2002); Burda et al. (1994); Jones et al. (2001).

SEX DYSFUNCTION

Binik et al. (1988, 1989, 1994, 1996); Ochs and Binik (1998); Ochs, Meana, Mah, and Binik (1993); Ochs et al. (1994).

SMOKING AND SUBSTANCE MISUSE

Cobb et al. (2005); Cunningham et al. (2000, 2005); Etter (2005); Feil et al. (2003); Hester and Delaney (1997); Hester and Miller (2006); Hester et al. (2005); Kypri et al. (2004); Lenert et al. (2003, 2004); Miller and Munoz (1982); Ondersma et al. (2005); Ondersma et al. (2006); Schinke and Schwinn (2005); Schinke et al. (2004a, 2004b, 2005, 2006); Schneider et al. (1990, 1995a, 1995b); Squires and Hester (2002, 2004); Strecher et al. (2005); Yates (1996a, 1996b, 1996c).

REVIEWS AND GENERAL ISSUES

Bower, Richards, and Lovell (2001); Cavanagh and Shapiro (2004); Cavanagh et al. (2003); Copeland and Martin (2004); Erwin, Turk, Heimberg, Fresco, and Hantula (2004); Eysenbach (2005); Finfgeld (1999); Gerson, Anderson, Graap, Zimand, Hodges, and Rothbaum (2002); Goss and Anthony (2003); Kaltenthaler et al. (2002); Kenardy and Adams (1993); Kirkby and Lambert (1996); Maheu et al. (2004); Marks (1999); Marks et al. (1998a, 1998b); Murray et al. (2005); Newman (2004); NICE (2002, 2006); Oakley-Browne and Toole (1994); Proudfoot (2004); Przeworski and Newman (2004); Ritterband et al. (2003a); Shapiro et al. (2003); Slack (2000); Tate and Zabinski (2004); Whitfield and Williams (2004); Wooton et al. (2003); Wright (2004); Wright and Katz (2004).

References

Abascal, L.B., Bruning-Brown, J., Winzelberg, A.J., Dev, P., and Taylor, C.B. (2003). Combining universal and targeted prevention for school-based eating disorder programs. *International Journal of Eating Disorders, 35*, 1–9.

Agras, W.S., Taylor, C.B., Feldman, D.E., Losch, M., and Burnett, K.F. (1990). Developing computer assisted therapy for the treatment of obesity. *Behavior Therapy, 21*, 99–109.

Andersson, G., Bergstrom, J., Hollandare, F., Carlbring, P., Kaldo, V., and Ekselius, L. (2005). Internet-based self-help for depression: RCT. *British Journal of Psychiatry, 187*, 456–461.

Andersson, G., Bergstrom, J., Hollandare, F., Ekselius, L., and Carlbring, P. (2004). Delivering CBT for mild to moderate depression via the internet: Predicting outcome at 6-month follow-up. *Verhaltenstherapie, 14*, 185–189.

Andersson, G., Carlbring, P., Holmström, A., Sparthan, E., Furmark, T., Nilsson-Ihrfelt, E., et al. (2006). Internet-based self-help with therapist feedback and in-vivo group exposure for social phobia: a RCT. *Journal of Consulting and Clinical Psychology, 74*, 677–686.

Andersson, G., Lundstrom, P., and Ström, L. (2003). Internet-based treatment of headache: Does telephone contact add anything? *Headache, 43*, 353–361.

Andersson, G., Stromgren, T., Ström, L., and Lyttkens, L. (2002). RCT of internet-based CBT for distress associated with tinnitus. *Psychosomatic Medicine, 64*, 810–816.

Andrewes, D.G., Sat, S., and McLennan, J. (1995). A self administered computer based educational program about eating-disorder risk factors. *Australian Psychologist, 30*, 210–212.

Andrewes, D.G., O'Connor, P., Mulder, C., McLennan, J., Derham, H., Weigall, S., et al. (1996). Computerised psychoeducation for patients with eating disorders. *Australia and New Zealand Journal of Psychiatry, 30*, 492–497.

Bachofen, M., Nakagawa, A., Marks, I.M., Park, J.M., Greist, J.H., Baer, L., et al. (1999). Home self-assessment and self-treatment of OCD using a manual and a computer-conducted telephone interview: Replication of a US–UK study. *Journal of Clinical Psychiatry, 60*, 8, 545–549.

240 REFERENCES

Baer, L., Minichiello, W.E., and Jenike, M.A. (1987). Use of a portable-computer program in behavioral treatment of OCD. *American Journal of Psychiatry*, *144*, 1101.

Baer, L., Minichiello, W.E., Jenike, M.A., and Holland, A. (1988). Use of a portable-computer program to assist behavioral treatment in a case of OCD. *Journal of Behaviour Therapy and Experimental Psychiatry*, *19*, 237–240.

Baer, L. and Surman, O.S. (1985). Microcomputer-assisted relaxation. *Perceptual & Motor Skills*, *61*, 499–522.

Bara-Carril, N., Williams, C., Pombo-Carril, M.G., Reid, Y., Murray, K., Aubin, S., et al. (2004). A preliminary investigation into the feasibility and efficacy of a CD-ROM-based cognitive-behavioral self-help intervention for bulimia nervosa. *International Journal of Eating Disorders*, *35*, 538–548.

Barlow, D.H. and Craske, M.G. (2000). *Mastery of Your Anxiety and Panic (Map-3): Client Workbook for Anxiety and Panic* (3rd ed). New York: Oxford University Press.

Barlow, D.H., Gorman, J.M., Shear, M.K., and Woods, S.W. (2000). Cognitive-behavioral therapy, imipramine, or their combination for panic disorder: A randomized controlled trial. *Journal of the American Medical Association*, *283*, 2529–2536.

Bartholomew, L.K., Gold, R.S., Parcel, G.S., Czyzewski, D.I., Sockrider, M.I., Fernandez, M., et al. (2000). *Watch, Discover, Think, and Act*: Evaluation of computer-assisted instruction to improve asthma self-management in inner-city children. *Patient Education and Counseling*, *39*, 269–280.

Bauer, S., Percevic, R., Okon, E., Meermann, R., and Kordy, H. (2003). Use of text messaging in the aftercare of patients with bulimia nervosa. *European Eating Disorders Review*, *11*, 279–290.

Bell, M., Bryson, G., Greig, T., Cocoran, C., and Wexler, B.E. (2001). Neurocognitive enhancement therapy with work therapy. *Archives of General Psychiatry*, *58*, 763–768.

Bellucci, D.M., Glaberman, K., and Haslam, N. (2002). Computer assisted cognitive rehabilitation reduces negative symptoms in the severely mentally ill. *Schizophrenia Research*, *59*, 225–232.

Bergh, C., Brodin, U., Lindberg, G., and Södersten, P. (2002). RCT of a treatment for anorexia and bulimia nervosa. *Proceedings of the National Academy of Sciences*, *14*, 9486–9491.

Biglan, A., Vilwock, C., and Wick, S. (1979). Computer controlled program for treatment of test anxiety. *Journal of Behavioural Therapy and Experimental Psychiatry*, *10*, 47–49.

Binik, Y.M., Meana, M., and Sand, N. (1994). Interaction with a sex-expert system changes attitudes and may modify sexual behaviour. *Computers in Human Behavior*, *10*, 395–410.

Binik, Y.M., Ochs, E.P., and Meana, M. (1996). Sexpert: An expert system for sexual assessment, counseling and treatment. In M.J. Miller, K.W. Hammond, and G. Hile (Eds.), *Mental Health Computing*. New York: Springer.

Binik, Y.M., Servan-Schreiber, D., Freiwald, S., and Hall, K. (1988). Intelligent computer-based assessment and psychotherapy: An expert system for sexual dysfunction. *Journal of Nervous and Mental Disease*, *176*, 387–400.

Binik, Y.M., Westbury, C.F., and Servan-Schreiber, D. (1989). Interaction with a 'sex-expert' system enhances attitudes towards computerized sex therapy. *Behaviour Research and Therapy*, *27*, 302–306.

Bornas, X., Fullana, M.A., Tortella-Feliu, M., Llabrés, J., and de la Banda, G.G. (2001a). Computer-assisted therapy in the treatment of flight phobia: Case report. *Cognitive & Behavioral Practice*, *8*, 234–240.

Bornas, X., Tortella-Feliu, M., and Llabrés, J. (2003). Computer-assisted therapy for fear of flying. In A.R. Bor and L. van Gerwen (Eds.), *Psychological perspectives on the fear of flying* (pp. 199–210). Aldershot: Ashgate.

Bornas, X., Tortella-Feliu, M., and Llabrés, J. (2006). Do all treatments work for flight

REFERENCES 241

phobia? Computer-assisted exposure vs a brief multi-component non-exposure treatment. *Psychotherapy Research, 16*, 41–50.

Bornas, X., Tortella-Feliu, M., Llabrés, J., and Fullana, M.A. (2001b). Computer-assisted exposure treatment for flight phobia: Controlled study. *Psychotherapy Research, 11*, 259–273.

Bornas, X., Tortella-Feliu, M., Llabrés, J., Mühlberger, A., Pauli, P., and Barcelo, F. (2002). Clinical usefulness of a simulated exposure treatment for fear of flying. *International Journal of Clinical & Health Psychology, 2*, 247–252.

Botella, C., Villa, H., Banos, R., Perpina, C., and Garcia-Palacios, A. (1999). Treatment of claustrophobia with VR: Changes in other phobic behaviors not specifically treated. *CyberPsychology & Behavior, 2*, 135–141.

Bower, P., Richards, D., and Lovell, K. (2001). Clinical and cost-effectiveness of self-help treatments for anxiety and depression in primary care: A systematic review. *British Journal of General Practice, 51*, 838–845.

Bowers, W., Stuart, S., and McFarlane, R. (1993). Use of computer-administered cognitive-behaviour therapy with depressed patients. *Depression, 1*, 294–299.

Bruning-Brown, J., Winzelberg, A.J., Abascal, L.B., and Taylor, C.B. (2004). An evaluation of an internet-delivered eating disorder prevention program for adolescents and their parents. *Journal of Adolescent Health, 35*, 290–296.

Buhrman, M., Faltenhag, S., Ström, L., and Andersson, G. (2004). Controlled trial of internet-based treatment with telephone support for chronic back pain. *Pain, 111*, 368–377.

Bulik, C.M. (1997). *Cognitive-behavioural modules for successful weight control.* In unpublished manual. Eating Disorders, MCV Hospitals at Virginia Commonwealth University.

Burda, P.C., Starkey, T.W., Dominguez, F., and Vera, V. (1994). Computer-assisted cognitive rehabilitation of chronic psychiatric inpatients. *Computers in Human Behavior, 10*, 359–368.

Burgess, M., Gill, M., and Marks, I.M. (1998). Postal self-exposure treatment of recurrent nightmares: Randomised controlled trial. *British Journal of Psychiatry, 172*, 257–262.

Burnett, K.F., Taylor, C.B., and Agras, W.S. (1985). Ambulatory computer-assisted therapy for obesity: A new frontier for behavior therapy. *Journal of Consulting and Clinical Psychology, 53*, 698–703.

Burnett, K.F., Taylor, C.B., and Agras, W.S. (1992). Ambulatory computer-assisted behavior therapy for obesity: An empirical model for examining behavioral correlates of treatment outcome. *Computers in Human Behavior, 8*, 239–248.

Campbell, J.O., Lison, C.A., Borsook, T.K., Hoover, J.A., and Arnold, P.H. (1995). Using computer and video technologies to develop interpersonal skills. *Computers in Human Behavior, 11*, 223–239.

Carlbring, P. (2004). *Panic! Its prevalence, diagnosis and treatment via the internet.* PhD thesis. http://urn.kb.se/resolve?urn=urn:nbn:se:uu:diva-4148 (2004-06-02).

Carlbring, P., Bjornstjerna, E., Bergstrom, A.F., Waara, J., and Andersson, G. (2007a). Applied relaxation: Experimental analogue study of therapist vs computer administration. *Computers in Human Behavior, 23*, 2–10.

Carlbring, P., Bohman, S., Brunt, S., Buhrman, M., Westling, B.E., Ekselius, L., et al. (2006a). Remote treatment of panic disorder: A randomized trial of internet-based CBT supplemented with telephone calls. *American Journal of Psychiatry, 163*, 2119–2125.

Carlbring, P., Ekselius, L., and Andersson, G. (2003). Treatment of panic disorder via the internet: A randomized trial of CBT vs applied relaxation. *Journal of Behaviour Therapy and Experimental Psychiatry, 34*, 129–140.

Carlbring, P., Furmark, T., Steczkó, J., Ekselius, L., and Andersson, G. (2006b). An open study of Internet-based bibliotherapy with minimal therapist contact via e-mail for social phobia. *Clinical Psychologist, 10*, 30–38.

Carlbring, P., Gunnarsdóttir, M., Hedensjö, L., Andersson, G., Ekselius, L., and Furmark, T.

242 REFERENCES

(2007b). Treatment of social phobia from a distance: A randomized trial of internet delivered CBT and telephone support. *British Journal of Psychiatry*. In press.

Carlbring, P., Nilsson-Ihrfelt, E., Waara, J., Kollenstam, C., Buhrman, M., Kaldo, V., et al. (2005). Treatment of panic disorder: Live therapy vs self-help via internet. *Behaviour Research and Therapy*, *43*, 1321–1333.

Carlbring, P., Westling, B.E., Ljungstrand, P., Ekselius, L., and Andersson, G. (2001). Treatment of panic disorder via the internet: Randomized trial of a self-help program. *Behavior Therapy*, *32*, 751–764.

Carlin, A.S., Hoffman, H.G., and Weghorst, S. (1997). VR and tactile augmentation in the treatment of spider phobia: case report. *Behaviour Research and Therapy*, *35*, 153–158.

Carr, A.C., Ghosh, A., and Marks, I.M. (1988). Computer supervised exposure treatment for phobias. *Canadian Journal of Psychiatry*, *33*, 112–117.

Cash, T.F. (1991). *Body-image therapy: A program for self-directed change*. New York: Guilford Press.

Cavanagh, K. and Shapiro, D.A. (2004). Computer treatment for common mental health problems. *Journal of Clinical Psychology*, *60*, 239–251.

Cavanagh, K., Shapiro, D.A., Van den Berg, S., Swain, S., Barkham, M., and Proudfoot, J.G. (2006a). Effectiveness of CCBT in routine primary care. *British Journal of Clinical Psychology*, *45*, 499–514.

Cavanagh, K., Shapiro, D.A., Van den Berg, S., Swain, S., Barkham, M., and Proudfoot, J.G. (2006b). *Computerised CBT in routine primary care: Acceptability and satisfaction*. Manuscript submitted for publication.

Cavanagh, K., Zack, J.S., Shapiro, D.A., and Wright, J.H. (2003). Computer programs for psychotherapy: The computer plays therapist. In S. Goss and K. Anthony (Eds.), *Technology in counselling and psychotherapy: A practitioner's guide* (pp. 141–164, 165–194). Basingstoke: Palgrave Macmillan.

Celio, A.A., Winzelberg, A.J., Dev, P., and Taylor, C.B. (2002). Improving compliance in on-line, structured self-help programs: Evaluation of an eating disorder prevention program. *Journal of Psychiatric Practice*, *8*, 14–20.

Celio, A.A., Winzelberg, A.J., Wilfley, D.E., Eppstein-Herald, D., Springer, E., Dev, P., et al. (2000). Reducing risk factors for eating disorders: Comparison of an internet and a classroom delivered psychoeducational program. *Journal of Consulting and Clinical Psychology*, *68*, 650–657.

Chandler, G.M., Burck, H.D., and Sampson, J. (1986). Generic computer program for systematic desensitization: Description, construction and case study. *Journal of Behavior Therapy and Experimental Psychiatry*, *17*, 171–174.

Chandler, G.M., Burck, H.D., Sampson, J., and Wray, R. (1988). Effectiveness of a generic computer program for systematic desensitization. *Computers in Human Behaviour*, *4*, 339–346.

Choi, Y.H. (2005, July). *Development and effects of experiential cognitive therapy for the treatment of panic disorder with agoraphobia*. Paper presented to the World Congresss of Behavior and Cognitive Therapy, Kobe, Japan.

Christensen, H. and Griffiths, K.M. (2002). Prevention of depression using the internet. *Medical Journal of Australia*, *177*, S122–S125.

Christensen, H., Griffiths, K.M., and Jorm, A.F. (2004a). Delivering interventions for depression by using the internet: Randomised controlled trial. *British Medical Journal*, *328*, 265–269.

Christensen, H., Griffiths, K.M., and Korten, A. (2002). Web-based CBT: Analysis of site usage and changes in depression and anxiety scores. *Journal of Medical Internet Research*, *4*, 3.

REFERENCES 243

Christensen, H., Griffiths, K.M., Korten, A., Brittliffe, K., and Groves, C. (2004b). Comparison of changes in anxiety and depression symptoms of spontaneous users and trial participants of a CBT website. *Journal of Medical Internet Research*, 6, 46.

Claassen, C.A. and Larkin, G.L. (2005). Occult suicidality in an emergency department population. *British Journal of Psychiatry*, 186, 352–353.

Clark, A., Kirkby, K.C., Daniels, B.A., and Marks, I.M. (1998). A pilot study of computer-aided vicarious exposure for OCD. *Australian & New Zealand Journal of Psychiatry*, 32, 268–275.

Clarke, G., Eubanks, D., Reid, E., Kelleher, C., O'Connor, E., DeBar, L.L., et al. (2005). Overcoming depression on the internet (ODIN) (2): A randomized trial of a self-help depression skills program with reminders. *Journal of Medical Internet Research*, 7(2), e16.

Clarke, G., Reid, E., Eubanks, D., O'Connor, E., DeBar, L.L., Kelleher, C., et al. (2002). Overcoming depression on the internet (ODIN): RCT of an internet depression skills intervention program. *Journal of Medical Internet Research*, 4, 14.

Clarke, G. (unpublished – a). *MoodHelper*. Kaiser-Permanente, USA.

Clarke, G. (unpublished – b). *ParentHelper*. Kaiser-Permanente, USA.

Cobb, N., Graham, A.L., Bock, B.C., Papandonatos, G., and Abrams, D.B. (2005). Initial evaluation of a real-world internet smoking cessation system. *Nicotine and Tobacco Research*, 7, 207–216.

Colby, K.M. (1995). Computer program using cognitive therapy to treat depressed patients. *Psychiatric Services*, 46, 1223–1225.

Colby, K.M. and Colby, P.M. (1990). *Overcoming depression*. Malibu: Malibu Artificial Intelligence Works.

Colby, K.M., Gould, R.L., and Aronson, G. (1989). Some pros and cons of computer-assisted psychotherapy. *Journal of Nervous and Mental Disease*, 177, 105–108.

Coldwell, S.E., Getz, T., Milgrom, P., Prall, C.W., Spadafora, A., and Ramsay, D.S. (1998). CARL: A LabVIEW 3 computer program for conducting exposure therapy for the treatment of dental injection fear. *Behaviour Research and Therapy*, 36, 429–441.

Coldwell, S.E., Wilhelm, F.H., Milgrom, P., Prall, C.W., Getz, T., Spadafora, A., et al. (2007). Combining alprazolam with systematic desensitization therapy for dental injection fear. *Journal of Anxiety Disorders*. In press.

Connelly, M., Rapoff, M.A., Thompson, N., and Connelly, W. (2006). *Headstrong*: A pilot study of a cd-rom intervention for recurrent pediatric headache. *Journal of Pediatric Psychology*, 31, 737–747.

Copeland, J. and Martin, G. (2004). Web-based interventions for substance abuse disorder: Qualitative review. *Journal of Substance Abuse Treatment*, 26, 109–116.

Craighead, W.E. and Nemeroff, C.B. (1994). *Concise Corsini Encyclopedia of Psychology and Behavioural Sciences*. Chichester: Wiley.

Cunningham, J.A., Humphreys, K., and Koski-James, A. (2000). Providing personalised assessment feedback for problem drinking on the internet: Pilot project. *Journal of Studies on Alcohol*, 61, 794–798.

Cunningham, J.A., Humphreys, K., Koski-James, A., and Cordingley, J. (2005). Internet and paper self-help materials for problem drinking: Is there an additive effect? *Addictive Behaviors*, 30, 1517–1523.

Cunningham M. et al. (unpublished). *Cool teens*. University of Macquarie, Australia.

Davis, R., Dearing, S., Faulkner, J., Jasper, K., Olmsted, M., Rice, C., et al. (1989). *The road to recovery: A manual for participants in the psychoeducation group for bulimia nervosa*. Toronto: The Toronto Hospital, Toronto General Division.

Delichatsios, H.K., Friedman, R.H., Glanz, K., Tennstedt, S., Smigelski, C., Pinto, B.M., et al. (2001). Randomized trial of a 'talking computer' to improve adults' eating habit. *American Journal of Health Promotion*, 15, 215–224.

244 REFERENCES

Devineni, T. and Blanchard, E.B. (2004). RCT of an internet-based treatment for chronic headache. *Behaviour Research and Therapy*, *43*, 277–293.

Dewis, L.M., Kirkby, K.C., Martin, F., Daniels, B.A., Gilroy, L.G., and Menzies, R.G. (2001). Computer-aided vicarious exposure versus live graded exposure for spider phobia in children. *Journal of Behaviour Therapy and Experimental Psychiatry*, *32*, 17–27.

Difede, J. and Hoffman, H.G. (2002). VR exposure therapy for World Trade Center post-traumatic stress disorder: Case report. *Cyberpsychology & Behavior*, *5*(6), 529–535.

Dolezal-Wood, S., Belar, C.D., Snibbe, J.R. (1996). Comparison of computer-assisted psychotherapy and CBT in groups. *Journal of Clinical Psychology in Medical Settings*, *5*, 103–115.

Elkin, I., Shea, M.T., Watkins, J.T., Imber, S.M., Sotsky, J.F., Collins, D.R., et al. (1989). Treatment of depression collaborative research program: General effectiveness of treatments. *Archives of General Psychiatry*, *46*, 971–982.

Erwin, B.A., Turk, C.L., Heimberg, R.G., Fresco, D.M., and Hantula, D.A. (2004). The internet: Home to a severe population of individuals with social anxiety disorder. *Anxiety Disorders*, *62*, 629–646.

Etter, J.F. (2005). Comparing the efficacy of two internet-based computer-tailored smoking cessation programs: Randomised trial. *Journal of Medical Internet Research*, *7*, 6.

Eysenbach, G. (2005). The law of attrition. *Journal of Medical Internet Research*, *7*, 11.

Farchaus-Stein, K. and Corte, C.M. (2003). Ecological momentary assessment of eating-disordered behaviours. *International Journal of Eating Disorders*, *34*, 349–360.

Farvolden, P., Denissof, E., Selby, P., Bagby, R.M., and Rudy, L. (2005). Usage and longitudinal effectiveness of a web-based self-help CBT behavioural therapy program for panic disorder. *Journal of Medical Internet Research*, *7*, 7.

Feil, E.G., Noell, J., Lichtenstein, E., Boles, S.M., and McKay, H.G. (2003). Evaluation of an internet-based smoking cessation program: Lessons learned from a pilot study. *Nicotine and Tobacco Research*, *5*, 189–194.

Finfgeld, D.L. (1999). Computer-assisted therapy: Harbinger of the 21st century? *Archives of Psychiatric Nursing*, *13*, 303–310.

Fox, E., Acton, T., Wilding, B., and Corcoran, S. (2004). Service development report: An assistant psychologist's persective on the use of computerised CBT in a GP practice in Barnet. *Quality in Primary Care*, *12*, 161–165.

Fraser, J., Kirkby, K.C., Daniels, B.A., Gilroy, L.G., and Montgomery, I.M. (2001). Three versus six sessions of computer-aided vicarious exposure treatment for spider phobia. *Behaviour Change*, *18*, 213–224.

Fullana, M.A. and Tortella-Feliu, M. (2001). Predictores de resultado terapéutico en el miedo a volar en avión. [Therapeutic outcome predictors in flight phobia]. *Psicothema*, *13*, 617–621.

Garcia-Palacios, A., Hoffman, H.G., Kwong-See, S., et al. (2001). Redefining therapeutic success with VR exposure therapy. *CyberPsychology and Behavior*, *4*, 341–348.

Gega, L., Kenwright, M., Mataix-Cols, D., Cameron, R., and Marks, I.M. (2005). Screening people with anxiety/depression for suitability for guided self-help. *Cognitive Behaviour Therapy*, *34*, 16–21.

Gega, L., Marks, I.M., and Mataix-Cols, D. (2004). Computer-aided CBT self-help for anxiety and depressive disorders: Experience of a London clinic and future directions. *Journal of Clinical Psychology/In Session*, *60*, 1–11.

Gega, L., Norman, I.J., and Marks, I.M. (2007). Computer-aided vs tutor-delivered teaching of exposure therapy for phobia/panic: RCT with pre-registration nursing students. *International Journal of Nursing Studies*, *44*, doi:10.1016/j.ijnurstu.2006.02.009

Gerson, J., Anderson, P.L., Graap, K., Zimand, E., Hodges, L.F., and Rothbaum, B.O. (2002). VR exposure therapy in the treatment of anxiety disorders. *Scientific Review of Mental Health*, *1*(1), 78–83.

REFERENCES 245

Ghosh, A. and Marks, I.M. (1987). Self-treatment of agoraphobia by exposure. *Behavior Therapy, 18*, 3–16.

Ghosh, A., Marks, I.M., and Carr, A.C. (1984). Controlled study of self-exposure treatment for phobics: Preliminary communication. *Journal of the Royal Society of Medicine, 77*, 483–487.

Ghosh, A., Marks, I.M., and Carr, A. (1988). Therapist contact and outcome of self-exposure treatment for phobias. *British Journal of Psychiatry, 152*, 234–238.

Gilroy, L.G., Kirkby, K.C., Daniels, B.A., Menzies, R.G., and Montgomery, I.M. (2000). Controlled comparison of computer-aided vicarious exposure versus live exposure in the treatment of spider phobia. *Behavior Therapy, 31*, 733–744.

Gilroy, L.G., Kirkby, K.C., Daniels, B.A., Menzies, R.G., and Montgomery, I.M. (2003). Long-term follow-up of computer-aided vicarious exposure versus live graded exposure in the treatment of spider phobia. *Behavior Therapy, 34*, 65–76.

Glazebrook, C., McPherson, A., Forster, D., James, C., Crook, I., and Smyth, A. (2004). The Asthma Files: Randomised controlled trial of interactive multimedia program to promote self-management skills in children. *Respiratory and Critical Care Medicine, 169*, A877.

Gortner, E.T., Gollan, J.K., Dobson, K.S., and Jacobson, N.S. (1998). CBT for depression: Relapse prevention. *Journal of Consulting and Clinical Psychology, 66*, 377–384.

Goss, S. and Anthony, K. (Eds.). (2003). *Technology in counselling and psychotherapy: A practitioner's guide*. Basingstoke: Palgrave Macmillan.

Greeno, C.G., Wing, R.R., and Shiffman, S. (2000). Binge antecedents in obese women with and without binge eating disorder. *Journal of Consulting and Clinical Psychology, 68*, 95–102.

Greist, J.H., Marks, I.M., Baer, L., Parkin, R., Manzo, P., Mantle, J., et al. (1998). Self-treatment for OCD using a manual and a computerized telephone interview: A US–UK Study. *MD Computing, 15*, 149–157.

Greist, J.H., Gustafson, D.H., Stauss, F.F., Rowse, G.L., Laughren, T.P., and Chiles, J.A. (1973). Computer interview for suicide-risk prediction. *American Journal of Psychiatry, 130*, 1327–1332.

Greist, J.H., Marks, I.M., Baer, L., Kobak, K.A., Wenzel, K.W., Hirsch, M.J., et al. (2002). Behaviour therapy for obsessive compulsive disorder guided by a computer or by a clinician compared with relaxation as a control. *Journal of Clinical Psychiatry, 63*, 138–145.

Griffiths, K.M., Christensen, H., Jorm, A.F., Evans, K., and Groves, C. (2004). Effect of web-based depression literacy and CBT interventions on stigmatising attitudes to depression. *British Journal of Psychiatry, 185*, 342–349.

Grime, P. (2003). Computerised CBT at work: A randomized controlled trial in employees with recent stress-related absenteeism. *Occupational Medicine, 53*, 538.

Gruber, K., Moran, P., Roth, W.T., and Taylor, C.B. (2001). Computer-assisted CBT for social phobia. *Behavior Therapy, 32*, 155–165.

Grundy, L. (2004). *Beating the Blues: Clinical psychology service evaluation*. Unpublished manuscript.

Haaga, D.A.F. (2000). Introduction to special section on stepped care models in psychotherapy. *Journal of Consulting and Clinical Psychology, 68*, 547–548.

Haddock, C.K., Rowan, A.B., Andrasik, F., Wilson, P.G., Talcott, G.W., and Stein, R.J. (1997). Home-based behavioral treatments for chronic benign headache: A meta-analysis of controlled trials. *Cephalalgia, 17*, 113–118.

Harcourt, L., Kirkby, K.C., Daniels, B.A., and Montgomery, I.M. (1998). Differential effect of personality on computer-based treatment of agoraphobia. *Comprehensive Psychiatry, 39*, 303–307.

Hassan, A.A.M. (1992). *Comparison of computer-based symbolic modelling and conventional methods in treatment of spider phobia*. PhD dissertation, University of Leeds, England.

246 REFERENCES

Hayward, L., MacGregor, A.D., Peck, D.F., and Wilkes, P. (2007). Feasibility and effectiveness of computer-guided CBT (*FearFighter*) in a rural area. *Behavioural and Cognitive Psychotherapy*. In press.

Heading, K., Kirkby, K.C., Martin, F., Daniels, B.A., and Gilroy, L.G. (2001). Controlled comparison of single-session treatments for spider phobia: Live graded exposure alone versus computer-aided vicarious exposure. *Behaviour Change*, *18*, 103–113.

Hepburn, E. (2004). *Effect of taking part in a computerised CBT package, while on the waiting list of a clinical psychology service, on length and outcome of subsequent individual treatment*. Unpublished manuscript, University of Glasgow.

Hester, R.K. and Delaney, H.D. (1997). Behavioral self-control program for windows: Results of a controlled clinical trial. *Journal of Consulting and Clinical Psychology*, *65*, 686–693.

Hester, R.K. and Miller, J.H. (2006). Computer-based interventions for diagnosis and treatment of alcohol problems. *Alcohol Research and Health*, *29*, 36–40.

Hester, R.K., Squires, D.D., and Delaney, H.D. (2005). The computer-based Drinker's Check-Up: 12-month outcomes of a controlled clinical trial with problem drinkers. *Journal of Substance Abuse Treatment*, *28*, 159–169.

Hirai, M. and Clum, G.A. (2005). Internet-based self-change program for traumatic event related fear, distress and maladaptive coping. *Journal of Traumatic Stress*, *18*, 631–636.

Hodge, J.G., Gostin, L.O., and Jacobson, P.D. (1999). Legal issues concerning electronic health information: Privacy, quality and liability. *Journal of the American Medical Association*, *282*, 1466–1471.

Hoffman, H.R. (2004). Virtual reality. *Scientific American*, August, 58–65.

Homer, C., Susskind, O., Alpert, H.R., Owusu, C., Schneider, L., Rappaport, L.A., et al. (2000). An evaluation of an innovative multimedia educational software program for asthma management: Report of a randomized, controlled trial. *Pediatrics*, *106*, 210–215.

Hunt, S., Howells, E., and Stapleton, B. (2006). The addition of computerised CBT program, to a stepped care, primary care mental health service. *Journal of Primary Care Mental Health*, *9*, 34–38.

Jacobi, C., Morris, L., Bronisch-Holtze, J., Winter, J., Winzelberg, A.J., and Taylor, C.B. (2005). Reduktion von Risikofaktoren für gestörtes Essverhalten: Adaptation und erste Ergebnisse eines Internet-gestützten Präventionsprogramms. *Zeitschrift für Gesundheitspsychologie*, *13*, 92–101.

Jacobs, M.K., Christensen, A., Snibbe, J.R., Dolezal-Wood, S., Huber, A., and Polterok, A. (2001). A comparison of computer-based versus traditional individual psychotherapy. *Professional Psychology*, *32*, 92–96.

Jacobson, N.S., Dobson, K.S., Truax, P.A., Addis, M.E., Koerner, K., Gollan, J.K., et al. (1996). Component analysis of CBT for depression. *Journal of Consulting and Clinical Psychology*, *64*, 295–304.

Jager, J., Emmelkamp, P.M.G., and Lange, A. (2004). Agoraphobia – internet treatment: Case study. *Verhaltenstherapie*, *14*, 200–205.

Jones, R.B., White, J., Kamarzaman, Z., Naven, L., Morton, A.R., Mariott, C., et al. (2006). *Cognitive behavioural computer therapy for anxiety in primary care: Difficulties in carrying out a randomised trial and lessons learned*. Manuscript submitted for publication.

Jones, R.B., Atkinson, M., Coia, A., Paterson, L., Morton, A.R., McKenna, K., et al. (2001). Randomised trial of personalised computer based information for patients with schizophrenia. *British Medical Journal*, *322*, 835–840.

Kaldo, V., Levin, S., Widarsson, J., Buhrman, M., Larsen, H.C., and Andersson, G. (2006). *Internet versus group CBT of distress associated with tinnitus. A RCT*. Manuscript submitted for publication.

Kaldo-Sandström, V., Larsen, H.C., and Andersson, G. (2004). Internet-based cognitive-

REFERENCES 247

behavioral self-help treatment of tinnitus: Clinical effectiveness and predictors of outcome. *American Journal of Audiology*, *13*, 185–192.

Kaltenthaler, E., Shackley, K., Beverley, C., Parry, G., and Chilcott, J. (2002). *Computerised cognitive behaviour therapy for depression and anxiety: Final assessment report*. London: NICE. http://www.nice.org.uk/pdf/ccbtassessmentreport.pdf.

Kaltenthaler, E. et al. (2005). Retrieved November 1, 2006, from http://www.nice.org.uk/page=aspx?o=247657.

Kenardy, J.A. and Adams, C. (1993). Computers in CBT. *Australian Psychologist*, *28*, 189–194.

Kenardy, J.A., Dow, M.G.T., Johnston, D.W., Newman, M.G., Thompson, A., and Taylor, C.B. (2003a). A comparison of delivery methods of cognitive behavioural therapy for panic disorder: An international multi-centre trial. *Journal of Consulting and Clinical Psychology*, *71*, 1068–1075.

Kenardy, J.A., McCafferty, K., and Rosa, V. (2003b). Internet-delivered indicated prevention for anxiety disorders: A RCT. *Behavioural & Cognitive Psychotherapy*, *31*, 279–289.

Kenwright, M. et al. (2006). *Preference trial in a CBT specialist service: Beating the Blues versus bibiotherapy*. Manuscript submitted for publication.

Kenwright, M., Gega, L., Mataix-Cols, D., and Marks, I.M. (2004). Computer-aided self-help for phobia/panic via home internet or standalone computer at a clinic: Pilot study. *British Journal of Psychiatry*, *184*, 448–449.

Kenwright, M., Liness, S., and Marks, I.M. (2001). Reducing demands on clinicians by offering computer-guided self-help for phobia-panic: Feasibility study. *British Journal of Psychiatry*, *11*, 456–459.

Kenwright, M., Marks, I.M., Graham, C., Franses, A., and Mataix-Cols, D. (2005). Brief scheduled phone support from a clinician to enhance computer-aided self-help for OCD: RCT. *Journal of Clinical Psychology*, *61*, 1499–1508.

Khan, K.S., ter Riet, G., Glanville, J., Sowden, A.J., and Kleijnen, J. (2001). *Undertaking Systematic Reviews of Research on Effectiveness: CRD's Guidance for those Carrying out or Commissioning Reviews* (2nd ed). CRD Report no. 4. York: NHS Centre for Reviews and Dissemination, University of York, UK.

Killen, J.D., Hayward, C., Wilson, D.M. Taylor, C.B., Hammer, L.D., Litt, I., et al. (1994). Factors associated with eating disorder symptoms in a community sample of 11- and 12-year-old girls. *International Journal of Eating Disorders*, *15*(4), 357–367.

Kirkby, K.C. and Lambert, T.J. (1996). Computer aids to treatment in psychiatry. *Australia and New Zealand Journal of Psychiatry*, *30*, 142–145.

Kirkby, K.C., Berrios, G.E., Daniels, B.A., Menzies, R.G., Clark, A., and Romano, A.J. (2000). Process-outcome analysis in computer-aided treatment of OCD. *Comprehensive Psychiatry*, *41*, 259–265.

Kirkby, K.C., Daniels, B.A., Harcourt, L., and Romano, A.J. (1999). Behavioral analysis of computer-administered vicarious exposure in agoraphobia subjects: Effect of personality on in-session treatment process. *Comprehensive Psychiatry*, *40*, 386–390.

Klein, B. and Richards, J.C. (2001). A brief internet-based treatment for panic disorder. *Behavioural and Cognitive Psychotherapy*, *29*, 131–136.

Klein, B., Richards, J.C., and Austin, D.W. (2006). Efficacy of internet therapy for panic disorder. *Behavior Therapy & Experimental Psychiatry*, *37*, 213–238.

Krishna, S., Francisco, B.D., Bala, A., Konig, P., Graff, G.R., and Masden, R.W. (2003). Internet-enabled interactive multimedia asthma education program: Randomized trial. *Pediatrics*, *111*, 503–510.

Kypri, K. and McAnally, H. (2005). Randomized control trial of a web-based primary care intervention for multiple health risk behaviours. *Preventive Medicine*, *41*, 761–766.

Kypri, K., Saunders, J.B., Williams, S.M., McGee, R.O., Langley, J.D., Cashnell-Smith, M.L.,

248 REFERENCES

et al. (2004). Web-based screening and brief intervention for hazardous drinking: A double-blind randomized controlled trial. *Addiction, 99*, 1410–1417.

Lange, A., Schrieken, B.A.L., van den Ven, J.-P., Bredeweg, B., Emmelkamp, P.M.G., van der Kolk, J., et al. (2000a). 'Interapy': The effects of a short protocolled treatment of post-traumatic stress and pathological grief through the internet. *Behavioural and Cognitive Psychotherapy, 28*, 175–192.

Lange, A., van den Ven, J.-P., Schrieken, B.A.L., Bredeweg, B., and Emmelkamp, P.M.G. (2000b). Internet-mediated, protocol-driven treatment of psychological dysfunction. *Journal of Telemedicine and Telecare, 6*, 15–21.

Lange, A., van den Ven, J.-P., Schrieken, B.A.L., and Emmelkamp, P.M.G. (2001). Interapy: Treatment of posttraumatic stress through the internet: Controlled trial. *Journal of Behaviour Therapy and Experimental Psychiatry, 32*, 72–90.

Lange, A., Schoutrop, M., Schrieken, B.A.L., and van den Ven, J.-P. (2002). Interapy: A model for therapeutic writing through the internet. In S.J. Lepore and J.M. Smyth (Eds), *The writing cure: How expressive writing promotes health and emotional well being.* Washington, DC: American Psychiatric Association.

Lange, A., Rietdijk, D., Hudcovicova, M., van den Ven, J.-P., Schrieken, B.A.L., and Emmelkamp, P.M.G. (2003). Interapy: RCT of the standardized treatment of posttraumatic stress through the internet. *Journal of Consulting and Clinical Psychology, 71*, 901–909.

Lange, A., van den Ven, J.-P., Schrieken, B.A.L., and Smit, M. (2004). 'Interapy' burn-out: Prevention and therapy of burnout via the internet [in German]. *Verhaltenstherapie, 14*, 190–199.

LeGrange, D., Gorin, A., Catley, D., and Stone, A.A. (2001). Does momentary assessment detect binge eating in overweight women that is denied at interview? *European Eating Disorders Review, 9*, 309–324.

LeGrange, D., Gorin, A., Dymek, M., and Stone, A.A. (2002). Does ecological momentary assessment improve CBT for binge eating disorder? A pilot study. *European Eating Disorders Review, 10*, 316–328.

Lenert, L., Munoz, R.F., Stoddard, J., Delucchi, K., Banson, A., Skoczen, S., et al. (2003). Design and pilot evaluation of an internet smoking cessation program. *Journal of the American Medical Informatics Association, 10*, 16–20.

Lenert, L., Munoz, R.F., Perez, J.F., and Banson, A. (2004). Automated email messaging as a tool for improving quit rates in an internet smoking cessation intervention. *Journal of the American Medical Informatics Association, 11*, 235–240.

Lieberman, D.Z. (2003). Automated treatment for jet lag delivered through the internet. *Psychiatric Services, 54*, 394–396.

Low, K.G., Charanasomboon, S., Lesser, J., Reinhalter, K., Martin, R., Jones, H., et al. (2006). Effectiveness of a computer-based interactive eating disorders prevention program at long term follow up. *Eating Disorders, 14*, 17–30.

Luce, K.H., Osborne, M.L., Winzelberg, A.J., Das, S., Abascal, L.B., Celio, A.A., et al. (2005). Application of an algorithim-driven protocol to simultaneously provide universal and targeted prevention programs. *International Journal of Eating Disorders, 37*, 220–226.

Maheu, M.M., Pulier, P.L., Wilhelm, F.H., McMenamin, J.P., and Brown-Connolly, N.E. (2004). *The mental health professional and the new technologies: A handbook for practice today.* Mahwah, NJ: Lawrence Erlbaum Associates, Inc.

Maltby, N., Kirsch, I., Mayers, M., and Allen, G.J. (2002). Virtual reality exposure therapy for the treatment of fear of flying: A controlled investigation, *Journal of Consulting and Clinical Psychology, 70*, 1112–1118.

Marks, I.M. (1978). *Living with fear.* New York: McGraw-Hill.

Marks, I.M. (1999). Computer aids to mental health care. *Canadian Journal of Psychiatry, 44*, 548–555.

REFERENCES 249

Marks, I.M. (2002). The maturing of therapy: Some brief psychotherapies help anxiety/depressive disorders but mechanisms of action are unclear. *British Journal of Psychiatry, 180*, 200–204.

Marks, I.M., Baer, L., Greist, J.H., Park, J.M., Bachofen, M., Nakagawa, A., et al. (1998a). Home self-assessment of OCD. Use of a manual and a computer-conducted telephone interview: Two US–UK studies. *British Journal of Psychiatry, 172*, 406–412.

Marks, I.M., Shaw, S.C., and Parkin, R. (1998b). Computer-aided treatments of mental health problems. *Clinical Psychology: Science & Practice, 5*, 151–170.

Marks, I.M. and Dar, R. (2000). Editorial: Fear reduction by psychotherapies: Recent findings, future directions. *British Journal of Psychiatry, 176*, 507–511.

Marks, I.M., Kenwright, M., McDonough, M., Whittaker, M., and Mataix-Cols, D. (2004). Saving clinicians' time by delegating routine aspects of therapy to a computer: A randomised controlled trial in phobia/panic disorder. *Psychological Medicine, 34*, 9–18.

Marks, I.M., Mataix-Cols, D., Kenwright, M., Cameron, R., Hirsch, S., and Gega, L. (2003). Pragmatic evaluation of computer-aided self-help for anxiety and depression. *British Journal of Psychiatry, 183*, 57–65.

Mataix-Cols, D., Cameron, R., Gega, L., Kenwright, M., and Marks, I.M. (2006). Effect of referral source on outcome with CBT self-help. *Comprehensive Psychiatry, 47*, 241–245.

Matthews, A.J., Kirkby, K.C., and Martin, F. (2002). Effects of single-dose lorazepam on memory and behavioural learning. *Journal of Psychopharmacology, 16*, 343–352.

McCrone, P., Knapp, M., Proudfoot, J.G., Ryden, C.C.E.B., Cavanagh, K., Shapiro, D., et al. (2004). Cost-effectiveness of computerised CBT for anxiety and depression in primary care. *British Journal of Psychiatry, 185*, 55–62.

McCrone, P., Marks, I.M., Greist, J.H., Baer, L., Kobak, K.A., Wenzel, K.W., et al. (2007). Cost-effectiveness of computer-aided behavior therapy for OCD. *Psychotherapy and Psychosomatics*. In press.

McCrone, P., Marks, I.M., Kenwright, M., McDonough, M., Whittaker, M., and Mataix-Cols, M. (2006). *Cost-effectiveness of computer-aided therapy for phobia/panic disorder*. Manuscript submitted for publication.

McDonough, M. and Marks, I.M. (2002). Teaching medical students exposure therapy – randomised comparison of face-to-face versus computer instruction. *Medical Education, 36*, 1–6.

McGarry, E., Jones, R., Cowan, B., and White, J. (1998). Multimedia system for personalised treatment of anxiety in primary care. *Healthcare Computing*, 21–29.

McPherson, A., Forster, D., Glazebrook, C., and Smyth, A. (2002a). The Asthma Files: Evaluation of a multimedia package for children's asthma education. *Paediatric Nursing, 14*, 32–35.

McPherson, A., Glazebrook, C., Forster, D., James, C., and Smyth, A. (2006). Randomised controlled trial of an interactive educational computer package for children with asthma. *Pediatrics, 117*, 1046–1054.

McPherson, A., Glazebrook, C., and Smyth, A. (2002b). Assessing what children know about asthma. *European Respiratory Journal, 20*, 331s.

McPherson, A., Glazebrook, C., and Smyth, A. (2003). Effectiveness of a multimedia education program for children with asthma. *European Respiratory Journal, 22*, 364s.

Meuret, A.E., Moscovitch, D.A., and Hofmann, S.G. (2006a). *Effects of physiologically oriented versus cognitive therapies on physiological and psychological parameters during in-vivo exposure*. Paper presented at the Annual Conference of Association for Advancement of Behavioral and Cognitive Therapy.

Meuret, A.E., Wilhelm, F.H., Ritz, T., and Roth, W.T. (2006b). Effect of capnometry-assisted breathing therapy on symptoms and respiration in panic disorder. *Archives of General Psychiatry*. In revision.

250 REFERENCES

Meuret, A.E., Wilhelm, F.H., and Roth, W.T. (2001). Respiratory biofeedback-assisted therapy in panic disorder. *Behavior Modification, 25*, 584–605.

Meuret, A.E., Wilhelm, F.H., and Roth, W.T. (2004). Respiratory feedback for treating panic disorder. *Journal of Clinical Psychology /In Session, 60*, 197–207.

Milgrom, P., Coldwell, S.E., Getz, T., Weinstein, P., and Ramsay, D.S. (1997). Four dimensions of fear of dental injections, *Journal of the American Dental Asssociation, 128*, 756–772.

Miller, W.R., Leckman, A.L., Delaney, H.D., and Tinkcom, M. (1992). Long-term follow-up of behavioral self-control training – group of two. *Journal of Studies on Alcohol, 53*, 249–261.

Miller, W.R. and Munoz, R.F. (1982). *Controlling Your Drinking: Tools to Make Moderation Work for You.* Albuquerque: CASAA Research Division, Dept. of Psychology, University of New Mexico.

Miller, W.R., Wilbourne, P.L., and Hettema, J.E. (2003). What works? A summary of alcohol treatment outcome research. In R.K. Hester and W.R. Miller (Eds.), *Handbook of Alcoholism Treatment Approaches: Effective Alternatives* (3rd ed., pp. 13–63). Boston, MA: Allyn & Bacon.

Mühlberger, A., Herrmann, M.J., Wiedemann, G., Ellgring, H., and Pauli, P. (2002). Repeated exposure of flight phobics to flights. *Behaviour and Research Therapy, 39*, 1033–1050.

Murray, E., Burns, J., See Tai, S., Lai, R., and Nazareth, I. (2005). Interactive health communication applications for people with chronic disease (review). *Cochrane Library, 4*.

Murray, K., Pombo-Carril, M.G., Bara-Carril, N., Grover, M., Reid, Y., and Langham, C., et al. (2003). Factors determining uptake of a CD-ROM-based CBT self-help treatment for bulimia: Patient characteristics and subjective appraisals of self-help treatment. *European Eating Disorders Review, 11*, 243–260.

Murray, K., Schmidt, U., Pombo-Carril, M.-G., Grover, M., Aleyna, J., Treasure, J., et al. (2007). Does therapist guidance improve uptake, adherence and outcome from a CD-ROM based cognitive-behavioural intervention for the treatment of bulimia nervosa? *Computers in Human Behaviour, 23*, 850–859.

Nakagawa, A., Marks, I.M., Park, J.M., Bachofen, M., Baer, L., Dottl, S.L., et al. (2000). Self treatment of OCD guided by a manual and computer-conducted telephone interview. *Journal of Telemedicine and Telecare, 6*, 22–26.

National Institute for Health and Clinical Excellence (NICE, 2002). *Guidance on the use of computerised cognitive behavioural therapy for anxiety and depression.* Technology Appraisal no. 51. London: NICE.

National Institute for Health and Clinical Excellence (NICE, 2006). *Computerised cognitive behaviour therapy (CCBT) for the treatment of depression and anxiety.* Technology Appraisal no. 97. London: NICE.

Nelissen, I., Muris, P., and Merkelbach, H. (1995). Computerized exposure and in vivo exposure treatments of spider fear in children: Two case reports. *Journal of Behaviour Therapy and Experimental Psychiatry, 26*, 153–156.

Newman, M.G. (2000). Recommendations for a cost-offset model of psychotherapy allocation using generalized anxiety disorder as an example. *Journal of Consulting and Clinical Psychology, 68*, 549–555.

Newman, M.G. (2004). Technology in psychotherapy: An introduction. *Journal of Clinical Psychology/In Session, 60*, 141–145.

Newman, M.G., Consoli, A.J., and Taylor, C.B. (1997a). Computers in assessment and CBT of clinical disorders: Anxiety as a case in point. *Behavior Therapy, 28*, 211–235.

Newman, M.G., Consoli, A.J., and Taylor, C.B. (1999). Palmtop computer program for treatment of generalised anxiety disorder. *Behavior Modification, 23*, 597–619.

Newman, M.G., Erickson, T., Przeworski, A., and Dzus, E. (2003). Self-help and minimal contact therapies for anxiety disorders: Is human contact necessary for therapeutic efficacy? *Journal of Clinical Psychology, 59*, 251–274.

Newman, M.G., Kenardy, J.A., Herman, S.W., and Taylor, C.B. (1996). Use of hand-held computers as an adjunct to CBT. *Computers in Human Behavior, 12*, 135–143.

Newman, M.G., Kenardy, J.A., Herman, S.W., and Taylor, C.B. (1997b). Comparison of palmtop-computer-assisted brief CBT to CBT for panic disorder. *Journal of Consulting and Clinical Psychology, 65*, 178–183.

Norton, M., Wonderlich, S.A., Myers, T., Mitchell, J.E., and Crosby, R.D. (2003). The use of palmtop computers in the treatment of bulimia nervosa. *European Eating Disorders Review, 11*, 231–242.

Oakley-Browne, M.A. and Toole, S. (1994). Computerised self-care programs for depression and anxiety disorders. In G. Andrews et al. (Eds.), *Computers in Mental Health* (pp. 96–102). Geneva: World Health Organization/Churchill Livingstone.

Ochs, E.P. and Binik, Y.M. (1998). A sex-expert computer system helps couples learn more about their sexual relationship. *Journal of Sex Education and Therapy, 23*, 145–155.

Ochs, E.P., Meana, M., Mah, K., and Binik, Y.M. (1993). Effects of exposure to different sources of sexual information on sexual behaviour: Comparing a 'sex-expert system' to other educational material. *Behaviour Research Methods, Instruments & Computers, 25*, 189–194.

Ochs, E.P., Meana, M., Pare, L., Mah, K., and Binik, Y.M. (1994). Learning about sex outside the gutter: Attitudes toward a computer sex expert system. *Journal of Sex and Marital Therapy, 20*, 86–102.

O'Kearney, R., Gibson, M., Christensen, H., and Griffiths, K.M. (2006). Effects of a cognitive-behavioural internet program on depression, vulnerability to depression and stigma in adolescent males: A school based controlled trial. *CBT*. In press.

Ondersma, S.J., Chase, S.K., Svikis, D.S., and Schuster, C.R. (2005). Computer-based brief motivational intervention for perinatal drug use. *Journal of Substance Abuse Treatment, 28*, 305–312.

Ondersma, S.J., Svikis, D.S., and Schuster, C.R. (2006, June). *Leveraging technology: Evaluation of a computer-based brief intervention for post-partum drug use and a dynamic predictor of treatment response*. Poster at 68th Annual Scientific Meeting of College on Problems of Drug Dependence, Scottsdale, Arizona.

Osgood-Hynes, D.J., Greist, J.H., Marks, I.M., Baer, L., Heneman, S.W., Wenzel, K.W., et al. (1998). Self-administered psychotherapy for depression using a telephone-accessed computer system plus booklets: An open US–UK study. *Journal of Clinical Psychiatry, 58*, 358–365.

Palermo, T. (unpublished). *Chronic pain program*. Case Western Reserve University, USA.

Palmer, S., Bor, R., and Josse, J. (2000). A self-help tool kit for conquering fears and anxieties about flying. *Counselling Psychology Review, 15*, 18–29.

Parkin, R., Marks, I.M., and Higgs, R. (1995). Development of a computerised aid for anxiety management in primary care. *Primary Care Psychiatry, 1*, 115–118.

Pivee, C. (1990). CARL: A nondirective counsellor based on Weizenbaum's ELIZA [computer program]. Melbourne: University of Melbourne.

Proudfoot, J.G. (2004). Computer-based treatment for anxiety and depression: Is it feasible? Is it effective? *Neuroscience and Biobehavioural Reviews, 28*, 353–363.

Proudfoot, J.G., Goldberg, D., Mann, A., Everitt, B., Marks, I.M., and Gray, J. (2003b). Computerized, interactive, multimedia cognitive behavioural therapy reduces anxiety and depression in general practice: A RCT. *Psychological Medicine, 33*, 217–227.

Proudfoot, J.G., Ryden, C.C.E.B., Everitt, B., Shapiro, D.A., Goldberg, D., Mann, A., et al. (2004). Clinical effectiveness of computerized cognitive behavioural therapy for anxiety and depression in primary care. *British Journal of Psychiatry, 185*, 46–54.

Proudfoot, J.G., Swain, S., Widmer, S., Watkins, E., Goldberg, D., Marks, I.M., et al. (2003a).

252 REFERENCES

Development and beta-test of a computer-therapy program for anxiety and depression: Hurdles and preliminary outcomes. *Computers in Human Behavior, 19,* 277–289.

Przeworski, A. and Newman, M.G. (2004). Palmtop computer-assisted group therapy for social phobia. *Journal of Clinical Psychology, 60,* 179–180.

Przeworski, A. and Newman, M.G. (2006). Efficacy and utility of computer-assisted CBT for anxiety disorders. *Clinical Psychologist, 10*(2), 43–53.

Ready, D.J., Rothbaum, B.O., and Hodges, L. (2001). VR based exposure therapy with Vietnam veterans who suffer from PTSD. *PTSD Clinical Quarterly, 10*(4), 62–66.

Richards, C., Cannon, N., and Scott, E. (unpublished – a). *Stress and anxiety in teenagers.* Young People's Unit, Royal Edinburgh Hospital, Tipperlinn Road, Edinburgh EH10 5HF.

Richards, C., Cannon, N., and Scott, E. (unpublished – b). *Depression in teenagers.* Young People's Unit, Royal Edinburgh Hospital, Tipperlinn Road, Edinburgh EH10 5HF. http://www.depressioninteenagers.com/.

Richards, D. (2002, September). *Access and effectiveness in psychological therapies: Self-help as a routine health technology.* Paper presented at the 32nd EABCT conference, Maastricht, Netherlands.

Richards, J.C. and Alvarenga, M.E. (2002). Extension and replication of an internet-based treatment programme for panic disorder. *Scandinavian Journal of Behaviour Therapy, 30,* 41–47.

Richards, J.C., Klein, B., and Carlbring, P. (2003). Internet-based treatment for panic disorder. *Cognitive Behavioral Therapy, 32,* 125–135.

Richards, J.C., Klein, B., and Austin, D.W. (2006). Internet CBT for panic disorder: Does the inclusion of stress management information improve end-state functioning? *Clinical Psychologist, 10,* 2–15.

Rifas-Shiman, S.L., Willett, W.C., Lobb, R., Kotch, J., Dart, C., and Gillman, M.W. (2001). PrimeScreen a brief dietary screening tool: Reproducibility and comparability with both a longer food frequency questionnaire and biological markers. *Public Health and Nutrition, 4,* 249–254.

Rimm, E.B., Giovannucci, E.L., Stampfer, M.J., Colditz, G.A., Litin, L.B., Willett, W.C., et al. (2002). Reproducibility and validity of an expanded self-administered semi-quantitative food frequency questionnaire among male health professionals. *American Journal of Epidemiology, 135,* 114–126.

Riper, J., Kramer, J., Conyn, B., Cuijpers, P., and Schipper, G. (2007). *Drinking Less: RCT on the effectiveness of a web-based self-help intervention for problem drinkers.* Manuscript submitted for publication.

Ritterband, L.M., Cox, D.J., Walker, L.S., Kovatchev, B., McKnight, L., Patel, K., et al. (2003a). An internet intervention as adjunctive therapy for childhood encopresis. *Journal of Consulting and Clinical Psychology, 71,* 910–917.

Ritterband, L.M., Gonder-Frederick, L.A., Cox, D.J., Clifton, A.D., West, R.W., and Borowitz, S.M. (2003b). Internet interventions: In review, in use, and into the future. *Professional Psychology: Research and Practice, 34,* 527–534.

Riva, G., Molinari, E., Vincelli, F. (2001). VR as communicative medium between patient and therapist. In G. Riva and F. Davide (Eds.), *Communications through Virtual Techologies. Identity, Community and Technology in the Communication Age. Studies in New Technologies and Practices in Communication* (pp. 87–100). Amsterdam: IOS Press.

Robinson, A. et al. (unpublished). *Stressbusters.* Institute of Psychiatry, London.

Rothbaum, B.O., Hodges, L.F., Alarcon, R.D., Ready, D.J., Shahar, F., Graap, K., et al. (1999a). VR exposure programme for PTSD Vietnam veterans: A case study. *Journal of Traumatic Stress, 12*(2), 263–271.

Rothbaum, B.O., Hodges, L.F., Anderson, P.L., and Price, L. (2002). 12-month follow-up of

VR and standard exposure therapies for the fear of flying. *Journal of Consulting and Clinical Psychology*, 70, 428–432.

Rothbaum, B.O., Hodges, L.F., and Kooper, R. (1999b). The use of virtual reality exposure in the treatment of anxiety disorders. *Behavior Modification*, 23, 507–525.

Rothbaum, B.O., Hodges, L.F., Ready, D.J., Graap, K., and Alarcon, R.D. (2001). Virtual reality exposure therapy for Vietnam veterans with posttraumatic stress disorder. *Journal of Clinical Psychiatry*, 62, 617–622.

Rothbaum, B.O., Hodges, L.F, and Smith, S.G. (1999c). Virtual reality exposure therapy abbreviated treatment manual: Fear of flying application. *Cognitive and Behavioral Practice*, 6, 234–244.

Rothbaum, B.O., Hodges, L.F., Smith, S.G., and Lee, J.H. (2000). A controlled study of virtual reality exposure therapy for the fear of flying. *Journal of Consulting Clinical Psychology*, 68, 1020–1026.

Rubin, D.H., Leventhal, J.M., Sadock, R.T., Letovsky, E., Schottland, P., Clemente, I., et al. (1986). Educational intervention by computer in childhood asthma: A randomized clinical trial testing the use of a new teaching intervention in childhood asthma. *Pediatrics*, 77, 1–10.

Ryden, C.C.E.B (2005). *Predictors of response to computerised cognitive therapy: RCT.* Unpublished doctoral thesis (Psych.D. in Clinical Psychology). University of Surrey, Guildford.

Sanchez-Craig, M. (1997). *DrinkWise: How to quit drinking or cut down. A self-help book.* Toronto: Addiction Research Foundation.

Sandford, J.A. and Browne, R.J. (1988). *Captain's Log Cognitive System.* Richmond: Brain Train.

Schinke, S.P., Di Noia, J., and Glassman, J.R. (2004b). Computer mediated intervention to prevent drug abuse and violence among high-risk youth. *Addictive Behaviors*, 29, 225–229.

Schinke, S.P. and Schwinn, T. (2005). Gender-specific computer-based intervention for preventing drug abuse among girls. *American Journal of Drug and Alcohol Abuse*, 31, 609–616.

Schinke, S.P., Schwinn, T.M., and Cole, K.C. (2006). Preventing alcohol abuse among early adolescents through family and computer-based interventions: four-year outcomes and mediating variables. *Journal of Developmental and Physical Disabilities*, 18, 149–161.

Schinke, S.P., Schwinn, T.M., Di Noia, J., and Cole, K.C. (2004a). Reducing the risks of alcohol use among urban youth: Three-year effects of a computer based interevention with and without parent involvement. *Journal of Alcohol Studies*, 65, 443–449.

Schinke, S.P., Schwinn, T.M., and Ozanian, A.J. (2005). Alcohol abuse prevention among high-risk youth: Computer based intervention. *Journal of Prevention & Intervention in Community*, 29, 117–130.

Schneider, A.J., Mataix-Cols, D., Marks, I.M., and Bachofen, M. (2005). RCT in phobia/panic disorder of two forms of net-guided self-help, each with brief live phone support. *Psychotherapy & Psychosomatics*, 74, 154–164.

Schneider, S.J. (1986). Trial of an on-line behavioural smoking cessation program. *Computers in Human Behavior*, 2, 277–286.

Schneider, S.J., Schwartz, M.D., and Fast, J. (1995a). Computerized, telephone-based health promotion: 1. Smoking cessation program. *Computers in Human Behavior*, 11, 135–148.

Schneider, S.J., Schwartz, M.D., and Fast, J. (1995b). Computerized, telephone-based health promotion: 2. Stress management program. *Computers in Human Behavior*, 11, 205–214.

Schneider, S.J., Walter, R., and O'Donnell, R. (1990). Computerized communication as a medium for behavioural smoking cessation treatment: Controlled trial. *Computers in Human Behaviour*, 6, 141–151.

Selmi, P.M., Klein, M.H., Greist, J.H., Sorrell, S.P., and Erdman, H.P. (1990). Computer-administered CBT for depression. *American Journal of Psychiatry*, 14, 51–56.

254 REFERENCES

Shapiro, D.A., Cavanagh, K., and Lomas, H. (2003). Geographic inequity in the availability of CBT in England and Wales. *Behavioral and Cognitive Psychotherapy*, *31*, 185–192.

Shapiro, H., Reba, L., Dymek-Valentine, M., Hamer, R.M., and Bulik, C.M. (2005). *CD-ROM and web-based cognitive behavioural treatment for binge eating disorder and obesity*. AED conference report. http://www.aedweb.org/newsletters/September_05.pdf.

Shaw, S.C., Marks, I.M., and Toole, S. (1999). Lessons from pilot tests of computer self-help for agoraphobia/claustrophobia and panic. *MD Computing*, *7*(8), 44–48.

Silver, M. and Oakes, P. (2001). Evaluation of a new computer intervention to teach people with autism or Asperger syndrome to recognise and predict emotions in others. *Autism*, *5*, 299–316.

Slack, W.V. (2000). Patient–computer dialogue: A review. In *Yearbook of Medical Informatics 2000: Patient-centred systems* (pp. 71–78). Stuttgart: Schattauer.

Slack, W.V., Porter, D., Balkin, P., Kowaloff, H.B., and Slack, C.W. (1990). Computer-assisted soliloquy as an approach to psychotherapy. *MD Computing*, *7*, 37–42, 58.

Slack, W.V., Porter, D., Witschi, J., Sullivan, M., Buxbaum, R., and Stare, F.J. (1976). Dietary interviewing by computer: An experimental approach to counseling. *Journal of the American Dietetic Association*, *69*, 514–517.

Slack, W.V. and Slack, C.W. (1972). Patient and computer dialogue. *New England Journal of Medicine*, *286*, 1304.

Slack, W.V. and Slack, C.W. (1977). Talking to a computer about emotional problems: A comparative study. *Psychotherapy: Theory, Research, and Practice*, *14*, 156–164.

Smith, K.L., Kirkby, K.C., Montgomery, I.M., and Daniels, B.A. (1997). Computer-delivered modeling of exposure for spider phobia: Relevant versus irrelevant exposure. *Journal of Anxiety Disorders*, *11*, 489–497.

Smith, S.G., Rothbaum, B.O., and Hodges, L.F. (1999). Treatment of fear of flying using virtual reality exposure therapy: A single case study. *The Behavior Therapist*, *22*, 154–160.

Spence, S.H., Holmes, J.M., March, S., and Lipp, O.V. (2006). Clinic versus internet-assisted treatment of childhood anxiety. *Journal of Consulting and Clinical Psychology*, *74*, 614–621.

Squires, D.D. and Hester, R.K. (2002). Computer-based brief intervention for drinkers: Increasing role for computers in the assessment and treatment of addictive behaviours. *The Behavior Therapist*, *23*, 59–65.

Squires, D.D. and Hester, R.K. (2004). Using technical innovations in clinical practice: The drinker's check-up software program. *Journal of Clinical Psychology*, *60*, 159–169.

Stone, L.A. and Kristjanson, R.W. (1975). Computer-assisted group encounter. *Small Group Behaviour*, *6*, 457.

Strecher, V.J., Shiffman, S., and West, R. (2005). RCT of a web-based computer-tailored smoking cessation program as a supplement to nicotine patch therapy. *Addiction*, *100*, 682–688.

Ström, L., Pettersson, R., and Andersson, G. (2000). A controlled trial of self-help treatment of recurrent headache conducted via the internet. *Journal of Consulting and Clinical Psychology*, *68*, 722–727.

Ström, L., Pettersson, R., and Andersson, G. (2004). Internet-based treatment for insomnia: A controlled evaluation. *Journal of Consulting and Clinical Psychology*, *72*, 113–120.

Stuart, S. and LaRue, S. (1996). Computerized cognitive therapy: The interface between man and machine. *Journal of Cognitive Psychotherapy*, *10*, 181–191.

Talley, J.L. (1987). *Interactive health systems: Therapeutic learning program evaluation*. Unpublished manuscript, Interactive Health Systems, Santa Monica, CA.

Tate, D.F., Jackvony, E.H., and Wing, R.R. (2003). Effects of internet behavioral counseling on weight loss in adults at risk for type 2 diabetes: A randomized trial. *Journal of the American Medical Association*, *289*, 1833–1836.

Tate, D.F., Wing, R.R., and Winett, R.A. (2001). Using internet technology to deliver a

REFERENCES 255

behavioural weight loss program. *Journal of the American Medical Association, 285,* 1172–1177.

Tate, D.F. and Zabinski, M.F. (2004). Computer and internet applications for psychological treatment: Update for clinicians. *Journal of Clinical Psychology/In Session, 60,* 209–220.

Taylor, C.B., Agras, W.S., Losch, M., and Plante, T.G. (1991). Improving the effectiveness of computer-assisted weight loss. *Behavior Therapy, 22,* 229–236.

Taylor, C.B., Bryson, S., Luce, K.H., Cunning, D., Celio, A.A., Abascal, L.B., et al. (2006). Prevention of eating disorders in at-risk college-age women. *Archives of General Psychiatry, 63,* 881–888.

Telch, C.F. and Agras, W.S. (1992). *CBT for binge eating disorder: Therapist manual.* Stanford: Stanford University Press.

Van den Berg, S., Shapiro, D.A., Bickerstaffe, D., and Cavanagh, K. (2004). Computerised CBT for anxiety and depression: A practical solution to the shortage of trained therapists. *Journal of Psychiatric and Mental Health Nursing, 11,* 508–513.

Wade, S.L., Carey, J., and Wolfe, C.R. (2005). Putting the pieces together: The efficacy of an online family intervention to reduce parental distress following pediatric brain injury RCT. *Journal of Pediatric Psychology, 30,* 1–6.

Wade, S.L., Carey, J., and Wolfe, C.R. (2006). The efficacy of an online family intervention to reduce parental distress following pediatric brain injury. *Journal of Consulting and Clinical Psychology.* In press.

Wade, S.L., Wolfe, C.R., Maines Brown, T., and Pestian, J.P. (2005a). Putting the pieces together: Preliminary efficacy of a web-based family intervention for children with traumatic brain injury. *Journal of Pediatric Psychology, 30*(5), 1–6.

Wade, S.L., Wolfe, C.R., and Pestian, J.P. (2004). A web-based family problem solving intervention for families of children with traumatic brain injury. *Behavior Research Methods, Instruments and Computers, 36,* 261–269.

Wade, S.L., Wolfe, C.R., Pestian, J.P., and Brown, T. (2005b). Can a web-based family problem-solving intervention work for children with traumatic brain injury? *Rehabilitation Psychology, 50,* 337–345.

Wagman, M. and Kerber, K.W. (1984). PLATO DCS, an interactive computer system for personal counseling: Further development and evaluation. *Journal of Counseling & Clinical Psychology, 27,* 31–39.

Waller, R. and Gilbody, S. (2006). *Barriers to the uptake of CCBT: A systematic review of the quantitative and qualitative evidence.* Manuscript submitted for publication.

Weizenbaum, J. (1976). Eliza – a computer program for the study of natural language communication between man and machine. In J, Weizenbaum, *Computer power and human reason.* San Francisco: Freeman.

Whitby, P. and Allcock, K. (1994). *Spider phobia control. Computerized behavioural treatment for fear of spiders.* Newport: Gwent Psychology Services.

White, J. (1998). 'Stresspac': Three-year follow-up of a controlled trial of a self-help package for the anxiety disorders. *Behavioural and Cognitive Psychotherapy, 26,* 133–141.

White, J., Jones, R.B., and McGarry, E. (2000). Cognitive behavioural computer therapy for anxiety disorders: A pilot study. *Journal of Mental Health, 9,* 505–516.

Whitfield, G., Hinshelwood, R., Pashely, A., Campsie, L., and Williams, C. (2006). Impact of a novel computerised CBT CD-ROM (Overcoming Depression) offered to patients referred to clinical psychology. *Behavioural and Cognitive Psychotherapy, 34,* 1–13.

Whitfield, G. and Williams, C. (2004). If the evidence is so good why doesn't anyone use them? A national survey of CCBT. *Behavioural and Cognitive Psychotherapy, 32,* 57–65.

Wiederhold, B.K. and Wiederhold, M.D. (2000). Lessons learned from 600 VR sessions. *CyberPsychology and Behavior, 3,* 393–400.

Winzelberg, A.J., Eppstein, D., Eldredge, K.L., Wilfley, D.E., Dasmahapatra, R., Dev, P., et

256 REFERENCES

al. (2000). Effectiveness of an internet based program for reducing risk factors for eating disorders. *Journal of Consulting and Clinical Psychology, 68,* 346–350.

Winzelberg, A.J., Taylor, C.B., Sharpe, T., Eldredge, K.L., Dev, P., and Constantinou, P.S. (1998). Evaluation of a computer mediated eating disorder intervention program. *International Journal of Eating Disorders, 24,* 339–349.

Witschi, J., Porter, D., Vogel, D., Buxbaum, R., Stare, F.J., and Slack, W.V. (1976). A computer-based dietary counseling system. *Journal of the American Dietetic Association, 69,* 385–390.

Wooton, R., Yellowlees, P., and McLaren, P. (2003). *Telepsychiatry and e-mail health.* London: Royal Society of Medicine Press.

Wright, J.H. (2004). Computer-assisted cognitive-behavior therapy. In J.H. Wright (Ed.), *Cognitive-behavior therapy* (pp. 55–82). Washington, DC: American Psychiatric Publishing.

Wright, J.H. and Katz, M. (2004). Computer-assisted psychotherapy. In E.W. Craighead and C.B. Nemeroff (Eds.), *The concise Corsini encyclopedia of psychology and behavioral science* (3rd ed). New York: Wiley.

Wright, J.H., Wright, A.S., Albano, A.M., Basco, M.R., Raffield, T., and Otto, M.W. (2005). Computer-assisted cognitive therapy for depression: Maintaining efficacy while reducing therapist time. *American Journal of Psychiatry, 162,* 1158–1164.

Wright, J.H., Wright, A.S., and Beck, A.T. (2003). Good days ahead: The multimedia program for cognitive therapy. Louisville: Mindstreet.

Wright, J.H., Wright, A.S. Salmon, P., Beck, A.T., Kuykendall, J., Goldsmith, L.J., et al. (2002). Development and initial testing of a multimedia program for computer-assisted cognitive therapy. *American Journal of Psychotherapy, 56,* 76–86.

Yates, F.E. (1996a). Developing therapeutic computer programmes with particular reference to a programme to teach coping strategies to problem drinkers. *Journal of Mental Health, 5,* 57–63.

Yates, F.E. (1996b). *Evaluation of the balance computer intervention.* Mental Health Foundation report (the author died before it became a peer-reviewed publication).

Yates, F.E. (1996c). Fast idiot or friendly helper? Development of a problem-solving client program. In F.E. Yates (Ed.), *Creative computing in health and social care.* Chichester: Wiley.

Yawn, B.P., Algatt-Bergstrom, P.J., Yawn, R.A., Wollan, P., Greco, M., Gleason, M., et al. (2000). An in school CD-ROM asthma education program. *Journal of School Health, 70,* 153–159.

Zabinski, M.F., Celio, A.A., Wilfley, D.E., and Taylor, C.B. (2003). Prevention of eating disorders and obesity via the internet. *Cognitive and Behavioral Therapy, 32,* 137–150.

Zabinski, M.F., Pung, M., Wilfley, D.E., Eppstein, D., Winzelberg, A.J., Celio, A., et al. (2001). Reducing risk factors for eating disorders: Targeting women with a computerised psycho-educational program. *International Journal of Eating Disorders, 29,* 401–408.

Zarr, M.L. (1984). Computer-mediated psychotherapy: Toward patient-selection guidelines. *American Journal of Psychotherapy, 37,* 47–61.

Zeiss, A.M., Lewinsohn, P.M., and Munoz, R.F. (1979). Nonspecific improvement effects in depression using interpersonal skills training, pleasant activity schedules, or cognitive training. *Journal of Consulting and Clinical Psychology, 47,* 427–439.

Zetterqvist, K., Maanmies, J., Ström, L., and Andersson, G. (2003). Randomised controlled trial of internet-based stress management. *Cognitive and Behavioral Therapy, 32,* 151–160.

Author index

Note: For publications with three or more authors the full list of authors is only mentioned in the first text citation of the reference and drops to first author name followed by et al. and year for all subsequent text citations. This author index includes entries for third, fourth, fifth, and sixth authors wherever the reference is cited throughout the main text, but *please note* that *only* the first text citation will show the name list in full and the first author name and year can be used as a marker for all subsequent page entries.

For example:

Cordingley, J. 7, 153, 159, 214, 231, 237

The full list of names is mentioned on p. 7 as Cunningham, Humphreys, Koski-James, and Cordingley (2005). All subsequent text page entries for Cordingley should be traced by using Cunningham et al. (2005).

Abascal, L. B. 123, 124, 130–132, 236
Abrams, D. B. 141, 148, 149, 237
Acton, T. 93, 96, 235
Adams, C. 237
Addis, M. E. 102
Agras, W. S. 110, 111, 115, 117, 229, 230, 236
Alarcon, R. D. 19, 237
Albano, A. M. 87, 97, 235
Aleyna, J. 120, 121, 236

Algatt-Bergstrom, P. J. 200, 205, 229, 235
Allcock, K. 19, 56, 230, 237
Allen, G. J. 236
Alpert, H. R. 200, 203, 235
Alvarenga, M. E. 33, 39, 218, 237
Anderson, P. L. 19, 60, 237
Andersson, G. 18, 31–38, 74, 76, 78, 83, 84, 88, 105, 170–173, 176–178, 213, 215, 216, 235, 236
Andrasik, F. 174

AUTHOR INDEX

Andrewes, D. G. 110, 114, 230, 236
Anthony, K. 237
Arnold, P. H. 78, 231, 236
Aronson, G. 74, 75, 79, 236
Atkinson, M. 17, 184, 186, 230, 237
Aubin, S. 120, 121, 236
Austin, D. W. 12, 33, 40, 41, 232, 236

Bachofen, M. 18, 19, 26, 27, 30, 32, 46, 47, 59, 62, 63, 64, 65, 68, 102, 115, 211, 225, 231, 236, 237
Baer, L. 12, 18, 19, 25, 38, 62–68, 74, 78, 86, 102, 106–108, 211, 213, 215, 216, 218, 225, 232, 235, 236, 237
Bagby, R. M. 8, 18, 33, 42, 104, 236
Bala, A. 198, 199, 229, 231, 235
Balkin, P. 11, 74, 77, 235
Banos, R. 236
Banson, A. 141, 142 149, 150, 232, 237
Bara-Carril, N. 120, 121, 236
Barcelo, F. 19, 55, 57, 58, 236
Barkham, M. 92, 93, 95, 235
Barlow, D. H. 48
Bartholomew, L. K. 199, 202, 233, 235
Basco, M. R. 87, 97, 235
Bauer, S. 112, 119, 232, 236
Beck, A. T. 87, 97, 218, 235
Belar, C. D. 75, 79, 236
Bell, M. 184, 185, 237
Bellucci, D. M. 184, 237
Bergh, C. 6, 112, 118, 236
Bergstrom, A. F. 32, 78, 236
Bergstrom, J. 88, 105, 215, 235
Berrios, G. E. 18, 50, 52, 63, 69, 236
Beverley, C. 2, 3, 237
Bickestaffe, D. 93, 96, 235
Biglan, A. 53, 54, 230, 236
Binik, Y. M. 179–183, 232, 237
Bjornstjerna, E. 32, 78, 236
Blanchard, E. B. 170, 172, 173, 231, 236
Bock, B. C. 141, 148, 149, 237
Bohman, S. 7, 35, 38, 236
Boles, S. M. 141, 147, 232, 237
Bor, R. 237
Bornas, X. 19, 46, 55, 57–59, 229, 230, 236
Borowitz, S. M. 237
Borsook, T. K. 78, 231, 236
Botella, C. 236
Bower, P. 237
Bowers, W. 4, 86, 90, 232, 235

Bredeweg, B. 18, 63, 69, 70, 231, 237
Brittliffe, K. 8, 18, 88, 103, 235
Brodin, U. 6, 112, 118, 236
Bronisch-Holtze, J. 124, 131, 236
Brown, T. 190, 194, 231, 235
Brown-Connolly, N. E. 2, 237
Browne, R. J. 183
Bruning-Brown, J. 123, 131, 132, 236
Brunt, S. 7, 35, 38, 236
Bryson, G. 184, 185, 237
Bryson, S. 124, 130, 236
Buhrman, M. 7, 18, 31, 32, 34, 35, 38, 105, 171, 175, 177, 236
Bulik, C. M. 121, 126, 236
Burck, H. D. 19, 53, 54, 230, 236
Burda, P. C. 183, 184, 237
Burgess, M. 213
Burnett, K. F. 110, 111, 115, 229, 230, 236
Burns, J. 2, 3, 237
Buxbaum, R. 110, 113, 230, 236

Cameron, R. 14, 15, 26, 27, 29, 62, 67, 68, 75, 81, 86, 90, 108, 210–212, 218, 236
Campbell, J. O. 78, 231, 236
Campsie, L. 86, 90, 236
Cannon, N. 235
Carey, J. 190, 195, 235
Carlbring, P. 7, 18, 31–38, 74, 78, 88, 105, 215, 216, 235–237
Carlin, A. S. 236
Carr, A. 5, 24, 25, 40, 216, 236
Carr, A. C. 24, 25, 27, 236
Cash, T. F. 127, 236
Cashnell-Smith, M. L. 153, 158, 232, 237
Catley, D. 111, 117, 231, 236
Cavanagh, K. 2, 92–96, 235, 237
Celio, A. A. 122–124,128–130, 132, 236
Chandler, G. M. 19, 53, 54, 230, 236
Charanasomboon, S. 124, 129, 236
Chase, S. K. 12, 162, 165, 166, 231, 237
Chilcott, J. 2, 3, 237
Chiles, J. A. 211
Choi, Y. H. 19, 236
Christensen, A. 75, 79, 235
Christensen, H. 4, 8, 18, 38, 87, 88, 100, 101, 103, 104, 192, 235
Claassen, C. A. 212
Clark, A. 18, 50, 52, 63, 69, 236

AUTHOR INDEX

Clarke, G. 87, 98, 99, 101, 104, 235
Clemente, I. 199, 201, 202, 229, 235
Clifton, A. D. 237
Clum, G. A. 63, 71, 237
Cobb, N. 141, 148, 149, 237
Cocoran, C. 184, 185, 237
Coia, A. 17, 184, 186, 230, 237
Colby, K. M. 74, 75, 79, 89, 233, 235, 236
Colby, P. M. 89, 233, 235
Colditz, G. A. 236
Coldwell, S. E. 54, 56, 57, 230, 236
Cole, K. C. 152, 156, 157, 232, 237
Collins, D. R. 107
Connelly, M. 172, 189, 193, 231, 235
Connelly, W. 172, 189, 193, 231, 235
Consoli, A. J. 2, 43, 44, 75, 83, 84, 232, 236, 237
Constantinou, P. S. 122, 127, 236
Conyn, B. 153, 160, 230
Copeland, J. 2, 237
Corcoran, S. 93, 96, 235
Cordingley, J. 7, 153, 159, 214, 231, 237
Corte, C. M. 111, 117, 232, 236
Cowan, B. 236
Cox, D. J. 191, 197, 235, 237
Crook, I. 235
Crosby, R. D. 236
Cuijpers, P. 153, 160, 230
Cunning, D. 124, 130, 236
Cunningham, J. A. 7, 153, 159, 214, 231, 237
Cunningham, M. 235
Czyzewski, D. I. 199, 202, 233, 235

Daniels, B. A. 18, 46, 49–52, 63, 69, 188, 189, 236, 237
Dar, R. 47, 59
Dart, C. 236
Das, S. 123, 132, 236
Dasmahapatra, R. 122, 128, 236
Davis, R. 127, 236
de la Banda, G. G. 19, 55, 57, 58, 229, 230, 236
Dearing, S. 127, 236
DeBar, L. L. 87, 98, 99, 101, 104, 235
Delaney, H. D. 151, 154, 155, 237
Delichatsios, H. K. 112, 119, 233, 236
Delucchi, K. 141, 149, 150, 232, 237

Denissof, E. 8, 18, 33, 42, 104, 236
Derham, H. 110, 114, 230, 236
Dev, P. 122, 123, 127–129, 131, 236
Devineni, T. 170, 172, 173, 231, 236
Dewis, L. M. 50, 52, 188, 189, 236
Di Noia, J. 152, 156, 157, 161, 232, 233, 237
Difede, J. 19, 237
Dobson, K. S. 102
Dolezal-Wood, S. 75, 79, 235, 236
Dominguez, F. 183, 184, 237
Dottl, S. L. 19, 62, 65, 211, 236
Dow, M. G. T. 18, 43, 44, 216, 236
Dymek, M. 111, 117, 231, 236
Dymek-Valentine, M. 121, 126, 236
Dzus, E. 212, 237

Ekselius, L. 7, 31–35, 37, 38, 74, 88, 105, 215, 216, 235, 236
Eldredge, K. L. 122, 127, 128, 236
Elkin, I. 107
Ellgring, G. 237
Emmelkamp, P. M. G. 18, 63, 69, 70, 231, 237
Eppstein, D. 122, 128, 236
Eppstein-Herald, D. 122, 128, 236
Erdman, H. P. 86, 89, 230, 235
Erickson, T. 212, 237
Erwin, B. A. 237
Etter, J. F. 140, 146, 237
Eubanks, D. 87, 98, 99, 101, 104, 235
Evans, K. 87, 100, 101, 235
Everitt, B. 91, 92, 94, 216, 217, 235
Eysenbach, G. 8, 237

Faltenhag, S. 171, 175, 236
Farchaus-Stein, K. 111, 117, 232, 236
Farvolden, P. 8, 18, 33, 42, 104, 236
Fast, J. 12, 139, 144, 237
Faulkner, J. 127, 236
Feil, E. G. 141, 147, 232, 237
Feldman, D. E. 110, 115, 236
Fernandez, M. 199, 202, 233, 235
Finfgeld, D. L. 2, 237
Forster, D. 200, 204, 235
Fox, E. 93, 96, 235
Francisco, B. D. 198, 199, 229, 231, 235
Franses, A. 62, 63, 93, 104, 213, 218

AUTHOR INDEX

Fraser, J. 18, 50, 51, 236
Freiwald, S. 179, 180, 232, 237
Fresco, D. M. 237
Friedman, R. H. 112, 119, 233, 236
Fullana, M. A. 19, 55, 57, 58, 229, 230, 236
Furmark, T. 32, 33, 35–37, 236

Garcia-Palacios, A. 236
Gega, L. 12, 14, 15, 17, 18, 26, 27, 29, 30, 32, 62, 67, 68, 75, 81, 86, 90, 108, 210–212, 218, 236
Gerson, J. 237
Getz, T. 54, 56, 57, 230, 236
Ghosh, A. 5, 24, 25, 27, 40, 216, 236
Gibson, M. 88, 104, 192, 235
Gilbody, S. 217
Gill, M. 213
Gillman, M. W. 236
Gilroy, L. G. 18, 49, 50–52, 188, 189, 236
Giovannucci, E. L. 236
Glaberman, K. 184, 237
Glanville, J. 226
Glanz, K. 112, 119, 233, 236
Glassman, J. R. 152, 161, 232, 233, 237
Glazebrook, C. 200, 204, 235
Gleason, M. 200, 205, 229, 235
Gold, R. S. 199, 202, 233, 235
Goldberg, D. xiii–xiv, 17, 91, 92, 94, 216, 217, 235
Goldsmith, L. J. 87, 97, 218, 235
Gollan, J. K. 102
Gonder-Frederick, L. A. 237
Gorin, A. 111, 117, 231, 236
Gorman, J. M. 48
Gortner, E. T. 102
Goss, S. 237
Gould, R. L. 74, 75, 79, 236
Graap, K. 19, 237
Graff, G. R. 198, 199, 229, 231, 235
Graham, A. L. 141, 148, 149, 237
Graham, C. 62, 63, 93, 104, 213, 218
Gray, J. 91, 92, 216, 235
Greco, M. 200, 205, 229, 235
Greeno, C. G. 111, 116, 231, 236
Greig, T. 184, 185, 237
Greist, J. H. 12, 19, 25, 38, 62–68, 86, 89, 102, 106–108, 211, 213, 215, 216, 218, 225, 230, 235–237

Griffiths, K. M. 4, 8, 18, 38, 87, 88, 100–104, 192, 235
Grime, P. 93, 95, 235
Grover, M. 120, 121, 236
Groves, C. 8, 18, 87, 88, 100, 101, 103, 235
Gruber, K. 45, 46, 232, 236
Grundy, L. 93, 96, 235
Gunnarsdóttir, M. 33, 37, 236
Gustafson, D. H. 211

Haaga, D. A. F. 9
Haddock, C. K. 174
Hall, K. 179, 180, 232, 237
Hamer, R. M. 121, 126, 236
Hammer, L. D. 132
Hantula, D. A. 237
Harcourt, L. 46, 50, 52, 236
Haslam, N. 184, 237
Hassan, A. A. M. 19, 53, 54, 230, 236
Hayward, C. 132
Heading, K. 18, 49, 51, 236
Hedensjö, L. 33, 37, 236
Heimberg, R. G. 237
Heneman, S. W. 12, 19, 38, 86, 102, 106–108, 213, 218, 235
Hepburn, E. 86, 90, 235
Herman, S. W. 43, 44, 232, 237
Herrmann, M. J. 237
Hester, R. K. 151, 154, 155, 237
Hettema, J. E. 156
Higgs, R. 75, 80, 233, 236
Hinshelwood, R. 86, 90, 236
Hirai, M. 63, 71, 237
Hirsch, M. J. 19, 62, 66, 68, 102, 213, 215, 216, 218, 236
Hirsch, S. 14, 15, 26, 27, 29, 62, 67, 68, 75, 81, 86, 108, 210, 212, 236
Hodges, L. F. 19, 60, 237
Hoffman, H. G. 19, 236, 237
Hoffman, H. R. 7, 19, 60, 171, 175, 232, 236
Hofmann, S. G. 231
Holland, A. 18, 62, 64, 232, 236
Hollandare, F. 88, 105, 215, 235
Holmes, J. M. 188, 189, 229, 235
Holmström, A. 32, 33, 35, 36, 236
Homer, C. 200, 203, 235
Hoover, J. A. 78, 231, 236
Howells, E. 93, 96, 235

AUTHOR INDEX

Huber, A. 75, 79, 235
Hudcovicova, M. 63, 69, 70, 237
Humphreys, K. 7, 153, 159, 214, 231, 237
Hunt, S. 93, 96, 235

Imber, S. M. 107

Jackvony, E. H. 125, 134, 231, 236
Jacobi, C. 124, 131, 236
Jacobs, M. K. 75, 79, 235
Jacobson, N. S. 102
Jager, J. 237
James, C. 200, 204, 235
Jasper, K. 127, 236
Jenike, M. A. 18, 62, 64, 232, 236
Johnston, D. W. 18, 43, 44, 216, 236
Jones, H. 124, 129, 236
Jones, R. B. 17, 76, 82, 184, 186, 216, 230, 236, 237
Jorm, A. F. 4, 18, 38, 87, 100, 101, 103, 235
Josse, J. 237

Kaldo, V. 18, 31, 32, 34, 38, 88, 105, 177, 215, 235, 236
Kaldo-Sandström, V. 176, 177, 236
Kaltenthaler, E. 2, 3, 237
Kamarzaman, Z. 17, 76, 82, 216, 236
Katz, M. 2, 17, 237
Kelleher, C. 87, 98, 99, 101, 104, 235
Kenardy, J. A. 18, 43, 44, 76, 83, 216–218, 232, 236, 237
Kenwright, M. 14, 15, 17, 18, 25–30, 32, 46, 62, 63, 67, 68, 75, 81, 86, 90, 93, 96, 104, 108, 115, 210–213, 216–218, 235, 236
Kerber, K. W. 74, 78, 232, 236
Khan, K. S. 226
Killen, J. D. 132
Kirkby, K. C. 2, 18, 46, 49, 50–52, 63, 69, 188, 189, 236, 237
Kirsch, I. 236
Kleijnen, J. 226
Klein, B. 12, 18, 33, 39–41, 216, 232, 236, 237
Klein, M. H. 86, 89, 230, 235
Knapp, M. 92, 94, 235
Kobak, K. A. 19, 25, 62, 66–68, 102, 213, 215, 216, 218, 236, 237
Koerner, K. 102

Kollenstam, C. 18, 31, 32, 34, 38, 105, 236
Konig, P. 198, 199, 229, 231, 235
Kooper, R. 237
Kordy, H. 112, 119, 232, 236
Korten, A. 8, 18, 88, 103, 235
Koski-James, A. 7, 153, 159, 214, 231, 237
Kotch, J. 236
Kovatchev, B. 191, 197, 235
Kowaloff, H. B. 11, 74, 77, 235
Kramer, J. 153, 160, 230
Krishna, S. 198, 199, 229, 231, 235
Kristjanson, R. W. 78, 230, 236
Kuykendall, J. 87, 97, 218, 235
Kwong-See, S. 236
Kypri, K. 153, 158, 232, 237

Lai, R. 2, 3, 237
Lambert, T. J. 2, 237
Lange, A. 18, 63, 69, 70, 231, 237
Langham, C. 120, 121, 236
Langley, J. D. 153, 158, 232, 237
Larkin, G. L. 212
Larsen, H. C. 176, 177, 236
Laughren, T. P. 211
Leckman, A. L. 154
Lee, J. H. 19, 60, 237
LeGrange, D. 111, 117, 231, 236
Lenert, L. 141, 142, 149, 150, 232, 237
Lesser, J. 124, 129, 236
Letovsky, E. 199, 201, 202, 229, 235
Leventhal, J. M. 199, 201, 202, 229, 235
Levin, S. 177, 236
Lewinsohn, P. M. 4
Lichtenstein, E. 141, 147, 232, 237
Lierberman, D. Z. 171, 178, 236
Lindberg, G. 6, 112, 118, 236
Liness, S. 25, 27, 28, 236
Lipp, O. V. 188, 189, 229, 235
Lison, C. A. 78, 231, 236
Litin, L. B. 236
Litt, I. 132
Ljungstrand, P. 31, 32, 34, 38, 105, 216, 236
Llabrés, J. 19, 46, 55, 57, 58, 59, 229, 230, 236
Lobb, R. 236
Lomas, H. 237
Losch, M. 110, 115, 236
Lovell, K. 237

AUTHOR INDEX

Low, K. G. 124, 129, 236
Luce, K. H. 123, 124, 130, 132, 236
Lundstrom, P. 35, 170, 171, 172, 173, 213, 236
Lyttkens, L. 18, 176, 177, 236

Maanmies, J. 76, 83, 84, 236
Mah, K. 181, 182, 237
Maheu, M. M. 2, 237
Maines Brown, T. 190, 194, 231, 235
Maltby, N. 236
Mann, A. 91, 92, 94, 216, 217, 235
Mantle, J. 62, 63, 68, 102, 236
Manzo, P. 62, 63, 68, 102, 236
March, S. 188, 189, 229, 235
Mariott, C. 17, 76, 82, 216, 236
Marks, I. M. 2, 4, 5,6, 10, 12, 14, 15, 17–19, 24–30, 32, 38, 40, 46, 47, 50, 52, 59, 62–69, 75, 80, 81, 86, 90–93, 102, 104, 106–108, 115, 150, 210–213, 215–218, 225, 231, 233, 235–237
Martin, F. 18, 49, 50, 51, 52, 188, 189, 236, 237
Martin, G. 2, 237
Martin, R. 124, 129, 236
Masden, R. W. 198, 199, 229, 231, 235
Mataix-Cols, D. 14, 15, 17, 18, 25–30, 32, 46, 47, 59, 62, 63, 67, 68, 75, 81, 86, 90, 93, 102, 104, 108, 115, 210–213, 216–218, 231, 236, 237
Matthews, A. J. 236
Mayers, M. 236
McAnally, H. 153, 158
McCafferty, K. 76, 83, 216, 217, 218, 236
McCrone, P. 25, 28, 62, 67, 92, 94, 235–237
McDonough, M. 12, 17, 25, 26, 28–30, 46, 115, 216, 217
McFarlane, R. 4, 86, 90, 232, 235
McGarry, E. 17, 76, 82, 236
McGee, R. O. 153, 158, 232, 237
McKay, H. G. 141, 147, 232, 237
McKenna, K. 17, 184, 186, 230, 237
McKnight, L. 191, 197, 235
McLaren, P. 2, 237
McLennan, J. 110, 114, 230, 236
McMenamin, J. P. 2, 237
McPherson, A. 200, 204, 235
Meana, M. 179–182, 232, 237

Meermann, R. 112, 119, 232, 236
Menzies, R. G. 18, 49–52, 63, 69, 188, 189, 236
Merkelbach, H. 54, 56, 188, 189, 230, 237
Meuret, A. E. 19, 45, 47, 48, 231, 237
Milgrom, P. 54, 56, 57, 230, 236
Miller, J. H. 237
Miller, W. R. 154, 156, 237
Minichiello, W. E. 18, 62, 64, 232, 236
Mitchell, J. E. 236
Molinari, E. 237
Montgomery, I. M. 18, 46, 49–52, 236, 237
Moran, P. 45, 46, 232, 236
Morris, L. 124, 131, 236
Morton, A. R. 17, 76, 82, 184, 186, 216, 230, 236, 237
Moscovitch, D. A. 231
Mühlberger, A. 19, 55, 57, 58, 236, 237
Mulder, C. 110, 114, 230, 236
Munoz, R. F. 4, 141, 142, 149, 150, 154, 232, 237
Muris, P. 54, 56, 188, 189, 230, 237
Murray, E. 2, 3, 237
Murray, K. 120, 121, 236
Myers, T. 236

Nakagawa, A. 19, 62–65, 68, 211, 225, 236, 237
National Institute for Health and Clinical Excellence (NICE) 2, 218, 237
Naven, L. 17, 76, 82, 216, 236
Nazareth, I. 2, 3, 237
Nelissen, I. 54, 56, 188, 189, 230, 237
Newman, M. G. 2, 18, 43–46, 75, 83, 84, 212, 216, 232, 236, 237
Nilsson-Ihrfelt, E. 18, 31–36, 38, 105, 236
Noell, J. 141, 147, 232, 237
Norman, I. J. 12, 29, 236
Norton, M. 236

Oakes, P. 191, 196, 235
Oakley-Brown, M. A. 2, 237
Ochs, E. P. 179, 181–183, 232, 237
O'Connor, E. 87, 98, 99, 101, 104, 235
O'Connor, P. 110, 114, 230, 236
O'Donnell, R. 139, 143, 231, 232, 237
O'Kearney, R. 88, 104, 192, 235

AUTHOR INDEX

Okon, E. 112, 119, 232, 236
Olmsted, M. 127, 236
Ondersma, S. J. 12, 162, 163, 165, 166, 231, 237
Osborne, M. L. 123, 132, 236
Osgood-Hynes, D. J. 12, 19, 38, 86, 102, 106–108, 213, 235
Otto, M. W. 87, 97, 235
Owusu, C. 200, 203, 235
Ozanian, A. J. 152, 156, 157, 237

Palermo, T. 235
Palmer, S. 237
Papandonatos, G. 141, 148, 149, 237
Parcel, G. S. 199, 202, 233, 235
Pare, L. 181, 182, 237
Park, J. M. 19, 62–65, 68, 211, 225, 236, 237
Parkin, R. 2, 6, 10, 62, 63, 68, 75, 80, 102, 150, 225, 233, 236, 237
Parry, G. 2, 3, 237
Pashely, A. 86, 90, 236
Patel, K. 191, 197, 235
Paterson, L. 17, 184, 186, 230, 237
Pauli, P. 19, 55, 57, 58, 236, 237
Percevic, R. 112, 119, 232, 236
Perez, J. F. 142, 150, 232, 237
Perpina, C. 236
Pestian, J. P. 190, 194, 231, 235
Pettersson, R. 18, 170–172, 177, 178, 213, 236
Pinto, B. M. 112, 119, 233, 236
Pivee, C. 114
Plante, T. G. 236
Polterok, A. 75, 79, 235
Pombo-Carril, M. G. 120, 121, 236
Porter, D. 11, 74, 77, 110, 113, 230, 235, 236
Prall, C. W. 54, 56, 57, 230, 236
Price, L. 19, 60, 237
Proudfoot, J. G. 2, 17, 91–95, 216, 217, 235, 237
Przeworski, A. 2, 45, 46, 212, 232, 237
Pulier, P. L. 2, 237
Pung, M. 236

Raffield, T. 87, 97, 235
Ramsay, D. S. 54, 56, 57, 236
Rapoff, M. A. 172, 189, 193, 231, 235
Rappaport, L. A. 200, 203, 235
Ready, D. J. 19, 237

Reba, L. 121, 126, 236
Reid, E. 87, 98, 99, 101, 104, 235
Reid, Y. 120, 121, 236
Reinhalter, K. 124, 129, 236
Rice, C. 127, 236
Richards, C. 235
Richards, D. 237
Richards, J. C. 12, 18, 33, 39–41, 216, 218, 232, 236, 237
Rietdijk, D. 63, 69, 70, 237
Rifas-Shiman, S. L. 236
Rimm, E. B. 236
Riper, J. 153, 160, 230
Ritterband, L. M. 191, 197, 235, 237
Ritz, T. 45, 47, 48, 231
Riva, G. 237
Robinson, A. 235
Romano, A. J. 18, 50, 52, 63, 69, 236
Rosa, V. 76, 83, 216, 217, 218, 236
Roth, W. T. 19, 45, 46, 47, 48, 231, 232, 237
Rothbaum, B. O. 19, 60, 237
Rowan, A. B. 174
Rowse, G. L. 211
Rubin, D. H. 199, 201, 202, 229, 235
Rudy, L. 8, 18, 33, 42, 104, 236
Ryden, C. C. E. B. 92, 94, 217, 235

Sadock, R. T. 199, 201, 202, 229, 235
Salmon, P. 87, 97, 218, 235
Sampson, J. 19, 53, 54, 230, 236
Sanchez-Craig, M. 159
Sand, N. 180, 182, 232, 237
Sandford, J. A. 183
Sat, S. 110, 114, 230, 236
Saunders, J. B. 153, 158, 232, 237
Schinke, S. P. 152, 156, 157, 161, 164, 231–233, 237
Schipper, G. 153, 160, 230
Schmidt, U. 120, 121, 236
Schneider, A. J. 18, 26, 27, 30, 32, 46, 47, 59, 102, 115, 231, 237
Schneider, L. 200, 203, 235
Schneider, S. J. 12, 139, 143, 144, 231, 232, 237
Schottland, P. 199, 201, 202, 229, 235
Schoutrop, M. 63, 69, 70, 237
Schrieken, B. A. L. 18, 63, 69, 70, 231, 237
Schuster, C. R. 12, 162, 163, 165, 166, 231, 237

AUTHOR INDEX

Schwartz, M. D. 12, 139, 144, 237
Schwinn, T. M. 152, 156, 157, 164, 231, 232, 237
Scott, E. 235
See Tai, S. 2, 3, 237
Selby, P. 8, 18, 33, 42, 104, 236
Selmi, P. M. 86, 89, 230, 235
Servan-Schreiber, D. 179, 180, 232, 237
Shackley, K. 2, 3, 237
Shaher, F. 237
Shapiro, D. A. 2, 92–96, 217, 235, 237
Shapiro, H. 121, 126, 236
Sharpe, T. 122, 127, 236
Shaw, S. C. 2, 6, 10, 25, 27, 150, 225, 237
Shea, M. T. 107
Shear, M. K. 48
Shiffman, S. 111, 116, 140, 145, 231, 236, 237
Silver, M. 191, 196, 235
Skoczen, S. 141, 149, 150, 232, 237
Slack, C. W. 11, 74, 77, 235
Slack, W. V. v, 11, 15, 74, 77, 110, 113, 230, 235–237
Smigelski, C. 112, 119, 233, 236
Smit, M. 70, 237
Smith, K. L. 46, 49, 50, 51, 237
Smith, S. G. 19, 60, 237
Smyth, A. 200, 204, 235
Snibbe, J. R. 75, 79, 235
Sockrider, M. I. 199, 202, 233, 235
Södersten, P. 6, 112, 118, 236
Sorrell, S. P. 86, 89, 230, 235
Sotsky, J. F. 107
Sowden, A. J. 226
Spadafora, A. 54, 56, 57, 230, 236
Sparthan, E. 32, 33, 35, 36, 236
Spence, S. H. 188, 189, 229, 235
Springer, E. 122, 128, 236
Squires, D. D. 151, 155, 237
Stampfer, M. J. 236
Stapleton, B. 93, 96, 235
Stare, F. J. 110, 113, 230, 236
Starkey, T. W. 183, 184, 237
Stauss, F. F. 211
Steczkó, J. 33, 37, 236
Stein, R. J. 174
Stoddard, J. 141, 149, 150, 232, 237
Stone, A. A. 111, 117, 231, 236
Stone, L. A. 78, 230, 236
Strecher, V. J. 140, 145, 237

Ström, L. 18, 35, 76, 83, 84, 170–173, 175–178, 213, 236
Stromgren, T. 18, 176, 177, 236
Stuart, S. 4, 86, 90, 232, 235
Sullivan, M. 110, 113, 236
Surman, O. S. 74, 78, 236
Susskind, O. 200, 203, 235
Svikis, D. S. 12, 162, 163, 165, 166, 231, 237
Swain, S. 17, 91–93, 95, 235

Talcott, G. W. 174
Talley, J. L. 74, 235
Tate, D. F, 2, 125, 134, 231, 237
Taylor, C. B. 2, 18, 43–46, 75, 83, 84, 110, 111, 115, 122–124, 127, 129–132, 216, 229, 230, 232, 236, 237
Telch, C. F. 117, 236
Tennstedt, S. 112, 119, 233, 236
ter Riet, G. 226
Thompson, A. 18, 43, 44, 216, 236
Thompson, N. 172, 189, 193, 231, 235
Tinkcom, M. 154
Toole, S. 2, 25, 27, 237
Tortella-Feliu, M. 19, 46, 55, 57–59, 229, 230, 236
Treasure, J. 120, 121, 236
Truax, P. A. 102
Turk, C. L. 237

Van den Berg, S. 92, 93, 95, 235
van den Ven, J.-P. 18, 63, 69, 70, 231, 237
van der Kolk, J. 18, 63, 69, 70, 231, 237
Vera, V. 183, 184, 237
Villa, H. 236
Vilwock, C. 53, 54, 230, 236
Vincelli, F. 237
Vogel, D. 110, 113, 230, 236

Waara, J. 18, 31, 32, 34, 38, 78, 105, 236
Wade, S. L. 190, 194, 195, 231, 235
Wagman, M. 74, 78, 232, 236
Walker, L. S. 191, 197, 235
Waller, R. 217
Walter, R. 139, 143, 231, 232, 237
Watkins, E. 17, 91, 92, 235
Watkins, J. T. 107
Weghorst, S. 236
Weigall, S. 110, 114, 230, 236

AUTHOR INDEX

Weinstein, P. 56
Weizenbaum, J. 77, 114, 236
Wenzel, K. W. 12, 19, 25, 38, 62, 66–68, 86, 102, 106–108, 213, 215, 216, 218, 235–237
West, R. 140, 145, 237
West, R. W. 237
Westbury, C. F. 179, 180, 237
Westling, B. E. 7, 31, 32, 34, 35, 38, 105, 216, 236
Wexler, B. E. 184, 185, 237
Whitby, P. 19, 56, 230, 237
White, J. 17, 76, 82, 216, 236
Whitfield, G. 15, 86, 90, 236, 237
Whittaker, M. 17, 25, 28, 30, 46, 115, 216, 217
Wick, S. 53, 54, 230, 236
Widarsson, J. 177, 236
Widmer, S. 17, 91, 92, 235
Wiedemann, G. 237
Wiederhold, B. K. 237
Wiederhold, M. D. 237
Wilbourne, P. L. 156
Wilding, B. 93, 96, 235
Wilfley, D. E. 122, 128, 129, 236
Wilhelm, F. H. 2, 19, 45, 47, 48, 54, 56, 57, 230, 231, 236, 237
Willett, W. C. 236
Williams, C. 15, 86, 90, 120, 121, 236, 237

Williams, S. M. 153, 158, 232, 237
Wilson, D. M. 132
Wilson, P. G. 174
Winett, R. A. 125, 134, 231, 236
Wing, R. R. 111, 116, 125, 134, 231, 236
Winter, J. 124, 131, 236
Winzelberg, A. J. 122–124, 127–129, 131, 132, 236
Witschi, J. 110, 113, 230, 236
Wolfe, C. R. 190, 194, 195, 231, 235
Wollan, P. 200, 205, 229, 235
Wonderlich, S. A. 236
Woods, S. W. 48
Wooton, R. 2, 237
Wray, R. 19, 53, 54, 236
Wright, A. S. 87, 97, 218, 235
Wright, J. H. 2, 17, 87, 97, 218, 235, 237

Yates, F. E. 17, 75, 81, 150, 151, 230, 236, 237
Yawn, B. P. 200, 205, 229, 235
Yawn, R. A. 200, 205, 229, 235
Yellowlees, P. 2, 237

Zabinksi, M. F. 2, 122, 129, 237
Zack, J. S. 2, 237
Zarr, M. L. 236
Zeiss, A. M. 4
Zetterqvist, K. 76, 83, 84, 236
Zimand, E. 237

Subject index

Note: Entries shown in *italics* refer to names of CP systems and of books.

AA (*Air Academy*) xvii, 200, 205, 229

Abbreviations xvii–xix

AC (*Asthma Command*) xvii, 199–203, 205, 209, 229

Acceptability of CP 13, 22, 92, 95, 165, 179, 217, 225–227

Access to CP vii, 7, 9–11, 14, 16–20, 22–23, 30, 38–39, 64, 67, 70–71, 82–83, 96, 99–108, 119, 128–131, 134, 137, 143–147, 154, 158–160, 165, 177, 185, 188, 195, 197, 202, 204, 210–212, 216–218, 221–222, 226–227

ACont (*Asthma Control*) 200, 203–204, 229

AF (*Asthma Files*) 200, 204–205, 209, 229

Age of CP users ix, 12–13, 36–38, 41–42, 64, 69, 71, 83, 90, 97–99, 103–107, 110–112, 116–117, 119–120, 126, 129–134, 141, 146, 149–150, 152–155, 157–158, 166, 173, 177, 179, 182–183, 185, 189–197, 199–200, 203, 211, 215, 222, 226–227

Alcohol problems (*see also* Substance misuse) viii, xi, 3, 10, 11, 14, 137–138, 150–161, 164–165, 207–209, 211, 214, 222, 230–233

Anger control 164, 207, 209

Anonymity (*see also* Disclosure *and* Security *and* Password protection) 6, 20, 42, 70

Anorexia (*see also* Eating problems) 110–115, 209

Antisocial behaviour 194

Anxiety (*see also* GAD) vii, viii, xi, xii, xviii, 3, 8, 11–12, 17–19, 27, 30, 33, 35–42, 47, 51, 53, 56–57, 60–71, 73–84, 90, 92–96, 103–108, 176, 187–189, 192, 194–195, 201, 207–211, 225, 227, 229–233, 235–236

Assessment (*see also* Screening Questionnaire) ix, xviii, 3, 7–9, 11–12, 15, 20–21, 27, 30–31, 34–40, 59, 62–67, 71, 80, 90, 98–108, 110–112, 116, 119–127, 129–131, 138–142, 148, 151–167, 172, 175, 178, 185, 189–191, 193,

267

268 SUBJECT INDEX

197, 210–212, 217, 221–222, 226–227, 231–233, 239, 249

Asthma (*see also AA, AC, ACont, AF*) viii, xii, xvii, 3, 8, 187–188, 198–206, 208–209, 222, 229, 231, 233

Attrition (*see also* Completers, Dropout) 85, 88, 104, 160, 169, 217–218, 222

Audiotape 22, 24, 34, 45, 47–48, 51, 53–54, 62, 66

Audit *see* CP, monitoring of use

Autism viii, xii, 3, 187, 190, 193, 196, 230

Availability of CP systems 229–233

Back pain viii, 38, 169, 171, 175, 232

Balance, 81, 210, 229

Beating the Blues (BTB) xi, xiv, xvii, 2, 17, 85, 91–97, 120, 209, 212–218, 229

Behavioural activation (pleasant activities) 4, 89, 100–102, 212, 215

Bias in CP reports 5

Bibliotherapy *see* Books

Binge-eating disorder (BED) *see* Bulimia, *see also* Eating disorders

Biofeedback (*see also* Capnometer) 8, 16, 19, 170–171, 174, 225

Bipolar disorder 209

Blind ratings 3, 4, 25, 28, 30, 35, 40, 54–55, 66, 74–76, 98, 130, 159, 166, 185, 193, 202, 226

BluePages 87, 89, 101–104

Body Traps 122, 128–129

Books, self-help 5–7, 9, 11–20, 22, 24–27, 31–46, 59, 61–70, 74–76, 84–88, 94, 96, 101, 105, 107–108, 115, 117, 120–127, 138–147, 151–153, 158–160, 164, 172, 174–177, 180–182, 188, 191–192, 199–200, 204–205, 207, 212–216

Brain injury viii, xii, 3, 187, 191–195, 231

BRAVE 187–188, 192, 209, 218, 229

Broad-spectrum CP clinic 209–210

BSCPW (Behavioural Self-Control Program for Windows) xvii, 151, 154–155, 229

BTSteps (BTS, Behaviour Therapy Steps, OCFighter) xvi, xvii, 13–14, 19, 38, 61–69, 102, 104, 144, 173, 209–210, 213–217, 229, 231

BTWL (Behavior Therapy for Weight Loss) xvii, 125, 134–135, 209, 231

Bulimia (*see also* Eating problems, Obesity) 110–121, 209–210, 222

Burn wounds (CP for pain of) viii, 7, 169, 171, 175

Burnout 15, 231

CADET (Computer-Assisted Diet and Exercise Training) xviii, 110–111, 115–116, 229–230

CAE (computer-aided exposure) 55–59, 229

Capnometer 18, 24, 45–48

CARL (Computer Assisted Relaxation Training) 54–57, 212, 230

CARM (Computer-Aided Relapse Management) 150–151, 230

CAVE (computer-aided vicarious exposure) xi, xvii, 2, 6, 17, 19, 22, 24, 46, 48–52, 61, 63, 69, 189, 201, 217, 230

CD-ROM (compact disk) viii, xi, xviii, 7, 16–17, 22–26, 74–76, 81–82, 86–88, 90, 109–113, 120–128, 151–153, 156–157, 161, 164, 187–193, 199–200, 204–205, 208, 218, 229, 231–233, 240

Children and adolescents, CP with viii, xii, 3, 13, 23–24, 52, 56, 71, 103, 114, 127, 131, 136, 138, 152, 156–157, 161, 164, 187–208, 215, 222, 229–232, 235, 239

CLCS (Captain's Log Cognitive System) xvii, 183–186, 230

Clinician (therapist) contact ix, xiii–xiv, 3, 6, 7–18, 20–63, 66–89, 82–83, 92–98, 102–109, 113, 115, 119–126, 134–135, 150, 152, 160, 155, 165, 169–179, 183, 188–198, 209, 211–222, 225–227

Clinician (therapist) time 7, 24, 31, 35, 53, 54, 57–73, 79–80, 85, 87, 92, 114, 173–174, 178, 192, 196–198, 209, 212– 215

Clinician (therapist), travel to 10, 21–22, 60, 210

SUBJECT INDEX 269

Cochrane reviews 3–4
Completers (*see also* Attrition,
Dropout) 25–26, 27, 31, 32–35,
44–50, 62–63, 66, 68, 70–71,
75–76, 81–82, 84–91, 93–94, 96,
99, 101, 106–112, 115, 121–123,
127, 129, 131, 134, 139–142,147,
151–153, 157, 160–163, 170–178,
180–181, 184, 189, 191, 199–200,
215, 216
Components (ingredients) of CP 4, 8,
12, 14, 41,47, 51, 59, 89, 97, 102,
106, 144–150, 222
Computer games 199–200, 208, 229
Confidentiality (*see also* Password
protection) 4, 9–11, 14, 20–21, 64,
188
Controls, aim of 4
Cope xvi, 13–14, 19, 38, 86, 102,
106–108, 144, 173, 210–217,
230
CP
central vs peripheral 16–17, 21
commercially available 24, 98, 145,
218–219
content 212
cost 6, 14–15, 40, 60, 67, 84, 94–95,
98, 115, 146–147, 173–174, 213,
218
credibility 38, 95
definition of 6–8
functions of vii, 20–22
interactivity 9, 21
monitoring of use 12, 20
reviews of 2–5, 237
screening of users for (*see also*
Screening Questionnaire) ix, 8,
16, 20, 21, 49–50, 70, 79, 96, 113,
160, 173, 210–212, 221
types of system vii, 7, 16–19, 23–60,
uptake of 85, 90–91, 120, 134, 217
CQ (*Committed Quitters Stop-Smoking
Plan*) xvii, 140, 145–146, 230

DAVP (*Drug Abuse and Violence
Prevention*) xvii, 161, 187
DCS (*PLATO Dilemma Counselling
System*) xvii, 74, 78, 232
DCU (*Drinker's Check-Up*) xvii, 151,
155–157, 230
Deafness 10

Definition of
CP 6–8
mental health problems 8
psychotherapy 8
Dependence *see* Alcohol, Drug misuse,
Substance misuse
Depression viii, 2–4, 14, 17–19, 22, 24,
30–31, 36–38, 42, 68, 70, 71, 73–76,
79, 81, 82, 85–108, 116, 173, 176,
187, 189–195, 207–212, 215,
221–222, 225, 227, 229–233, 235,
239
Desensitization 53, 230
Desktop computer vii, viii, xi, 23–25,
79, 89, 110–114, 208, 230
Diaries *see* Homework
DIET 110, 230
Digital videodisk *see* DVD
Disincentives to CP 219
Display CP systems vii, 19, 24, 48–60,
189
DL (*Drinking Less*) xvii, 138, 153,
160–161, 209, 213, 230
Dose-response to CP 102, 104, 106–107,
134, 139, 144–145, 149, 199
Dropout ix, xviii, 3–4, 8, 15, 25–35, 42,
44–50, 53, 62–63, 66, 68–71,
74–76, 79, 81–96, 98, 101–118,
120–129, 131, 134, 137–142,
146–157, 160–164, 169, 170–178,
180–182, 184–186, 189–192, 195,
199–202, 210, 215, 217–218, 222,
226–227
Drinkwise 153, 159
Drug misuse (*see also* Substance
misuse) viii, xi, xvii, 3, 10, 12,
138, 152–157, 161, 161–168,
207–209, 211, 231–233 Drug
treatment (Prescribed drugs) *see*
Medication
Duration of problem 11, 36–37, 39–41,
107
DVD (Digital videodisk) xviii, 7, 16–17,
23, 97–98, 231

Eating problems (*see also* Obesity) viii,
xi, xviii, 3, 6, 22, 109–135, 207–209,
211–212, 221–222, 230–232, 236,
239
Ecological momentary assessment *see*
IOSR

270 SUBJECT INDEX

Education
of professionals by CP 12, 24, 26,
28–29, 31, 214–215, 222,
226–227
of lay people to support CP 102
level of CP users xvii, ix, 6–7, 9, 13,
17, 20, 23, 30–31, 37, 39, 41–43,
56, 59–60, 64, 73, 83, 85, 97,
101–103, 106–107, 109, 114, 116,
119–120, 128, 132–133, 137–138,
149–150, 160–161, 166, 172–173,
175, 177, 179, 186–188, 193, 198,
201, 203–205, 212, 215–216, 219,
230
Effect size (ES) 3, 25–30, 32–39, 44–46,
49–52, 59, 62–63, 66, 69, 70–71,
75–76, 81, 83, 86–87, 93, 95, 98,
100, 101, 108, 122–124, 128,
130–133, 143, 153, 156–157, 161,
163, 166, 170–171, 174, 177–178,
186, 216–217, 222
ELIZA 77, 110, 114, 230
Email xv, 1, 6–7, 10–11, 13, 15–16, 18,
20–24, 31–42, 61, 63, 70–71, 76, 83,
7, 98–100, 104, 105, 113, 121,
124–125, 128–129, 131, 134–135,
137,141, 145, 147–150, 153, 158,
169,–170–178, 192, 210–214, 222,
227, 229
Emotion trainer 190, 196, 230
Encopresis viii, xii, 3, 187, 190, 197–198,
209, 233
Enuresis 209
Epilepsy 209
*ESPWC (Empowerment Solution for
Permanent Weight Control)* xvii,
121, 126–127, 218, 230

Face-to-face (ftf) care vs CP xiv,
xvii–xviii, 4, 6–7, 10–11, 15, 18,
20–21, 25–29, 34, 36, 38, 41, 43, 46,
49, 59, 66–70, 80, 86–90, 96, 98,
100, 102, 104, 107, 110, 113,
116–117, 121, 126, 128, 145, 152–
154, 156, 177, 183, 187–192, 211,
215–218, 222
Family involvement in therapy 101, 152,
157, 189–191, 195
FearFighter (FF) xi, xvi, xvii, 2, 14,
17–18, 24–32, 38, 46, 102, 129, 173,
209–219, 231

Feasibility of CP 155, 165, 179
FPS (Family Problem Solving) xvii, 191,
194–195, 231–232

Generalised Anxiety Disorder (GAD,
general anxiety) viii, xi, xiv, xviii, 3,
17–18, 35–38, 42, 46, 73–84,
207–210, 225, 229, 232–233, 236
GDA (Good Days Ahead) xvii, 17, 85,
87, 89, 97–98, 212, 218, 231
Goal setting 20, 22, 210, 213
Go Nosmoke 139, 143–144
Grief 18, 63, 70, 166, 231
GSI (Girls' Stress Intervention) xvii, 152,
164–165, 187, 231

Handheld devices (*see also* Palmtop) vii,
viii, xi, 16, 18, 22–24, 43–48, 62, 64,
84, 109–111, 115–118, 208, 216,
231
Hawthorne effect *see* Placebo effect
Headache viii, xii, 3, 8, 18, 35, 169–174,
187, 189, 193, 231, 239
Headstrong 189, 193, 231
Homework (*see also* Handheld devices
and Palmtop
Human support *and* Clinician *and*
Clinician time *and* Support of CP
users) xi, 4, 9, 11, 13, 14, 18, 21–24,
27, 30, 43–48, 52, 55, 58–59, 64, 75,
79–80, 83–84, 86, 89–91, 94, 97,
106, 109–112, 126, 128, 132–134,
144, 172, 176–179, 187, 192–193,
212–213, 215–216

*IMPACT (Interactive Multimedia
Program for Asthma Control and
Tracking)* xvii, 198–199, 201, 209,
231
Implementation of CP 218–221
Independent testing of CP 5, 30, 78
Insomnia viii, xi, 3, 18, 38, 70, 82, 91,
105, 169–171, 176–178, 207–209,
232, 236
Interactive Voice Response (IVR) viii,
xviii, 6, 9–10, 12, 14, 16, 18–22,
61–65, 68–69, 85–86, 104, 106–108,
112, 119, 137–139, 144–145, 208,
210–211, 216, 222, 229–230,
232–233
Interapy 61, 63, 69–70, 212, 231

SUBJECT INDEX   271

Internet (net, web) (*see also* Online therapy) vii, viii, xi, xviii, 1, 5–7, 9–10, 15–20, 22–42, 57, 60–61, 63–64, 69–70, 73, 76, 78, 81, 83–87, 98–105, 107–109, 121–142, 145–150, 153, 155, 158, 159–161, 169–178, 185, 187–199, 207–208, 210–222, 225–226, 229, 230–232, 239

IOSR (immediate on-site recording) 111

IRCAE (Internet Relaxation Computer-Aided Exposure) xviii, 55, 58

Jetlag viii, xi, 3, 8, 169, 171, 178–179, 208, 231, 236

Job satisfaction of therapists 15

Laptop 17–18, 61, 64, 200, 204, 232

Living With Fear 27

MA (Managing Anxiety) xviii, 26, 30, 231

Mandometer 6, 6, 112, 118, 231

Manual *see* Books

MAP (Mastery of your Anxiety and Panic) xviii, 33, 40

Medication 2, 5, 7, 13, 15, 22, 40, 43, 54, 56–57, 65, 86, 91, 94, 97, 101, 106–108, , 165–166, 170, 172, 174, 178, 183, 193, 198–203, 216–219, 221

Meditation 89

Meta-analysis (systematic analysis), pros and cons 3–4

MES (Motivational Enhancement System) 12, 162–167, 231

MoodGYM 85, 87–89, 100–105, 212–213, 215, 217, 231

Motivation of CP users 12, 62, 132, 162, 138, 211–212

Motivational therapy xviii, 12, 115, 120, 131–132, 154–155, 161–167, 231

Multimedia use in CP xvii, 22, 109, 187, 198–199, 222, 225, 231–232

NAPFD (Net Assessment and Personalised Feedback for Problem Drinking) xviii, 7, 153, 159, 213–215, 231

NET (*Neurocognitive Enhancement Therapy*) xviii, 184, 185

Net *see* Internet

Net Assessment and Personalised Feedback for Problem Drinking (see NAPFD)

NICE (National Institute for Clinical Excellence) xv, xviii, 2–4, 24, 31, 61, 67, 85, 91, 209, 213, 218, 237

Nightmares 209, 213

OAPP (Online Anxiety Prevention Program) 76, 83, 217, 231

OB (Overcoming Bulimia) xviii, 120–121, 126, 212, 232

Obesity, 3, 110, 113–118, 121–125, 126, 209, 239, *see also* Eating problems

Obsessions *see* Ruminations

Obsessive-compulsive disorder (OCD) vii, xi, xviii, xix, 3, 14, 18–19, 42, 50–54, 61–69, 102, 104, 207–210, 213, 215, 222, 225, 229–230, 232, 236, 239–240

OCCheck 62, 232

OCFighter (*see also* BTSteps (BTS)) 23

OD1 (Overcoming Depression1, by Bowers) xviii, 86, 89–90, 232

OD2 (Overcoming Depression2, by Calypso) xviii, 86, 90–91, 232

ODIN (Overcoming Depression on the Internet) xviii, 85, 87, 89, 98–101, 104, 212, 217, 232

Online support (*see also* Internet) xviii, 10, 15, 18, 24, 31–42, 63, 76, 79, 83, 88, 98–106, 113, 123–143, 147–150, 153, 158–161, 212–214, 225, 231–232

Overcoming Depression
by Bowers *see OD1*
by Calypso *see OD2*

Pain (*see also* Back pain *and* Headache) viii, xi, 3, 7, 38, 60, 101, 169–175, 193–194, 208, 231–232, 236

Palmtop (*see also* Handheld devices) viii, 7, 14, 18, 43–47, 61–64, 75, 83–84, 111, 117–118, , 216–217, 222, 232

Panic *see* Phobia, agoraphobia

272 SUBJECT INDEX

Panic Program 18, 24, 42, 212, 217, 232
Password protection (*see also*
  Confidentiality) 14, 17, 20, 31,
  34–35, 39, 64, 68, 70–71, 83, 103,
  107–108, 145, 158, 160, 177–178,
  188, 210, 218
PC (personal computer) vii, viii, xi, xix,
  7, 13, 16–19, 23ff, 208
Personality disorders 209
Pharmacotherapy *see* Medication
Phobia vii–viii, 2, 6, 17, 19, 23–60,
  188–191, 207–210, 222, 236
  agoraphobia, vii, xi, xviii, 2–3, 10, 14,
    17–19, 22–60, 102–105, 207–219,
    222, 225, 231–232, 236
  dental injection 23, 54, 56–57
  flying 19, 23–24, 46, 55, 58–60,
    229–230
  heights 60
  snake 38
  social phobia (social anxiety) 24,
    35–36, 38, 42, 46, 60, 232, 239
  spider phobia 17, 19, 23–24, 38, 46,
    49–56, 54 188, 230, 189
  test (examination) 23, 53–54
Phone support (*see also* Interactive
  Voice Response) viii, 4, 6–7, 9–25,
  29–41, 63–64, 67–69, 77, 80–81,
  87, 89, 93, 96, 98–108, 169,
  112–113, 119, 129, 131, 137, 144,
  156, 158, 164–165, 169–173, 175,
  177, 197, 202–203, 210–214, 216,
  221–222, 227, 232–233, 239
Phone support, scheduled vs requested
  63, 67–68, 104, 213–214
Placebo (attention) effect 3–4, 24, 28,
  30, 34, 37, 48, 57, 85, 03, 97,
  114–115, 131, 155–156, 172–178,
  185–186, 202, 207, 209, 216, 222,
  227
Panic Online (*PO*) xviii, 18, 24, 33,
  39–41, 212, 232
Preferences of CP users ix, 3, 9, 12, 90,
  93, 96, 126–127, 143, 146, 162–163,
  176, 195, 216, 221–222, 225, 226,
  227
Prevention
  of problems xv, 83, 104–105,
    122–127, 130–134, 151–157,
    161–167, 187, 208–209, 221–222,
    231–232, 239

of relapse 31, 36, 40, 68, 105, 138, 143,
  145, 154, 176, 212, 214
Privacy *see* Confidentiality
Psychosis (*see also* Schizophrenia) 154,
  209, 211
PTSD (Post-Traumatic Stress Disorder)
  see Traumatic stress

Quality of life 24, 35–36, 38, 95,
  106–107, 199, 201
Questionnaires in CP 7, 11, 41, 51, 58,
  70, 100–101, 131, 138, 148–149,
  159–160, 186, 203, 210–211
Quitn xviii, 141, 148–149, 213, 232
QSN (*Quit Smoking Network*) xviii, 141,
  147–149, 213, 232

RCT (randomised controlled trial), pros
  and cons 3
Referral source and outcome 210
Relapse prevention *see* Prevention of
  relapse
Relationship of patient–therapist 8, 11,
  215
Relaxation xvii, xviii, 8, 12, 25, 28, 30,
  25, 32–34, 38–29, 41, 48–59, 62,
  66–67, 69, 71, 73–74, 76, 78, 82–83,
  101, 164, 170, 172, 174–177, 193,
  216, 230, 240
Ruminations 53–54

Satisfaction of CP users 28–29, 67–79,
  80, 96, 128–129, 177, 192, 216, 218,
  222, 225–227
SB (*Student Bodies*) xviii, 112–124,
  127–134, 209, 213, 232
SBI (*Screening and Brief Intervention*)
  xviii, 153, 158–159, 213, 232
Schizophrenia (*see also* Psychosis) viii,
  xi, 3, 17, 169, 183–186, 207–208,
  230, 237
Screening *see* Assessment *and* CP,
  screening of users for
Screening and Brief Intervention see
  SBI
Screening Questionnaire 210
Search for CP studies 225–228
Security of CP systems *see*
  Confidentiality
Sexpert 179–183, 209, 232
Sexual abuse 80

SUBJECT INDEX   273

Sexual problems viii, xi, 3, 169, 179–183, 208–209, 237
SHTC (Self-Help Traumatic Consequences) 63, 71
Smoking (*see also* Substance misuse) viii, xi, 3, 137–153, 157–159, 164–165, 207–209, 214, 217, 230–233, 237
SMS (Text messaging) xix, 20, 34, 112, 119–120, 210, 214, 232
SODAS (Stop, Options, Decide, Act, Self-Praise to think, not drink) xviii, 138, 152, 156–157, 187, 209, 232
Soliloquy, computer–aided 77–78
SS (Stop Smoking) xviii, 74, 142, 149–150, 217, 232
Stage of change 147, 160
Stammering 209
Stigma 10, 14, 20–21, 87, 101, 210
Stop Tabac 140, 146–147, 232
Stress management 73, 76, 83–84, 164–165
Stresspac 17, 76, 82, 212, 232
Substance misuse (*see also* Drugs, Alcohol, Smoking) viii, 137–167, 187, 237
Suicide 11, 13, 16, 89, 90, 211–212, 221
Support of CP users (*see also* Clinician *and* Therapist time) 212–215, 222–223, 239
Swedish CP 31–39, 76, 83–84, 88, 105–106, 169–178, 209, 212–218, 232

TC (Totally Cool) xviii, 152, 161, 164, 233
Teaching *see* Education
Ted 139, 144–145, 232
Telephone *see* Phone
Text messaging *see* SMS

Therapist *see* Clinician *and* Clinician time
Tics 209
Tinnitus distress viii, xi, 3, 8, 18, 169, 171, 176–177, 208, 236, 239
TLC–Eat (Telephone-Link-Communications-Eat) xviii, 112, 119, 233
TLP (Therapeutic Learning Program) xviii, 74–75, 79–80, 233
Training using CP *see* Education, of professionals
Traumatic stress (Post-Traumatic Stress Disorder, PTSD) vii, xi, xviii, xix, 3, 14, 18, 42, 60–61, 65, 67, 69–71, 195, 207, 208–210, 225, 237

UCPT (U-Can-Poop-Too) 190, 197–198, 209, 233

Videophone 1
Video for therapy 6, 9–11, 17, 22, 23, 5658, 60, 78, 90–93, 96–97, 127, 156–157, 164, 182–183, 187, 191, 194–195, 212–213
Virtual clinic 210
Virtual reality (VR) (*see also* Display systems) vii, xix, 7, 19, 23, 60, 169, 175, 200, 208, 225 Voicemail 18, 20–21, 144, 213–214

Waitlist (WL) control 32–36, 40–41, 46, 49, 52–55, 61, 63, 71, 75–76, 83–89, 93, 97, 106–107, 118, 127, 131, 133, 138, 154–156, 169, 172, 174–175, 178, 189, 191–193, 207, 209, 216–217, 222
WDTA (Watch, Discover, Think & Act) xviii, 199, 202–203, 205, 233
Workbooks *see* Books
Worrytel 75, 80–81, 233